OXFORD LEGAL PHILOSOPHY

Series Editors: Timothy Endicott, John Gardner, and Leslie Green

Law and Morality at War

OXFORD LEGAL PHILOSOPHY

Series editors: Timothy Endicott, John Gardner, and Leslie Green

Oxford Legal Philosophy publishes the best new work in philosophically-oriented legal theory. It commissions and solicits monographs in all branches of the subject, including works on philosophical issues in all areas of public and private law, and in the national, transnational, and international realms; studies of the nature of law, legal institutions, and legal reasoning; treatments of problems in political morality as they bear on law; and explorations in the nature and development of legal philosophy itself. The series represents diverse traditions of thought but always with an emphasis on rigour and originality. It sets the standard in contemporary jurisprudence.

ALSO AVAILABLE IN THE SERIES

Law and Morality at War

Adil Ahmad Haque
Professor of Law and Judge Jon O. Newman Scholar
Rutgers Law School

OXFORD

UNIVERSITY PRESS

Great Clarendon Street, Oxford, OX2 6DP,
United Kingdom

Oxford University Press is a department of the University of Oxford.
It furthers the University's objective of excellence in research, scholarship,
and education by publishing worldwide. Oxford is a registered trade mark of
Oxford University Press in the UK and in certain other countries

First Edition published in 2017

Impression: 1

Published in the United States of America by Oxford University Press
198 Madison Avenue, New York, NY 10016, United States of America

British Library Cataloguing in Publication Data
Data available

Library of Congress Control Number: 2016959974

ISBN 978–0–19–968739–8

Printed and bound by
CPI Group (UK) Ltd, Croydon, CR0 4YY

For my mother, Rehana, and my father, Aijaz

Series Editors' Preface

In this landmark in the philosophy of violence, Adil Haque resolves tensions between the law and the morality of war. And he offers a new and discerning critique of the law, at points where the tension is irresoluble.

The field has been turned upside-down by revisionists who have challenged the conventional idea that, in a conflict that has credentials as a war, combatants on each side can rightly and lawfully kill each other even if (and this is the case in every such conflict) it is unjust for at least one side to be engaged in the war. The revisionists have said that it may be lawful for combatants to slaughter each other, but it is not right.

Haque's subject is the unbearable hostility that seems to result–a war–between law and morality. His argument has crucial implications at every stage of the apparent conflict. He argues that the law does not authorise immorality, as you may think, because it does not actually authorize the use of violence in an unjust cause. He argues that at some points, morality supports the law more fully than the revisionists have thought (for example, he says that the general legal protection for civilians gives effect to moral principles). And he argues that the law can and should be reformed where the conflict with morality is genuine. In particular, he advocates new and more stringent legal restraints on the use of force against combatants.

A war fought in accordance with the law of war is still a war. Haque takes an appropriately realistic approach to the potential of the law: he counts it as a great success–for legal thought and for legal practice–if ever the law has the result that an innocent person is spared from slaughter or rape or torment or enslavement. And even so, he sets aspirations for the law of war very high: where others have thought that the law can only constrain, he thinks that the law should *serve* combatants who are committed to acting justifiably. The result is a highly realistic anti-scepticism about international law.

In this original account, reconciling the law and the morality of war becomes a viable and an essential pursuit for philosophers, lawyers, combatants, and non-combatants. We are very glad to be able to publish a major contribution to the understanding and the critique of the law of war.

T.A.O. Endicott

J. Gardner

L. Green

Author's Preface

As a scholar, writing about the law and ethics of war, I do not expect to dramatically alter the behavior of states or armed groups. Mostly, I hope to help move the needle. Once in a long while, the needle moves.

On June 12, 2015, the United States Department of Defense issued its long-awaited Law of War Manual. Ten days later, I began publishing a series of essays, criticizing various aspects of the Manual, on the national security law blog *Just Security*. I focused particular attention on the Manual's alarming claim that collateral harm to civilians forced to serve as involuntary human shields would not prohibit an attack under the proportionality rule, no matter how great the expected harm or how small the anticipated military advantage. A lengthy article followed in *International Law Studies*, a journal published by the U.S. Naval War College. Other scholars and practitioners offered their own criticisms of the Manual, on this point and many others.

On November 25, 2016, as this book was in proofs, Jennifer O'Connor, General Counsel of the Department of Defense, announced that her office is revising the Manual to clarify that the proportionality rule applies to civilians used as human shields. As of this writing, the text of the revisions has not been released. For that reason, among others, I have decided not to amend my discussion of this issue in Chapter 9. At the very least, I hope that it will prove instructive to examine the Manual's original mistakes.

When I began writing this book, I believed that the United States generally complies with international law *as understood by the United States government*. Accordingly, if we correct the misunderstandings of the United States government, then compliance with international law, properly understood, will follow.

As this book goes to press, my country's future compliance with the rule of law—international or domestic—seems very much in doubt. We are reminded that decades of legal progress can be reversed. Laws can be changed, or ignored. Manuals interpreting the law can be revised, only to be revised again.

What remains constant are the moral norms to which the law is, even at its best, an imperfect guide. By revealing the moral foundations of the law, we may better defend those laws that should not be changed, propose those changes to the law that should be made, and better interpret those laws whose meaning determines who lives and who dies. We may also encourage compliance with the law out of moral conviction, quite apart from any expectation of reciprocity or fear of punishment.

Now, perhaps more than before, we must articulate and defend a vision of law that reflects our moral values. This book is one contribution to that broader effort.

Adil Ahmad Haque
Brooklyn, New York, USA
November 30, 2016

Acknowledgments

My sincere thanks to Milton Regan for organizing a wonderful workshop on the manuscript at Georgetown University; to Yitzhak Benbaji, Janina Dill, David Luban, Jeff McMahan, Jens Ohlin, and Jeremy Waldron for their insightful comments; and to Jovana Davidovic, Ashley Deeks, Jesse Kirkpatrick, Marty Lederman, Hadassa Noorda, Michael Robillard, and Michael Skerker for lively discussion.

Special thanks to Jeff McMahan for first igniting my interest in the contemporary ethics of war and for later offering me the advice and encouragement that enabled me to move between two worlds. Only Antony Duff has done as much to help launch my academic career, in my other life as a criminal law theorist.

Special thanks also to Seth Lazar and Helen Frowe. Seth read and commented on much of the manuscript in various forms. Although Seth and I differ on some fine points, we remain fellow travelers. Helen and I disagree about a great deal, including civilian immunity and the relative merits of coffee and wine. No one has offered me greater encouragement or more opportunities to attempt what she calls "proper philosophy."

Thanks to Saba Bazargan, Vera Bergelson, Krister Bykvist, Lars Christie, Roger Clark, Harlan Cohen, Evan Criddle, Margaret deGuzman, John Dehn, Kai Draper, Charles Dunlap, Kimberly Ferzan, David Glazier, Stuart Green, Alexander Greenawalt, Amos Guiora, Andrew Hayashi, Lisa Hecht, Kevin Heller, Alan Hyde, Kyron Huigens, Col Richard Jackson, Maximo Langer, Adriaan Lanni, John Leubsdorf, Dan Markel, Richard McAdams, Maj Richard Meyer, Mary Ellen O'Connell, Brandon Paradise, Jonathan Parry, Massimo Renzo, Sam Rickless, Alice Ristroph, Leila Sadat, Michael Schmitt, Mark Shulman, Daniel Statman, Bradley Strawser, Beth Van Schaack, Horacio Spencer, Victor Tadros, François Tanguay-Renaud, Gerardo Vildostegui, Alec Walen, Lt Col Jeffery Walker, Mathew Waxman, Alan Weiner, and Steve Woodside for stimulating conversations over the years.

Thanks also to audiences at the American Society of International Law, Benjamin N. Cardozo School of Law, Carnegie Council for Ethics and International Affairs, George Washington University Law School, New Voices in Legal Theory Roundtable, Osgoode Hall Law School, Rutgers Law School, St John's University School of Law, Stockholm Centre for the Ethics of War and Peace, University of California, San Diego, University of Pennsylvania Law School, Universidad Torcuato di Tella, Washington University School of Law, William & Mary Law School, and Yale Law School.

Thanks as well to Nicole Barna, Capt Edward Westfall, and Kenneth Wagner for their excellent research assistance at various times.

Thanks most of all to Saumya Manohar, whose love and support has made writing this book, among other things, a joy.

Contents

1

Introduction

In the middle of Aleppo's Souq al-Madina, a tailor invited me to share a cup of tea with him, as merchants had invited travelers for over five hundred years. His name was Abdul Karim and he had served in the Syrian Army during its occupation of Lebanon. While stationed there, he fell in love with a young woman. She was from a different sect and their families forbade them to marry. Abdul Karim adored his wife and children, but not a day went by in which he did not think of the woman whom he had loved and lost. After chatting for an hour or so, I thanked Abdul Karim for his company and for his tea, took his business card, and continued on my way.

Seven years later, most of the Souq al-Madina and much of Aleppo is rubble and ash. Abdul Karim does not answer his phone. I fear that he and his family are among the hundreds of thousands of men, women, and children who have been killed by one side or another of the conflict that has torn apart two countries and now threatens the surrounding region.

Human beings have long sought to constrain the conduct of war through legal as well as moral norms. In the seventh century, the caliph Abu Bakr instructed his army as follows:

Stop, O people, that I may give you ten rules for your guidance in the battlefield. Do not commit treachery or deviate from the right path. You must not mutilate dead bodies. Neither kill a child, nor a woman, nor an aged man. Bring no harm to the trees, nor burn them with fire, especially those which are fruitful. Slay not any of the enemy's flock, save for your food. You are likely to pass by people who have devoted their lives to monastic services; leave them alone.[1]

In issuing these rules, Abu Bakr claimed to follow the example of his son-in-law and predecessor, Muḥammad ibn ʿAbd Allāh, who in turn claimed to follow truths revealed to him by God. These rules, and others like them, later surfaced in

---

[1] Malik ibn Anas (ed), *Al-Muwatta* (circa 767 CE) (Diwan 4th edn 2015) Book 21, Number 21.3.10. See also UK Ministry of Defence, *Law of Armed Conflict Manual* (OUP 2005) 1.16 ("It is said, however, that the first systematic code of war was that of the Saracens, based on the Koran, and principles of the law of armed conflict presented themselves in many different parts of the world").

European codes of chivalry, in the just war tradition, in customary international law, and finally in the Hague and Geneva Conventions.

The contemporary international law of war both constrains and protects every person who finds himself or herself on one side of a conflict or trapped between opposing sides of a conflict. Similarly, the modern, secular ethics of war addresses all parties to armed conflict and all participants in hostilities.

It is natural to view this legal and moral project with skepticism. Each year, thousands of men and women, girls and boys, are killed, maimed, and driven from their homes by opposing combatants. One objection to the project is that much of this violence flouts applicable moral and legal rules. This fact can make the project seem irrelevant. Another objection to the project is that much of this violence satisfies applicable moral and legal rules. This fact can make the project seem perverse.

It seems likely that no war has ever been fought in full compliance with the law of war. It seems certain that even a war fought in full compliance with the law would not be fully just. War can never be fully just because war inevitably infringes the human rights of civilians and inflicts undeserved suffering on combatants. At best, the resort to war can be morally justified only as the lesser of two great evils, perhaps when the only alternative is surrender to aggression or genocide. Similarly, the conduct of war can be morally justified only if it targets individuals who have forfeited or compromised their right not to be harmed while collaterally harming the innocent only to prevent substantially greater harm to others.

It is unfortunate that the moral theory of war is so often referred to as "just war theory." This label suggests that just wars are real things that could be the subjects of a theory—like politics, decisions, or music. In my view, moral theory should aim to identify and analyze the most serious injustices perpetrated in war. Many of these injustices—such as torture, rape, and enslavement—require little theoretical illumination. In contrast, launching indiscriminate attacks and inflicting disproportionate civilian losses are clearly unjust but they are not, one might say, unjust clearly. What makes an attack "indiscriminate"? What makes civilian losses "disproportionate"? These are the sorts of questions that the moral theory of war should address. Perhaps a better name for the field would be "unjust war theory."

Law can never make war just. However, law can make war less unjust than it would be otherwise. Law can prohibit the intentional, indiscriminate, unnecessary, and disproportionate killing of civilians, almost all of whom, I will argue, retain their fundamental moral rights. Law can also, I will argue, prohibit the unnecessary killing of opposing combatants. Combatants who try to follow such laws may still inflict wrongful harm—at the very least by mistake—but they will inflict less wrongful harm than they would without the law to guide them. Individuals protected by such laws may still suffer infringements of their fundamental rights but these infringements will be less morally arbitrary than they would be without these laws.

Unfortunately, the law governing the conduct of hostilities—the *jus in bello*—cannot prohibit all killing of civilians or combatants in pursuit of an unjust cause, though most such killing violates their fundamental moral rights. Fortunately, this prohibition resides, at least to an extent, in the law governing the use of armed force between states—the *jus ad bellum* or *jus contra bellum*—with which the law governing the conduct of hostilities shares a division of moral labor. If each body of law does its job, then those combatants who perfectly conform to both bodies of law will avoid wrongful killing. The majority of combatants—who imperfectly conform to one body or both bodies of law—will commit less wrongful killings than they would otherwise.

While no body of law receives full compliance, partial compliance with the law of war is vastly preferable to there being no law of war with which to comply. The law of war is respected by some, distorted by others, and ignored by many. If the law is shown to rest on a strong moral foundation, then perhaps the law will be more often respected, less often distorted, and harder to ignore. In particular, if it can be shown that the law provides combatants with sound moral guidance, then combatants may be more willing to obey the law even when their adversaries do not. The practical efficacy of the law would then rest on humanity rather than reciprocity.

The law of war is often presented in terms of a balance between humanitarian considerations and military considerations, implying that the two are opposing forces locked in perpetual conflict. In fact, a law of war that neglects humanitarian considerations would often impair rather than enhance military effectiveness. If the law of war loses its moral credibility, then combatants will not trust that they can obey lawful orders in good conscience. They will hesitate, question, and dissent, looking elsewhere for the normative guidance that law ought to provide. Instead of relying on the law to strike a reasonable balance between competing considerations, combatants will have no choice but to strike their own.

The law of war may influence behavior by eliciting compliance, mere conformity, or near-conformity. Some seek, in good faith, to comply with the law for reasons given or endorsed by the law. Others seek merely to conform to the law for reasons independent of the law.[2] Still others seek, in bad faith, not to violate the law so flagrantly that any legal defense they might offer would be implausible on its face. In my view, every innocent person spared rather than killed due to the influence of law represents a resounding success.

This legal and moral project sometimes involves defending established legal principles—such as civilian immunity—from attempts to undermine or corrupt their moral foundations. At other times, this project involves developing new legal principles—such as restraints on the use of force against opposing combatants—to

---

[2] For the distinction between compliance and conformity, see Joseph Raz, *Practical Reason and Norms* (OUP 1999) 178–9.

legally recognize moral wrongs long ignored. Most often, this project involves interpreting ambiguous legal principles—such as proportionality or precautions in attack—in their morally best light, using moral concepts, principles, and arguments to give the law more determinate content, combatants clearer guidance, and civilians more robust protection. This book is my contribution to this ongoing legal and moral project.

Aim and Scope

The laws are not silent in war. But what do they say? What should they say? What is the moral function of the law of war? Should the law protect civilians who do not fight but help those who do? Should the law protect soldiers who perform noncombat functions or who may be safely captured? How certain should a soldier be that a person is a combatant rather than a civilian before using lethal force? Which weapons are so inaccurate as to be intolerably indiscriminate? What risks should soldiers take on themselves to avoid harming civilians? When is "collateral damage" to civilians disproportionate? Should civilians lose their rights when they serve—voluntarily or involuntarily—as human shields? Finally, when should killing civilians constitute a war crime?

These questions have always been with us, but they may have seemed less pressing during an era of regular armed conflicts between states, often conducted at sea, in the air, or on distant battlefields. Unfortunately, more than ever before, today's combatants fight where civilians live. These questions take on new urgency in our own era of irregular armed conflicts between states and organized armed groups, in which the latter often wear no uniforms, conceal their weapons, and operate among the civilian population. These changes in the nature of warfare have exposed gaps and ambiguities in the law of war that leave civilians without adequate legal protection and leave combatants without adequate legal guidance.

These are the questions that this book seeks to answer, drawing on and contributing to both international law and moral philosophy in equal measure. In Chapter 2, I argue that the law of war should be defended, interpreted, and developed so as to serve combatants by providing them with moral guidance, thereby helping them to conform as closely as possible to their moral obligations. I defend a broad principle of civilian immunity in Chapter 3, while proposing new restraints on the use of force against combatants in Chapter 4. I explore a new account of epistemic moral permissibility in order to develop new approaches to distinguishing civilians from combatants in Chapter 5, and to indiscriminate attacks in Chapter 6. I appeal to the moral asymmetry between doing harm and allowing harm in order to advance a new understanding of precautions in attack in Chapter 7, and a new standard of proportionality in Chapter 8. Resisting some disturbing trends, I argue in Chapter 9 that civilians used as human shields generally retain their moral and legal rights.

Finally, in Chapter 10, I argue that the Rome Statute of the International Criminal Court fails to recognize and punish serious violations of the law of armed conflict and must be amended.

This book examines those legal principles that promise "[t]he civilian population and individual civilians . . . general protection against dangers arising from military operations."[3] These legal principles—civilian immunity, distinction, discrimination, precautions, and proportionality—constitute only part of the law of war. I will say little about the *jus ad bellum* and nothing about the law of occupation. Even within the *jus in bello*, I will say little about the treatment of prisoners, the sick, and the wounded; the legal status of medical, religious, and civil defense personnel; prohibitions on specific weapons; or damage to civilian property, cultural property, and the environment. Instead, I will focus my attention on the law of targeting and attack that protects individual human beings from death and serious physical injury. My aim is not to touch on every part of the law of war but to focus on what I consider its moral core.

Each chapter contains both legal analysis and moral argument. The relationship between the two varies somewhat from chapter to chapter. In some chapters, I offer moral arguments in *defense* of existing law. In others, I offer moral arguments for *reform* of existing law. In most chapters, I offer moral arguments for *interpreting* existing law in its morally best light.

Over the last two decades, philosophical enquiry into the ethics of war has reached an unprecedented level of rigor and sophistication. In my view, it is high time that we integrate the concepts, methods, and insights of moral theory into contemporary legal discourse.

I hope that this book will contribute to both international law and moral philosophy while perhaps bringing these two fields closer together. If a few international lawyers come to see moral philosophy as a valuable resource, while a few moral philosophers come to see international law as an exciting opportunity to put their theoretical skills to practical use, then writing this book will have been time well spent.

Accordingly, I hope that this book will prove both accessible and interesting to readers from a variety of disciplines, provided that they are willing to familiarize themselves with a few legal terms and moral concepts. Most of these terms and concepts are used in ordinary language, though often imprecisely. Admittedly, a few are rather esoteric, but I hope will earn their keep. I introduce many of them here so that readers will not feel ambushed when I reintroduce them in later chapters. Readers should feel no need to memorize each term or concept now, but instead should refer back to the following sections as needed.

---

[3] Protocol Additional to the Geneva Conventions of August 12, 1949, and relating to the Protection of Victims of International Armed Conflicts (Protocol I) (adopted June 8, 1977, entered into force December 7, 1978) 1125 UNTS 3, art 51(1).

Legal Terms

I use the labels "law of war," "law of armed conflict" (or LOAC), and "international humanitarian law" (or IHL) interchangeably. The term "war" may seem both narrow and antiquated, suggesting either formal declarations of war by opposing states or the large-scale use of military force by opposing states. Nevertheless, the term "war" remains ubiquitous in ordinary language, in state practice, in international law, and in moral philosophy.[4] For its part, "law of armed conflict" underscores the *scope* of the relevant legal principles, which regulate any use of significant military force between states as well as intense armed violence between states and organized armed groups or between such groups. In contrast, "international humanitarian law" underscores the *purpose* of the relevant legal principles, which is to protect human beings in armed conflict. Since none of these labels appear obviously superior to the others, I will use each as seems appropriate.

I will use the term "combatant" to refer to members of the armed forces of parties to international armed conflicts as well as to members of both state armed forces and organized armed groups representing parties to non-international armed conflicts.[5] Civilians who take a direct part in hostilities are not, strictly speaking, combatants. This legal distinction is highly relevant to lawful detention and criminal prosecution, but it is largely irrelevant to lawful targeting, attack, and collateral harm. Accordingly, unless otherwise indicated, my moral and legal claims regarding combatants apply also to civilians directly participating in hostilities, while my moral and legal claims regarding civilians apply only to civilians not directly participating in hostilities. I sometimes refer to members of state armed forces as "soldiers" irrespective of their service branch.

I refer to harm inflicted on individuals who are not the object of an attack either as "collateral" harm or as "incidental" harm. Both terms have unfortunate connotations in ordinary language but are unavoidable in legal discourse and military practice.

I typically use "harm" or "losses" to refer to death and serious physical injury. In addition, my legal and moral claims regarding killing extend, with appropriate modifications, to nonlethal injury as well. I make a few comments regarding damage to civilian property in Chapter 8.

I often use "attacking forces" or "attackers" to refer to combatants planning or carrying out acts of violence and often use "defending forces" or "defenders" to

---

[4] International law continues to refer to "war crimes" as well as "prisoners of war," while philosophers continue to refer to "just war theory," "war ethics," and "the deep morality of war." On some views, the law of war includes the law governing the resort to military force as well as the law of neutrality, while the law of armed conflict and international humanitarian law include only the law governing the conduct of hostilities. See, eg, US Department of Defense, *Law of War Manual* (2015) 1.3.1.2.

[5] Some authors refer to the latter as "fighters," since they are not entitled to combatant immunity from criminal prosecution or to treatment as prisoners of war. Respectfully, I find this proliferation of terms unnecessary.

refer to combatants who are the targets of those acts of violence. These terms apply strictly at the tactical and operational levels of warfare. In any given engagement or campaign, forces fighting in national self-defense may be on the attack while forces participating in a war of aggression may be on the defensive. These terms simply identify the party to whom relevant legal principles apply at any given moment.

Finally, unless otherwise noted, the legal norms that I will discuss apply in international armed conflicts between states as well as in non-international conflicts between states and organized armed groups or between such groups. Many of these norms have been codified in conventional (treaty) law, most notably in the Additional Protocols to the Geneva Conventions. All of them reflect customary international law and therefore apply to all states independently of their treaty obligations.

Moral Concepts

On any moral view, you have *reasons* not to kill an innocent person that are grounded in her interests in living. In addition, you owe her a *duty* not to kill her that is grounded in her *right* against you that you not kill her. Her right that you not kill her both protects her interests in living and reflects her moral status. Your corresponding duty not to kill her is owed to her as an individual and gives you reasons not to kill her that are distinct from your reasons to ensure that as few innocent people die as possible. Since the duties I discuss are grounded on rights, all of my moral claims using one concept may be reframed using the other.

Rights are *infringed* when we act as someone has a right that we not act, for example, when we harm an innocent person. Rights are *violated* when they are unjustifiably infringed, for example, when we harm an innocent person for a trivial, insufficient, or wicked reason. Rights may be *overridden*—and therefore infringed but not violated— when the moral reasons in favor of infringing them outweigh the moral reasons against infringing them, for example, when we collaterally harm an innocent person as an unintended side effect of preventing far greater harm to others.

Any threat to infringe a right is an *unjust threat*. In contrast, only a threat to violate a right is an *unjustified threat*. It follows that unjust threats may be justified when the right that they threaten to infringe is overridden, to use the same example, when we threaten to infringe the rights of an innocent person as a side effect of preventing far greater harm to others.

An *innocent* person retains her basic rights. A person *forfeits* her rights when she loses them through her own voluntary conduct, for example, by culpably attempting to kill an innocent person.[6] A person who forfeits a right makes herself *morally liable* to be treated as she previously had a right not to be treated, for example, to

---

[6] Forfeiture of a right may be intentional or unintentional. In contrast, a person *waives* her rights only when she intentionally loses them through her voluntary conduct.

be (defensively) restrained, harmed, or even killed. It follows that treating someone as she has made herself morally liable to be treated does not infringe her rights and is not unjust.

Moral reasons are reasons for action, while *epistemic reasons* are reasons for belief. A *conclusive* reason confronts no opposing reasons. A *decisive* reason outweighs or otherwise defeats opposing reasons. A *strongly decisive* reason far outweighs opposing reasons. An *undefeated* reason is neither outweighed nor otherwise defeated.

An act is *objectively permissible* if and only if it is permissible given all the morally relevant facts. An act is *subjectively permissible* if and only if it would be objectively permissible were the agent's beliefs about the morally relevant facts true. An act is *epistemically permissible* only if it would be objectively permissible were the morally relevant facts as the available evidence suggests.[7] I offer a more detailed account of epistemic permissibility in Chapter 5.

While permissibility and impermissibility are binary, *wrongfulness* comes in degrees.[8] In one sense—call it the *pro tanto* sense—the stronger the moral reasons to refrain from an act, the more wrongful it is. In this sense, killing five innocent people is worse than killing one innocent person. In a different sense—call it the *all-things-considered* sense—the more decisively the reasons to refrain from the act outweigh the reasons to perform that act, the more wrongful it is. In this sense, killing five innocent people to save one innocent person is worse than killing five innocent people to save two innocent people. When I refer to the wrongfulness of an act, the context will indicate which sense I intend.

Similarly, one act is morally *worse* than another in the *pro tanto* sense when the moral reasons to refrain from the former are stronger than the moral reasons to refrain from the latter. In this sense, one act is morally worse than another when the former is harder to justify than the other, as it would take stronger opposing reasons to render the former permissible than to render the latter permissible. One act is morally worse than another in the all-things-considered sense when the final balance of moral reasons more strongly disfavors the former than the latter. When I say that one act is worse than another, the context will indicate which sense I intend.

Finally, *just combatants* are combatants whose armed forces fight for a just cause, while *unjust combatants* are combatants whose armed forces fight for an unjust cause. These designations refer to the strategic level of warfare at which the resort to military force is permitted or prohibited by the *jus ad bellum*. In particular tactical engagements, individual just combatants may pose unjust threats to innocent people while individual unjust combatants may pose justified threats to such just combatants. Almost all wars are morally heterogeneous to one extent or another.[9]

---

[7] These distinctions correspond to the distinctions between fact-relative, belief-relative, and evidence-relative wrongfulness in Derek Parfit, *On What Matters*, vol 1 (OUP 2011) 151.

[8] See Seth Lazar, *Sparing Civilians* (OUP 2016) 5.

[9] See Saba Bazargan, "Morally Heterogeneous Wars" (2013) 41 Philosophia 959.

War and Defensive Killing

Every moral argument begins somewhere. The moral arguments in this book begin with three claims. First, the moral norms governing violence in war are continuous with the moral norms governing violence outside of war. Second, the moral norms governing violence in war regulate not only the consequences of our actions but also their causal and intentional structure. Finally, the moral norms governing violence in war generally reflect our moral status as human beings and only interstitially reflect our special relationships. We may refer to these claims as *reductive individualism, nonconsequentialism,* and *cosmopolitanism* respectively. Since each of these claims has been admirably defended elsewhere by others, I will only present them in what I hope will prove a morally attractive light.[10]

On my view, almost all morally permissible killing in war is either defensive killing or a side effect of defensive killing. In general, individuals are morally liable to killing in war only if they unjustly threaten to kill or seriously injure innocent people or are sufficiently responsible for similar unjust threats posed by others. Relatedly, innocent people may be justifiably killed in war only if their deaths are an unavoidable side effect of defending other innocent people from such unjust threats. On my view, the law of war should help combatants target only those morally liable to defensive killing and collaterally harm the innocent only in defense of other innocent people.

Importantly, this approach does not entail that the law of war should track national criminal law rules governing self-defense and defense of others or track international human rights law rules governing the use of force by law enforcement. In ordinary life, it is hardly ever necessary to kill someone who poses no immediate threat or from whom one could safely retreat. In contrast, combatants who currently pose no threat often pose serious threats in the near future. Similarly, safely retreating from opposing forces in one engagement often means facing greater danger in the next engagement.

Nor does this approach entail that the law of war should track abstract moral principles without regard to the epistemic, pragmatic, cognitive, and emotional constraints under which combatants fight. On the contrary, the law of war should address combatants roughly as they are and in the circumstances in which they typically find themselves. Similarly, rules of engagement should provide simple guidance that combatants can understand, internalize, and apply under fire.

Finally, this approach does not deny that war may be a continuation of politics by other means. Instead, this approach emphasizes that war is a continuation of

---

[10] On reductive individualism, see Jeff McMahan, *Killing in War* (OUP 2009); Helen Frowe, *Defensive Killing* (OUP 2014). On nonconsequentialism, see FM Kamm, *Intricate Ethics: Rights, Responsibility, and Permissible Harm* (OUP 2007). On cosmopolitanism, see Cécile Fabre, *Cosmopolitan War* (OUP 2012).

politics by means of violence. If a state or non-state actor uses or threatens violence to achieve its political aims, then it may be permissible to use violence to stop or prevent such violence. In contrast, generally it is not permissible to use violence merely to prevent an adversary from achieving political aims—assuming these aims are not inherently violent—or merely to achieve one's own political aims. There may be cases in which it is permissible to resort to lethal force to protect or secure the political rights of many individuals. However, even in such cases, once war begins the rules governing the conduct of hostilities will be the rules governing defensive killing.[11]

Moral Asymmetries

On any nonconsequentialist view of ethics, the consequences of our actions always matter, but how we bring those consequences about often matters more. On most such views, intentionally harming innocent people is morally much worse (that is, much harder to justify) than unintentionally harming innocent people, which in turn is substantially morally worse (that is, substantially harder to justify) than allowing harm to innocent people. On such views, we may not unintentionally harm innocent people except as an unavoidable side effect of preventing substantially greater harm to other innocent people. In contrast, we may not intentionally harm innocent people except as a necessary means of preventing far greater harm to other innocent people.

International law reflects the extreme wrongfulness of intentionally harming innocent people in its categorical prohibition on targeting civilians. In contrast, international law reflects the substantial but lesser wrongfulness of unintentionally harming innocent people in its conditional prohibition on launching attacks that may be expected to cause harm to civilians that would be disproportionate or excessive in relation to the anticipated military advantage.

The substantial moral asymmetry between doing harm and allowing harm may be understood in a number of ways. Doing harm typically interferes with something else to which the person harmed has a right—typically her physical integrity—while allowing harm typically does not.[12] In addition, doing harm to someone typically leaves her worse off than she would have been in your absence, while allowing harm to someone typically fails to make her better off than she would have been in your absence. These considerations combine to make it substantially morally worse to harm an innocent person, even unintentionally, than to allow harm to another innocent person. For example, it would be wrong to protect

---

[11] Conditional threats of violence also introduce some complications. See generally Cécile Fabre and Seth Lazar (eds), *The Morality of Defensive War* (OUP 2014).

[12] See, eg, Kai Draper, *War and Individual Rights* (OUP 2016) 53–6.

one innocent person from being killed if, as a foreseeable side effect, you will kill another innocent person. Though the consequences are equally bad, one way of bringing about those consequences would be worse than the other.

The compound moral asymmetry between intentionally doing harm and foreseeably allowing harm also may be understood in a number of ways. In many cases, intentionally harming someone uses her as a means of achieving aims that you could not achieve in her absence. Such *opportunistic, manipulative*, or *exploitative* harming wrongfully involves her in your plans without her consent and wrongfully uses her to benefit others at her expense.[13] Paradigmatically, it would be wrong to intentionally kill an innocent, healthy person in order to distribute her organs to five deserving patients who will die without them. Though the consequences would be better, this way of bringing them about would be worse.

International law recognizes the special wrongfulness of opportunistically harming innocent people by categorically prohibiting "[a]cts or threats of violence the primary purpose of which is to spread terror among the civilian population."[14] International law also recognizes the special wrongfulness of opportunistically using innocent people—endangering them though not directly harming them—by forbidding combatants from using civilians as human shields.

In rare cases, the presence of an innocent person can make you worse off than you would be in her absence. For example, her presence may physically prevent you from achieving your aims. Intentionally harming her may remove the obstacle that she presents. Such *eliminative* harming would not use her as a means of achieving your aims but would still harm her, or affect her in a way that harms her, as a means of achieving your aims. Eliminative harming remains a form of instrumental harming that wrongfully involves the victim in your plans without her consent as a means of preventing harm to others at her expense. These considerations typically make eliminative harming harder to justify than collateral harming but not as hard to justify as opportunistic harming.[15]

To illustrate these moral distinctions in wartime contexts, compare the following cases:

> *Flush Out*: A military sniper deploys to kill an opposing combatant. The combatant is in a house, so the sniper has no clear shot. Just then, a passing civilian unwittingly walks by the front door. If the sniper shoots the civilian, then the combatant will run out to try to help the civilian, allowing the sniper to kill the combatant.

[13] See, eg, Warren S Quinn, "Actions, Intentions, and Consequences: The Doctrine of Double Effect" (1989) 18 Philosophy & Public Affairs 334; Victor Tadros, "Wrongful Intentions without Closeness" (2015) 43 Philosophy & Public Affairs 52.

[14] Protocol I art 51(2); International Committee of the Red Cross, *Customary International Humanitarian Law*, vol 1 (CUP 2009) 8.

[15] See Quinn, "Actions, Intentions, and Consequences"; Tadros "Wrongful Intentions." In some cases, one person intentionally kills another person as an end in itself, neither as a

Clear Shot: A military sniper has a clear shot at an opposing combatant. Just as the combatant is about to leave, a passing civilian unwittingly walks directly in the line of fire. If the sniper shoots the civilian, then the civilian will drop to the ground, giving the sniper a clear shot to kill the combatant.

Drone Strike: A drone pilot tracks an opposing combatant to an otherwise empty house and prepares to launch a missile strike. Just then, a passing civilian unwittingly stops by the side of the house to rest in the shade. The pilot can launch a missile at the house, killing the combatant and wounding the civilian.

Holding constant the harm to the civilian and the military advantage of killing the combatant, it seems somewhat worse to harm the civilian in *Flush Out* than in *Clear Shot* and much worse to harm the civilian in *Clear Shot* than in *Drone Strike*. In *Flush Out*, the sniper would opportunistically harm the civilian as a means of achieving an aim that the sniper could not achieve in the civilian's absence. In *Clear Shot*, the sniper would eliminatively harm the civilian as a means of achieving an aim that the sniper could achieve in the civilian's absence. Finally, in *Drone Strike*, the pilot would collaterally harm the civilian as a foreseen but unintended side effect of achieving an aim that the pilot could achieve in the civilian's absence.

Importantly, in some cases, it is possible to opportunistically harm someone without deliberately targeting her or directly attacking her. Consider the following scenario:

Collateral Terror: An attack on a munitions factory will also kill some innocent civilians nearby. The damage to the factory will confer little military advantage; there are many other munitions factories and this factory will be quickly repaired. This military advantage alone would not justify the civilian deaths, leaving the attack disproportionate. However, the deaths of the civilians will terrorize and demoralize the rest of the civilian population.

Suppose that attackers strike the factory not *in order to* kill the civilians but only *because* or *on the condition* that the civilians will be killed. In other words, the attackers would not attack the civilians in the factory's absence but neither would they attack the factory in the civilians' absence. In my view, the civilians are still killed opportunistically, taking advantage of their presence to obtain benefits that could not be obtained in their absence.[16]

More broadly, when we consider the permissibility of an act that infringes the rights of an innocent person—either intentionally or unintentionally—generally we should exclude the downstream consequences of that infringement from

---

means of producing benefits nor as a means of preventing harms. Obviously, such wanton killings are necessarily unjustified.

[16] For a different view, see Kamm, *Intricate Ethics*. The scenario that I describe is adapted from one of Kamm's. I return to this issue in Chapter 9.

justifying that infringement.[17] If such consequences could justify such infringements, then morality itself would regard the infringement of rights as an appropriate causal means of producing good consequences and as an opportunity to be exploited for the greater good. The exclusion of such consequences—at least below some significant threshold—partly constitutes our moral status as presumptively inviolable beings, generally entitled to decide for ourselves which ends we will serve and which sacrifices we will make. It is wrong to kill in order to bring about such consequences, or on the condition that killing will bring about such consequences, because in either case we fail to act on morally valid grounds.

Fellow Soldiers, Fellow Citizens, and Foreign Civilians

In international armed conflict, combatants must often choose between launching attacks that collaterally harm foreign civilians or refraining from such attacks and thereby—sooner or later—allowing opposing combatants to kill their comrades or their own civilians. Some scholars argue that, in such cases, combatants have *special duties* to protect their comrades and fellow citizens. These special duties may be associative obligations based on shared nationality or role–responsibilities voluntarily undertaken. Importantly, these scholars argue that the special duties of combatants offset or override the general moral asymmetry between doing harm and allowing harm. On these views, special duties make it morally permissible for combatants to collaterally harm foreign civilians rather than allow comparable or even lesser harm from befalling their comrades or their civilians.[18]

I reject all such views. No doubt, combatants generally bear special duties to protect their comrades and civilians from harm. These duties may be very stringent. Indeed, combatants may be morally required to risk or sacrifice their own lives to discharge their special duties. However, it does not follow that combatants are morally permitted to risk or sacrifice the lives of foreign civilians simply to discharge their own special duties.[19] In general, I may not force others to bear the costs of discharging my duties. Since these are my duties, the costs of discharging them should

[17] See Adil Ahmad Haque, "Torture, Terror, and the Inversion of Moral Principle" (2007) 10 New Criminal Law Review 613; Howard Nye, "Objective Double Effect and the Avoidance of Narcissism," in Mark Timmons (ed), *Oxford Studies in Normative Ethics*, vol 3 (2013) 280 ("All else held equal, the fact that an act or omission will result in benefits for some individuals at the expense of other individuals weakens the extent to which those benefits count in favour of the act or omission").

[18] See, eg, Thomas Hurka, "Proportionality in the Morality of War" (2005) 33 Philosophy & Public Affairs 34, 63–4.

[19] Seth Lazar helpfully distinguishes between the stringency of special duties, which determines "the costs they can justify imposing on the duty-bearer" and the gravity of

fall on me alone. To force others to bear these costs is tantamount to forcing others to discharge my duties on my behalf. It follows that combatants are permitted to kill foreign civilians only according to the general morality of doing and allowing harm, unaffected by their special duties to their comrades and civilians.

Here is another way of seeing that special duties cannot affect the moral permissibility of killing. Suppose that an innocent stranger is about to be harmed and asks me to defend her. She retains her right to use force in self-defense and may transfer that right to me to exercise on her behalf. However, my general duty to defend her is not very stringent. I may decline to defend her if doing so would place me at grave personal risk. Now suppose that an innocent civilian is about to be harmed by a foreign combatant and asks a soldier in her state's armed forces to defend her. The soldier's special duty to defend her may be very stringent, such that the soldier must defend her even at grave personal risk. But notice that what the soldier is required to do—the content of the special duty—is to exercise the civilian's right of self-defense on her behalf. It follows that the soldier may not do for the civilian what the civilian may not do for herself. If the civilian may not inflict a greater harm on a foreign civilian as a side effect of defending herself from a lesser harm, then the soldier may not do so on her behalf. After all, no one can transfer a right that she does not possess.[20]

The opposing view, that special relationships significantly affect the morality of killing and letting die, may seem attractive when we imagine our loved ones in peril. When considering such cases, we may feel that it would be permissible for us to kill an innocent bystander in order to save our loved one, if not as a means then perhaps as a side effect.[21] However, when we imagine *ourselves* in peril and our loved ones in a position to save us, it seems clearly wrong to ask our loved ones to kill an innocent bystander to save us, either as a means or as a side effect. Yet it seems hard to believe that others may do for us what we may not ask them to do for us. Put another way, the extra weight that we may place on each other's lives, due to our special relationships, should not exceed the extra weight that we may each place on our own life. Accordingly, in my view, our special duties to protect others do not give us special rights to harm others.

---

special duties, which determines their "relative weight when they clash with other moral reasons" ("Associative Duties and the Ethics of Killing in War" (2013) 1 Journal of Practical Ethics 3, 14). On my view, the special duties of soldiers are very stringent but not sufficiently grave to justify killing foreign civilians when doing so would otherwise be morally impermissible.

[20] See Jeff McMahan, "The Just Distribution of Harm Between Combatants and Noncombatants" (2010) 38 Philosophy & Public Affairs 342, 366. See also David Lefkowitz, "Partiality and Weighing Harm to Non-Combatants" (2009) 6 Journal of Moral Philosophy 298.

[21] McMahan, "Just Distribution," 377. McMahan notes that such cases are largely irrelevant to the case of war, "since the relations between just combatants and just civilians are in general far less morally significant than the relation between a parent and child."

The Road Ahead

In Chapter 2, I argue that the central debate in contemporary just war theory—between conventionalists led by Michael Walzer and revisionists led by Jeff McMahan—rests, in part, on a mistake. Conventionalists argue that both the law of war and the morality of war grant opposing combatants symmetrical permissions to fight irrespective of the cause for which they fight. Revisionists argue that combatants have no moral permission to fight for an unjust cause and conclude that the law of war sharply diverges from the deep morality of war. Indeed, many revisionists argue that the law of war should not even aim to track the deep morality of war but instead should aim to reduce wrongful suffering in war to the greatest extent practically possible—what I call *the humanitarian view*.

In contrast, I argue that the law of war does not, in fact, permit combatants to fight for an unjust cause. The legal equality of combatants does not consist in symmetrical legal permissions to fight but instead in symmetrical legal prohibitions on certain means of fighting as well as symmetrical legal immunities from criminal prosecution for acts that are not prohibited by the law of war. On this view, the law of war applies alongside other legal and moral norms, including human rights law, rather than displacing them. Accordingly, conventionalists who seek to defend the war convention need not defend moral permissions to fight for an unjust cause. At the same time, revisionists who reject such moral permissions need not resign themselves to a sharp divergence between law and morality.

Finally, I reject the humanitarian view and defend *the service view*, according to which the law of war should aim to help combatants better conform to their moral obligations. The law of war achieves its aim to the extent that just combatants are more likely to avoid acting wrongfully if they obey the law and unjust combatants will act less wrongfully if they obey the law. We should defend, interpret, and develop the law of war by reference to the service view. Though apparently heterodox, the service view gives moral content to the orthodox view that we should purposively interpret the law of war by balancing humanitarian and military considerations.

In Chapter 3, I offer a moral defense of the legal principle of civilian immunity. Civilians enjoy general legal protection from intentional, unnecessary, and disproportionate harm unless and for such time as they take a direct part in hostilities. A number of revisionists, particularly Jeff McMahan and Helen Frowe, reject the deep moral basis of civilian immunity, arguing that many civilians who contribute to an unjust war effort are morally liable to defensive killing. I directly address their arguments in an Appendix at the end of the book. In Chapter 3, I present my affirmative moral argument that civilians generally are morally liable to defensive killing only if they pose unjust threats directly, jointly with others, or indirectly through others they control. Suitably interpreted, the legal standard of direct participation in hostilities closely tracks deep moral principles. Just combatants who obey the law will avoid wrongful killing while unjust combatants will kill less wrongfully if they obey the law than if they break the law.

In Chapter 4, I argue that the moral status of combatants is more complex than is generally believed, and that we should reform the law to reflect this complexity. While unjust combatants who perform combat functions are morally liable to defensive killing, unjust combatants who perform noncombat functions are not. At the same time, I argue that it is much less wrongful to kill unjust combatants who perform noncombat functions than to kill civilians. It follows that one need not presume that unjust combatants perform noncombat functions in case of doubt or take risky precautions to avoid mistakenly killing such combatants. In addition, collateral harm to such combatants will seldom render acts of war—or the resort to war—disproportionate. Nevertheless, it is epistemically impermissible to target unjust combatants if one has decisive reason to believe that they perform non-combat functions. International law should therefore prohibit intentionally killing combatants "if it becomes apparent" that they perform noncombat functions. Such a prohibition will help just combatants avoid wrongful killing and will help unjust combatants avoid particularly wrongful killings. Human rights law may also pro-hibit such killings.

In addition, it is objectively impermissible to unnecessarily kill opposing com-batants whom one could safely capture. With some regret, I conclude that recent arguments that the law of war already prohibits such unnecessary killing do not succeed. Such combatants are not *hors de combat* and the principle of humanity does not directly obligate individuals to refrain from such killings. Instead, I argue that the principle of humanity legally obligates states to instruct their armed forces to refrain from such killings. Over time, convergent state practice and opinion will generate specific rules of customary international law, binding on individuals, that prohibit such killings.

In Chapter 5, I argue that the principle of distinction requires more than not intentionally targeting known civilians. In addition, attackers must not intentionally target a person unless they are sufficiently certain that the individual is a combat-ant and not a civilian. Unfortunately, international law does not identify the level of certainty required to lawfully attack a person. Some experts propose a balancing approach, according to which the required level of certainty varies with the relative risks of mistakenly killing a civilian or mistakenly sparing an opposing combatant. Unfortunately, the balancing approach quickly generates intolerable results. Instead, I argue that it is epistemically permissible to target a person only if your epistemic reasons to believe that she is liable to targeting are stronger than your epistemic reasons to believe that she is not liable to targeting. In particular, combatants must presume that persons are civilians unless the behavior of those individuals provides decisive reason to believe that they are combatants. Above this *reasonable belief thresh-old*, the required level of certainty varies with the relative moral costs of mistakenly killing an innocent person or mistakenly allowing innocent people to be killed.

These moral costs reflect the moral asymmetry between doing harm and allowing harm. I illustrate how my approach would operate in practice, proposing new interpretations of existing law as well as model rules of engagement.

In Chapter 6, I explore two possible justifications for the legal prohibition on the use of indiscriminate weapons. The prohibition may be justified instrumentally, as an indirect strategy of implementing more fundamental prohibitions on inflicting intentional, unnecessary, and disproportionate harm on civilians. In particular, the prohibition can assist in preventing attacks that are *expectably* disproportionate, that is, whose possible military benefits, discounted by their probability, are outweighed by their possible humanitarian costs, discounted by their probability. However, I argue that it is intrinsically morally wrong to use weapons that, either by their general nature or by their particular use, are more likely to strike civilians or civilian objects than to strike combatants or military objectives. I argue that, pursuant to the service view, such use of inaccurate weapons should be considered unlawfully indiscriminate.

In Chapter 7, I reject the view of some states and scholars that attacking forces are legally and morally permitted to forgo precautions in attack that would avoid harm to civilians if these precautions carry significant risk to attacking forces or to the success of their mission. A better view is that a precaution is "feasible" and therefore required if the humanitarian considerations in favor of taking the precaution outweigh the military considerations against taking the precaution. On a "risk-egalitarian" interpretation of this view, we should place equal weight on the lives and welfare of combatants and civilians and require those precautions that maximize expected value. Unsurprisingly, my own view is that the feasibility of a precaution should reflect the moral asymmetry between doing and allowing harm. On my view, a precaution should be considered feasible unless taking the precaution would increase the marginal risk of allowing harm to combatants substantially more than forgoing the precaution would increase the marginal risk of harming civilians. In addition, I reject arguments that precautionary obligations should be less stringent in humanitarian interventions that often endanger the very civilian populations that they seek to protect.

In Chapter 8, I examine the most elusive concept in the law of war—though perhaps the most important—namely the concept of proportionality. I argue that an attack that inflicts incidental harm on civilians is objectively proportionate only if it prevents opposing forces from inflicting substantially greater harm on attacking forces or civilians in current or future military operations. This account reflects the moral asymmetry between doing harm and allowing harm while looking beyond particular tactical engagements to the broader operational picture. I argue that an attack is epistemically proportionate only if the attacker reasonably believes—on the basis of decisive epistemic reasons—that the attack will prove objectively proportionate. Put another way, an attacker must reasonably believe that, of all the possible outcomes of the attack, it is probable that the actual outcome of the attack will be objectively proportionate.

My account of *jus in bello* proportionality is in one way more determinate than existing accounts—for example, it does not compare incommensurable values but instead compares immediate losses to civilians with future losses to civilians and to attacking forces. At the same time, my account must still grapple with the predictive uncertainty inherent in determining whether immediate losses inflicted will be redeemed by future losses prevented. I therefore explore a number of decision procedures and rules of engagement that combatants may use to make the best possible decision given the limited information available to them.

In Chapter 9, I reject the view of some states and scholars that attackers may partly discount or entirely disregard collateral harm to human shields in determining the proportionality of an attack. Instead, I argue that civilians who are used as involuntary shields retain their ordinary legal and moral protection. Here, as elsewhere, attackers must weigh the collateral harm that they reasonably expect to inflict on civilians—who have done nothing to lose their legal or moral rights—against the military advantage that they reasonably anticipate.

More controversially, I reject the popular view that all civilians who serve as voluntary shields directly participate in hostilities and thereby lose their civilian immunity entirely. Instead, I argue that voluntary shields directly participate in hostilities only for such time as their physical presence is an integral part of a coordinated military operation that is likely to directly cause serious harm. At the same time, I argue that collateral harm to voluntary shields may be discounted—though not entirely disregarded—in determining the proportionality of an attack. Since positive legal materials alone leave the legal status of voluntary shields indeterminate, I argue that we should interpret the law in its morally best light, thereby giving combatants the best possible moral guidance.

Finally, in Chapter 10, I argue that the Rome Statute of the International Criminal Court fails to enforce the fundamental rules of distinction, discrimination, precautions, and proportionality. Defendants will often escape criminal liability for recklessly attacking civilians; using indiscriminate weapons; forgoing feasible precautions; and foreseeably causing excessive harm to civilians. We should revise the Rome Statute, bringing it into alignment with the law of war as well as with customary international criminal law. We should recognize violations of these fundamental rules as war crimes, thereby underscoring the moral seriousness of these violations, affirming the moral legitimacy of the law of war, and reinforcing the moral guidance that the law of war aims to provide.

We have much to discuss. Let us begin.

2

Law and Morality

International law prohibits the use of military force by states on the territory of other states except with the consent of the territorial state, with the authorization of the United Nations Security Council, or in individual or collective self-defense against an armed attack.[1] Importantly, the law governing the conduct of hostilities (the *jus in bello*) applies independently of the law governing the resort to military force (the *jus ad bellum* or *jus contra bellum*) and applies symmetrically to all sides irrespective of the legality of their respective war aims.

In international armed conflicts, international law grants combatants "the right to participate directly in hostilities," irrespective of the party for which they fight, so long as they distinguish themselves from the civilian population while they are engaged in an attack or in military operations preparatory to an attack.[2] Similarly, international law protects civilians, as well as combatants who surrender, are taken prisoner, or are wounded, sick, or shipwrecked, "without any adverse distinction based on the nature or origin of the armed conflict or on the causes espoused by or attributed to the Parties to the conflict."[3] In short, international law accepts both the *legal equality of combatants* and the *legal equality of noncombatants*.

For some time, just war theory was dominated by *the conventionalist view* according to which the morality of war tracks the law of war in most respects.[4] On the conventionalist view, combatants on all sides enjoy symmetrical moral permissions while noncombatants on all sides enjoy symmetrical moral protections. All combatants are morally permitted to intentionally harm opposing combatants and to inflict necessary and proportionate collateral harm on noncombatants. All noncombatants are morally protected from intentional, unnecessary, or disproportionate harm. In

---

[1] United Nations Charter arts 2(4), 42, 51.

[2] Protocol Additional to the Geneva Conventions of 12 August 1949, and relating to the Protection of Victims of International Armed Conflicts (Protocol I) (adopted 8 June 1977, entered into force 7 December 1978) 1125 UNTS 3, arts 43(2), 44; International Committee of the Red Cross, *Customary International Humanitarian Law*, vol 1 (CUP 2009) 11, 384.

[3] Protocol I preamble.

[4] In important respects, the conventionalist view itself departed from traditional just war theory. See Gregory M Reichberg, "Just War and Regular War: Competing Paradigms," in David Rodin & Henry Shue (eds), *Just and Unjust Warriors: The Moral and Legal Status of Soldiers* (OUP 2008) 193.

Law and Morality at War. First Edition. Adil Haque. © Adil Haque 2017. Published 2017 by Oxford University Press

short, the conventionalist view accepts both the *moral equality of combatants* and the *moral equality of noncombatants*.

Since roughly the turn of the century, a number of *revisionist* scholars have systematically attacked the conventionalist view and with it the moral foundations of the law of war. Revisionists deny that the moral norms governing armed conflict are symmetrical in the conventionalist sense. Most revisionists deny the moral equality of combatants and many deny the moral equality of noncombatants as well. On the revisionist view, only combatants pursuing a just cause are morally permitted to intentionally harm opposing combatants or to inflict necessary and proportionate collateral harm on noncombatants. Some revisionists also argue that noncombatants who indirectly contribute to an unjust war effort are morally liable to intentional or collateral harm.

Importantly, most revisionists agree that the legal norms governing armed conflict should remain symmetrical, not as a matter of moral principle but for pragmatic and epistemic reasons. On the revisionist view, the law of war must diverge from the deep morality of war. The law must permit what morality forbids—killing in pursuit of an unjust cause—and forbid what some revisionists believe that morality permits—killing civilians who support an unjust war effort.

Many revisionists, convinced that law and morality must diverge, are driven to embrace *the humanitarian view* that the law of war should aim to reduce unnecessary suffering in war to the greatest extent practically possible. According to the humanitarian view, while the deep morality of war may protect the moral rights of individuals, the law of war can at best reduce aggregate harm. On this view, armed forces convinced (or at least claiming) that they fight for a just cause will simply ignore legal constraints that make military victory impossible. It follows that the law of war can only effectively prohibit militarily unnecessary harm.

In this chapter, I argue that the debate between conventionalists and revisionists regarding the morality of war rests, in part, on a mistake. The legal equality of combatants does not consist in symmetrical legal permissions to fight but in symmetrical legal prohibitions on certain means and methods of fighting as well as symmetrical legal immunities from criminal prosecution for acts that do not violate those prohibitions. The law does not permit what morality forbids because the law does not, in fact, permit combatants to fight for an unjust cause. On my view, the law of targeting and attack contains no permissions but instead contains only prohibitions. Conventionalists committed to the convergence of law and morality need not defend symmetrical moral permissions to fight irrespective of one's war aims. At the same time, revisionists who reject such symmetrical moral permissions need not insist on a sharp divergence between law and morality.

Finally, I reject the humanitarian view and defend the *service view*, according to which the law of war should aim to help combatants better conform to their moral obligations. On the service view, individuals generally have decisive moral reason to obey the law only if they will better conform to their moral obligations by following the law than by following their own moral judgment. The law of war achieves its aim to the extent that just combatants are more likely to *avoid* acting wrongfully if they obey the law while unjust combatants will act *less* wrongfully if they obey the law.

The service view can accommodate the revisionist insight that the deep morality of war is asymmetrical while providing a non-consequentialist defense of a symmetrical law of war. The contingent aim of many states in developing the law of war may be to reduce unnecessary suffering in war, but the constitutive aim of the law of war itself is to provide a moral service to combatants. We should defend, interpret, and develop the law of war by reference to the service view.

Conventionalists and Revisionists

The conventionalist view, that combatants are both legally and morally permitted to fight irrespective of their war aims, is most closely associated with Michael Walzer. In *Just and Unjust Wars*, Walzer offers a critical interpretation and qualified defense of "the war convention," which Walzer describes as "the set of articulated norms, customs, professional codes, legal precepts, religious and philosophical principles, and reciprocal arrangements that shape our judgments of military conduct."[5] According to Walzer, "the task of the moral theorist is to study the pattern as a whole, reaching for its deepest reasons."[6]

Since Walzer views the law of war as an integral part of the war convention, it is no surprise that his interpretation and defense of the latter reads like an interpretation and defense of the former. Famously, Walzer argues that the moral principles governing the resort to war and the moral principles governing the conduct of war are "logically independent. It is perfectly possible for a just war to be fought unjustly and for an unjust war to be fought in strict accordance with the rules."[7] In particular, Walzer argues that combatants on all sides of a conflict possess "an equal right to kill" opposing combatants as well as an equal (though limited) right to collaterally kill noncombatants.[8] Finally, Walzer argues that all noncombatants retain an equal right not to be intentionally killed or to be collaterally killed unnecessarily or disproportionately.

---

[5] Michael Walzer, *Just and Unjust Wars* (2nd edn Basic Books 1992) 44.

[6] Walzer, *Just and Unjust Wars*, 45.

[7] Walzer, *Just and Unjust Wars*, 21; see also 136 ("The rules of war apply with equal force to aggressors and their adversaries . . . . Soldiers fighting for an aggressor state are not themselves criminals: hence their war rights are the same as those of their opponents").

[8] Walzer, *Just and Unjust Wars*, 41; see also 36 ("Though there is no license for war-makers, there is a license for soldiers, and they hold it without regard to which side they are on; it is the first and most important of their war rights. They are entitled to kill").

On Walzer's view, combatants are morally equal because they pose threats to others, while noncombatants are morally equal because they pose no threats to anyone. According to Walzer, the "right not to be attacked . . . is lost by those who bear arms 'effectively' because they pose a danger to other people."[9] It follows that opposing combatants have "an equal right to kill" one another because they pose lethal threats to one other (as well as to noncombatants) and thereby lose their right not to be killed by one another. Importantly, combatants lose their right not to be killed even if they do not act wrongfully. "Simply by fighting," combatants lose "their title to life and liberty, . . . even though, unlike aggressor states, they have committed no crime."[10] Conversely, since noncombatants pose no threats, they retain their ordinary rights not to be intentionally or unnecessarily killed.

The revisionist view, that combatants are only morally permitted to fight for a just cause, is most closely associated with Jeff McMahan. In *Killing in War*, McMahan argues that human beings lose their moral right not to be killed by posing unjust threats but not by posing just threats. Combatants who fight for an unjust cause (such as territorial conquest) typically pose unjust threats to opposing combatants and thereby lose their moral right not to be killed. In contrast, combatants who fight for a just cause (such as national self-defense) typically pose just threats to opposing combatants and therefore retain their moral right not to be killed. On the revisionist view, the soldier fighting in national self-defense and the soldier fighting for territorial conquest do not have an "equal right to kill" one another. The former has a right to kill the latter and the latter has no right to kill the former.[11]

McMahan grants that combatants are legally permitted to inflict collateral harm on civilians irrespective of their war aims, but argues that combatants are only morally permitted to inflict collateral harm on civilians in pursuit of a just cause. Soldiers fighting in national self-defense can sometimes morally justify collaterally harming civilians as a necessary and proportionate side effect of preventing a greater evil. In contrast, soldiers fighting for territorial conquest can never morally justify collaterally harming civilians as a side effect of achieving an even greater evil.

While McMahan rejects the moral equality of combatants on deontological grounds, he accepts the legal equality of combatants on broadly consequentialist

---

[9] Walzer, *Just and Unjust Wars*, 145. Similarly, Walzer writes that a combatant may "be personally attacked only because he already is a fighter. He has been made into a dangerous man" (145).

[10] Walzer, *Just and Unjust Wars*, 136.

[11] Jeff McMahan, *Killing in War* (OUP 2009). McMahan allows that combatants fighting for a just cause may pose unjust threats in particular cases, for example by threatening to intentionally, unnecessarily, or disproportionately harm innocent civilians. Conversely, combatants fighting for an unjust cause may pose just threats in particular cases, for example in the course of protecting innocent civilians from intentional, unnecessary, or disproportionate harm. However, McMahan argues that such cases do not amount to a general moral equality of combatants.

grounds. As McMahan observes, a legal prohibition on killing in pursuit of an unjust cause will do little good and may do great harm. Most combatants, who believe that they fight for a just cause, will simply ignore such a prohibition. Worse, if combatants fear that they will be punished merely for fighting, then they may be less willing to surrender and more willing to win at all costs.[12] As Vattel observed, "each party asserting that they have justice on their own side, will arrogate to themselves all the rights of war, and maintain that their enemy has none."[13] It follows that, perhaps counter-intuitively, the legal equality of combatants reduces wrongful suffering in war.

For McMahan, the deep morality of war reflects the moral rights and duties of each affected individual. In contrast, McMahan writes that "the law of war is designed not to protect rights but to prevent harm."[14] On this view, "the laws of war are conventions that we design for ... mitigating the savagery of war, seeking to bring about outcomes that are more rather than less just or morally desirable."[15] In such passages, McMahan suggests that the legal equality of combatants rests not on the deep morality of war but on *the humanitarian view* of the law of war.

I will have more to say about the humanitarian view shortly, but first things first. In the next section, I reject the premise that the legal equality of combatants consists in symmetrical legal permissions to fight irrespective of one's war aims. If I am right then the dispute between conventionalists and revisionists, as well as the appeal of the humanitarian view, partly rests on a mistake.

The Right to Fight: An Immunity, Not a Privilege

As noted at the outset, international law grants lawful combatants "the right to participate directly in hostilities" irrespective of the party for which they fight.[16] Importantly, this legal right is granted to lawful combatants but denied to civilians. Indeed, international law positively defines combatants as those with a right to fight and negatively defines civilians as those who are not combatants. In this respect, the right to participate directly in hostilities contrasts with the right to be treated as a prisoner of war

---

[12] McMahan, *Killing in War*, 190–1.
[13] Emer de Vattel, *The Law of Nations* (1758) (Thomas Nugent trans, Liberty Fund 2008) book III, §188.
[14] McMahan, *Killing in War*, 107.
[15] Jeff McMahan, "The Morality of War and the Laws of War," in David Rodin and Henry Shue (eds), *Just and Unjust Warriors* (OUP 2008) 19, 34–5 ("My suggestion, then, is that we distinguish sharply and explicitly between the morality of war and the law of war"). See also Jeff McMahan, "The Ethics of Killing in War" (2004) 114 Ethics 693, 730.
[16] Protocol I art 43(2).

upon capture, which is granted both to lawful combatants and to certain categories of civilians.[17]

The right to participate directly in hostilities is often referred to as "the combatant's privilege" or as "the privilege of belligerency." As David Rodin writes:

The legal privilege functions as a positive right to kill, much in the way that the liberty to kill in self-defence functions as a right within domestic criminal law. It functions as a codified exception to an established prohibition . . . .[18]

Similarly, Jeremy Waldron writes that

The default position, apart from any convention, is that intentionally killing or attacking any human being is prohibited as murder. The laws of armed conflict provide an exception to that; they establish what we call in the trade a Hohfeldian privilege in relation to what is otherwise forbidden. And the rule about civilians is to be understood as a limitation on the scope of that privilege.[19]

On this view, international law grants all combatants a limited legal permission to target opposing combatants and to inflict necessary and proportionate collateral harm on noncombatants. Simply put, international law grants lawful combatants a "license to kill."[20]

In sharp contrast, on my view, international law does not grant lawful combatants a symmetrical legal privilege to fight but instead grants lawful combatants a symmetrical legal immunity from criminal prosecution. To see this, recall that international law grants "the right to participate directly in hostilities" exclusively to combatants and not to civilians. If this exclusive legal right involves a legal permission, then it should follow that combatants are legally permitted to fight while civilians are legally forbidden to fight. However, international law nowhere forbids civilians from participating directly in hostilities. Civilians do not violate international law simply by taking up arms and joining the fight.[21]

---

[17] See Geneva Convention (III) relative to the Treatment of Prisoners of War (opened for signature August 12, 1949, entered into force October 21, 1950) 75 UNTS 135. Protocol I clearly distinguishes between the right to be a combatant and the right to be a prisoner of war. See Protocol I, art 43(2) (stating that members of armed forces "are combatants, that is to say, they have the right to participate directly in hostilities"), art 44(1) ("Any combatant, as defined in Article 43, who falls into the power of an adverse Party shall be a prisoner of war"), arts 44(2), 44(5), and 47(1) (distinguishing the right to be a combatant from the right to be a prisoner of war).

[18] David Rodin, "Morality and Law in War," in H Strachan & S Scheipers (eds), *The Changing Character of War* (OUP 2011) 446, 455.

[19] Jeremy Waldron, *Torture, Terror, and Trade-offs* (OUP 2010) 107. But see Jeremy Waldron, "Responses to Zedner, Haque and Mendus" (2014) 8 Criminal Law and Philosophy 137 (writing that "Haque's account of this in terms of a ban on prosecutions is more accurate and more precise than my characterization in terms of a Hohfeldian privilege").

[20] Yoram Dinstein, *The Conduct of Hostilities under the Law of International Armed Conflict* (CUP 2010) 33.

[21] See, eg, International Committee of the Red Cross, *Interpretive Guidance on the Notion of Direct Participation in Hostilities Under International Humanitarian Law* (ICRC 2009) 83–4

It follows that the legal "right to participate directly in hostilities" conferred on combatants but denied to civilians cannot be a *privilege* or *liberty-right* to participate directly in hostilities, that is, the absence of a legal duty not to fight.[22] After all, neither combatants nor civilians have a legal duty under international law not to fight. Of course, this legal right also cannot refer to a *claim-right* that imposes on others legal duties of non-interference (let alone positive assistance). Obviously, opposing combatants have no legal duty not to prevent each other from fighting.

Instead, international law confers a limited legal immunity on lawful combatants, but not on civilians, from subsequent criminal prosecution.[23] International law prohibits states from criminally prosecuting combatants for acts that may violate national law but do not violate international law. In contrast, international law does not prohibit states from criminally prosecuting civilians under national law merely for participating directly in hostilities. Civilians may be criminally prosecuted for acts that do not violate international law but that violate national law, including killing opposing combatants. The right of combatants, but not civilians, "to participate directly in hostilities" is simply the right not to be criminally prosecuted merely for participating directly in hostilities.[24]

As Seth Lazar observes, "immunity from prosecution can be justified on its own terms; it need not be grounded in a right to fight."[25] Lazar writes that disconnecting combatant immunity from the right to fight "would not need too radical a change in the laws of war as they currently stand." On my view, no change in the laws of war is necessary because the right to fight just is a limited legal immunity from prosecution for fighting.

(stating that "civilian direct participation in hostilities is neither prohibited by IHL nor criminalized under the statutes of any prior or current international criminal tribunal or court"); Philip Alston, Report of the Special Rapporteur on Extrajudicial, Summary or Arbitrary Executions, Study on Targeted Killings, Human Rights Council, UN Doc A/HRC/14124/ Add.6 (May 28, 2010), para 71 ("Under IHL, civilians . . . are not prohibited from participating in hostilities").

[22] See generally Wesley Hohfeld, *Fundamental Legal Conceptions* (1919).

[23] See, eg, ICRC, *Interpretive Guidance* 83 ("This right [to directly participate in hostilities] . . . merely provides combatants with immunity from domestic prosecution for acts which, although in accordance with IHL, may constitute crimes under the national criminal law of the parties to the conflict (the so-called combatant privilege)"); Alston, Study on Targeted Killings, para 71 ("the consequence of participation is two-fold. First, . . . [civilian participants] may themselves be targeted and killed. Second, [civilian participants] do not have immunity from prosecution under domestic law for their conduct")).

[24] Notice that civilians may be criminally prosecuted for directly participating in hostilities irrespective of *jus ad bellum* considerations, while lawful combatants may not be criminally prosecuted for directly participating in hostilities irrespective of *jus ad bellum* considerations.

[25] Seth Lazar, "The Morality and Law of War," in Andrei Marmor (ed), *Routledge Companion to Philosophy of Law* (Routledge 2012) 376. See also Adil Ahmad Haque, "International Crime: In Context and in Contrast," in RA Duff, Lindsay Farmer, SE Marshall, Massimo Renzo, & Victor Tadros (eds), *The Structures of Criminal Law* (OUP 2011) 106; Adil Ahmad Haque, "Law and Morality at War" (2014) 8 Criminal Law & Philosophy 79.

Importantly, this legal immunity is limited in several ways. First, combatants forfeit their legal immunity by failing to distinguish themselves from civilians.[26] Second, this legal immunity only exists in international armed conflicts between state armed forces, not in non-international armed conflicts between states and organized armed groups or between such groups.[27] Most importantly, combatants are only legally immune from criminal prosecution by foreign states under their domestic criminal law. Conversely, combatants may be criminally prosecuted by their own state under its domestic criminal law.[28] Paradigmatically, lawful combatants fighting for their own state may be criminally prosecuted by their own state for violating rules of engagement that are more restrictive than international law. In addition, combatants fighting against their own state may be criminally prosecuted—most notably for treason—merely for directly participating in hostilities.[29]

As we have seen, combatants have no general "right to fight." Instead, lawful combatants in international armed conflicts have specific rights against foreign governments not to prosecute them for acts that violate domestic criminal law but do not violate international law. Vattel seemed to express this view when he wrote that the law of nations

does not, to him who takes up arms in an unjust cause, give any real right that is capable of justifying his conduct or acquitting his conscience, but merely entitles [an unjust combatant] to the benefit of the external effect of the law, and to impunity among mankind.[30]

It seems that, according to Vattel, only the *jus ad bellum* promises a justification for fighting, while the *jus in bello* offers only immunity from punishment.

States and scholars often use the terms "combatant's privilege" and "combatant immunity" interchangeably. As should now be clear, this lack of precision is apt to mislead. Strictly speaking, international law confers no legal privilege on

---

[26] Protocol I, art 44(3).

[27] See ICRC, *Customary IHL Study*, 12 ("Persons taking a direct part in hostilities in non-international armed conflicts are sometimes labelled "combatants" ... but [this] does not imply a right to combatant status or prisoner-of-war status, as applicable in international armed conflicts .... The lawfulness of direct participation in hostilities in non-international armed conflicts is governed by national law").

[28] See, eg, Lassa Oppenheim, *International Law, Volume II: Disputes, War and Neutrality* (Hersch Lauterpacht ed, 7th edn 1952) 115 ("The privileges of members of armed forces cannot be claimed by members of the armed forces of a belligerent who go over to the forces of the enemy and are afterwards captured by the former. They may be, and always are, treated as criminals").

[29] See Waldemar A Solf, "The Status of Combatants in Non-International Armed Conflicts under Domestic Law and Transnational Practice" (1983) 33 American University Law Review 53, 59.

[30] Vattel, *Law of Nations*, book III, §192. According to an alternative translation, the law of war "does not confer upon him whose cause is unjust any true rights capable of justifying his conduct and appeasing his conscience, but merely makes his conduct legal in the sight of men, and exempts him from punishment" (Emer de Vattel, *The Law of Nations* (1758) (Charles G Fenwick trans, Carnegie 1916) book III, §192).

combatants to fight irrespective of their war aims. International law does not permit what a combatant's own state forbids. States are free to punish their own citizens for acts that violate national law but not international law. On the contrary, international law prohibits what a combatant's own state might permit. States are free to punish combatants of any nationality for acts that violate international law even if those acts were authorized under national law. International law only prohibits states from punishing foreign lawful combatants for acts that violate national law but do not violate international law.

This dual function of international law—imposing legal prohibitions on all participants in hostilities while granting limited legal protections to lawful combatants—belies the notion that killing in war is presumptively lawful,[31] or, as Jeremy Waldron describes it, "a model that assumes that the default position is that you can kill anyone you like in wartime."[32] On the contrary, killing in war, as elsewhere, is presumptively criminal. International law bars the prosecution of foreign combatants for such presumptively criminal acts only when the latter kill in conformity with international law. In contrast, the ordinary law of criminal homicide remains in effect during war and may be applied to lawful combatants who kill in violation of international law, to unlawful combatants, to combatants who fight against their own state, and to civilians who directly participate in hostilities.

Importantly, a legal immunity is not a legal permission or an exemption from a legal prohibition. A legal immunity is not a justification (like self-defense), an excuse (like duress), or a denial of responsibility (like insanity). On the contrary, a legal immunity is a bar to criminal prosecution that applies irrespective of the wrongdoing and blameworthiness of the actor.

To illustrate, consider that diplomats are immune from criminal prosecution even if they satisfy all the elements of a criminal offense and can offer no exculpatory defense on their behalf. Of course, diplomatic immunity does not rest on a special legal permission conferred on diplomats but denied to ordinary citizens.[33] Instead, diplomatic immunity is a non-exculpatory public policy defense that allows an individual to "escape[] conviction in spite of [] culpability."[34] As Antony Duff explains

someone who claims diplomatic immunity when charged with an offense is not claiming that she was authorized to engage in that conduct, or that her conduct was legally

[31] For an example of this view, see George P Fletcher & Jens David Ohlin, *Defending Humanity* (OUP 2008) 100.

[32] Waldron, *Torture, Terror, and Trade-offs*, 109–11.

[33] See, eg, Vienna Convention on Consular Relations (opened for signature April 18, 1961, April 24, 1964) 500 UNTS 95, art 55(1) ("Without prejudice to their privileges and immunities, it is the duty of all persons enjoying such privileges and immunities to respect the laws and regulations of the receiving State").

[34] Paul H Robinson, "Criminal Law Defenses: A Systematic Analysis" (1982) 82 Columbia Law Review 199, 229–32. Prior acquittal is another example of a bar to prosecution that does not reflect on the legal or moral guilt of the accused.

permissible—indeed, she might admit that what she did was culpably criminal: but she is denying that this court has the authority to call her to account for her conduct.[35]

Put another way, justifications and excuses answer a criminal charge, while immunities entail that the accused need not answer the charge. Accordingly, legal immunities are typically raised and adjudicated on prior to trial and, if sustained, result in dismissal of charges. In contrast, justifications and excuses are typically raised and adjudicated on during trial and, if sustained, result in a verdict of acquittal.

Although justifications, excuses, denials of responsibility, and bars to prosecution allow the accused to avoid conviction, they each express a distinct moral message. Justifications express the message that the accused acted permissibly, all things considered, and that no one has a legitimate grievance or complaint against her. Excuses express the message that the accused acted impermissibly but she does not deserve blame. Bars to prosecution express the message that the accused may have acted impermissibly and may deserve blame but that there are other reasons why the state should not punish her. Less is required to morally justify bars to prosecution because bars to prosecution make relatively modest moral claims.

On my view, we should understand lawful combatant immunity as a bar to prosecution that rests on prosaic considerations of treaty and custom, reciprocity and impartiality, marginal incentives and aggregate consequences. No state wants its own soldiers prosecuted by its adversaries, and so all states agree not to prosecute the soldiers of their adversaries. In addition, such a legal immunity gives soldiers determined to fight an incentive to fight within the constraints of international law. If combatants will act less wrongfully if they obey the law than if they violate the law, then the law should create such incentives.

Revisionists may be right that such prosaic considerations are too weak to morally justify a legal permission to kill in pursuit of an unjust cause. Perhaps, as Rodin argues, a legal system that "creates a legal right for certain people to violate the moral rights of others, as a means to achieving a broader desirable end" thereby violates rights itself.[36] However, such prosaic considerations may be strong enough to ground a prohibition on criminally prosecuting foreign combatants who kill in pursuit of an unjust cause but who do not violate international law. Put another way, if the law claims that combatants are morally permitted to kill in pursuit of an unjust cause, then law's claim is false. If law claims only that states are morally prohibited from prosecuting combatants for fighting for an unjust cause, then law's claim may be redeemed. Those killed in pursuit of an unjust cause have a legitimate moral grievance or complaint—one that a legal permission would deny—but not necessarily one that their state may vindicate through domestic criminal prosecution.

---

[35] RA Duff, "'I Might Be Guilty, But You Can't Try Me': Estoppel and Other Bars to Trial" (2003) 1 Ohio State Journal of Criminal Law 245, 247.

[36] Rodin, "Morality and Law in War," 455.

On many jurisprudential views, including my own, law necessarily makes moral claims. On such views, a legal right is a (putative) moral right claimed by law.[37] In some cases, the law purports to identify and protect a pre-legal moral right, such as the right not to be tortured. In other cases, the law purports to create a new moral right, such as the right to vote, by changing the moral reasons that apply to those subject to the law. On such views, if the law permits some actor to perform some act, then the law claims that actor is morally permitted to perform that act. In particular, if international law confers a symmetrical legal permission to fight then it asserts a symmetrical moral permission to fight. Indeed, if international law did not make such moral claims, then conventionalists would not consider it part of the war convention that conventionalists seek to interpret and defend.[38]

Thankfully, on my view, international law does not claim that killing in pursuit of an unjust cause is morally permissible, that combatants are exempt from ordinary moral constraints, or that combatants are always or even typically justified or excused. International law claims only that states are morally prohibited from criminally prosecuting lawful combatants for acts that conform to international law. Put another way, international law does not purport to change the moral reasons that apply to combatants but rather to change the moral reasons that apply to states. Accordingly, Walzer was incorrect when he wrote that combatants who kill in pursuit of an unjust cause "have committed no crime." Often they have committed crimes, albeit crimes for which they may not be prosecuted.

No doubt, the legal immunity of combatants carries a moral cost. Many combatants know or should know that they fight for an unjust cause. They may believe that their war is unlawful or their war may be manifestly unlawful. There may be retributive reasons to allow states to punish such combatants in proportion to the wrongs they commit and their degree of moral fault. However, there are also retributive reasons against allowing such prosecutions. Such prosecutions would often be misdirected or abused—particularly by states prosecuting enemy soldiers—resulting in the unjust punishment of combatants who fought for a just cause or who reasonably believed that they fought for a just cause. In addition, such prosecutions would often result in disproportionate punishment of combatants who unreasonably but sincerely believed that they fought for a just cause. In

---

[37] See, eg, John Gardner, "How Law Claims, What Law Claims," in *Law as a Leap of Faith* 133 (OUP 2012); Joseph Raz, "Law, Morality and Authority," in *Ethics in the Public Domain* (OUP 1994).

[38] But see McMahan, *Killing in War*, 105 ("The law of war does not assert the *moral* equality of combatants but it does assert the *legal* equality of combatants"). On the contrary, by asserting the legal equality of combatants the law of war necessarily asserts the moral equality of combatants. It is just that the legal equality of combatants consists in immunities from prosecution rather than in permissions to fight. Accordingly, the law of war necessarily asserts that states have decisive moral reasons not to criminally prosecute opposing combatants for acts not prohibited by the law of war.

any event, even if the retributive reasons against combatant immunity outweigh the retributive reasons supporting combatant immunity, it is hard to believe that the former outweigh both the latter and the instrumental reasons supporting combatant immunity.

Importantly, combatant immunity does not entail general impunity for harms inflicted in pursuit of an unjust cause. International law recognizes the crime of aggression, which imposes criminal liability on political and military leaders for the use of force in manifest violation of the United Nations Charter.[39] Such political leaders do not enjoy combatant immunity and such military leaders may not claim combatant immunity with respect to the crime of aggression. If the crime of aggression is indeed "the supreme international crime differing only from other war crimes in that it contains within itself the accumulated evil of the whole" then by punishing the whole we punish its constituent parts, at least to a degree.[40] We will not thereby punish all those directly responsible for each killing in an unjust war, but we will punish those ultimately responsible for all killing in that unjust war.[41]

To conclude, international law does not prohibit lawful combatants from participating in aggression, and immunizes them from prosecution for acts that international law does not prohibit. The non-prohibition and the immunity are conceptually distinct but inextricably linked. If international law prohibited lawful combatants from participating in aggression, then foreign states would be free to prosecute them on that basis. No doubt, such a prohibition would have considerable expressive value. However, there is no combatant immunity for acts prohibited by international law. We must choose between the proposed prohibition and the existing immunity and, as we have seen, the reasons for the immunity are weighty indeed.

Prohibitions and Permissions

In my view, "the law relating to the conduct of hostilities is primarily a law of prohibition: it does not authorize, but prohibits certain things."[42] While the *jus ad*

---

[39] See, eg, Rome Statute of the International Criminal Court (opened for signature July 17, 1998, entered into force July 1, 2002) 2187 UNTS 3, art 8 *bis*.

[40] Judgment of the International Military Tribunal for the Trial of German Major War Criminals 421 (1946). See also Vattel, *Law of Nations*, book III, §§183–4.

[41] While threatening leaders with prosecution for the crime of aggression carries costs and risks—including creating incentives to win by any means necessary and thereby avoid trial and punishment—the strong retributive reasons to punish such leaders may justify such costs and risks. Thanks to Yitzhak Benbaji for pressing this point.

[42] Protocol I Commentary para 2238. See also Richard R Baxter, "So-Called 'Unprivileged Belligerency': Spies, Guerillas, and Saboteurs" (1951) 28 British Yearbook of International Law 323, 324 ("The law of war is . . . 'prohibitive law' in the sense that it forbids rather than

bellum sometimes authorizes the use of force by states, the *jus in bello* never authorizes acts of violence by armed forces. Under international law, authorization for acts of violence, if any, must come from the *jus ad bellum*.

As we have seen, international law applies the *jus in bello* equally to parties conforming to the *jus ad bellum* and to parties violating the *jus ad bellum*. Yet it would be illogical for international law to prohibit a use of force under the *jus ad bellum* while authorizing the acts of violence that make up that use of force under the *jus in bello*. The prohibition of aggressive force under the *jus ad bellum*, the equal application of the *jus in bello*, and the notion that the *jus in bello* authorizes acts of violence form a logically inconsistent set. In my view, we should reject the final proposition.

Similarly, international law applies the *jus in bello* equally to state armed forces and to non-state armed groups. Yet international law hardly gives non-state armed groups a legal right to wage war against their governments.

The law of armed conflict (LOAC) does not tell combatants what they may do, only what they may not do.[43] The LOAC prohibits the intentional, unnecessary, or disproportionate killing of civilians. However, no rule of the LOAC authorizes or justifies the unintentional, unavoidable, and proportionate killing of civilians. Similarly, the LOAC prohibits the intentional killing of combatants who have surrendered or are incapacitated by injury or illness. However, no rule of the LOAC authorizes or justifies the intentional killing of combatants who have not surrendered or been incapacitated. When we say that the LOAC "permits" such killings we refer either to the absence of a prohibition in international law or to lawful combatant immunity from prosecution for violations of domestic law. Indeed, it would be more precise to describe acts not prohibited by the LOAC as merely "tolerated" rather than as "permitted."[44]

Along similar lines, John Westlake wrote of the laws of war that

These rules are always restrictive, never permissive in any other sense than that of the absence of prohibition, for law can give no positive sanction to any act of force of which it cannot secure the employment on the side of justice alone, even if the particular act be not one which the law would prohibit both to the just and to the unjust if it could. Whenever

authorizes certain manifestations of force"); Derek Jinks, "International Human Rights Law in Time of Armed Conflict," in Andrew Clapham et al, *Oxford Handbook of International Law in Armed Conflict* 656 (OUP 2014).

[43] The law of detention and occupation may both authorize and constrain. On this view, detaining and occupying powers temporarily assume responsibility for the wellbeing of those detained or occupied, and therefore must have the legal power to issue authoritative directives until the end of detention or occupation. See, eg, Geneva Convention (III), art 21; Geneva Convention (IV) relative to the Protection of Civilian Persons in Time of War (opened for signature August 12, 1949, entered into force October 21, 1950), art 42. But see Jinks, "International Human Rights Law in Time of Armed Conflict," 666–7.

[44] See Accordance with International Law of the Unilateral Declaration of Independence in Respect of Kosovo, Advisory Opinion, 2010 ICJ Rep 403, paras 8–9 (declaration of Judge

therefore in speaking of the laws of war it is said that a belligerent may do this or that, it is always only the absence of prohibition that must be understood.[45]

Put another way, the law of targeting and attack confers no *strong* permissions. As Joseph Raz explains, "an act is strongly permitted only if its being permitted is entailed by a norm. It is permitted in the weak sense if the permission ... is simply a consequence of there being no norms prohibiting the performance of the action."[46] For example, the oft-cited *Lotus* principle—that states are permitted to do what international law does not prohibit—clearly refers to weak permissions rather than to strong permissions.[47]

Infelicitously, some legal prohibitions are phrased as legal requirements, which may in turn suggest implicit legal permissions. As we will see in Chapters 5 and 7, international law requires attackers to take feasible precautions to avoid mistakenly targeting civilians, unnecessarily harming civilians, or disproportionately harming civilians. However, combatants are not authorized to attack so long as they take these precautions. Instead, combatants are prohibited from attacking without taking these precautions. Put another way, these legal requirements are conditional—*if* you attack, *then* you must take these precautions—and entail no unconditional permissions to attack.[48] Similarly, combatants "shall at all times distinguish between [civilians or] civilian objects and military objectives and accordingly shall direct their operations only against military objectives."[49] Obviously, this basic rule means that combatants *shall not* direct their operations against civilians or civilian objects. The rule was hardly intended to encourage combatants to kill each other.

It is sometimes claimed that "the principle of military necessity in the customary law of war may be viewed as justifying or permitting certain acts."[50] Since military necessity is not defined in any treaty, proponents of this claim typically draw on two sources. In my view, neither source supports this claim.

First, the so-called Lieber Code states that

Military necessity, as understood by modern civilized nations, consists in the necessity of those measures which are indispensable for securing the ends of the war, and which are lawful according to the modern law and usages of war.[51]

Simma) (criticizing the view that "everything which is not expressly prohibited carries with it the same colour of legality; [this view] ignores the possible degrees of non-prohibition, ranging from 'tolerated' to 'permissible' to 'desirable' ... That an act might be 'tolerated' would not necessarily mean that it is 'legal,' but rather that it is 'not illegal'").

[45] John Westlake, II *International Law* (1907) 52.

[46] Joseph Raz, *Practical Reason and Norms* 86 (OUP 1999).

[47] See *SS "Lotus" (France v Turkey)* (Judgment) [1927] ICGJ 248.

[48] See, eg, Protocol I art 57(5) ("No provision of this Article may be construed as authorizing any attacks against the civilian population, civilians or civilian objects").

[49] Protocol I art 48.

[50] US Department of Defense, *Law of War Manual* 1.3.3.2.

[51] Instructions for the Government of Armies of the United States in the Field, General Order No 100, art. 14 (April 24, 1863).

By the terms of this definition, measures are militarily necessary only if they are lawful. However, measures are not lawful in virtue of military necessity. Measures derive their lawfulness not from military necessity but "according to the laws and usages of war," that is, according to the specific legal rules that other provisions of the Code purport to list. Military necessity is not a source of legal authority or even part of the law of war.

The Lieber Code states that "Military necessity admits of all direct destruction of life or limb of armed enemies, and of other persons whose destruction is incidentally unavoidable in the armed contests of the war."[52] However, these acts are not lawful because they are "admitted" by military necessity. On the contrary, military necessity "admits" these acts because they are lawful (that is, not prohibited) according to the law and usages of war. Similarly, the Lieber Code states that military necessity "does not admit" of cruelty, unnecessary suffering, torture, poison, or perfidy.[53] However, these tactics are not unlawful because military necessity does not "admit" them. On the contrary, military necessity "does not admit" of these tactics because these tactics are not "lawful according to the modern law and usages of war." Each of these tactics is specifically prohibited in other articles of the Code, by reference to the laws of war rather than to military necessity.[54]

Almost a century later, the American Military Tribunal at Nuremberg wrote that

Military necessity permits a belligerent, subject to the laws of war, to apply any amount and kind of force to compel the complete submission of the enemy with the least possible expenditure of time, life, and money.[55]

As before, by the terms of this definition, military necessity permits force only if that force is lawful. However, force is not lawful because it is militarily necessary. Instead, every amount and kind of force is "subject to the laws of war," with which military necessity is partially contrasted.

Importantly, the Tribunal repeatedly states that "international law is prohibitive law."[56] On this view, international law is a source of legal prohibitions, not a source of legal authority.[57] Accordingly, states are *always* (weakly) permitted to do what

---

[52] Instructions for the Government of Armies of the United States in the Field, General Order No 100, art 15.

[53] Instructions for the Government of Armies of the United States in the Field, General Order No 100, art 16.

[54] Instructions for the Government of Armies of the United States in the Field, General Order No 100, arts 44, 56, 65, 70.

[55] *US v List* (American Military Tribunal, Nuremberg, 1948), 11 NMT 1230, at 1253.

[56] *US v List* (American Military Tribunal, Nuremberg, 1948), at 1247, 1252, 1256. See also at 1236 ("acts done in time of war . . . cannot involve any criminal liability . . . if the acts are not prohibited by the conventional or customary rules of war").

[57] The Tribunal did not mistake the absence of a legal prohibition for an affirmative authorization or endorsement. The Tribunal condemned reprisals against civilian hostages as "a barbarous relic of ancient times" and bemoaned the "complete failure on the part of the nations of the world to limit or mitigate the practice by conventional rule" (at 1249, 1251).

international law does not prohibit them from doing. It is in this sense that belligerent states are (weakly) permitted to use force subject to the laws of war. We do not need to invoke military necessity to explain this result.

As the Tribunal observed, the laws of war prohibit the destruction or seizure of property "unless such destruction or seizure be imperatively demanded by the necessities of war."[58] Other legal rules "make no such exceptions to [their] enforcement."[59] Today, specific legal prohibitions contain exceptions for cases of military necessity, public necessity, medical and investigative necessity, or the necessity of providing for the civilian population.[60] However, "The[se] prohibitions ... control, and are superior to military [or other] necessities of the most urgent nature except where the [prohibitions] themselves specifically provide the contrary."[61] Accordingly, military necessity, public necessity, medical and investigative necessity, and so forth are not free-standing sources of legal authority. These are non-legal concepts that must be incorporated into specific legal rules in order to have any legal effect.

Since the *jus in bello* applies equally to opposing states, military necessity cannot legally authorize the acts of violence that make up an unlawful act of aggression.[62] Since the *jus in bello* applies equally to state armed forces and non-state armed groups, military necessity cannot grant non-state armed groups a legal right to wage war against their governments. Accordingly, lawful combatants charged with murder in the criminal courts of an adversary would hardly claim that their killings were justified by military necessity. Instead, such lawful combatants would claim that they are immune from prosecution for acts not prohibited by the law of armed conflict.

To conclude, international law does not guarantee the equal legal status of combatants but only the equal application of the *jus in bello*.[63] Since the *jus in bello* is primarily prohibitive rather than permissive, combatants may conform to the *jus in bello* yet remain legally unequal under other branches of international or national law. Accordingly, common article 3 of the 1949 Geneva Conventions, as well as article 4 of Protocol I, underscore that their equal application "shall not affect the legal status of the Parties to the conflict."[64] The prohibitions contained in the LOAC

---

[58] *US v List* (American Military Tribunal, Nuremberg, 1948), at 1296.

[59] *US v List* (American Military Tribunal, Nuremberg, 1948), at 1256.

[60] See, eg, Protocol I, arts 34(4)(b), 63(5), 70(3)(c).

[61] *US v List* (American Military Tribunal, Nuremberg, 1948), at 1296.

[62] Note that the Lieber Code long predates the legal prohibition of aggression. See General Order No 100, art. 67 ("The law of nations allows every sovereign government to make war upon another sovereign state").

[63] I owe this crisp formulation to Dapo Akande.

[64] See, eg, Geneva Convention (I) for the Amelioration of the Condition of the Wounded and Sick in Armed Forces in the Field (opened for signature August 12, 1949, entered into force October 21, 1950), art 3; Protocol I, art 4.

apply alongside other applicable legal rules, working together "to ensure a better protection for the victims of those armed conflicts."[65]

Human Rights in War

Since the LOAC does not authorize or justify the killings that it does not specifically prohibit, it cannot permit killings that are prohibited by other bodies of law. Most importantly, international human rights law prohibits the arbitrary deprivation of life.[66] In armed conflict, this general prohibition on arbitrary killing applies alongside the specific prohibitions of the LOAC. As the Inter-American Commission on Human Rights observes, "humanitarian law generally afford[s] victims of armed conflicts greater or more specific protections than do the more generally phrased guarantees in . . . human rights instruments."[67] Importantly, these specific protections were designed to guide combatants and protect civilians in the unique circumstances of armed conflict.

Similarly, Protocol II states that "international instruments relating to human rights offer a basic protection to the human person" while the LOAC aims "to ensure a better protection for the victims of those armed conflicts."[68] As Protocol II makes clear, human rights law and the LOAC do not conflict, as both offer protections from violence rather than licenses to commit violence. Accordingly, "when Protocol II in its more detailed provisions establishes a higher standard than the Covenant [on Civil and Political Rights], this higher standard prevails," while "provisions of the Covenant . . . which provide for a higher standard of protection than the protocol should be regarded as applicable" in appropriate cases.[69] On this view, the LOAC can only add to, but can never subtract from, the protection that individuals enjoy under human rights law.

It is true that, in its *Nuclear Weapons* advisory opinion, the International Court of Justice (ICJ) famously wrote that

In principle, the right not arbitrarily to be deprived of one's life applies also in hostilities. The test of what is an arbitrary deprivation of life, however, then falls to be determined by

---

[65] Protocol Additional to the Geneva Conventions of August 12, 1949, and relating to the Protection of Victims of Non-International Armed Conflicts (Protocol II) (adopted June 8, 1977, entered into force December 7, 1978) 1125 UNTS 609, preamble.

[66] See, eg, International Covenant on Civil and Political Rights (ICCPR) (opened for signature December 19, 1966, entered into force March 23, 1976) 999 UNTS 171, art 6(1). Note that an act may be otherwise lawful yet arbitrary. See ICCPR, art 17(1) ("No one shall be subjected to arbitrary or unlawful interference with his privacy, family, home or correspondence").

[67] *Juan Carlos Abella v Argentina* (Case 11.137) Report No 55/97 [18 Nov 1997] OEA/Ser L/V/II.98, paras 159–60 ("It is, moreover, during situations of internal armed conflict that these two branches of international law most converge and reinforce each other").

[68] Protocol II, preamble.

[69] Michael Bothe, Karl Josef Partsch, and Waldemar A Solf, *New Rules for Victims of Armed Conflicts: Commentary on the Two 1977 Protocols Additional to the Geneva Conventions of 1949* (Martinus Nijhoff 1982) 636.

the applicable *lex specialis*, namely, the law applicable in armed conflict which is designed to regulate the conduct of hostilities.[70]

This passage suggests that, in the context of armed conflict, deprivations of life that do not violate the LOAC are *necessarily* non-arbitrary under human rights law. On this view, the LOAC does not need to permit what human rights law prohibits because the LOAC determines what human rights law prohibits in armed conflict. We should reject this view.

In its advisory opinion, the ICJ took for granted the *contingent* content of the LOAC, namely that its "cardinal principles" prohibit weapons "that are incapable of distinguishing between civilian and military targets" or that "cause unnecessary suffering to combatants."[71] Understandably, the ICJ considered these cardinal principles sufficient to adjudicate the legality of the threat or use of nuclear weapons. However, if these cardinal principles never entered the LOAC then clearly the LOAC would not prohibit all or even most arbitrary deprivations of life in armed conflict.

The extent to which the LOAC prohibits arbitrary killing in armed conflict is contingent on the content of the LOAC, which is itself contingent on treaty and custom, which is in turn contingent on what states agree to, how states behave, and what states believe. There is no reason why such contingencies should determine the content of human rights law.

Of course, it is hard to imagine the LOAC without the prohibitions on indiscriminate weapons and unnecessary suffering. A different example may help illustrate that the content of the LOAC is a contingent matter. Protocol I provides that

When a choice is possible between several military objectives for obtaining a similar military advantage, the objective to be selected shall be that the attack on which may be expected to cause the least danger to civilian lives and to civilian objects.[72]

Strikingly, the US Department of Defense denies that this rule reflects customary international law.[73] This view seems clearly mistaken.[74] But imagine if this view were true. Imagine that attacking forces could cut off an enemy supply route by destroying either of two bridges, the first with no civilian traffic and the second full of civilians on their way to work, school, or their homes. Assume that the military advantage of destroying the second bridge would render the collateral harm to civilians *proportionate*. However, such collateral harm would be *unnecessary*, since destroying the first bridge would yield the same advantage. Clearly, if attacking forces strike the second bridge rather than the first, then they would kill the civilian travelers *arbitrarily* whether or not they would thereby violate the LOAC.

---

[70] *Legality of the Threat or Use of Nuclear Weapons*, Advisory Opinion, 1996 ICJ Rep 226, para 25.

[71] *Legality of the Threat or Use of Nuclear Weapons*, Advisory Opinion, para 78.

[72] Protocol I, art 57(3).

[73] US Department of Defense, *Law of War Manual* (2015) 5.11.5.

[74] See Adil Ahmad Haque, "Off Target: Selection, Precaution, and Proportionality in the DoD Manual" (2016) 92 International Law Studies 31.

Alternatively, assume for the sake of argument that Protocol I crystallized the precautions rule for the first time.[75] Now imagine that the Diplomatic Conference that produced Protocol I never convened. If wartime killings are arbitrary only if they are prohibited by the LOAC, then careless and easily avoidable killings would not be arbitrary. Put another way, on this view, Protocol I did nothing to make the LOAC more respectful of human rights or to limit arbitrary killing in armed conflict. Similarly, if Protocol I had omitted the precautions rule, then this omission would not have affected Protocol I's human rights credentials. This seems impossible to believe.

When applying human rights law, we should ask whether a particular deprivation of life was arbitrary given the circumstances. While we may certainly look to the LOAC to inform our interpretation of which deprivations of life are arbitrary in armed conflict, there is no reason to assume that the LOAC is so perfect that it effectively prohibits all arbitrary deprivation of life in armed conflict. In the end, whether a particular deprivation of life is arbitrary remains a question of human rights law, not of the LOAC. Our best interpretation of human rights law, informed but not determined by looking to the LOAC, should prevail.

During armed conflict, the LOAC may or may not prove sufficient to prohibit arbitrary killing. That will depend on the contingent content of the LOAC, as well as on the factual circumstances, not on some a priori relationship between the LOAC and human rights law. Outside of armed conflict, killing is almost always arbitrary unless it follows strict rules governing self-defense or law enforcement. During armed conflict, killing opposing combatants may seldom prove arbitrary. However, as we shall see in Chapter 4, killing a combatant whom one could safely capture may not violate the LOAC but may fail to respect the human right to life.

The relationship between the LOAC and human rights is teleological, not constitutive. The LOAC aims to protect human rights to the greatest extent possible in armed conflict, not to define what human rights mean in armed conflict.[76] It is not an a priori or conceptual truth that the LOAC, whatever its content, prohibits arbitrary killing. If the LOAC prohibits even most arbitrary killing in armed conflict, then this is a contingent and reversible human achievement. Accordingly, we may draw on the LOAC to interpret human rights law, or draw on human rights law to interpret the LOAC, but neither body of law determines the content of the other.[77]

---

[75] This assumption is probably correct, but I do not wish to argue for it here. A very limited version of the precautions rule is found in Hague Convention (IX) concerning Bombardment by Naval Forces in Time of War (opened for signature October 18, 1907, entered into force January 26, 1910), art 2.

[76] See, eg, UK Ministry of Defense, *Law of Armed Conflict Manual* (OUP 2005) 1.8 (one purpose of the law of armed conflict is "to safeguard the fundamental human rights of persons who are not, or are no longer, taking part in the conflict . . . and of civilians").

[77] The European Convention on Human Rights prohibits intentional deprivation of life, with narrow exceptions, but permits measures derogating from that obligation "in respect of deaths resulting from lawful acts of war." Convention for the Protection of Human Rights and Fundamental Freedoms, 213 UNTS 222, entered into force September 3, 1953, art 15.

The Humanitarian View

As we have seen, revisionists assume that combatants are legally permitted to fight for an unjust cause, argue that combatants are not morally permitted to fight for an unjust cause, and conclude that law and morality sharply diverge. Moreover, revisionists argue that law and morality *must* diverge, since a legal prohibition on fighting for an unjust cause will either be ignored or create perverse incentives. These revisionists conclude that, while the deep morality of war is concerned with individual rights and directed duties, the law of war should content itself with the consequentialist aim of reducing wrongful suffering in war to the greatest extent practically possible.

As we have seen, this revisionist argument rests on a false premise. Combatants are not legally permitted to fight for an unjust cause, though lawful combatants are legally immune from criminal prosecution so long as they fight according to the rules. It follows that revisionists should not feel compelled to embrace the humanitarian view. At the same time, the humanitarian view can seem plausible—even attractive—on its face. As a general matter, the aim of reducing wrongful suffering in war is one that we should all share. We should therefore evaluate the humanitarian view on its own merits.

According to the humanitarian view, the guiding aim of international humanitarian law (IHL) should be to reduce wrongful suffering in war by prohibiting *militarily unnecessary* killing, maiming, and destruction. More precisely, IHL should aim to prohibit types of harmful acts that are generally or typically militarily unnecessary. For example, on this view, IHL rightly prohibits targeting civilians because generally it is unnecessary to target civilians in order to defeat opposing armed forces. The humanitarian view is sometimes expressed in terms of striking a *balance* between military and humanitarian considerations. Unfortunately, the rhetoric of balancing often proves empty. When military and humanitarian considerations directly and broadly conflict, military considerations always seem to prevail.

The humanitarian view was elegantly expressed by Vattel, who held that

All acts of hostility which injure the enemy without necessity, or which do not tend to procure victory and bring about the end of the war, are unjustifiable, and as such condemned by the natural law.[78]

Importantly, such measures are permitted only "to the extent strictly required by the exigencies of the situation" (art 15). On my view, a court applying the Convention may find that intentional killings that conform to the law of war nevertheless violate the Convention because the measures taken were not strictly necessary. For example, a court may find that measures derogating from the Convention are strictly required only in certain parts of a state's territory, or only in certain situations. In other areas or situations, the Convention may very well apply with full force.

[78] Vattel, *Law of Nations*, book III, §172.

At the same time, Vattel saw that warring parties should not be left free to judge the necessity or utility of their own military operations on a case-by-case basis, since such an open-ended principle would invite self-serving judgments and endless recriminations. Instead,

> as between Nation and Nation, we must lay down general rules, independent of circumstances and of certain and easy application .... Hence, ... the voluntary Law of Nations limits itself to forbidding acts that are essentially unlawful and obnoxious .... On the other hand, it permits or tolerates every act which in its essential nature is adapted to attaining the end of the war; and it does not stop to consider whether the act was unnecessary, useless or superfluous in a given case unless there is the clearest evidence that an exception should have been made in that instance; for where the evidence is clear freedom of judgment cannot be exercised.[79]

On this view, international law should prohibit acts of war that are typically militarily unnecessary while tolerating acts of war that are typically militarily necessary.

The humanitarian view later found expression in several foundational treaties. Most notably, the St Petersburg Declaration states that "the progress of civilization should have the effect of alleviating as much as possible the calamities of war," that law must fix "the technical limits at which the necessities of war ought to yield to the requirements of humanity," and that the parties will continue to work "to conciliate the necessities of war with the laws of humanity."[80] Similarly, the fourth Hague Convention was "inspired by the desire to diminish the evils of war, as far as military requirements permit."[81]

Recently, Janina Dill and Henry Shue have offered a vigorous philosophical defense of the humanitarian view. On their account, the aim of IHL should be "to limit *all* killing [in armed conflict] as much as possible."[82] It is not possible to limit killing in ways that make winning impossible, because parties determined to win will simply ignore such limitations. However, it is possible to limit killing in ways that make winning more difficult. Dill and Shue reason that the law is right to categorically prohibit targeting civilians because this prohibition limits the killing of a large category of individuals and generally it is possible to win without targeting civilians. In some cases, it may be *easier* to win by targeting civilians, but this is an option that the law can foreclose without being systematically ignored. The law is

---

[79] Vattel, *Law of Nations*, book III, §173.

[80] Declaration Renouncing the Use, in Time of War, of Explosive Projectiles Under 400 Grammes Weight [St Petersburg Declaration], Nov 29/Dec 11, 1868, 138 Consol TS 297, 18 Martens Nouveau Recueil (ser 1) 474, preamble.

[81] Hague Convention (IV) Respecting the Laws and Customs of War on Land (opened for signature October 18, 1907, entered into force January 26, 1910) 3 Martens Nouveau Recueil (ser 3) 461, preamble.

[82] Janina Dill & Henry Shue, "Limiting the Killing in War: Military Necessity and the St. Petersburg Assumption," (2012) 26 Ethics & International Affairs 311, 319.

also right not to prohibit targeting combatants because generally it is not possible to win without targeting combatants. According to Dill and Shue, "the rules for the conduct of war cannot in general restrict the killing of combatants" or they will be ignored.[83] Since all individuals are either civilians or combatants, it follows that the legal restrictions on killing civilians limit lawful killing in armed conflict as much as possible.[84]

Importantly, Dill and Shue argue that most combatants—just and unjust alike— are not morally liable to be killed. It seems to follows that, on their view, law and morality sharply conflict, since intentionally killing individuals who retain their moral right not to be killed is almost always morally wrong. Nevertheless, Dill and Shue argue that, by limiting lawful killing as much as possible, IHL indirectly reduces wrongful killing as much as possible.[85] Thus, rather than aiming to *prohibit* wrongful killing, IHL aims to *minimize* wrongful killing in part by *permitting* some wrongful killing.

As Dill and Shue observe, "even if we all agree on noncombatant immunity, it matters what underlies the application of discrimination."[86] As it happens, Dill and Shue provide the wrong explanation for the right result. After all, if many soldiers retain their moral rights then in some cases soldiers may violate fewer rights by targeting civilians than by targeting combatants. In these cases, by limiting *lawful* killing in war IHL may increase *actual* killing. When means subvert ends in this way, rule-consequentialism seems like rule-fetishism. It is not clear why combatants who internalize the aim of reducing wrongful suffering in war will follow a legal rule prohibiting attacks on civilians when attacking civilians will in fact reduce wrongful suffering. Indeed, while the humanitarian view aims to reduce wrongful suffering in war, IHL in fact concentrates suffering in war on one category of individuals rather than another.

The deeper problem with the humanitarian view is that while the utility of targeting civilians varies, the morality of targeting civilians remains constant. To take an extreme example, suppose that if IHL does not prohibit the intentional killing of young children, then this will in fact reduce wrongful suffering in war. Such a position might deter states from initiating armed conflict and encourage belligerents to surrender more quickly when victory is in doubt. On the humanitarian view,

---

[83]   Dill & Shue, "Limiting the Killing in War," 323.

[84]   Interestingly, Dill and Shue write that "proportionality . . . prohibits conduct that, even though it might be necessary, can be expected to cause unintended but foreseeable civilian damage that is excessive" ("Limiting the Killing in War," 320). Presumably they believe that attacks that are tactically necessary to achieve concrete and direct military advantages are seldom strategically necessary to defeat opposing armed forces. Otherwise, on their assumptions, *jus in bello* proportionality would fail to constrain the conduct of parties determined to win.

[85]   Dill & Shue, "Limiting the Killing in War," 329.

[86]   Dill & Shue, "Limiting the Killing in War," 330.

IHL should adopt this position and not prohibit the intentional killing of young children. If this implication seems hard to accept, then civilian immunity likely does not rest on empirical contingencies in the way the humanitarian view suggests. I will have more to say about civilian immunity in Chapter 3.

Similarly, there is only an empirically contingent connection between the voluntary conduct of combatants and the utility of killing them, but there are morally necessary connections between the voluntary conduct of combatants and the morality of killing them. Many combatants pose unjust threats to civilians who retain their basic rights, while most civilians make indirect and superfluous contributions to their armed forces. In addition, combatants can avoid being eliminatively harmed more easily than civilians can avoid being opportunistically harmed, in part because combatants choose to make themselves lawful targets. I will say more about these considerations at the end of Chapter 3.[87]

These moral considerations systematically favor legal rules that prohibit targeting civilians but do not prohibit targeting combatants. Killing civilians is, at a minimum, intrinsically morally worse than killing combatants. It follows that IHL should not aim to limit all killing as much as possible and distribute lawful killing in whatever way will in fact minimize wrongful killing in war. At the very least, IHL should skew the distribution of actual killings by strictly limiting the more wrongful killings (of civilians) but not comparatively less wrongful killings (of combatants).

Indeed, in subsequently published work, Dill shows that law might limit killing as much as militarily possible in at least two very different ways.[88] According to the "logic of sufficiency," law should tolerate intentionally and collaterally killing combatants, as this is both necessary and sufficient for military victory. At the same time, the law should prohibit intentionally killing civilians, as this is generally unnecessary for military victory. In contrast, according to the "logic of efficiency," the law should allow each party to achieve its war aims in the quickest and least costly way possible, even if this means targeting civilians and civilian objects. Importantly, Dill argues that it is impossible to empirically determine which "logic" of warfare will best reduce killing in war, that is, whether "contained wars are the least destructive" or whether "sharp wars are brief."

Accordingly, Dill argues that we should prefer the logic of sufficiency to the logic of efficiency because generally it is morally worse to kill civilians than to kill combatants. As Dill observes, civilians are often vulnerable, defenseless, and non-threatening. Moreover, a legal rule prohibiting attacks on civilians allows civilians to be secure in their expectations that they will not be attacked unless they exercise their agency in defined ways. This refinement of Dill's view is both significant and welcome. However, the "logic of sufficiency" remains grounded in rule-consequentialism.

---

[87] See also Seth Lazar, *Sparing Civilians* (OUP 2016).
[88] Janina Dill, *Legitimate Targets* (CUP 2015) 262–3.

Non-consequentialist considerations merely support one set of rules over another when we cannot tell which set of rules would yield better consequences.

It is not clear why individual soldiers would follow rules justified on rule-consequentialist grounds rather than follow their own moral judgment. After all, Dill and Shue do not argue that soldiers will wrongfully kill fewer people by following IHL than by violating IHL, or even that a smaller proportion of their killings will be wrongful killings if they follow IHL than if they violate IHL. They argue that soldiers who follow IHL will wrongfully kill one category of people but not another category of people. It is hard to see why a rational, moral soldier would abstain from militarily efficacious actions on such grounds. Presumably, such soldiers will be concerned primarily with the rights and duties they infringe and only secondarily with the aggregate consequences of general rules.

Soldiers are not computers, and legal norms are not software programs. Soldiers are human beings who bear moral obligations and exercise moral judgment. The law must address them as such. Soldiers need a reason to obey the law, and the most obvious reason to do so is that they will better fulfill their moral obligations by following the law than by following their independent moral judgment. As Seth Lazar nicely observes, rule-consequentialism is a third-person view of moral justification, while soldiers need a first-person view that addresses them as moral agents.[89]

None of this is to say that legal rules should never aim at producing good aggregate consequences, or that individuals never have reasons to obey such rules. Often, we have moral reasons to *cooperate* with others in order to achieve shared aims together that we could not achieve individually (think of making small contributions to the same charity). Similarly, we may have moral reasons to *coordinate* with others so that we can pursue our individual aims more effectively or more safely (think of driving on the same side of the road). In contrast, in war we *compete* with our adversary, and our moral reasons do not depend on their behavior. We can avoid targeting civilians, and have moral reasons to do so, irrespective of how our adversary behaves.

Of course, many scholars believe that rule-consequentialist sensibilities, whatever their normative credentials, drove the historical development of IHL. For example, David Luban argues that "humanitarianism in war is plainly a form of negative benthamism" aimed at reducing aggregate suffering.[90] Luban cites the preamble to the St Petersburg Declaration as evidence that the historical aim of IHL was "alleviating as much as possible the calamities of war."[91]

---

[89]   See Lazar, "The Morality and Law of War."
[90]   David Luban, "Human Rights Thinking and the Laws of War," in Jens David Ohlin (ed), *Theoretical Boundaries of Human Rights and Armed Conflict* (OUP 2016) 52.
[91]   St Petersburg Declaration, preamble.

In fact, the St Petersburg Declaration prohibited the use of a particular weapon—exploding bullets—thought to inflict suffering on *each* individual combatant unnecessary to incapacitate *him*. This suggests that the Declaration's purpose was to prevent unnecessary individual suffering, not to prevent unnecessary aggregate suffering. To see this, suppose that the drafters received credible reports that the use of exploding bullets actually reduces aggregate suffering, because the extreme suffering that they inflict on individual combatants encourages other combatants to surrender more quickly. It is far from clear that the drafters would have abandoned their project, allowing the infliction of unnecessary individual suffering in order to reduce aggregate suffering.

While the humanitarian view may or may not provide a historical explanation of how IHL developed, it certainly does not provide a moral explanation for why soldiers should follow IHL. The contingent aim of some states in developing IHL may have been to reduce aggregate suffering. However, I argue below that the constitutive aim of IHL itself is to provide a moral service to combatants.

The Service View

At times, McMahan suggests an alternative to the humanitarian view, writing that "Ideally we should establish laws of war best suited to get combatants on both sides to conform their action as closely as possible to the constraints imposed by the deep morality of war."[92] Importantly, McMahan observes that "combatants should be reluctant to give their individual judgment priority over the law, for the law has been designed in part precisely to obviate the need for resort to individual moral judgment in conditions that are highly unconducive to rational reflection."[93] These passages suggest that the aim of the law of war should not be to minimize wrongful harm overall. Instead, the law should aim to help combatants to conform to their moral obligations more closely than they would by relying on their individual moral judgment. This seems to me the better view.

Why should any individual follow the law rather than follow his or her own moral judgment? As moral agents, our ultimate aim should be to fulfill our moral obligations and conform to the strongest moral reasons that apply to us. We should follow our own moral judgment if and only if this is the best available means of achieving our ultimate aim. In some cases, we are more likely to fulfill our moral obligations if we defer to the moral judgment of another person who is better informed, more perceptive, more logical, or more virtuous. Similarly, sometimes we are more likely to fulfill our moral obligations if we follow a rule that directs the morally correct action more often than will a

---

[92] McMahan, "Ethics of Killing in War," 731.
[93] McMahan, "Morality of War and the Law of War," 38.

series of case-by-case judgments. Such a rule provides a service to moral agents by helping them to conform to their moral obligations better than they could on their own. According to the *service view*, the LOAC should aim to provide such a service to combatants.

Joseph Raz famously argues that law necessarily claims legitimate authority, that is, that those subject to the law morally ought to follow the law rather than their own moral judgment when the two conflict.[94] Of course, law's necessary claim is not necessarily true. Law has legitimate authority over an individual only if that individual "would better conform to reasons that apply to him anyway (that is, to reasons other than the directives of the authority) if he intends [or tries] to be guided by the authority's directives than if he does not."[95] When this *normal justification* condition is met, law's claim to legitimate authority is vindicated by the service that it provides those subject to the law by helping them conform to the reasons that apply to them independently of the law. Accordingly, Raz names his account of legitimate authority *the service conception*.

The service conception eases the tension between legal authority and individual autonomy. First, we must exercise our own moral judgment in order to determine that the normal justification condition is satisfied and only then accept the law as a legitimate authority over us. Second, if the normal justification condition is satisfied, then the law is "simply one device, one method, through the use of which people can achieve the goal (*telos*) of their capacity for rational action, albeit not through its direct use."[96] In other words, we can choose to comply with the law as an indirect strategy for pursuing our ultimate aim of fulfilling our moral obligations.

Let me elaborate on the idea of an indirect strategy. As moral agents, our ultimate aim is to act permissibly in the *objective* or *fact-relative* sense, that is, to conform to the moral reasons that objectively apply to us given all the morally relevant facts. Since we do not have unmediated access to the moral reasons that objectively apply to us, we can only pursue our ultimate aim indirectly, by way of our beliefs, the evidence available to us, or the rules applicable to us. We might pursue our ultimate aim by acting permissibly in the *subjective* or *belief-relative* sense, that is, by doing what would conform to the moral reasons that would apply to us if the morally relevant

---

[94] Joseph Raz, *The Morality of Freedom* (OUP 1986).

[95] Joseph Raz, *Between Authority and Interpretation* (OUP 2009) 136–7. Raz also describes an *independence condition* according to which authority is not legitimate if it encroaches on a domain in which the value of your actions depends on your reasons for acting. For example, the value of proposing marriage depends on your subjective judgment that your partner is right for you. In contrast, the value of avoiding unjustified harm does not depend on your subjective judgment that the harm is unjustified. It is much more important that combatants avoid inflicting morally unjustified harm than that combatants decide for themselves which harms are morally unjustified.

[96] Raz, *Between Authority and Interpretation*, 140.

facts were as we believe. We might pursue our ultimate aim by acting permissibly in the *epistemic* or *evidence-relative* sense, that is, by doing what would conform to the moral reasons that would apply to us if the morally relevant facts were as our evidence suggests.[97]

However, often our subjective beliefs are unreliable, the available evidence is incomplete or misleading, or our moral reasoning is distorted by emotion or bias. In such cases, we may better pursue our ultimate aim not by following our beliefs or our evidence but by following a rule. Following a rule is just another indirect strategy for conforming to the moral reasons that objectively apply to us.

Put another way, individuals always have decisive reason to *do* what is objectively morally required but sometimes have decisive reason not to *try* to do what is objectively morally required. In some cases, if they try to do what is objectively morally required, then they are likely to fail, but if they try to follow a rule, then they are more likely to succeed in doing what is objectively morally required. In other words, often we are more likely to satisfy the moral standards that apply to us, not by applying those standards, but instead by following a well-designed decision procedure. In such cases, we have decisive reason to adopt that decision procedure rather than exercise our (more fallible) moral judgment on a case-by-case basis. We may say that an act that is permissible under a rule or decision procedure that we have decisive reason to adopt is permissible in the *instrumental* sense.

Importantly, in exceptional cases, generally reliable rules may provide no service to their subjects and obedience would only lead them astray.[98] If a generally reliable rule prohibits an act that is clearly morally required, or requires an act that is clearly morally prohibited, then individuals have no reason to defer to that rule rather than follow their own moral judgment. Individuals should neither blindly follow generally reliable rules in morally clear cases nor second-guess generally reliable rules in morally unclear cases. Instead, individuals should exercise their moral judgment when they adopt generally reliable rules, trust in those rules in morally unclear cases, and trust in their moral judgment when those rules yield clearly wrong results.[99]

Like all law, the LOAC claims legitimate authority over those subject to it. The LOAC claims that combatants should follow the law rather than their own moral judgment when the two conflict. According to the service conception, this claim is vindicated only to the extent that combatants will better conform to the moral reasons that apply to them by following the law than by trying to act directly on

---

[97] See Derek Parfit, *On What Matters*, vol 1 (OUP 2011) 151.

[98] See Raz, *Morality of Freedom*, 62.

[99] Lazar is therefore incorrect when he writes that "if other moral reasons could justify disobedience to the law, then we would have to consult those reasons in any situation to determine whether it is exceptional" ("Morality and Law of War," 368). In morally unclear cases, we should not trust own judgment that a given situation is exceptional.

those reasons. Put another way, combatants have decisive reason to follow the law only if doing so will help them fulfill their moral obligations. If combatants will make morally better decisions by ignoring the law and relying on their own moral judgment, then they have decisive reason to do just that.

In war, moral judgment is easily misled by limited or unreliable information; clouded by stress, fatigue, anger, and fear; and distorted by all-too-familiar psychological dynamics. Combatants are human beings and, like the rest of us, too readily obey authority; conform to group behavior; and rationalize wrongdoing, for example, by adverting to the wrongful conduct of our adversaries, to the moral guilt of our victims, or to our own feelings of victimization. As one important study concluded:

> While attempts at justification such as those referred to can enable combatants to switch off guilt feelings in the face of inhuman acts and to stretch moral values by legitimizing such acts, they cannot confer legality on such behaviour. The [law] draws an easily identifiable red line, whereas [moral] values represent a broader spectrum which is less focused and more relative.[100]

In other words, rather than attempt sound moral reasoning in such adverse circumstances, combatants may better conform to their moral obligations by following the law.

Throughout this book, I appeal to the service view to evaluate apparent gaps between the law of war and the morality of war. For example, in Chapter 3, I defend the legal prohibition of direct attacks on civilians not directly participating in hostilities. I will argue, against many revisionists, that almost all such civilians retain their ordinary moral rights. I then appeal to the service view to show that combatants will best conform to their moral obligations by following the general legal prohibition rather than by trying to identify and target civilians who have forfeited their ordinary moral rights. Very few civilians forfeit their moral rights, these civilians are very difficult to distinguish from the majority of civilians who retain their moral rights, and killing these civilians is seldom necessary to prevent harm to others. If soldiers try to target morally liable civilians, then they are much more likely to wrongfully kill than to prevent wrongful killing. It follows that soldiers will better conform to their moral obligations by following the law than by following their own moral judgment.

In contrast, in Chapter 4, I propose a limited legal prohibition of directing attacks at members of armed forces or armed groups whom the attacker knows or has decisive reason to believe perform noncombat functions. Often it is objectively wrong to kill noncombat personnel. At the same time, if combatants must positively

---

[100] Daniel Muñoz-Rojas & Jean-Jacques Frésard, "The Roots of Behaviour in War: Understanding and Preventing IHL Violations" (2004) 86 International Review of the Red Cross 189, 203.

identify opposing combat personnel, distinguishing them from opposing noncombat personnel, then they will often hesitate to use objectively permissible force and
allow their fellow soldiers or civilians to be harmed. Moreover, in general, noncombat personnel can avoid being mistaken for combat personnel more easily than can
civilians, simply by conforming to more stringent moral duties than civilians bear. It
follows that attackers need not take the same precautions to avoid mistakenly killing
such individuals that they must take to avoid mistakenly killing civilians. However,
if an attacker knows or has decisive reason to believe that a person performs a noncombat function, then the moral costs of restraint are low relative to the moral costs
of attack. I argue that such a limited legal prohibition will help combatants better
conform to their moral obligations.

It might appear that on these issues the service view simply requires epistemic
permissibility. If most civilians are not morally liable, then perhaps it is presumptively unreasonable to believe that any particular civilian is morally liable. Similarly,
if most unjust combatants are morally liable, then perhaps it is presumptively reasonable to believe that each particular combatant is morally liable.[101] However,
this is not quite correct. Objective permissibility depends on intrinsically morally
relevant facts. Epistemic permissibility depends on one's evidence regarding such
intrinsically morally relevant facts. In contrast, the rule prohibiting attacks on civilians makes no reference to intrinsically morally relevant facts, such as the moral
rights or liabilities of particular individuals. Instead, the rule refers to facts that reliably indicate that such intrinsically morally relevant facts exist or do not exist.[102] The
point of relying on IHL is to allow combatants to bypass individualized assessments
of intrinsically morally relevant facts when the moral stakes are high but directly
relevant evidence is weak. Moreover, combatants should not *trust* the reasonableness
of their beliefs regarding the moral liability of civilians, which are susceptible to
distortion by non-rational factors. Combatants would better avoid killing morally
protected civilians by following IHL than by following their own judgment. This is
the service that IHL should aim to provide combatants.

Importantly, some rules of IHL invite combatants to exercise moral judgment.
Most notably, the proportionality rule invites attackers to judge whether the collateral harm they expect their attack will inflict on civilians would be *excessive* in
relation to the concrete and direct military advantage they anticipate. The proportionality rule nevertheless performs an important guidance function by framing
the relevant moral issue and focusing moral deliberation. The proportionality rule
directs attackers to consider only two morally relevant variables—expected civilian
losses and anticipated military advantage—while excluding all others. Moreover,

---

[101]   See, eg, Jeff McMahan, "Innocence, Self-Defense, and Killing in War" (1994) 2 Journal
of Political Philosophy 193, 218.
[102]   cf Donald H. Regan, "Authority and Value: Reflections on Raz's Morality of Freedom"
(1989) 62 Southern California Law Review 1003, 1007.

the proportionality rule directs attackers to consider only military advantages that are both concrete and direct, and to resist wishful thinking. Finally, combatants may receive moral guidance from the rule itself, from authoritative interpretations of the rule, and from rules of engagement that implement the rule. In these ways, moral guidance and moral judgment may be mutually reinforcing rather than mutually exclusive.

Revisionists might argue that the LOAC can only help just combatants to conform to their moral obligations. On their view, unjust combatants cannot conform to their moral obligations except by laying down their arms, which the law does not require. Yet the law does not claim legitimate authority only over just combatants or only over combatants who believe—rightly or wrongly—that their cause is just. The law also claims legitimate authority over combatants who are not sure whether their cause is just or unjust and seek to hedge against the moral risk that they fight for an unjust cause. Finally, the law claims legitimate authority over combatants who believe that their cause is unjust, elect to fight under duress or out of excessive partiality, yet wish to limit the kind and degree of their own wrongdoing.

On one view, the LOAC should prohibit those acts that would be morally impermissible if committed by combatants fighting for a just cause. The law should then simply apply those prohibitions to the just and the unjust alike, on the assumption that all combatants believe that they fight for a just cause.[103] Though attractive, this view seems too elegant to cope with a messy reality. The truth is that many combatants fight despite grave doubts regarding the war as a whole. They may doubt that they fight for a just cause, or that war was necessary or proportionate. They may suspect that justice favors their adversary, or that justice condemns both parties. Nevertheless, they may choose to fight in order to protect their friends, families, and communities from the consequences of their government's decision to go to war. The LOAC must speak to these combatants as well, by showing them that, even in an unjust war, there are rules worth following.

On the service view, the legitimate authority of law does not require that individuals who conform to the law will never perform objectively impermissible acts, only that they will perform fewer or less wrongful objectively impermissible acts than they would by relying on their own moral judgment. As noted in Chapter 1, while permissibility is all-or-nothing, wrongfulness is a matter of degree. An act is objectively impermissible only if the moral reasons against its performance outweigh the moral reasons in favor of its performance. In contrast, the wrongfulness of an impermissible act depends on the degree to which the moral reasons against its performance outweigh the moral reasons in favor of its performance. Although the balance of reasons matters most, it still matters whether the balance of reasons is

---

[103] See, eg, Vattel, *Law of Nations* §191.

tipped by a penny or by a pound. Even when we fall short of our moral obligations, it matters whether we fall short by an inch or by a mile.

To vindicate the legitimate authority of the LOAC, it is enough to show that combatants fighting for an unjust cause will act less wrongfully if they follow the law than if they follow their own moral judgment and violate the law. In other words, it is enough to show that killings in pursuit of an unjust cause are morally worse if they also violate the law than if they at least conform to the law.

As we will see in Chapter 3, targeting civilians is morally worse than targeting combatants even when neither has forfeited their moral right not to be killed. Just combatants often pose unjust threats to civilians who have a moral right not to be killed. It follows that there are moral reasons to kill just combatants that offset the moral reasons not to kill just combatants. In addition, combatants can avoid eliminative harm more easily than civilians can avoid opportunistic harm and, on a related though distinct point, forgo fair opportunities to avoid making themselves lawful targets. It follows that the moral reasons not to kill just combatants are weaker than the moral reasons not to kill civilians. In these ways, among others, it is less wrongful to kill just combatants than to kill civilians.[104] It follows that unjust combatants will act less wrongfully by following the law than by targeting combatants and civilians without distinction.

As we will see in Chapter 8, *jus in bello* proportionality is best understood to prohibit attacks that inflict greater collateral harm on civilians than they prevent the opposing force from inflicting on civilians and combatants in current or future military operations. Since there are strong moral reasons to prevent harm to civilians as well as significant moral reasons to prevent harm to most unjust combatants, an attack that satisfies *jus in bello* proportionality is generally less wrongful than one that does not. Such attacks may remain all-things-considered impermissible, but the balance of reasons is hardly one-sided. The moral reasons to launch such attacks partially offset the moral reasons not to launch such attacks. It follows that unjust combatants will act less wrongfully by following the law than by inflicting disproportionate harm on civilians.

Revisionists may be right that it is objectively morally impermissible to fight for a party pursuing an unjust cause. Nevertheless, ordinary combatants cannot force their political leaders to abandon their war aims and make peace. Instead, ordinary combatants must choose between killing opposing combatants and foreign civilians or allowing opposing combatants to kill their fellow soldiers and their own civilians. Over the remainder of the book I hope to demonstrate what I have already suggested: that by following the LOAC (suitably interpreted and developed) all combatants can ensure that they will fight, if not permissibly, then less wrongfully than they would otherwise. In other words, I hope to vindicate the LOAC's claim to legitimate authority over just and unjust combatants alike.

---

[104] See also Lazar, *Sparing Civilians*.

Interpretation and Justification

As we have seen, Raz's service conception provides an analysis of law's claim to legitimate authority as well as a standard by which to evaluate that claim. My own view is that we should interpret and develop the LOAC so as to vindicate the law's claim of legitimate authority. We should interpret and develop the law such that the law satisfies the normal justification condition with respect to as many combatants as possible.

The constitutive aim of all law is to guide human conduct through positive normative standards. The positive nature of law distinguishes law from morality while the normative nature of law distinguishes law from a system of mere incentives. For law to succeed in its constitutive aim, it must provide those subject to the law with decisive reasons to accept its guidance. On my view, the basic task of legal interpretation is to help law to achieve its constitutive aim by casting positive legal materials in their morally best light, that is, in the light that gives those subject to the law the strongest moral reasons to obey the law.

Of course, some laws are both legally unambiguous and morally indefensible. In such cases, positive legal materials make a morally attractive interpretation unsustainable. The failure of such laws to achieve their constitutive aim is so complete that the failure cannot be cured through interpretation alone. But if the content of a particular law is ambiguous then interpretation can serve the constitutive aim of all law without directly contradicting the contingent aim of the law in question. Put another way, if the specific aim of the drafters of a law is indeterminate then it is appropriate to revert to the constitutive aim that the drafters implicitly adopted as their own general aim when they chose to pursue their specific aims through law.

The states that create international law through treaty and custom have a variety of contingent aims, including the humanitarian aim of reducing wrongful suffering in war. However, these states chose to pursue their contingent aims through law, and the constitutive aim of law is to give those subject to the law decisive reason to follow the law rather than their own moral judgment. Our aim in interpreting the LOAC should be to ensure that the law achieves its constitutive aim.

It might seem that mine is a heterodox approach to the interpretation of international law. According to the orthodox approach, the terms of a treaty should be "interpreted in good faith in accordance with the[ir] ordinary meaning ... in their context and in the light of its object and purpose."[105] If this

---

[105] Vienna Convention on the Law of Treaties (opened for signature May 23, 1969, entered into force January 27, 1980) 1155 UNTS 331, art 31. Since the customary law that I will discuss in this book tracks treaty law, particularly Protocol I, I will only discuss treaty interpretation here. For a view similar to mine regarding the identification and interpretation of customary international law, see John Tasioulas, "Custom, *Jus Cogens*, and Human Rights," in Curtis Bradley (ed), *Custom's Future: International Law in a Changing World* (CUP 2016).

textual–purposive approach "[l]eaves the meaning" of these terms "ambiguous or obscure" or "[l]eads to a result which is manifestly absurd or unreasonable," then their meaning may be determined by "supplementary means of interpretation" such as preparatory materials and concluding commentary.[106] This textual–purposive approach is appropriate in most cases, since lawmakers can only exercise legitimate practical authority if they can anticipate how the laws they make will be interpreted.[107]

As we shall see in later chapters, the drafters of Protocol I deployed evaluative terms such as "feasible," "reasonable," and "excessive"—and introduced such terms into customary law—without explicitly defining these terms or coming to a consensus regarding their intended meaning. Neither ordinary meaning nor context provides these terms with determinate content. Relevant preparatory materials and concluding commentary shed little additional light. In each case, we must interpret these terms in light of the object and purpose of Protocol I, namely "protecting the victims of armed conflicts,"[108] as well as the purpose of the LOAC as a whole, namely "to protect combatants and non-combatants from unnecessary suffering and to safeguard the fundamental human rights of persons who are not, or are no longer, taking part in the conflict . . . and of civilians."[109]

As David Luban observes, the difficulty with purposive interpretation "lies in what you take the purpose of laws of war to be. Is it to protect civilians, even at cost to military effectiveness, or is it to give full sway to military necessity and protect civilians (only) against military excess?"[110]

Endorsing the former view, the International Criminal Tribunal for the former Yugoslavia (ICTY) controversially held that "a rule of international humanitarian law [that] is not sufficiently rigorous or precise . . . must be interpreted so as to construe as narrowly as possible the discretionary power [of] belligerents and, by the same token, so as to expand the protection accorded to civilians."[111]

Endorsing the latter view, Michael Schmitt posits that states, as authors of international law, would never agree to legal norms that "unduly restrict their freedom of action on the battlefield, such that national interests might be affected."[112] Schmitt concludes that sound interpretation of international law should reflect "a

---

[106] Vienna Convention art 32.
[107] See, eg, Raz, *Between Authority and Interpretation*, ch 11.   [108] Protocol I Preamble.
[109] UK Ministry of Defense, *Law of Armed Conflict Manual* (OUP 2005) 1.8. Note that the first clause refers to protecting each individual combatant and non-combatant from unnecessary suffering, not to minimizing aggregate suffering.
[110] David Luban, "Military Necessity and the Cultures of Military Law" (2013) 26 Leiden Journal of International Law 315, 323.
[111] *Prosecutor v Kupreškić* (Judgment) IT-95-16-T (Jan 14, 2000), para 525.
[112] Michael N Schmitt, "Military Necessity and Humanity in International Humanitarian Law: Preserving the Delicate Balance" (2010) 50 Virginia Journal of International Law 795, 801.

reasonable balance between military necessity and humanity," that is, a balance that leaves "states . . . reasonably free to conduct their military operations effectively."[113]

These dueling approaches may seem worlds apart both from each other and from the service view. But things are not as they appear. Perhaps surprisingly, my apparently heterodox approach to purposive interpretation both captures and reconciles what is attractive in these dueling mainstream approaches while leaving behind their excesses.

According to the service view, we should indeed interpret imprecise legal norms so as to legally protect civilians—from objectively impermissible harm, epistemically impermissible harm, and instrumentally impermissible harm. At the same time, according to the service view, we should indeed interpret imprecise legal norms so as to balance military and humanitarian considerations—by reference to their respective moral weight.

On my view, military considerations support a permissive interpretation to the extent that they reflect moral reasons to perform the type of act in question, such as the losses that such acts might prevent to the attacking force or to its civilian population. Humanitarian considerations support a restrictive interpretation to the extent that they reflect moral reasons to refrain from the type of act in question, such as the losses that such acts might inflict on the civilian population of the opposing party. We balance military and humanitarian considerations by balancing the moral reasons for and against performing the act in question. When the former outweigh the latter we should adopt a permissive interpretation; when the latter outweigh the former we should adopt a restrictive interpretation.

Crucially, when adopting either a permissive or a restrictive interpretation we should consider not only whether the act in question is morally permissible in the objective and epistemic senses but also whether the act in question is morally permissible in the instrumental sense. In other words, we should adopt the interpretation that will best help combatants to conform to their objective moral obligations. Sometimes that will mean tracking the conditions of objective or epistemic permissibility; often it will mean departing from those conditions. As we have seen, combatants are sometimes more likely to act objectively permissibly if they follow the law rather than their own moral judgment. We should interpret imprecise laws so that they provide combatants with the best possible moral guidance, understood in this instrumental sense.

There is another reason to interpret the LOAC in its morally best light, namely to narrow the gap between the LOAC and human rights law. Since human rights are moral rights that we all posses in virtue of our humanity, morally unjustified killings violate our right not to be arbitrarily deprived of our lives. Accordingly, we should interpret the LOAC so as to prohibit morally unjustified killings. Evidently, a killing that is morally permissible in the objective, epistemic, or instrumental sense

---

[113] Schmitt, "Military Necessity and Humanity," 837.

is not morally unjustified and should not be considered arbitrary. For example, a wartime killing that is morally permissible in the instrumental sense should not be considered arbitrary because, by hypothesis, following the relevant rule is the best way to avoid violating the human rights of others, such that one could not better respect human rights by relying on one's own moral judgment. Accordingly, we should interpret the LOAC so that it helps combatants avoid violating human rights better than they could on their own.

International Law and National Law

The discussion so far raises important questions regarding the relationship between international law and national law. Does national law permit combatants to fight, or merely bar their prosecution for fighting? When international law and national law diverge, which should combatants follow? Let us take each question in turn.

Under the national law of many states, soldiers are justified in fighting to the extent that they exercise lawful authority or obey lawful orders. For example, according to the United States *Manual for Courts-Martial*, "A death, injury, or other act caused or done in the proper performance of a legal duty is justified and not unlawful."[114] In particular, "killing an enemy combatant in battle is justified."[115] In addition, the US *Manual* provides that "An act performed pursuant to a lawful order is justified."[116] Accordingly, under national law, US soldiers who kill enemy combatants in conformity with the LOAC are typically justified and not merely immune from prosecution. In contrast, under national law, foreign combatants who kill US soldiers in conformity with the LOAC are typically not justified but merely immune from prosecution.[117] While the LOAC applies symmetrically, national law typically applies asymmetrically.

As we have seen, law necessarily makes moral claims. Accordingly, a legal justification is a moral justification claimed by law. It is hardly surprising that states claim that their soldiers are justified in fighting. Nor is it surprising that states do not claim that opposing soldiers are justified in fighting but instead claim only that opposing soldiers are immune from prosecution. After all, states invariably claim that they are waging a just war while their adversaries are waging an unjust war. Indeed, a state that orders its soldiers to war, authorizes them to use lethal force, and obligates them

---

[114] United States Manual for Courts-Martial §916(c) (2012).

[115] United States Manual for Courts-Martial §916(c) Discussion.

[116] United States Manual for Courts-Martial §916(d) Discussion (in contrast, "An act performed pursuant to an unlawful order is excused unless the accused knew it to be unlawful or a person of ordinary sense and understanding would have known it to be unlawful").

[117] For a recent US case in which an individual fighting for a foreign armed force asserted a justification defense, which the court denied, see *United States v Hamidullin*, 114 F Supp 3d 365, 382 (ED Va 2015).

to follow orders necessarily claims that its soldiers are morally permitted (indeed, morally required) to fight. Of course, most such claims turn out to be false.[118]

Under national law, soldiers have a legal duty to obey general orders, including rules of engagement, as well as specific orders. According to the service conception of legitimate authority, soldiers morally should defer to their superiors only if they are more likely to conform to the moral reasons that apply to them by obeying their orders than by relying on their own moral judgment. Conversely, soldiers should not defer to their superiors if ordered to commit acts that are clearly immoral, or if important new information or circumstances arise that their superiors did not anticipate, or if they know that their superiors issued their orders arbitrarily or in bad faith.[119]

If a soldier's orders prohibit what international law tolerates, then there is no true conflict. As we have seen, international law does not authorize or entitle soldiers to kill in ways that it does not prohibit, or give soldiers a right to kill that national law might infringe. Typically, soldiers morally ought to follow orders that are more restrictive than international law. Following such orders will help soldiers avoid wrongful killing and, of course, satisfy their oath. Moreover, since armed forces typically have an interest in using as much force as law and morality permit, a decision by military commanders to issue such restrictive orders warrants significant deference.

In contrast, if a soldier's orders require what international law prohibits, then there is a true conflict. As Raz observes, "When several authorities pronounce on the same matter and their directives conflict, we must decide, to the best of our ability, which is more reliable as a guide."[120] Typically, soldiers morally ought to refuse to obey orders that violate international law. As we will see throughout this book, almost all killings that violate the LOAC are seriously wrongful, such that a soldier's promissory obligation to obey her superiors cannot render these killings morally permissible. Moreover, since armed forces typically have an interest in using more force than morality permits, a decision by military commanders to issue such permissive orders warrants little deference.

Fortunately, under the national law of most states, soldiers have no duty to obey orders that violates international law. Unfortunately, in many states, soldiers may be punished for disobeying orders that they believe (rightly or wrongly) violate international law but that a court-martial later decides (rightly or wrongly) do not violate international law.[121] Accordingly, a soldier may be punished under national

---

[118] As McMahan observes, all wars are unjust on at least one side, and some wars are unjust on all sides.

[119] See Raz, *Morality of Freedom*, 46.

[120] Raz, *Between Authority and Interpretation*, 143.

[121] See, eg, United States Manual for Courts-Martial §14(c)(2)(a)(i) ("An order requiring the performance of a military duty or act may be inferred to be lawful and it is disobeyed at the peril of the subordinate").

law if she disobeys an order to perform an act that violates international law but that conforms to her state's mistaken interpretation of international law. Conversely, that same soldier may be punished under international law if she obeys that same order, provided that she believes that the ordered act is unlawful or the ordered act is manifestly unlawful. For this reason, among many others, it is imperative that states adopt reasonable interpretations of international law that bring national law, international law, and morality into alignment.

Conclusion

International law does not confer on combatants a legal permission to fight for an unjust cause and therefore does not claim that combatants are morally permitted to fight for an unjust cause. Conventionalists need not defend such a moral permission in order to defend international law. Revisionists need not insist on a sharp divergence between law and morality or feel compelled to embrace the humanitarian view that the law should aim to reduce wrongful suffering in war to the greatest extent practically possible. The law of armed conflict is prohibitive, not permissive, and applies alongside other applicable moral and legal norms. Accordingly, acts not prohibited by the law of armed conflict may be prohibited by human rights law or by moral rules.

Though initially attractive, the humanitarian view does not stand up to critical scrutiny. Instead, we should accept the service view that the law should aim to provide moral guidance to combatants, helping them to conform as closely as possible to their moral obligations. Ideally, combatants on all sides will commit fewer and less serious moral wrongs by following the law than they would by violating the law and following their own moral judgment. Finally, wherever possible, we should interpret and develop the law so as to vindicate the law's claim to legitimate authority and provide the best possible moral guidance to combatants.

3

Civilians

Civilians are all persons who are neither members of the armed forces of a party to an armed conflict nor participants in a *levée en masse*. Under international law, civilians "shall enjoy general protection against dangers arising from military operations."[1] It is "[t]o give effect to this general protection" that international law specifically prohibits making civilians the object of attack, employing indiscriminate methods or means of combat, and launching attacks which may be expected to cause excessive civilian losses. Simply put, international law grants civilians legal immunity from intentional, indiscriminate, unnecessary, and disproportionate harm. The legal rules of distinction, discrimination, precautions, and proportionality all rest on the fundamental principle of civilian immunity.

The moral basis of civilian immunity is both obvious and profound. Civilians are, first and foremost, human beings who possess certain basic moral rights simply in virtue of their humanity. First among these rights is the right not to be killed. The right not to be maimed is not far behind. As Michael Walzer reminds us, "[w]e are all immune to start with; our right not to be attacked is a feature of normal human relationships."[2] Accordingly, "the theoretical problem is not to describe how immunity is gained, but how it is lost."

How, then, can human beings lose their moral rights not to be harmed? Presumably, rights so fundamental are as hard to forfeit as they are to override. If killing other people is ordinarily the gravest moral wrong that we can commit, then doing so requires an exceptionally strong moral justification. Put another way, the grounds of moral liability to defensive killing must be sufficiently powerful to overturn the compound moral asymmetry between intentionally doing harm and unintentionally allowing harm. After all, it is impermissible to intentionally kill innocent people except (perhaps) as a necessary means of preventing far greater harm to others. In contrast, it is permissible to intentionally kill those morally liable

---

[1] Protocol Additional to the Geneva Conventions of August 12, 1949, and relating to the Protection of Victims of International Armed Conflicts (Protocol I) (adopted June 8, 1977, entered into force December 7, 1978) 1125 UNTS 3, art 51(1). See also International Committee of the Red Cross, *Customary International Humanitarian Law*, vol 1 (CUP 2009) 19 ("Rule 6. Civilians are protected against attack unless and for such time as they take a direct part in hostilities").

[2] Michael Walzer, *Just and Unjust Wars* (2nd edn Basic Books 1992) 145.

Law and Morality at War. First Edition. Adil Haque. © Adil Haque 2017. Published 2017 by Oxford University Press

to defensive killing as a means of preventing comparable harm to only one other person. Indeed, on most views, it is permissible to kill many culpable aggressors to defend a single innocent victim. What could explain such a dramatic reversal of ordinary moral principles?

Under international law, civilians enjoy general protection from targeting and collateral harm "unless and for such time as they take a direct part in hostilities."[3] Civilians directly participate in hostilities by performing specific acts likely to directly cause harm to one party to the conflict in support of another. In contrast, civilians retain their legal immunity if they merely contribute to the general war effort, for example through the design, production, and shipment of weapons and military equipment; or if they merely engage in war-sustaining activities including political advocacy, voting, and paying taxes. Let us call civilians who directly participate in hostilities *participant civilians* and civilians who do not directly participate in hostilities *non-participant civilians*.

Several revisionist moral philosophers, most notably Jeff McMahan, Cécile Fabre, and Helen Frowe, argue that many non-participant civilians are morally liable to defensive killing. On their views, civilians lose their moral right not to be intentionally killed as a means of preventing the unjust threats posed by their armed forces by making political, material, strategic, and financial contributions to those threats. Let us call civilians who make such contributions *contributing civilians*.

Revisionists often add that, for pragmatic and epistemic reasons, the legal immunity of non-participant civilians should remain absolute. In my preferred terms, soldiers who try to identify and kill morally liable civilians are much more likely to kill wrongfully than to prevent wrongful killing. In many cases, such instrumentalist considerations would prove decisive on their own. However, I will argue that civilian immunity primarily rests on deep moral principles and that instrumental considerations play an important but subordinate role.

On my view, almost all non-participant civilians retain their moral right not to be killed. In general, persons are morally liable to defensive killing only if they pose unjust threats directly, jointly with others, or indirectly through others they control. Suitably interpreted, the current legal standard maps closely onto these deep moral principles. In addition, it is less wrongful for combatants fighting for an unjust cause to kill participant civilians than to kill non-participant civilians. It follows that just and unjust combatants alike will better conform to their moral obligations if they respect the legal immunity of non-participant civilians than if they target non-participant civilians whom they judge morally liable to be killed.

The body of this chapter presents my account of civilian immunity and its loss. I offer my response to the revisionist challenge in an appendix. Philosophically

---

[3] Protocol I art 51(3); ICRC, *Customary International Humanitarian Law*, 19.

inclined readers may wish to read the appendix before turning to Chapter 4. Readers who are primarily interested in international law may wish to read the first section below and then move directly to Chapter 4. Finally, I will avoid several difficult philosophical issues by ignoring cases of involuntariness, ignorance, insanity, and the like and focusing on the liability of persons who exercise responsible moral agency.

Direct Participation in Hostilities

To evaluate the legal standard of direct participation in hostilities we must first understand it. Unfortunately, "a clear and uniform definition of direct participation in hostilities has not been developed in State practice."[4] For example, in 1976, the United States Air Force took the view that

taking a direct part in hostilities covers acts of war intended by their nature and purpose to strike at enemy personnel and material. Thus a civilian taking part in fighting, whether singly or as a member of a group, *loses* the immunity given civilians.[5]

Similarly, the International Criminal Tribunal for the former Yugoslavia (ICTY) has held that "[t]o take a 'direct' part in the hostilities means acts of war which by their nature or purpose are likely to cause actual harm to the personnel or matériel of the enemy armed forces."[6]

In contrast, the recent US Department of Defense Law of War Manual asserts that it is lawful to target civilians who "effectively and substantially contribute to an adversary's ability to conduct or sustain combat operations."[7] Obviously, there are significant differences between "directly" and "effectively and substantially"; between "participate" and "contribute"; and between "hostilities" and "the ability to conduct or sustain combat operations." The Manual illustrates its position with the rather chilling example of Vietnamese villagers "of all ages and sexes [who], willingly or under duress, served as porters [for] . . . communist forces. It is well established that once civilians act as support personnel they cease to be noncombatants and are subject to attack."[8] It seems that, according to the Manual, children forced to serve as porters for opposing forces are lawful targets and may be intentionally killed. More broadly, it seems that all civilians who perform acts of service and support lose their immunity from attack.

---

[4] ICRC, *Customary International Humanitarian Law*, vol 1, 23.

[5] Department of the Air Force, AFP 110-31, International Law—The Conduct of Armed Conflict and Air Operations 5–8 (1976).

[6] *Prosecutor v Galić* (Judgment) IT-98-29-T (December 5, 2003), para 48. See also *Prosecutor v Rutaganda* (Judgment) ICTR-96-3-T (December 6, 1999), para 100.

[7] US Department of Defense, *Law of War Manual* (2015) para 5.9.3.

[8] US Department of Defense, *Law of War Manual*, para 5.9.3 n 227.

Finally, some states seem reluctant to adopt any general criteria. For example, the United Kingdom's law of armed conflict manual says simply that

Whether civilians are taking a direct part in hostilities is a question of fact. Civilians manning an anti-aircraft gun or engaging in sabotage of military installations are doing so. Civilians working in military vehicle maintenance depots or munitions factories or driving military transport vehicles are not, but they are at risk from attacks on those objectives since military objectives may be attacked whether or not civilians are present.[9]

Importantly, contrary to the US Defense Department Manual, the UK Manual suggests that civilians lose their immunity from attack if they act as combat personnel but not if they act as service or support personnel.

My own view, roughly, is that direct participation *in hostilities* means direct participation *in attacks and detention*: that is what hostilities *are*, that is what the law governing the conduct of hostilities *regulates*, and that is what combatants but not civilians have a "right" to directly participate *in*.[10] In filling out this rough outline, I will draw on the most rigorous legal analysis of direct participation to date, accepting some parts while modifying others.

According to the International Committee of the Red Cross (ICRC), direct participation in hostilities involves the preparation, execution, or command of specific acts likely to (i) directly cause (ii) harm meeting a relevant threshold (iii) in support of one party to the conflict and in opposition to another.[11] I will discuss these elements in turn.

A civilian can satisfy the requirement of *direct causation* in three ways. First, a civilian may cause harm without further intervening agency, for example by firing a weapon or by laying a mine. Second, a civilian may play an integral part in a coordinated military operation—for example by identifying targets or providing coordinates for bombardment—which in turn causes harm without further intervening agency. Finally, a civilian may command others to perform harmful acts or jointly carry out harmful military operations, for example when a civilian intelligence officer orders a targeted killing operation or when a head of state, acting as commander in chief of the armed forces, approves a broader military campaign.

Borrowing some terms from international criminal law, civilians become lawful targets only through *direct perpetration* of a harmful act as an individual, *joint perpetration* of a harmful act with others, or *indirect perpetration* of a harmful act through another person whom they effectively control.[12] Indeed, members of a military unit

---

[9] UK Ministry of Defense, *Law of Armed Conflict Manual* (OUP 2005) 5.3.3.
[10] In international law, "attacks" are "acts of violence against the adversary, whether in offence or in defence" (Protocol I art 49(1)).
[11] International Committee of the Red Cross, Interpretive Guidance on the Notion of Direct Participation in Hostilities Under International Humanitarian Law (ICRC 2009) 46.
[12] See, eg, Rome Statute of the International Criminal Court (opened for signature July 17, 1998, entered into force July 1, 2002) 2187 UNTS 3, art 25(3) ("a person shall be

performing coordinated roles in a combat operation are paradigmatic joint perpetrators, while military commanders directing their subordinates to conduct combat operations are paradigmatic indirect perpetrators.[13] Naturally, when civilians perform similar roles they incur similar liability. Importantly, jointly perpetrating a crime with others and indirectly perpetrating a crime through others contrast with aiding and abetting the crimes of others. Joint perpetration and indirect perpetration involve direct liability for one's own acts, not derivative liability for the acts of others. When we act jointly, your act is my act; when you act on my orders, your act is my act. More on this below.

There is one apparent disanalogy between participation in hostilities and perpetration of crimes. According to the ICRC, an individual may perform an integral part in a coordinated military operation even if she does not make a necessary contribution to the operation's success. For example:

a person serving as one of several lookouts during an ambush would certainly be taking a direct part in hostilities although his contribution may not be indispensable to the causation of harm.[14]

In contrast, the International Criminal Court has written that

when the objective elements of an offence are carried out by a plurality of persons acting within the framework of a common plan, only those to whom essential tasks have been assigned – and who, consequently, have the power to frustrate the commission of the crime by not performing their tasks – can be said to have joint control over the crime.[15]

On the latter view, criminal perpetration requires control over the crime. Direct perpetrators control the crime by either performing or not performing the criminal act. Indirect perpetrators control the crime by either inducing or not inducing those they control to perform the criminal act. Similarly, joint perpetrators control the crime by either performing or not performing essential tasks. On this view, individuals who do not perform essential tasks may aid and abet the crimes of others but do not perpetrate crimes with others.

The control theory of perpetration yields implausible results in cases of preemptive and simultaneous overdetermination. If a person performs the task assigned her by a common plan, then she may be a joint perpetrator even if someone else would perform that task if she did not. Similarly, if a person conditionally intends to

criminally responsible . . . if that person: (a) Commits such a crime, whether as an individual, jointly with another or through another person, regardless of whether that other person is criminally responsible").

[13] In such cases, international criminal law draws on the German theory of *Organisationsherrschaft*, that is, perpetration through another person by means of an organized apparatus of power.

[14] ICRC, Interpretive Guidance, 54.

[15] *Prosecutor v Lubanga*, Decision on the Confirmation of Charges, 01/04-01/06, Pre-Trial Chamber, January 29, 2007, para 347.

perform the task assigned her by a common plan should the need arise (say to alert the others if the police arrive) then she is a joint perpetrator even if the need does not arise (since no police arrive).[16] International criminal law should understand "an essential task" simply as a task that the participants believe one of them may have to perform for the plan to succeed.[17] Similarly, international humanitarian law (IHL) should understand "an integral part" of a military operation as one that the participants believe one of them may have to fulfill for the operation to succeed.

In its Commentary to Protocol I, the ICRC took the position that an act satisfies the relevant *threshold of harm* only if it is likely to kill or injure military personnel or damage military equipment.[18] It quickly became apparent that the threshold of harm may be satisfied by acts likely to harm civilians or damage civilian property. More recently, the ICRC took the position that the threshold of harm is satisfied by acts likely to cause "harm of a military nature," that is, by acts likely to "adversely affect" a party's military operations or military capacity.[19] Surprisingly, the ICRC took the position that military harm *always* satisfies the threshold of harm "regardless of quantitative gravity." On this view, "large numbers of unarmed civilians who deliberately gather on a bridge in order to prevent the passage of governmental ground forces in pursuit of an insurgent group would probably have to be regarded as directly participating in hostilities."[20] It follows that, on this view, it is lawful to intentionally kill all of these civilians; to forsake feasible precautions to avoid or reduce collateral harm to them; and to collaterally harm them in pursuit of comparatively trivial military advantage.

In my view, lowering the threshold of harm in this way is both a doctrinal mistake and a policy miscalculation. I suspect that the ICRC accepts a broad interpretation of military harm only because it elsewhere takes the position that the principle of humanity imposes legal restraints on the use of force (RUFs) against direct participants in hostilities.[21] In particular, the ICRC takes the position that it is unlawful to kill direct participants in hostilities unnecessarily, that is, to kill when capture, non-lethal incapacitation, or avoidance will not endanger one's forces or

---

[16] Importantly, Saba Bazargan argues that unjust combatants may be morally liable to be killed even if they do not causally contribute to unjust threats if they assume a role the function of which is to pose or causally contribute to threats ("Complicitous Liability in War" (2013) 165 Philosophical Studies 177–95). Bazargan describes this as complicitous liability, but it is more precise to call it liability based on joint perpetration.

[17] On my view, the distinction between joint perpetration and complicity is not one of control but one of coordination, between our acting together and my helping you act. The fact that the right distinction is sometimes hard to draw is no reason to always draw the wrong distinction instead. More on this below.

[18] International Committee of the Red Cross, Commentary on the Additional Protocols of June 8, 1977 to the Geneva Conventions of August 12, 1949 (1987) para 1944.

[19] ICRC, Interpretive Guidance, 47.   [20] ICRC, Interpretive Guidance, 81.

[21] Tellingly, the ICRC writes that "[t]he concerns expressed by some experts that the criterion of 'adversely affecting' military operations or military capacity was too wide and vague and could be misunderstood to authorize the killing of civilians without any military necessity are addressed below in Section IX [discussing RUFs]" (Interpretive Guidance, 47–8, fn 97).

civilians. I suspect that the ICRC hoped to offset a lower threshold of direct participation with greater RUFs against direct participants. If adopted, the ICRC's two-pronged approach might result in a similar level of effective protection as a high threshold of harm and avoid the disturbing implications described above. For example, the ICRC writes that it would be unlawful to kill the civilians on the bridge in the previous example. Though they satisfy the threshold of military harm, "[i]n most cases, . . . it would be reasonably possible for the armed forces to remove the physical obstacle posed by these civilians through means less harmful than a direct military attack on them."[22]

Unfortunately, leading military lawyers have almost uniformly rejected the ICRC's position that IHL imposes RUFs against direct participants.[23] I will discuss the merits of this dispute in the next chapter, but the very existence of the dispute is significant. If two legal frameworks yield similar legal results, then we should prefer the framework that plausibly interprets an uncontroversial legal norm to a framework that rests on a putative legal norm whose very existence is hotly disputed. Moreover, there is a grave danger that armed forces will help themselves to the ICRC's broad interpretation of military harm while rejecting the ICRC's proposed RUFs. Other things equal, we should prefer a framework that is less susceptible to predictable misunderstanding and conscious manipulation. In my view, the ICRC adopted a broad interpretation of military harm on the assumption that its breadth would be limited by a complementary prohibition of unnecessary killing. If that prohibition is widely rejected, then the broad interpretation of military harm should be rejected as well.

On my view, a civilian who directly causes "military harm" thereby directly participates in hostilities only if she does so as an integral part in a coordinated military operation likely to kill or injure persons or destroy, capture, or neutralize military objectives. For example, a civilian who blocks a street with a truck directly participates' in hostilities if she does so as part of an ambush but not if she does so simply to disrupt a routine patrol. Any lower standard would permit armed forces to intentionally kill civilians whose actions are neither intended nor likely to result in comparable harm to others. No serious account of morally permissible killing would support such conduct. We will consider RUFs against combatants and direct participants in Chapter 4. In the meantime, we should not compromise the principle of civilian immunity.

Finally, an act constitutes direct participation in hostilities only if it is specifically designed to support one party to the conflict to the detriment of another. The existence of such a *belligerent nexus* ensures that civilians lose their immunity only by taking sides between the warring parties and fighting with an armed force

---

[22] ICRC, Interpretive Guidance 81.
[23] See, eg, US Department of Defense, *Law of War Manual*, 2.2.3.1; Michael N Schmitt, "Military Necessity and Humanity in International Humanitarian Law: Preserving the Delicate Balance" (2010) 50 Virginia Journal of International Law 795, 834–5.

against its adversaries. A belligerent nexus thereby distinguishes military acts that form part of an armed conflict from criminal acts that occur during armed conflict. Criminal acts may trigger ordinary principles of self-defense, defense of others, or law enforcement within the framework of human rights law. Only military acts trigger the application of IHL. Importantly, absent a belligerent nexus, it might violate international human rights law to kill civilians who do not threaten to kill or seriously injure others but whose actions may adversely affect military capacity or operations. It is lawful to kill such civilians only if their actions are designed to help one party and hinder the other party in military operations.

Helen Frowe writes that the legal standard of direct participation in hostilities "is clearly mistaken as a picture of liability to defensive harm":

If being directly involved in the hostilities means firing weapons on the front line, then most combatants will not be involved in the hostilities either. And if we broaden the meaning of 'hostilities' to include the military activities behind the front line that provide intelligence, training, and supplies, such that we cover all combatants, it seems arbitrary to exclude the non-combatants playing comparable roles.[24]

Frowe's objection seems misplaced. The law does not inconsistently apply the same basis of liability to both civilians and combatants but instead consistently applies a different basis of liability to each. Civilians are lawful targets only while they directly participate in hostilities. In contrast, regular combatants are lawful targets even if they never directly participate in hostilities. In other words, civilians are lawful targets in virtue of their conduct while combatants are lawful targets in virtue of their status or function. The law may be mistaken on this point, but it is not confused.

In the remainder of this chapter, I argue that civilians who do not directly participate in hostilities are not morally liable to defensive killing. In the next chapter, I consider the claim that combatants whose function does not include direct participation in hostilities are nevertheless morally liable to defensive killing.

Offensive Killing and Defensive Killing

Paradigmatically, defensive killing aims to prevent non-defensive killing or, more simply, offensive killing. Before we consider possible extensions of the paradigm we should understand the paradigm itself. Moreover, to understand the permissibility of defensive killing we must first understand the wrongfulness of offensive killing. After all, it is the wrongfulness of offensive killing that generates moral liability to defensive killing.

The most obvious reason why it is presumptively impermissible to kill another human being is that doing so deprives her of all the goods that she otherwise

---

[24] Helen Frowe, *Defensive Killing* (OUP 2014) 165.

would have enjoyed, thereby making her much worse off than she otherwise would have been. However, killing another human being not only *harms* her but also *wrongs* her, infringing her right that you not kill her. While her right that you not kill her protects her interest in living, the strength of the former does not vary directly with the strength of the latter. The right not to be killed is held equally by the young and the old, the healthy and the sick, the lavishly rich and the desperately poor. Put another way, rights are *opaque* rather than *transparent* to the interests that they protect. Killing harms some more than others, but killing wrongs everyone just the same.[25]

While we often refer to a "right not to be killed," this phrase is elliptical. More precisely, V has a right against A that A not kill her, a right against B that B not kill her, and so on. These directed rights ground corresponding directed duties. A has a duty to V not to kill V, B has a duty to V not to kill V, and so on. These rights reflect V's moral status while these duties reflect each duty-bearer's moral relationship to V. In technical terms, these duties are victim-centered but agent-relative.

On my view, permissible defensive killing is the mirror image of impermissible offensive killing. Permissible defensive killing prevents others from lethally wronging us and from lethally harming us. Defensive killing enforces our rights against others that those others not kill us. Put the other way around, defensive killing enforces their corresponding duties, owed to us, not to kill us. For these reasons, defensive killing does not wrong those who threaten to wrong us in these ways. In addition, defensive killing typically prevents others from making us much worse off than we would be in their absence. This *eliminative* dimension of typical defensive killing contributes to making it all-things-considered permissible to harm others rather than allow them to harm us. I will say more about both ideas below.

First, we should clarify what our right that others not kill us—and their corresponding duty not to kill us—involves. One person *directly* kills another by performing an act that causes the other's death without intervening agency and, ordinarily, without which the victim would not have died.[26] Direct killers both infringe their victims' rights and make their victims much worse off.

In addition, one person *indirectly* kills another by inducing someone she effectively controls to directly kill the other person. Indirect killers infringe their victims' rights and make their victims worse off through or by means of the person they effectively control. Importantly, the person controlled functions less as an intervening agent than as an instrument or tool in the hands of the controller. In some cases, indirect killers manipulate innocent or irresponsible agents (such children or the

---

[25] Frances Kamm suggests that my right that you not kill me loses its ordinary force if I will die very soon anyway. I doubt it. For example, if A tries to murder V, a terminally ill patient, then A is not wronged if B kills A in V's defense. In some cases, it may be all-things-considered impermissible to kill A (for example, if A is very young and can be rehabilitated) but that is a separate question.

[26] I will consider cases of simultaneous and preemptive overdetermination shortly.

mentally ill) to do their bidding. In other cases, indirect killers command subordinates committed to obey their orders. Of course, subordinates generally are not automatons but instead are moral agents who view their orders as reasons for action rather than as causal constraints. Crucially, superiors decide what reasons to give their subordinates and tell their subordinates what to do and intend. Subordinates commit to obey their superior and are thereby rationally constrained to either obey or rescind their commitment. So long as subordinates remain committed to obey, superiors can manipulate these rational constraints as if they are causal constraints. In this sense, indirect killers kill their victims through or by means of the person whom they control, much as direct killers may kill their victims through or by means of non-human weapons.[27]

Finally, several people *jointly* kill another by together performing a joint action that causes the other's death, without subsequent intervening agency by others and, typically, without which the victim would not have died. Joint killers together infringe the rights of their victim and together make their victim worse off. For example, if A restrains V while B stabs V to death, each performing coordinated roles in a common plan, then A and B together kill V. Importantly, joint actions are the actions of each participant, not solely the actions of the last participant to perform her role or only the actions of those participants without whose participation the plan would not have succeeded. For example, in the previous case, A and B together kill V even if B's participation was counterfactually unnecessary because V would not have resisted. What we do, I do. When we kill, I kill.

The nature of joint agency is, of course, the subject of long-running philosophical debate.[28] Indeed, joint agency may be a primitive and irreducible concept, difficult to elucidate in a non-circular fashion. For example, successful joint action requires the coordinated execution of joint intentions, that is, individual intentions to act jointly. We walk together only if we each intend to walk together, we each walk in execution of our respective intentions to walk together, and we are each mutually responsive to each other's attempts to execute our respective intentions to walk together.[29] If the concept of joint agency is indeed primitive, it will be difficult

---

[27] See also Kai Draper, *War and Individual Rights* (OUP 2015) 213–14. As we shall see in the Appendix, the concept of indirect perpetration provides one way to defend David Rodin's account of civilian immunity against the objections of Helen Frowe.

[28] See, eg, Margaret Gilbert, "Shared Intention and Personal Intention" (2009) 144 Philosophical Studies 167; Christopher Kutz, "Acting Together" (2000) 61 Philosophy and Phenomenological Research 1; John Searle, "Collective Intentions and Actions," in P Cohen, J Morgan, & M Pollack (eds), *Intentions in Communication* (MIT 1990) 401; Scott Shapiro, "Massively Shared Agency," in Manuel Vargas & Gideon Yaffe (eds), *Rational and Social Agency: The Philosophy of Michael Bratman* (OUP 2014) 257.

[29] See Michael E Bratman, *Shared Agency: A Planning Theory of Acting Together* (OUP 2014). Bratman famously understands mutual responsiveness in terms of "meshing sub-plans." See

to classify borderline cases. For example, it is sometimes hard to say whether com-muters walk together or separately into the same train car. In contrast, it is clear that my friend and I walk together as we discuss our life plans. Conversely, it is clear that the construction worker who paved the street on which I walk does not thereby walk with me.

Those who directly, indirectly, or jointly kill others presumptively infringe their basic rights and make them much worse off. If anyone is liable to defensive killing, then direct, indirect, and joint killers are liable to defensive killing. Paradigmatically, defensive killing aims to prevent the infringement of basic rights and the infliction of lethal harms by killing those who would infringe these rights and inflict these harms by themselves, through others, or together with others. Importantly, when individuals indirectly or jointly threaten to kill they are *directly* liable rather than *derivatively* liable to defensive killing. In these cases, we do not kill one person to prevent another from killing; instead, we kill one person to prevent her from killing through or with others.

It follows that most direct participation in hostilities on behalf of an unjust cause falls within the paradigm case of moral liability to defensive killing. Those who threaten to kill or seriously injure innocent people—directly, indirectly, or jointly—are not wronged if they are killed to avert the threats they pose. Importantly, con-tributing civilians do not threaten to kill directly, indirectly, or jointly. Contributing civilians do not directly cause harm, command others to do so, or perform integral parts in coordinated military operations. For example, in paying their taxes, civil-ians do not jointly pose unjust threats together with their armed forces any more than they jointly build roads together with construction workers, jointly provide healthcare together with doctors and nurses, or jointly teach children together with teachers. There are borderline cases of joint agency and mere contribution, but these cases are not among them.

The burning question is whether contributing civilians nevertheless become morally liable to defensive killing by contributing to or enabling unjust threats posed by their armed forces. It is to this question that we now turn.

Eliminative Killing and Opportunistic Killing

Recall the distinction, drawn in Chapter 1, between *eliminative* harming and *oppor-tunistic* harming.[30] Eliminatively harming someone prevents her from making others worse off than they would be in her absence. Opportunistically harming

also Jens David Ohlin, "Joint Intentions to Commit International Crimes" (2011) 11 Chicago Journal of International Law 693–753.

[30] These terms originate with Warren Quinn, "Actions, Intentions, and Consequences: The Doctrine of Double Effect" (1989) 18 Philosophy & Public Affairs 344 (distinguishing between "direct agency that benefits from the presence of the victim (direct *opportunistic* agency) and . . . direct agency that aims to remove an obstacle or difficulty that the victim

someone makes others better off than they would be in her absence. Shooting an unjust attacker about to throw a grenade at you is an example of eliminative harming. Throwing an innocent bystander on top of the grenade is an example of opportunistic harming.

In general, a person is currently liable to opportunistic harming if and only if she was previously liable to eliminative harming (or would have been so liable had such harm been necessary to prevent an unjust threat).[31] In the previous example, the unjust attacker was liable to eliminative killing before she threw the grenade. If she has already thrown the grenade, then she is liable to opportunistic killing, for example by throwing her on top of the grenade. Throwing her on top of the grenade will make you better off than you would be were she not present at that moment, but not better off than you would have been had she not thrown the grenade in the first place. Overall, her presence makes you neither better nor worse off. This fact annuls the presumptive wrongfulness of using her for your benefit.

If we would not wrong someone by harming her at t_1 to prevent her from performing some action at t_2 that will make others worse off at t_4, then we do not wrong her at t_3 by comparably harming her to prevent her action at t_2 from making others worse off at t_4. If we opportunistically harm her at t_3 no more than she was liable to be eliminatively harmed at t_1, then we do not make her worse off than she has a right to be. Moreover, though we make use of her presence at t_3 to make ourselves better off than we would be in her absence at t_3, we do not make ourselves better off than we would be had she been absent at t_2. Put another way, it was just her good luck that we could not or did not (permissibly) eliminatively harm her earlier, so she has no grounds to complain if we opportunistically harm her to the same extent now.[32]

---

presents (direct *eliminative* agency)"). Seth Lazar essentially defines eliminative harming as non-opportunistic harming, that is, as harming that makes no one better off than they would have been in the victim's absence. See Lazar, *Sparing Civilians*, ch 3. This seems unfortunate. Harming that leaves no one better or worse off than they would have been in the victim's absence sets a moral baseline in relation to which opportunistic harming generally is *pro tanto* more wrongful, while eliminative harming is *pro tanto* less wrongful. It is best not to collapse these three important categories into only two.

[31] The latter clause accommodates the possibility that necessity is internal to liability, such that one can only be liable to defensive harms that are necessary to prevent unjust threats. For doubts about this possibility, see Frowe, *Defensive Killing*, ch 4.

[32] Compare Jeff McMahan, *The Ethics of Killing: Problems at the Margins of Life* (OUP 2002) 406 ("It is hard to see how this mere difference in timing—the difference between having caused a present threat and causing a present threat—could by itself make a decisive moral difference, making it permissible to kill one who is the present cause of a present threat ... when it is clearly impermissible to kill one who is the past cause of a present threat"). McMahan claims that non-liability to opportunistic killing entails non-liability to eliminative killing. I claim that non-liability to eliminative killing entails non-liability to opportunistic killing.

Conversely, if someone was not liable to eliminative killing to prevent her from performing an action that will make others worse off (and would not have been so liable had it been necessary to do so), then typically she is not liable to opportunistic killing to prevent that action from making others worse off. In such cases, her presence never threatens to make others worse off but only presents an opportunity to make others better off.

The vast majority of contributing civilians make no one worse off through their individual political, material, strategic, and financial contributions to their governments and armed forces. In the absence of any given contributing civilian, their armed forces would pose the same unjust threats to the same people. In other words, the vast majority of contributing civilians make superfluous contributions and no difference to the threats posed by their armed forces. It follows that intentionally killing contributing civilians cannot be eliminative and can only be opportunistic.

Jeff McMahan observes that contributing civilians are often killed opportunistically, on the grounds that their contributions lie in the past and that they are often killed as a means of spreading terror.[33] I am making the different point that intentionally killing contributing civilians cannot be eliminative and can only be opportunistic (or gratuitous) since contributing civilians make no one worse off. Helen Frowe responds to McMahan that we can be morally liable to opportunistic killing—perhaps even to terroristic killing—in virtue of doing something in the past that will make others worse off unless we are opportunistically killed now.[34] I am making the distinct point that no contributing civilian has done anything in the past that will make others worse off unless we opportunistically kill her now. Her past contributions will make no difference to what happens to anyone in the future.

Contributing civilians cannot be liable to eliminative killing since no contributing civilian makes anyone worse off than they would be absent that contributing civilian. It follows that contributing civilians cannot be liable to opportunistic killing either. If we may not eliminatively kill a civilian to prevent her from paying her taxes, voting for pro-war politicians, or working in war-related industries then we may not opportunistically kill a civilian who has already done so—not because her action lies in the past but because her action will make no one worse off. If she was never liable to eliminative killing to prevent her action, then she is not liable to opportunistic killing in virtue of her action.

It is true that contributing civilians sometimes *collectively* make others worse off, by collectively enabling their armed forces to pose unjust threats. I argue below that it does not follow that contributing civilians are liable to eliminative killing

---

[33] Jeff McMahan, *Killing in War* (OUP 2009) 226. Marty Lederman pointed out to me that, whether or not contributing civilians are liable to eliminative killing, they are almost always killed opportunistically, irrespective of their liability to eliminative killing.

[34] Frowe, *Defensive Killing*, 201.

in small numbers let alone in large numbers. But first we should attend to some other issues.

Elimination and Overdetermination

In cases of preemptive and simultaneous overdetermination, the permissibility of defensive killing comes apart from liability to eliminative killing. To see this, consider the following cases:

> *Preemptive*: A decides to shoot V. A then sees B about to shoot V. A resolves to shoot V if B does not. V cannot shoot A, but knows that shooting B will frighten off A.

> *Simultaneous*: A decides to shoot V. A then sees B about to shoot V. A resolves to shoot V at the same time as B. V cannot shoot A, but knows that shooting B will frighten off A.

In both cases, B does not threaten to make V worse off than V would be in B's absence. After all, in B's absence, A will kill V. Instead, B presents V with an opportunity to make V better off that V would be in B's absence. After all, killing B will prevent A from killing V, which V could not achieve in B's absence. Killing B therefore seems opportunistic rather than eliminative.

Nevertheless, it is morally permissible for V to kill B. In both cases, B threatens to directly kill V, violating V's right against B that B not kill V. In other words, B threatens to *wrong* V, albeit not to *harm* V. In my view, V would not wrong B by killing B, just as we would not wrong someone attempting to murder a terminally ill patient by killing the attacker.

Ordinarily, opportunistic killing violates both the right not to be killed and the right not to be used, compounding the wrongfulness of killing with the wrongfulness of using. However, since killing B does not wrong B, only using B stands in need of justification. In my view, killing B is the morally weighted lesser evil, since it is worse to allow A to gratuitously kill V while violating V's right not to be killed than for V to opportunistically use B without violating B's right not to be killed. It follows that it is both just and all-things-considered permissible for V to kill B.[35]

Of course, contributing civilians do not threaten to wrong innocent people by invading their rights that the contributing civilians not kill them individually, jointly, or indirectly. Since contributing civilians also make no one worse off, it follows that civilians are not morally liable to any form of defensive killing. Killing contributing civilians is always unjust and almost always all-things-considered impermissible.

---

[35] My approach to overdetermination both resembles and departs from Frowe's approach to what she calls broad and narrow liability. See Frowe, *Defensive Killing*, 189–94.

Duty and Liability

We all have moral rights against others that they not contribute to unjust threats against us. To contribute, even superfluously, to an unjust threat to another person for a trivial or wicked reason seems profoundly disrespectful. However, it does not follow that we have a right to defensively kill those who superfluously contribute to unjust threats against us. Put the other way around, we all have moral duties not to contribute to unjust threats posed by others. In particular, civilians have a moral duty not to contribute to unjust threats posed by their armed forces. Contributing civilians breach this duty. Yet the breach of this duty does not render contributing civilians morally liable to defensive killing.

For one thing, many contributing civilians are justified in breaching their duty not to contribute to unjust threats posed by their armed forces. In most countries, tax evasion is punished either by imprisonment or by heavy fine. Many employers withhold their employees' income tax liability from their paychecks. Most goods, including food and clothes, carry a sales tax. In my view, contributing civilians who pay income and sales taxes in order to avoid criminal punishment, keep their job, or feed and clothe themselves are justified in doing so. No contributing civilian makes anyone worse off by paying his or her taxes and any contributing civilian who fails to pay his or her taxes will be made much worse off. Though the war to which they contribute is unjust, their contribution is justified and not merely excused.

Of course, many contributing civilians pay their taxes out of a sense of duty, patriotism, or support for the policies of their government. Their contributions are not justified because the normative reasons that favor their actions are not the motivating reasons that explain their actions. The practical impossibility of distinguishing justified taxpayers from unjustified taxpayers probably renders it epistemically impermissible to target civilians on the basis of taxpaying and instrumentally justifies a legal rule to that effect. In any event, I hope to show that it is *objectively* impermissible to target contributing civilians. Indeed, I hope to show that even unjustified contributions to an unjust cause—including voting, advocacy, and the design or manufacture of weapons—do not render contributing civilians morally liable to defensive killing. In my view, the duty not to contribute to unjust threats posed by others is not sufficiently stringent for its violation to result in the loss of basic rights.

In general, the stringency of a moral duty should determine the moral consequences of its violation. Suppose that some moral duty is sufficiently important that I am morally required to suffer some harm rather than violate that duty. If I threaten to violate that duty, then you will not wrong me by inflicting comparable harm on me in order to prevent me from doing so. I have no moral right to be free from such harm since I am morally required to suffer comparable harm rather than violate my duty. In contrast, you would wrong me by inflicting a greater harm on me than I am morally required to suffer rather than violate my duty.[36]

Put another way, moral constraints protect moral prerogatives: I am under a moral constraint not to harm you as a means to some end if and only if you have a moral prerogative not to accept that harm as a means to that end. Conversely, if you are morally required to accept some harm as a means to some end, then I do not wrong you by inflicting that harm on you as a means to that end.[37]

For example, the duty not to kill the innocent is very stringent. In general, we are morally required to die rather than breach this duty. It follows that someone who tries to kill an innocent person is not wronged by defensive killing. Killing her to prevent her from breaching her duty merely inflicts a harm on her that she is morally required to accept rather than breach her duty. In contrast, the duty to save the innocent is much less stringent. In general, we are not morally required to die or suffer serious injury to save an innocent person from comparable harm. If follows that we wrong an innocent person by killing her to save another innocent person. Killing her imposes a harm on her that she is not morally required to accept.

Importantly, our moral duty not to contribute to the unjust threats posed by our armed forces is not very stringent. As we have seen, civilians are not morally required to die or suffer serious injury rather than make superfluous contributions to unjust threats. Indeed, our duty not to superfluously contribute to an unjust threat cannot be much stronger than our duty to save others from unjust threats. Both superfluously contributing to a threat and failing to stop a threat leaves the victim no worse off than she would be in our absence. Moreover, failing to prevent a threat makes the victim worse off than she would be had we acted differently, while making a superfluous contribution to a threat does not. Perhaps it matters whether we are active or passive in relation to harm to others. Surely it matters whether we control the occurrence of the harm. Failing to prevent harm makes a difference to the occurrence of the harm; superfluously contributing to harm does not. It is hard to believe that our duty to make a (positive) difference is less stringent than our duty not to make *no* (negative) difference.

If civilians need not risk death or serious injury to avoid superfluously contributing to an unjust war, then it is presumptively wrong to kill or seriously injure civilians who do so. Of course, contributing civilians generally do not contribute to an unjust war under threat of death. On my view, liability depends not on our motivations but on the stringency of the moral duty we threaten to violate. For

---

[36] I started thinking along these lines after reading Victor Tadros, *The Ends of Harm* (OUP 2011). Tadros focuses on our positive duties to accept harm. I focus on the stringency of our negative duties, as reflected in the harms that we must accept rather than violate these negative duties. Nevertheless, his influence is unmistakable.

[37] Of course, moral rights and moral constraints can be overridden, such that it may be permissible to harm one person to prevent greater harm to others even if she has no moral duty to accept that harm (that is, a moral prerogative not to accept that harm).

example, in my view, an adult who fails to save a drowning child for a trivial or wicked reason may not be intentionally killed as a means of saving that child. True, the adult does not fail to save the child in order to avoid being killed. However, the moral duty that the adult violates is insufficiently stringent to result, when violated, in moral liability to be killed. The adult's culpable breach of his duty to save the child may generate liability to moral condemnation or even criminal punishment but does not generate liability to defensive killing. The duty to save is much less stringent than the duty not to kill, and the unjustified breach of a much less stringent duty cannot have the same moral consequences as the unjustified breach of a much more stringent duty.[38]

In some cases, the wrongfulness of killing someone may be reduced by their unjustified breach of a less stringent duty. For example, it seems less wrongful to kill one adult who fails to save a drowning child at little cost to himself, as a means of saving the child, than to kill some other adult who had no reasonable opportunity to save the child. After all, the first adult creates a situation in which either he or the child will die and could avoid that situation by doing his duty and saving the child. In contrast, no contributing civilian creates a situation in which either she or some other innocent person will be killed. The threats posed by her armed forces, as well as the utility of harming her to prevent those threats, lie beyond her control and would exist whether or not she does her duty.

Once again, overdetermination complicates matters. Some readers may think that, in cases of preemptive or simultaneous overdetermination, we are not morally required to die rather than kill an innocent person who will be killed by others if we do not kill her. Consider the following case:

> *Erdemovic*: Drazen, a soldier, is ordered to participate in a massacre of civilians. If Drazen refuses to participate, then Draven's fellow soldiers will kill Drazen as well as the civilians.

Some readers may think that Drazen is justified in participating, since his participation will not make the civilians worse off than they would be in his absence and his refusal to participate will make him much worse off. Now consider the following variation:

> *Not Erdemovic*: As in *Erdemovic*, Drazen cannot stop the massacre by refusing to participate. However, we can stop the massacre by killing Drazen, frightening the other soldiers into retreat.

If Drazen agrees to participate in the massacre, jointly threatening to kill the civilians, then it seems permissible to intentionally kill Drazen. This pair of cases seems to drive a wedge between the stringency of Draven's duty not to kill and Draven's

---

[38] Helen Frowe disagrees. I take up her arguments in the Appendix. See also Christian Barry & Gerhard Øverland, "The Implications of Failing to Assist" (2014) 40 Social Theory and Practice 570–90.

liability to defensive killing. But things are not as they seem. Consider a final variation:

> *Also Not Erdemovic*: Drazen knows that, while he cannot stop the massacre by refusing to participate, we can stop the massacre by killing him. Drazen is standing in a place where we cannot kill him.

In my view, Draven's duty not to kill the civilians is sufficiently stringent that he is morally required to move where we can kill him and thereby prevent the massacre. Importantly, Drazen is not morally required to die in order to save the civilians, but instead is morally required to die rather than kill the civilians. If I am right, then the stringency of Draven's duty not to kill the civilians explains his liability to defensive killing in *Not Erdemovic*.

We may be misled in *Erdemovic* by the fact that the civilians may be morally required to waive their rights that Drazen not kill them, since they will be killed either way but he will be killed only if he refuses.[39] But if killing Drazen will save the civilians, then the civilians are morally permitted not to waive their rights not to be killed by Drazen and we do not wrong Drazen by killing him in their defense.

Unlike the duty not to kill innocent people—directly, indirectly, or jointly—the duty not to superfluously contribute to unjust threats posed by others is not sufficiently stringent for its breach to result in moral liability to defensive killing. It is therefore unjust to kill contributing civilians, on the basis of their superfluous contributions to the unjust threats posed by their armed forces, as a means of preventing those unjust threats. Contributing civilians neither threaten to violate the rights of others nor threaten to make others worse off. Contributing civilians therefore retain their moral right not to be killed for the sake of others.

Killing and Enabling

In rare cases, civilians who do not directly participate in hostilities *enable* their armed forces to pose unjust threats, making a necessary contribution to those unjust threats.[40] Most civilians who design or manufacture weapons make no difference to the unjust threats posed by their armed forces. In their absence, their armed forces would simply use other weapons to inflict the same harm on the same people. However, in rare cases, the design or production of weapons can make a difference to how many people—or at least to which people—will be

---

[39] cf Victor Tadros, "Duress and Duty" (unpublished manuscript).

[40] I use the term "enable" in its ordinary sense of making others able to do what they could not otherwise do, for example by providing a necessary means. Note that some philosophers use "enabling harm" to refer to double-preventing harm, that is, to preventing someone or something from preventing harm. See, eg, Samuel C Rickless, "The Moral Status of Enabling Harm" (2011) 92 Pacific Philosophical Quarterly 66.

killed. For example, a civilian scientist designing nuclear weapons during World War II might enable her armed forces to kill many more people than they could in her absence. Similarly, a civilian who sells improvised explosive devices (IEDs) to an organized armed group might enable that group to kill many more people than it could otherwise.

If such *enabling civilians* contribute to the general military capacity of their armed forces but do not perform an integral part in a coordinated military operation, then they do not directly participate in hostilities. Yet it is tempting to think that it is morally permissible to intentionally kill civilians who enable unjust threats and that it should be legally permissible to do so. Indeed, some military lawyers believe that the legal standard for direct participation in hostilities should be expanded to accommodate such cases.[41]

In my view, enabling civilians are not liable to defensive killing because the duty not to enable others to kill is both different from and less stringent than the duty not to kill. However, our duties not to enable others to kill sometimes *aggregate*. We owe each person a distinct, directed duty not to enable others to kill him or her. If we enable others to kill many innocent people, then we violate many such duties, each owed to a different innocent person. The cumulative stringency of these many duties not to enable killing can equal the stringency of the duty not to kill. Importantly, if we are morally required to die rather than enable the killing of many innocent people, then it is not unjust to kill us to prevent us from doing so. However, I will argue that we may not kill enabling civilians if we can prevent the unjust threats that those civilians enable by targeting the combatants who pose those unjust threats, by destroying the means by which civilians enable unjust threats, or by detaining or interning civilians who enable unjust threats.

To see that the duty not to enable others to kill is *different* from the duty not to kill, consider the following cases:

Necessity I: A demands that B kill V with B's long-range rifle. A threatens to kill C and D if B refuses to kill V.

Necessity II: A demands that B give B's long-range rifle to A so that A can kill V. A threatens to kill C and D if B refuses to give A the rifle.

In *Necessity I*, it seems that B may not kill V in order to prevent A from killing C and D. B's duty not to kill V seems stronger than B's reasons to save C and D. In contrast, in *Necessity II*, it seems that B may enable A to kill V in order to prevent A from killing C and D. B's duty not to enable A to kill V does not seem stronger

---

[41] See US Department of Defense, *Law of War Manual*, 5.9.3, 226, fn 232 (endorsing the view that "more than 900 of the World War II Project Manhattan personnel were civilians, and their participation in the US atomic weapons program was of such importance as to have made them liable to legitimate attack"); ICRC, Interpretive Guidance, 53, fn 122 and fn 123 (reporting but not endorsing this position).

than B's reasons to save C and D. Accordingly, it seems that B's duty not to kill V is different from and stronger than B's duty not to enable A to kill V.

To see that the duty not to enable others to kill is *less stringent* than the duty not to kill, consider the following cases:

> *Coercion I*: A threatens to kill B unless B kills V with B's long-range rifle. A cannot kill V himself or by means of anyone else except B.
>
> *Coercion II*: A threatens to kill B unless B gives B's long-range rifle to A so that A can use it to kill V. A cannot kill V without B's rifle.[42]

In *Coercion I*, it seems that B may not kill V in order to avoid being killed by A. In contrast, in *Coercion II*, it seems that B may enable A to kill V in order to avoid being killed by A. In *Coercion II*, B will not directly kill V by giving his rifle to A. Instead, A will directly kill V. Nor will B indirectly kill V through A. Evidently, B does not control A. Finally, B will not jointly kill V together with A. A and B will not perform coordinated roles in a common plan, mutually responding to each other's efforts to execute joint intentions. No doubt, there are borderline cases between jointly acting with others and enabling others to act, but this case should not be one of them. It follows that if B gives A the rifle, then killing V will not be B's action but A's. B's relationship with the unjust threat to V is mediated through A's intervening agency. B will neither infringe V's right that B not kill V nor breach B's directed duty not to kill V.

These cases indicate that the duty not to enable others to kill is less stringent than the duty not to kill. While we are morally required to die rather than kill, we are not morally required to die rather than enable others to kill. In my view, it follows that B is liable to defensive killing if B threatens to kill V in *Coercion I* but not if B enables A to kill V in *Coercion II*.

At the same time, it seems hard to deny that we are morally required to die rather than enable others to kill *many* innocent people. After all, we are probably morally required to die rather than *allow* others to kill *very many* innocent people. It seems that our directed duties to very many innocent people that we prevent them from being killed can aggregate to the point that we are morally required to die rather than breach these very many duties. Moreover, our duty not to enable others to kill is more stringent than our duty to prevent others from killing. Breaching the former duty, unlike breaching the latter duty, makes others worse off than they would be in our absence. It follows that our directed duties to many innocent people that we not enable others to kill them can aggregate to the point that we are morally required to die rather than breach these many duties.

In my view, it is not unjust to kill us to save very many innocent people or to prevent us from enabling others to kill many innocent people. However, it is clearly mistaken to describe such cases as instances of liability to *defensive* killing. Earlier, we

---

[42] I borrow these cases from Draper, *War and Individual Rights*, 207.

saw that combatants who pose overdetermined threats to innocent people are morally liable to non-eliminative defensive killing. We now see that individuals whose deaths will prevent the killing of very many innocent people are morally liable to non-defensive opportunistic killing, while individuals who enable threats to many innocent people are morally liable to non-defensive eliminative killing.

The distinction between liability to defensive killing and liability to non-defensive killing may seem to split hairs, but it has important implications. For example, if we can prevent unjust threats either by targeting those who pose them or by targeting those who enable them or fail to prevent them, then we should target the former rather than the latter. Given the choice, we should target those liable to defensive killing rather than those liable to non-defensive killing. Just as the duty not to kill takes priority over the duty not to enable others to kill, the liability generated by breach of the former duty takes priority over the liability generated by breach of the latter duty.[43]

In addition, if it is possible to prevent unjust threats to many innocent people without killing those who enable these threats, then we must try to do so, accepting a level of risk—both risk to ourselves and risk of failure—that we need not accept to avoid killing those who pose these threats. Finally, if we can destroy the means by which individuals enable unjust threats or detain or intern individuals who enable unjust threats then we must do so rather than kill them.

For example, it might be morally permissible to kill an IED supplier if, as a result, the armed group that he supplies will kill many fewer innocent people. At the same time, since the IED supplier is not morally liable to defensive killing, the opposing party may not kill the IED supplier if they can prevent the threats that he enables by targeting the combatants whom he supplies, by destroying his means of supplying IEDs, or by capturing him even at some risk to their own forces.

Enabling civilians do not directly participate in hostilities and are not lawful targets. This is as it should be. Enabling civilians are not morally liable to defensive killing. In most cases, we can prevent unjust threats enabled by civilians by targeting the combatants who pose those unjust threats, by destroying the means by which civilians enable unjust threats, or by detaining or interning civilians who enable unjust threats. Combatants who try to identify and target enabling civilians will often mistakenly target civilians who make little difference—and whose death will make little difference—to the unjust threats posed by their armed forces. In rare cases, enabling civilians may be morally liable to non-defensive eliminative killing. However, combatants who follow the law and refrain from targeting

---

[43]   See Victor Tadros, "Causal Contributions and Liability" (unpublished manuscript) (stipulating that "a person has greater *priority liability* to be killed than another person if she ought to be killed rather than another person where other things are equal"). Note that my position is consistent with the possibility that it may be morally preferable to kill one enabling civilian than to kill very many unjust combatants.

enabling civilians will commit many fewer wrongful killings than will combatants who break the law.

Collectively Enabling Unjust Threats

By this point, many readers may have observed that contributing civilians some-times *collectively* enable unjust threats. For example, although the contributions of individual taxpayers to their armed forces are each superfluous, the aggregate of these contributions may enable their armed forces to pose unjust threats. In many cases, their armed forces may rely exclusively on weapons and equipment obtained long before the current conflict began, just as their government may rely on tax revenues from past years or on loans that will be repaid long after the current con-flict ends. Nevertheless, in some cases, civilians may knowingly contribute to an imminent or ongoing unjust war effort.

In such cases, killing all or most of these contributing civilians might prevent their actions from collectively making others worse off. However, the perverse con-clusion that contributing civilians are liable to eliminative killing in large numbers but not in small numbers does not follow. After all, we lose our rights by our own actions, not by the independent actions of others. If you do not lose your rights by paying your taxes then you do not lose your rights by other people independently paying their taxes, even in sufficiently large numbers so as to collectively enable unjust threats. Whatever may be true of the collective, no individual taxpayer vio-lates a duty sufficiently stringent to ground liability to defensive killing.

Certainly, civilians do not *jointly* enable unjust threats by voting or by paying taxes. Elections and tax collection are paradigm cases of aggregating individual actions almost none of which are coordinated with one another. Of course, if my partner and I walk to the polling place and then go for lunch, or if we file a joint tax return, then we vote together or pay taxes together as the case may be. But there is no important sense in which I jointly vote with all other voters or jointly pay my taxes with all other taxpayers. I vote and they vote, I pay and they pay. We never meet or interact. My actions in no way depend on their actions nor theirs on mine. We have no conditional intention of helping each other to fulfill coordinated roles in a common plan. There is no common plan. There are no meshing sub-plans. There are no joint intentions. There are only similar plans, parallel sub-plans, and individual intentions. You and I do the same type of thing (vote, pay taxes) but we do not perform any token of that thing together.

To be clear, often we have duties to make or refrain from making individually superfluous contributions to certain outcomes, including to political and envi-ronmental outcomes.[44] Frequently, these duties are grounded in considerations of

---

[44] Thanks to Jeremy Waldron for pressing this point.

fair play, gratitude, solidarity, or expressive value. For example, we have duties to vote against political leaders likely to initiate unjust wars. These duties may be moderately stringent, requiring us to take time away from work or family in order to vote. We ought to reciprocate the efforts of our fellow citizens who take the time to vote, and show gratitude for the costs they bear (in part) for our sake. We ought to stand in solidarity with potential war victims, and express our disavowal and condemnation of unjust war. We have even more stringent duties not to vote for such politicians, on the grounds that it is even worse to be active rather than passive with respect to injustice. However, in my view, such duties are not so stringent that we are morally required to bear very great costs rather than breach them. Accordingly, in my view, the violation of such duties will not result in moral liability to lethal harm.

Since contributing civilians neither jointly pose unjust threats nor jointly enable unjust threats they are not morally liable to defensive killing or to non-defensive eliminative killing. Indeed, even if civilians jointly enabled unjust threats it would be wrong to target these civilians rather than their armed forces, who after all pose these unjust threats.

Symmetry and Avoidability

Civilians are lawful targets only if they directly participate in hostilities and are morally liable to defensive killing only if they do so for an unjust cause. It follows that just combatants have strong moral reasons to target civilians who fight alongside opposing armed forces but to spare civilians who do not fight at all. In contrast, civilians who fight for a just cause generally are not morally liable to defensive killing. It may seem to follow that combatants who know that they fight for an unjust cause, perhaps under duress, have no moral reason to target participant civilians but spare the rest. It may seem that the least wrongful way for such unjust combatants to fight is to kill as few people as possible, irrespective of whether they are combatants, participant civilians, or non-participant civilians. But things are not as they may seem.

For one thing, individuals who fight for a just cause sometimes pose unjust threats to civilians who do not fight at all. These threats may be *justified* as a lesser evil but they are not *just* because those threatened are not liable to harm. To see this, consider a classic case (albeit one involving a just combatant rather than a participant civilian):

> *Tactical Bomber*: A bomber pilot fighting for a just cause intends to bomb a legitimate military target. The attack will collaterally kill several innocent civilians as an unintended side effect. At the same time, the destruction of the target will prevent a substantially greater number of innocent people from being killed by the opposing party.

In this case, the pilot poses an unjust threat to the civilians that is justified as a lesser evil. The civilians retain their rights not to be killed but their rights are overridden. Such conflicts between justified threats and innocent victims are rare in ordinary life but all too common in war.

Now suppose that the civilians can shoot down the plane with anti-aircraft weapons that their armed forces have for some reason abandoned. The civilians have done nothing to lose their rights not to be killed or their rights to defend themselves from those who would infringe their rights not to be killed. In my view, the civilians are morally permitted to defend themselves from the pilot, even though the pilot is justified in threatening their rights and even though defending their rights will *double-prevent* (that is, prevent the prevention of) substantially greater harm to others. Importantly, if it is permissible for the civilians to shoot down the pilot in their own defense, then it seems permissible for their armed forces to shoot down the pilot in their defense.[45]

In my view, the pilot is morally liable to defensive killing simply in virtue of posing an unjust threat to the rights of the civilians. To see this, suppose that the pilot could destroy the target without killing any civilians but at the cost of his own life (say, by flying into the target rather than bombing it). The pilot seems morally required to do so, that is, to die rather than kill the civilians. We may not kill several innocent people, even with justification, rather than allow or occasion our own deaths. Whenever possible, we should bear the costs of our own permissible choices, as well as of discharging our own duties.[46] It follows that if the civilians could shoot down the pilot in a way that defends their rights but that does not double-prevent harm to others (say by forcing the plane to crash into the target, destroying it but avoiding the civilians) then doing so would not wrong the pilot. Importantly, the pilot is morally liable to defensive killing even if doing so will double-prevent harm to others. The fact that doing so will double-prevent harm to others is a separate objection, to which we now turn.

In my view, the duty not to double-prevent harm to others is more stringent than the duty to prevent harm to others but somewhat less stringent than the duty not to enable harm to others and significantly less stringent than the duty not to harm others.[47] On one hand, while both double-preventing harm and failing

---

[45] See Uwe Steinhoff, "Jeff McMahan on the Moral Inequality of Combatants" (2008) 16 Journal of Political Philosophy 220–6; Adil Ahmad Haque, "Rights and Liabilities at War," in Paul H Robinson, Stephen Garvey, & Kimberly Ferzan (eds), *Criminal Law Conversations* (OUP 2009) 395. See also Seth Lazar, *Sparing Civilians* (OUP 2016) 13.

[46] See Adam Hosein, "Are Justified Aggressors a Threat to the Rights Theory of Self-Defense?" in Helen Frowe & Gerald Lang (eds), *How We Fight: Ethics in War* (OUP 2014) 87.

[47] For the view that double-preventing harm is morally comparable to allowing harm, see Matthew Hanser, "Killing, Letting Die, and Preventing People from Being Saved" (1999) 11 Utilitas 277–95; Samuel C Rickless, "The Moral Status of Enabling Harm" (2011) 92 Pacific Philosophical Quarterly 66.

to prevent harm make others worse off than they could be, the former typically makes others worse off than they would be in your absence. On the other hand, while both double-preventing harm and enabling harm make others worse off indirectly—through the intervening agency of others—only the latter facilitates harm in the ordinary sense of providing or enhancing the means of inflicting harm. Accordingly, while we may be morally required to allow ourselves to be killed rather than enable much greater harm to others, we are not morally required to allow ourselves to be killed rather than double-prevent substantially greater harm to others. It follows that we may defend ourselves from unjust threats even if doing so will double-prevent substantially greater harm to others. Accordingly, the civilians may permissibly shoot down the plane, killing the pilot, even if doing so would double-prevent substantially greater harm to others.

The final question raised by this scenario is whether the pilot would be justified in intentionally killing the civilians to prevent them from shooting him down before he completes his mission. If the civilians are acting in self-defense, then they are not directly participating in hostilities—their actions lack a belligerent nexus—and are not lawful targets. Moreover, if the pilot is liable to defensive killing then he may not kill the civilians in self-defense. Finally, the pilot may not kill the civilians in defense of others, since the civilians do not pose unjust threats to those whom the pilot seeks to protect. Accordingly, the pilot may only intentionally kill the civilians if necessary to prevent far greater harm to others by completing his mission. Otherwise, the pilot must cancel or suspend the planned attack.

On my view, individuals who fight for a just cause are morally liable to defensive killing when they pose unjust threats to non-participant civilians, even if these unjust threats are justified as a lesser evil. Alternatively, it is possible that innocent people have agent-relative permissions to eliminatively kill those who pose unjust threats to them. Arguably, non-participant civilians may transfer such agent-relative permissions to their armed forces. Indeed, armed forces may have an associative obligation to exercise the agent-relative permissions of their citizens on their behalf.[48] On either account, it is sometimes permissible to kill just combatants to defend civilians from unjust but justified threats. Similarly, unjust combatants often have strong moral reason to target civilians who fight for a just cause rather than civilians who do not fight at all.

I wish to explore two additional reasons why killing civilians who fight for a just cause is less wrongful than killing civilians who do not fight at all. The first reason is that participant civilians can avoid being eliminatively or collaterally harmed more easily than non-participant civilians can avoid being opportunistically or collaterally harmed. The second reason is that participant civilians choose to make

---

[48] Seth Lazar, "Authorization and the Morality of War" (2016) 94 Australasian Journal of Philosophy 211; "Associative Duties and the Ethics of Killing in War" (2013) 1 Journal of Practical Ethics 3.

themselves lawful targets when they could easily avoid doing so. The first reason obtains prior to and independently of law. The second reason presupposes law. It is important to keep these reasons separate, lest it appear that I am double-counting or arguing in a circle. For each reason, independently, unjust combatants will act less wrongfully if they respect the legal immunity of civilians than if they simply kill the fewest people.

Seth Lazar argues that it is *contingently* true that non-participant civilians are generally killed opportunistically while combatants and participant civilians are generally killed eliminatively.[49] Opportunistically killing non-participant civilians is *pro tanto* morally worse than eliminatively killing participant civilians because the former compounds the wrongfulness of killing an innocent person with the wrongfulness of using an innocent person as a means to our ends. I have made the stronger claim it is *necessarily* true that non-participant civilians are intentionally killed opportunistically (or gratuitously) rather than eliminatively, since non-participant civilians do not threaten to make anyone one worse off. This stronger claim adds to the breadth of Lazar's argument.[50]

I now offer the further claim that it is easier for participant civilians to avoid being eliminatively killed than for non-participant civilians to avoid being opportunistically killed. In general, the wrongfulness of harming someone for some end varies somewhat with her ability to avoid being harmed for that end. Importantly, there is little that non-participant civilians can do to avoid being opportunistically killed, for example by somehow making killing them an ineffective means of spreading terror. In contrast, participant civilians can avoid being eliminatively killed simply by not threatening to make others worse off. This difference in avoidability adds to the intrinsic wrongfulness of opportunistically killing non-participant civilians and subtracts from the intrinsic wrongfulness of eliminatively killing participant civilians. This further claim adds to the depth of Lazar's argument.

Finally, participant civilians and non-participant civilians are both vulnerable to collateral killing due to their proximity to military targets. In most cases, it is harder for non-participant civilians to avoid military targets than for participant civilians to avoid military targets. In most cases, participant civilians actively go to military targets while non-participant civilians passively have military targets brought to them. When a military target is placed in a civilian area it is generally very costly for non-participant civilians to abandon their homes and livelihoods in order to avoid the target. In contrast, participant civilians typically place themselves near military targets voluntarily and could avoid doing so at little cost to themselves. These facts

---

[49] Lazar, *Sparing Civilians*, ch 3.

[50] At a symposium on Lazar's book, Victor Tadros observed that eliminatively killing just combatants furthers an unjust cause, making it somewhat worse than pointlessly killing civilians. Lazar responded that opportunistically killing civilians also furthers an unjust cause, preserving the general moral asymmetry between opportunistically killing civilians and eliminatively killing just combatants. As is often the case, I side with Lazar.

make collateral harm to non-participant civilians harder to justify than collateral harm to participant civilians even when none are liable to collateral harm.

In general, civilians choose to directly participate in hostilities and thereby make themselves lawful targets. Importantly, Lazar argues that, given background legal norms, just combatants "offer their opponents a limited waiver of their rights, in return for concentrating their fire."[51] According to Lazar, "[j]ust combatants who adhere to the laws of war implicitly say to their adversaries: 'you ought to put down your weapons. But if you are going to fight, then fight us.'"[52] Lazar emphasizes that "[t]he waiver is limited, and conditional: just combatants would of course prefer that unjust combatants not fight at all; but if they are going to fight, then they should target them exclusively."[53] Lazar's claims regarding just combatants apply to just participant civilians as well.[54]

Lazar might have made the stronger claim that combatants conditionally *request* that, if their adversaries target anyone, then their adversaries target them rather than their civilian population. While waivers of rights remove reasons to refrain from an act, requests generate reasons to perform an act. For example, in a match, boxers always waive their rights not to be hit but hardly ever ask to be hit. In contrast, while training, boxers often ask to be hit by their sparring partners as part of their conditioning. If combatants conditionally request to be targeted, then, counter-intuitively, combatants who target each other show each other a certain measure of respect.

In any event, on Lazar's view, the law should give civilians the opportunity to make themselves lawful targets and combatants should respect the choice of participant civilians to make themselves lawful targets. Of course, unjust combatants will best respect the wishes of participant civilians by not targeting anyone. However, unjust combatants will at least partially respect the wishes of participant civilians by targeting them rather than non-participant civilians. This small measure of respect for the conditional preferences of participant civilians reduces the wrongfulness of killing them to a small but significant extent.[55]

Rather than focus on the choice of participant civilians to make themselves lawful targets, I wish to focus on the opportunity of non-participant civilians to avoid becoming lawful targets. Obviously, if all civilians are lawful targets then no civilian has any opportunity to avoid becoming a lawful target. Similarly, if civilians become lawful targets by contributing to the threats posed by their armed forces, then most civilians will find it very difficult and very costly to avoid becoming a lawful target.

---

[51] Lazar, *Sparing Civilians*, 124.   [52] Lazar, *Sparing Civilians*, 127.

[53] Lazar, *Sparing Civilians*, 128. If the notion of a conditional waiver (or request) seems obscure, think of a tourist who asks a robber to take his money but leave his passport.

[54] Lazar, *Sparing Civilians*, 2.

[55] Put another way, there are moral reasons to give civilians the legal power to change their legal status. Arguably, the exercise of a morally justified legal power changes one's moral status as well as one's legal status.

Finally, if civilians become lawful targets by "effectively and substantially" contributing to the threats posed by their armed forces, then many civilians will find it difficult to predict which contributions will make them lawful targets.

In contrast, it is a virtue of the direct participation standard that it is both relatively clear and fairly narrow. Since the legal right not to be killed is so valuable, civilians should be able to reliably predict and easily avoid the loss of that legal right. No doubt, some borderline cases remain, particularly along the border of jointly participating in military operations and merely contributing to military operations. In general, we should resolve legal ambiguity in favor of civilian immunity in order to give civilians greater control over their legal status and their ultimate fate.

Given a legal standard that empowers individuals to become lawful targets or remain unlawful targets, unjust combatants who follow international law enable individuals to exercise a significant degree of control over their fate. In contrast, if unjust combatants simply aim to kill as few people as necessary to achieve their war aims, then no one can control whether he or she will be targeted or spared. We all have reason to want such control for ourselves and to respect the attempt to exercise such control by others. Targeting non-participant civilians denies them this small measure of control over their ex ante risk of being targeted and killed. This denial compounds the wrongfulness of killing non-participant civilians.

For these reasons, typically it is morally worse for unjust combatants to kill non-participant civilians than to kill participant civilians even if none are morally liable to defensive killing. It follows that unjust combatants will act less wrongfully if they obey international law and refrain from targeting non-participant civilians even if they could thereby reduce the overall harm that they inflict.

Conclusion

The legal principle of civilian immunity closely tracks deeper moral principles. Civilians retain their moral right not to be intentionally or collaterally killed unless and for such time as they directly participate in hostilities, threatening to directly, indirectly, or jointly harm others. In particular, ordinary civilians who make political, material, strategic, and financial contributions to an unjust war are not thereby morally liable to defensive killing. Those few civilians who enable their armed forces to pose unjust threats are sometimes morally liable to non-defensive eliminative killing but may not be killed if those unjust threats can be prevented by targeting their armed forces or by non-lethally preventing these civilians from enabling such unjust threats. Finally, both just and unjust combatants will better conform to their moral obligations and act less wrongfully by following the law protecting non-participant civilians than by breaking the law and following their own moral judgment.

4

Combatants

Combatants are members of the armed forces of a party to an armed conflict, excluding religious, medical, and civil defense personnel.[1] The law of armed conflict prohibits attacking combatants who are *hors de combat*, that is, who are in the power of their adversary, who clearly express an intention to surrender, or who are incapacitated by wounds or sickness.[2] It is also unlawful to use weapons that by their nature—rather than by their use in a particular case—inflict superfluous injury or unnecessary suffering.[3] Finally, it is unlawful to kill opposing combatants perfidiously, for example by feigning protected status.[4]

In contrast, international law does not otherwise prohibit intentionally killing combatants; does not require taking precautions to avoid or reduce harm to combatants; and does not consider disproportionate an attack that kills many combatants and achieves no further military advantage beyond removing them from the battlefield. In particular, it is not unlawful to intentionally kill soldiers who clearly perform service and support functions rather than combat functions. In addition, most experts believe that it is not unlawful to intentionally kill combatants whom one could safely capture.

Philosophers offer both moral and pragmatic justifications for the general lawfulness of killing combatants. As we have seen, Michael Walzer argues that combatants on all sides of a conflict forfeit their moral right not to be killed simply by posing a threat to others. In contrast, Jeff McMahan argues that all and only combatants who are morally responsible for *unjust* threats are morally liable to defensive killing. Importantly, McMahan argues that a *legal* norm prohibiting the killing of just combatants would do more harm than good. On his view, unjust combatants who mistakenly believe that they fight for a just cause will ignore such a norm while unjust combatants who know that they fight for an unjust cause will have no marginal incentive to fight with restraint.

---

[1] Protocol Additional to the Geneva Conventions of August 12, 1949, and relating to the Protection of Victims of International Armed Conflicts (Protocol I) (adopted June 8, 1977, entered into force December 7, 1978) 1125 UNTS 3, art 43(2); ICRC, *Customary International Humanitarian Law*, vol 1 (CUP 2009) 11.

[2] Protocol I art 41; ICRC, *Customary IHL*, 164.

[3] Protocol I art 35; ICRC, *Customary IHL*, 237.

[4] Protocol I art 37; ICRC, *Customary IHL*, 221.

Law and Morality at War. First Edition. Adil Haque. © Adil Haque 2017. Published 2017 by Oxford University Press

Importantly, Seth Lazar takes a fresh approach to the issue, arguing that, while many combatants are not morally liable to be killed, it is almost always *pro tanto* morally worse to kill civilians than to kill combatants. For example, Lazar argues that many unjust combatants make small contributions to the unjust threats posed by their compatriots, with a low degree of culpability, and therefore are not morally liable to defensive killing. Nevertheless, according to Lazar, "[k]illing soldiers is often necessary and eliminative."[5] Moreover, combatants "voluntarily put themselves in harm's way, trading a limited waiver of their right to life for a greater likelihood that their enemies will target them instead of their civilians."[6] For such reasons, Lazar argues that the legal distinction between civilians and combatants approximates deep moral principles.

In the previous chapter, I argued that individuals who directly participate in hostilities on behalf of an unjust cause typically are morally liable to defensive killing. It follows that unjust combatants who perform combat functions—that is, whose role is to directly participate in hostilities—typically are morally liable to defensive killing as well. Importantly, this basis of liability extends up the military chain of command to every unjust combatant who participates in the preparation, execution, or command of specific military operations at both the tactical level and the operational level of warfare.[7] In contrast, so long as combatants who perform noncombat functions—that is, whose role is to provide administrative, logistical, or other general service and support—do not directly participate in hostilities, they are not objectively morally liable to defensive killing. The fact that a majority of soldiers in modern militaries perform noncombat functions therefore poses a serious challenge to the law and morality of war.[8]

Importantly, generally noncombat personnel can avoid being mistaken for combat personnel—and can avoid being near combat personnel—more easily than civilians can, often simply by conforming to more stringent moral duties than civilians bear. These considerations reduce the objective moral wrongfulness of mistakenly or collaterally killing noncombat personnel, and with it the effect of such killings on both *jus ad bellum* and *jus in bello* proportionality.

Moreover, since the epistemic permissibility of an action depends in part on its possible moral costs, the reduced objective wrongfulness of killing such combatants entails that it may be epistemically permissible to kill such combatants based on weaker evidence of objective liability than morality ordinarily requires. In particular,

---

[5] Seth Lazar, *Sparing Civilians* (OUP 2016) 139.

[6] Lazar, *Sparing Civilians*, 139.

[7] Roughly, the tactical level of warfare involves discrete battles, engagements, and strikes while the operational level of warfare involves broader military campaigns.

[8] According to one report, combat personnel make up only 16% of the US military, 21% of the Russian military, 27% of the UK military, and 38% of the Israeli military. Scott Gebicke & Samuel Magid, "Lessons from around the World: Benchmarking Performance in Defense" (2010) 5 McKinsey on Government 3–4.

given decisive reason to believe that a person is a combatant, attacking forces may presume that person performs a combat function until they acquire decisive reason to believe that person performs a noncombat function. It follows that attackers need not take the same precautions to avoid mistakenly killing such combatants that they must take to avoid mistakenly killing civilians. However, attackers may not kill a combatant if they know or have decisive reason to believe that the combatant performs a noncombat function. A limited legal prohibition on knowingly targeting noncombat personnel will help attacking forces conform to their moral obligations more closely than will the legal *status quo*. On this basis, I argue that international law should prohibit targeting a combatant *if it becomes apparent* that he or she performs a noncombat function.[9]

Finally, I argue that international law should prohibit attacking forces from killing opposing combatants whom the attackers could capture or spare without significant risk to themselves or to civilians. Since attacking forces are already legally required to attempt capture, offer opportunity to surrender, and use non-lethal weapons when doing so would avoid or reduce harm to nearby civilians, such a proposal cannot be dismissed as impractical out of hand. At the same time, since killing combatants is much less wrongful than killing civilians, attacking forces are not morally required to attempt capture when doing so will endanger attackers or civilians. A limited legal prohibition on unnecessarily killing opposing combatants is therefore both practically possible and morally justified.

With some regret, I conclude that recent arguments that international law already prohibits such unnecessary killing do not succeed. Such combatants are not *hors de combat* and the principle of humanity does not directly obligate individuals to refrain from such killings. Instead, I argue that the principle of humanity legally obligates states to order their armed forces to refrain from such killings. Over time, convergent state practice and opinion will generate a specific rule of customary international law, binding on individuals, that prohibits such killings. Human rights law may also constrain such killings.

As elsewhere, I will use the term "combatant" to refer to members of the armed forces of parties to international armed conflicts as well as to members of organized armed groups who fight on behalf of non-state parties to non-international armed conflicts. There are important differences between the former and the latter. If captured, the former are presumptively entitled to lawful combatant immunity as well as to treatment as prisoners of war. The latter are entitled to neither. Indeed, the leading treaty governing non-international armed conflicts does not use, let alone define, the

---

[9] I first sketched this position in Adil Ahmad Haque, "Criminal Law and Morality at War," in RA Duff & Stuart Green (eds), *Philosophical Foundations of Criminal Law* (OUP 2011) 481. While that paper was in press, Gabriella Blum took a similar though distinct position, arguing that members of armed forces may be presumed to pose an immediate threat but individual members may not be targeted if there they pose no immediate threat. Gabriella Blum, "The Dispensable Lives of Soldiers" (2010) 2 Journal of Legal Analysis 69.

term "combatant."[10] However, since the same legal rules governing targeting, attack, and collateral harm apply to state armed forces and to organized armed groups, I will refer to members of both as "combatants." In addition, I sometimes refer to members of state armed forces as "soldiers" irrespective of their service branch.

Finally, unless otherwise noted, I will discuss the permissibility and relative wrongfulness of killing unjust combatants. Nevertheless, the rules that I propose will help both just and unjust combatants avoid, or at least minimize, seriously wrongful killing.

Soldiers, Irregulars, and Employees

According to the International Committee of the Red Cross (ICRC), there are three ways in which individuals become lawful targets: by joining the armed forces of a state, by assuming a "continuous combat function" within an organized armed group, or by directly participating in hostilities.[11] Within this framework, it is lawful to target members of state armed forces who perform combat, service, or support functions. In contrast, it is lawful to target "individuals whose continuous function involves the preparation, execution, or command of acts or operations amounting to direct participation in hostilities" on behalf of organized armed groups.[12] However, it is unlawful to target individuals who only perform service and support functions for such groups.[13] For targeting purposes, only the former are members of an organized armed group; the latter are members of the non-state party for whom the group fights, much like civilian employees of a governmental defense department or ministry. Finally, it is unlawful to target civilian employees who perform service or support functions for state armed forces.[14]

Influential military lawyers have objected to the ICRC's framework on the grounds that it unfairly grants greater protections to organized armed groups than it grants to state armed forces.[15] This objection seems incomplete. After all, we

---

[10] Protocol Additional to the Geneva Conventions of 12 August 1949, and relating to the Protection of Victims of Non-International Armed Conflicts (Protocol II) (adopted June 8, 1977, entered into force December 7, 1978) 1125 UNTS 609.

[11] See ICRC, Interpretive Guidance on the Notion of Direct Participation in Hostilities Under International Humanitarian Law (ICRC 2009).

[12] ICRC, Interpretive Guidance, 34.

[13] That is, unless and for such time as the latter directly participate in hostilities. This qualification is assumed but not repeated in the discussion below.

[14] Similarly, unless and for such time as they directly participate in hostilities.

[15] See, eg, Michael N Schmitt, "The Interpretive Guidance on the Notion of Direct Participation in Hostilities: A Critical Analysis" (2010) 1 Harvard National Security Journal 5, 23. See also US Department of Defense, Law of War Manual 5.9.2.1 ("The U.S. approach has been to treat the status of belonging to a hostile, non-State armed group as a separate basis upon which a person is liable to attack, apart from whether he or she has taken a direct part in hostilities").

might cure this apparent unfairness *either* by making it lawful to target those who service or support organized armed groups *or* by making it unlawful to target the service and support personnel of state armed forces. Alternatively, states could simply assign their service and support functions to civilian employees. For this objection to succeed, its proponents must first explain why the service and support personnel of state armed forces are lawful targets while civilian employees who perform service and support functions for state armed forces are not. Then they must show that those who service and support organized armed groups more closely resemble the former than the latter.

For example, according to the US Department of Defense:

> Membership in the armed forces or belonging to an armed group makes a person liable to being made the object of attack regardless of whether he or she is taking a direct part in hostilities. This is because the organization's hostile intent may be imputed to an individual through his or her association with the organization. Moreover, the individual, as an agent of the group, can be assigned a combat role at any time, even if the individual normally performs other functions for the group.[16]

With respect to the first point, the notion of imputing the hostile intent of an organization to its individual members seems obscure. It is not obvious that organizations have intentions, hostile or otherwise, and it seems unlikely that we may justify killing a person by imputing to her an intent that she does not in fact have. Moreover, individuals are not liable to lawful attack simply because they share the hostile intent of an organized armed group, namely that the group prevail over its adversaries. Instead, liability to lawful attack requires the hostile intent to perform specific acts likely to inflict serious harm, including as part of one's continuous function.

With respect to the second point, almost all members of state armed forces receive basic combat training and commit to directly participate in hostilities if ordered to do so; almost all civilian employees who perform service and support functions do not. Although I have not found an empirical study of the question, it seems unlikely that a comparable majority of those who perform service or support functions for organized armed groups receive such training or make such a commitment. It seems more likely that non-state actors draw their members from many walks of life and assign individuals to roles that align with their respective abilities and limitations. In this respect, those who perform service or support functions for organized armed groups seem to resemble civilian employees who perform similar functions more closely than they resemble members of state armed forces who perform similar functions. Fairness and consistency therefore suggest that, like civilian employees, those who provide service and support to organized armed groups should not be lawful targets unless and for such time as they directly participate in hostilities.

---

[16] US Dept of Defense, *Law of War Manual*, 5.8.1.

For its part, the ICRC defends its framework as a means of distinguishing between the *parties* to an armed conflict and their respective *armed forces*. Under international law, only the latter are liable to status-based targeting in addition to conduct-based targeting. Often, the informal structure of non-state parties to a conflict—ranging from revolutionary, secessionist, and national liberation movements to clans and tribes—makes it difficult to distinguish between their political or humanitarian wings and their armed forces. According to the ICRC, individuals who perform continuous combat functions on behalf of non-state parties are necessarily members of its armed forces. In contrast, targeting members of non-state parties who do not perform combat functions invites error, arbitrariness, and abuse.[17]

The ICRC's position seems like a sensible adaptation of the legal framework applicable to international armed conflict between states to the context of non-international armed conflicts involving non-state parties. At the same time, we cannot settle the question by reference to positive legal materials alone. No treaty establishes criteria for status-based targeting in non-international armed conflicts, and state practice remains unsettled. On my view, we should adopt the interpretation of existing law that is both consistent with positive legal materials and that will provide opposing forces with the best moral guidance practically possible. Since, on my view, individuals who do not directly participate in hostilities are not morally liable to defensive force in virtue of their conduct, it follows that persons who do not perform a combat function are not morally liable to defensive force in virtue of their status. We therefore should embrace the ICRC's position on moral as well as legal grounds.

Sparing Known Noncombat Personnel

The next question is whether IHL should extend greater legal protection to the service and support personnel of regular armed forces. Although almost all such personnel receive basic combat training and commit to directly participate in hostilities if ordered to do so, in practice they are rarely reassigned to combat duty. Modern armies rarely fight to the last man or woman. If combat personnel are unable to achieve military success, then reassigned service and support personnel are unlikely to do so. Simply put, if you have to hand rifles to cooks and clerks then typically you have already lost.

On my view, combatants who perform combat functions may be targeted even while they are not directly participating in hostilities on grounds of anticipatory self-defense. Although they currently pose no unjust threat, they are very likely to do so in the future. It is objectively permissible to kill such combatants when this will in fact prevent them from posing unjust threats in the future, and it is

[17] ICRC, Interpretive Guidance, 32–4.

epistemically permissible to kill such combatants when the attacker has decisive reason to believe that this will prevent them from posing unjust threats in the future. The fact that a combatant performs a combat function is very strong reason to believe that she will pose unjust threats in the future unless she is prevented from doing so. Since attackers hardly ever have stronger reasons to believe that such combatants will *not* pose unjust threats in the future, it is almost always epistemically permissible to kill such combatants.[18] Accordingly, a legal prohibition on targeting combatants who perform combat functions but who will never in fact pose threats to others would not help attackers conform to their moral obligations.

In contrast, it is hardly ever objectively permissible to kill combatants who perform noncombat functions since they rarely directly participate in hostilities or otherwise pose unjust threats to others. It is true that many combatants who perform service and support functions directly, indirectly, or jointly enable other combatants to pose unjust threats (think of a crew of mechanics repairing or maintaining a fighter jet). However, as we saw in Chapter 3, it is only objectively permissible to intentionally kill individuals who merely enable others to pose unjust threats if strictly necessary to prevent much greater harm to others. If those unjust threats can be prevented by targeting those who pose them, by destroying the means by which they are enabled, or by detaining or interning those who enable them, then that is what objective morality requires.

It is also plausible that combatants involved in a collective war effort, irrespective of their function, engage in "massively shared agency," coordinated not through mutual responsiveness to each other's intentions and actions but instead through a mutually accepted authority structure that assigns roles and integrates tasks.[19] These combatants may be said to collectively pursue unjust war aims. However, in my view, only those combatants who pursue unjust war aims by directly, indirectly, or jointly posing unjust threats are morally liable to defensive killing. While all those who pursue unjust political aims may be resisted by political means, only those who resort to unjust political violence may be resisted by violent means.

Relatedly, Helen Frowe observes that individuals who pose no unjust *micro-threat* of killing or injuring any innocent person may nevertheless "further the unjust *macro-threats* that are the ends of their country's aggressive war."[20] In my view, only individuals who further such unjust macro-threats by posing unjust micro-threats are morally liable to defensive killing. As we saw in Chapter 3, the constitutive aim of defensive killing is to protect our right not to be killed from those who would

---

[18] As Lazar observes, many combatants who perform combat functions are ineffective, "[w]hether through fear, disgust, principle, lack of opportunity or ineptitude" (*Sparing Civilians*, 12). However, since attackers hardly ever have strong reason to believe that such combatants are ineffective, it is epistemically permissible to kill such ineffective combatants.

[19] See Scott Shapiro, "Massively Shared Agency," in Manuel Vargas & Gideon Yaffe (eds), *Rational and Social Agency: The Philosophy of Michael Bratman* (OUP 2014) 257.

[20] Helen Frowe, *Defensive Killing* (OUP 2014) 194 (italics added).

infringe that right by killing us directly, indirectly, or jointly with others. Subject to those constraints, defensive killing inflicts no more harm on those who would kill us than they would be required to bear to avoid breaching their stringent duty not to kill. Accordingly, those who do not threaten to kill us are not objectively morally liable to defensive killing by us.

At the same time, killing combatants who perform noncombat functions is often epistemically permissible. The fact that a person is a combatant is strong reason to believe that he performs a combat function. Since attackers rarely have stronger reasons to believe that a particular combatant performs a noncombat function, generally it is epistemically permissible to kill such combatants. However, if an attacker has decisive reason to believe that a particular combatant performs a non-combat function then it is epistemically impermissible to kill that combatant. Such individualized knowledge is rare in conventional armed conflict but typifies tar-geted killing operations against named individuals—so-called "personality strikes." Accordingly, a legal prohibition on targeting combatants whom the attacker knows or has decisive reason to believe performs a noncombat function would help attack-ers conform to their moral obligations.

As we will see in the next chapter, attackers are legally required to "do every-thing feasible to verify" that their intended human targets are combatants rather than civilians.[21] On my view, this means that attackers must presume that persons are non-participant civilians until they acquire decisive reason to believe that they are either participant civilians or combatants. Above this epistemic threshold, the lower the risk that a person would pose if she turns out to be liable, the stronger the reasons to believe that she is liable must be to render targeting her epistemi-cally permissible. Simply put, we must weigh the moral costs of mistakenly killing a non-participant civilian against the moral costs of mistakenly allowing a participant civilian or combatant to kill those whom we seek to protect. For example, if the evidence available to an attacker is such that a person is either a non-participant civilian or an ordinary combatant who performs a combat function but poses no immediate threat—as in most "signature strike" targeted killing operations—then the attacker must have very strong, perhaps conclusive reason to believe that the individual is such a combatant. Or so I argue in the next chapter.

In contrast, international law should prohibit attacking properly identified com-batants only "if it becomes apparent" that they perform noncombat functions.[22] In other words, attackers may presume that combatants perform combat func-tions until they acquire decisive reasons to believe otherwise. For example, if the evidence available to an attacker is such that a person is either a combatant who performs a combat function or a combatant who performs a noncombat function,

---

[21] See Protocol I art 57(2)(a); ICRC, *Customary IHL*, 55.
[22] cf Protocol I art 57(2)(b) (providing that "an attack shall be cancelled or suspended if it becomes apparent that the objective is not a military one or is subject to special protection").

then the attacker is permitted to strike unless her reasons to believe the latter decisively outweigh her reasons to believe the former.[23] The threshold for epistemic permissibility is lower because the moral cost of killing a combatant who performs a noncombat function is lower than the moral cost of killing a non-participant civilian. Although such combatants are not morally liable to defensive killing, killing them is less wrongful than killing non-participant civilians. Or so I argue in the next section.

Liability and Wrongfulness

As we saw in Chapter 3, the wrongfulness of harming someone for some end depends in part on her ability to avoid being harmed for that end. In general, it is very difficult for civilians to avoid being reasonably mistaken for irregular combatants. Since irregular combatants either actively try to blend with civilians or passively fail to distinguish themselves from civilians, civilians can only avoid being mistaken for such combatants by changing their ordinary appearance and behavior. For example, for a young Afghan man to avoid being mistaken for a member of the Taliban, he might have to shave his beard and wear Western clothing, alienating himself from his religious beliefs and cultural identity. In contrast, combatants who perform noncombat functions generally can avoid being reasonably mistaken for combatants who perform combat functions simply by not joining their armed forces, not donning uniforms or distinctive emblems, and not accompanying combatants preparing for and returning from military operations.

In addition, to the extent that someone can avoid harm simply by doing her duty, the wrongfulness of harming her varies in proportion to the strength of the relevant duty.[24] In general, civilians have no stringent moral duty to actively distinguish themselves from irregular combatants and breach no stringent moral duty by passively failing to do so. Moreover, civilians are seldom reasonably mistaken for combatants as a result of actions that breach their moral duties. As we have seen, civilians have moral duties not to contribute to or enable unjust threats posed by their armed forces. However, civilians are not reasonably mistaken for irregular combatants as a result of paying their taxes, voting, or working in war-related industries. In general, contributing civilians are mistaken for irregular combatants as a result of maintaining their ordinary ways of life, no differently than civilians who do not or cannot contribute to such unjust threats. Generally, there is no causal connection between their contributions and their misidentification.

---

[23] When combatants wear uniforms, we rarely have decisive reason to believe that a uniformed individual is a non-participant civilian.

[24] See generally Victor Tadros, *The Ends of Harm* (OUP 2011) ch 8.

In contrast, unjust combatants who perform noncombat functions have stringent moral duties not to contribute to or enable unjust threats posed by their fellow combatants who perform combat functions. Moreover, combatants who perform noncombat functions are mistaken for combatants who perform combat functions as a result of their contributing actions. If such combatants did not breach their stringent duties, then they would not be reasonably mistaken for their dangerous compatriots. Although these duties are not sufficiently stringent for their violation to result in liability to defensive killing, the fact that these combatants could avoid being reasonably mistaken for their dangerous comrades simply by conforming to their stringent moral duties reduces the objective wrongfulness of mistakenly killing them.

For these reasons, it is objectively less wrongful to mistakenly kill combatants who perform noncombat functions than to mistakenly kill civilians.[25] If, as I argue in Chapter 5, the epistemic permissibility of an action depends on its possible moral costs, then it will be epistemically permissible to risk mistakenly killing combatants who perform noncombat functions when it would not be epistemically permissible to risk mistakenly killing civilians. Killing combatants who may or may not perform combat functions generally is less morally risky than killing individuals who may be civilians or may be combatants.

Importantly, attackers must presume that persons are civilians unless their conduct gives attackers decisive reason to believe that they are combatants. In contrast, attackers may not presume that persons are combatants based on characteristics that they cannot change (such as age, race, or ethnicity) or that they may not be required to change on pain of death (such as religion). Just as we cannot *actually* lose our right not be killed involuntarily, we should not *effectively* lose our right not be killed involuntarily. Since we all act based on the evidence available to us, if the epistemic permissibility of intentionally killing us is out of our control, then it would be little comfort that the objective permissibility of intentionally killing us remains in our control.

In contrast, attackers may presume that combatants perform a combat function unless attackers acquire decisive reason to believe that the combatants perform a noncombat function. By joining their armed forces, combatants knowingly give others strong reason to believe that they will perform combat functions. They thereby lose their right to be presumed innocent (that is, non-threatening).

Some scholars take the stronger position that combatants become *objectively* liable by giving attackers decisive reason to believe that they are objectively liable. According to Kim Ferzan, combatants thereby become objectively liable to defensive killing.[26] According to Helen Frowe, combatants thereby become objectively

[25] Of course, there may be others. See, eg, Seth Lazar, "Risky Killing and the Ethics of War" (2015) 126 Ethics 91–117.
[26] Kimberly Kessler Ferzan, "Culpable Aggression: The Basis for Moral Liability to Defensive Killing" (2012) 9 Ohio State Journal of Criminal Law 669.

liable to *attempted* defensive killing.[27] Both views seem mistaken. First, since the duty not to appear threatening is, in general, far less stringent than the duty not to threaten, it is hard to believe that the breach of the former duty results in objective liability to defensive killing. Second, an actual assailant might be objectively liable to killing in a futile attempt to prevent the threat that he in fact poses. However, it is hard to believe that a merely apparent assailant is objectively liable to killing in an attempt to prevent a threat that he does not in fact pose. Instead, we should accept that noncombat personnel are not objectively liable to be killed, although it is objectively less wrongful to kill them than to kill civilians and, in part for that reason, it is epistemically permissible to presume that they are objectively liable to be killed absent decisive evidence to the contrary.

So far I have argued that it is epistemically permissible, and should be legally permissible, to target opposing combatants unless it becomes apparent—that is, unless one acquires decisive reason to believe—that they perform noncombat functions. For the same reasons, it is epistemically permissible, and should be legally permissible, to disregard collateral harm to opposing combatants unless one has decisive reason to believe that they perform noncombat functions. However, suppose that you have decisive reason to believe that combatants near a military target perform noncombat functions. Should collateral harm to such combatants carry the same moral and legal weight as comparable collateral harm to civilians? I think not.

As we have seen, the wrongfulness of harming someone varies with how easily they could avoid being harmed and with how stringent a duty they have to do that which would avoid their being harmed.[28] Generally, it is easier for noncombat personnel than for civilians to avoid military targets. Typically, noncombat personnel go to military targets while civilians have military targets brought to them. Moreover, most noncombat personnel involved in an unjust war are near military targets in order to contribute to unjust threats, while most civilians remain near military targets for personal reasons unrelated to the conflict—for example, because they live or work where the targets have been placed. Put another way, civilians cannot avoid military targets by not paying their taxes, while combatants can avoid military targets by not performing service and support functions. Finally, noncombat personnel have more stringent duties than civilians not to contribute to unjust threats because the former are more likely than the latter to enable unjust threats, making a counter-factual difference to the unjust harms ultimately inflicted. It follows that it is objectively much less wrongful to collaterally harm noncombat personnel than to collaterally harm civilians.

---

[27] Frowe, *Defensive Killing*.

[28] To see this, consider a group of children who skip school and unwittingly play near a military target. Though they could have avoided the target had they conformed to their duty, the duty they violate is too trivial to affect the wrongfulness of harming them.

The fact that it is less wrongful to kill noncombat personnel than to kill civilians is relevant both to *jus in bello* proportionality and to *jus ad bellum* proportionality. Since many unjust combatants are not liable to defensive killing, the harm that just combatants inflict upon unjust combatants is often itself unjust. If the unjust harms inflicted on such unjust combatants are as seriously wrongful as the unjust harms inflicted on contributing civilians, then traditional just causes for war may prove insufficient to justify the total harm inflicted in their pursuit. On these facts, contingent pacifism might be the only morally sustainable position. However, the harms inflicted on such unjust combatants, though unjust, are not nearly as hard to justify as the harms inflicted on civilians. It follows that the pursuit of traditional just causes for war can satisfy both *jus in bello* proportionality and *jus ad bellum* proportionality. On my view, even a just war inflicts objectively unjust but epistemically justified harm on many unjust combatants. Indeed, only such a view reflects the moral tragedy of war.[29]

Unnecessarily Killing Combatants

The moral case against killing combatants whom one could safely capture, non-lethally incapacitate, or simply ignore seems straightforward. According to Jeff McMahan, liability to defensive killing is liability to killing that is *necessary* to prevent an unjust threat.[30] On this view, it is unjust to unnecessarily kill unjust aggressors. Put the other way around, even unjust aggressors do not forfeit their right to be killed for no reason. Alternatively, according to Helen Frowe, liability to defensive killing is liability to killing that is *sufficient* to prevent an unjust threat.[31] On this view, it is not unjust to unnecessarily kill unjust aggressors; doing so does not wrong them. However, according to Frowe, unnecessarily killing unjust aggressors is all-things-considered impermissible, on broadly consequentialist grounds, since the same benefit could be achieved at a lower cost. Put another way, unnecessarily kill unjust aggressors is not unjust but *inhumane*, inflicting gratuitous or pointless harm. On either view, it is morally wrong to unnecessarily kill either just combatants or unjust combatants. Indeed, unnecessarily killing opposing combatants is particularly morally risky, since it may turn out that we rather than they fight for an unjust cause.

At the same time, attackers need not take the same risks to avoid killing opposing combatants that they must take to avoid killing civilians. As I will argue in Chapter 7, attackers must select means, methods, and objectives—that is, weapons, tactics, and targets—that avoid harm to civilians unless doing so would increase the risk to attackers substantially more than doing so would decrease the risk to

---

[29] On this point, see Lazar, *Sparing Civilians*, 14–15.
[30] McMahan, *Killing in War*.   [31] See Frowe, *Defensive Killing*.

civilians. In contrast, just combatants need not take significant risks to avoid killing unjust combatants. In general, we need not accept significant risks of death or serious injury to avoid imposing a significant risk of death or serious injury on someone who could have avoided such risks simply by complying with their stringent moral obligations. Most unjust combatants will not be killed or maimed if they refuse to fight or to provide service and support those who do so. It follows that just combatants need not assume comparable risks to avoid imposing such risks on unjust combatants.[32]

Nevertheless, ground forces may come across opposing combatants while the latter are unarmed, unaware, or sleeping. Other combatants may be sufficiently separated from their weapons that there is no military disadvantage to offering them an opportunity to surrender: if they refuse and move for their weapons then they may be killed before they reach, aim, or fire them. Finally, one may be in such a dominant tactical position that even armed opponents pose no realistic threat and can be attacked just as easily with or without warning. There is no obvious moral reason not to offer such opposing combatants the opportunity to surrender.

The main objections to legally prohibiting killing combatants whom one could safely capture are practical. For example, attackers may find it cognitively burdensome to consider the feasibility of capturing their adversaries in addition to the various other moral, legal, and tactical considerations that they must constantly balance. In response, I would note that the precautions rule—discussed in Chapter 7—already requires attackers to determine the feasibility of capturing their adversaries *when doing so would reduce the risk of harming nearby civilians*. In mixed battle spaces, civilians are often in harm's way and attackers must therefore constantly consider what they can feasibly do to avoid harming civilians—including offering their opponents an opportunity to surrender. For example, if offering opposing combatants an opportunity to surrender would likely avoid an exchange of fire that would endanger civilians then such a precaution may be required. This suggests that it is not unduly burdensome to require attackers to consider the feasibility of capture even when there are *no* civilians in harm's way. The main difference would be that attackers must sometimes take substantial risks to avoid harming civilians, but need not take substantial risks to avoid harming their opponents.

In addition, maintaining prisoners may prove costly to an attacking force in terms of time, resources, personnel, or mobility. Importantly, international law excludes these costs from permitting attackers to kill combatants who have already

---

[32] On Frowe's view, just combatants do not wrong unjust combatants by unnecessarily killing them. It seems to follow that the risks and costs that just combatants must bear to avoid unnecessarily killing such unjust combatants are the same as the risks and costs that just combatants must bear to save such unjust combatants from being killed. On my view, this stronger claim is true only with respect to unjust combatants who perform combat functions.

surrendered or who have already been taken prisoner. It may seem inconsistent for international law to allow these same costs to permit attackers to kill combatants without offering them an opportunity to surrender and without attempting to take them prisoner. Logically, it seems that only the risks of taking combatants prisoner, not the costs of maintaining them as prisoners, should legally count in favor of killing them rather than attempting to capture them. In both contexts, it seems that attackers must either find a way to keep these combatants prisoner or release them, even if, once released, they will likely return to the battlefield. I suspect, however, that things are not quite as they seem.

Both the act of surrender and the relationship of captor and prisoner are morally significant. A surrendering combatant places her trust in her adversary. She gives up her power to protect herself—making herself utterly vulnerable and completely defenseless—and entrusts her adversary with total power over her fate. To kill such a combatant betrays that trust, exploits that vulnerability, and abuses that power. Similarly, captors already have total power over their prisoners, and with that power comes special duties to do for their prisoners what their prisoners cannot do for themselves—indeed, what captors prevent their prisoners from doing for themselves. These duties include feeding, sheltering, and clothing their prisoners as well as protecting them from harm. At a minimum, captors have special duties not to kill those whose lives are in their hands.[33]

For these reasons, international law might draw a morally credible distinction between combatants who have not surrendered or been taken prisoner and combatants who have surrendered or been taken prisoner. It is always wrong to kill combatants when doing so is unnecessary to avoid significant risk to attackers. In addition, it is wrong to kill combatants who have surrendered or been taken prisoner *even* when doing so is necessary to avoid significant risk to attackers. Such combatants must be treated humanely or released. However, it is not wrong to kill combatants who have not surrendered or been taken prisoner when doing so is necessary to avoid significant risk to attackers. What at first appears like a morally arbitrary distinction turns out, on closer examination, to track significant moral differences.

The pressing question is whether there is a basis within existing international law for a legal prohibition on killing combatants who could be taken prisoner and kept prisoner without significant risk. It is to this question that we now turn.

The Principle of Humanity

There is no specific rule of treaty or custom prohibiting attackers from killing opposing combatants whom the attackers could safely capture. At the same time, the *principle of humanity* "forbids the infliction of suffering, injury or destruction

---

[33] See also Larry May, *War Crimes and Just War* (CUP 2007) 150–4.

not actually necessary for the accomplishment of legitimate military purposes."[34] In 2009, the ICRC took the view that

> while operating forces can hardly be required to take additional risks for themselves or the civilian population in order to capture an armed adversary alive, it would defy basic notions of humanity to kill an adversary or to refrain from giving him or her an opportunity to surrender where there manifestly is no necessity for the use of lethal force.[35]

On this view, it is unlawful to kill an opposing combatant whom one could safely capture, effectively incapacitate using non-lethal means, or simply ignore.[36] The ICRC conceded that its proposed restraints on the use of force (RUFs) will seldom apply to the conduct of "classic large-scale confrontations between well-equipped and organized armed forces or groups." However, the ICRC predicted that such RUFs will often apply "where a party to the conflict exercises effective territorial control, most notably in occupied territories and non-international armed conflicts."[37] In such asymmetrical armed conflicts, occupying forces and counterinsurgents can often safely capture or arrest their adversaries, particularly when the latter are (perhaps temporarily) unarmed.

The principle of humanity is something of a jurisprudential puzzle. According to the famous Martens Clause

> In cases not covered by this Protocol or by other international agreements, civilians and combatants remain under the protection and authority of the principles of international law derived from established custom, from the principles of humanity and from the dictates of public conscience.[38]

On one reading of the Martens Clause, the principles of humanity do not rest on treaty or custom but rather constitute an independent source of international law alongside treaty and custom. Accordingly, acts that violate "the principles of humanity" necessarily violate "principles of international law" even if they violate no specific rule of international law. This appears to be the understanding of the ICRC.

On an alternative reading, humanitarian considerations may inform the development, interpretation, and application of specific rules of treaty or custom, but have no independent legal status. For example, Yoram Dinstein asserts that

---

[34] ICRC, Interpretive Guidance, 79; US Dept of Defense, *Law of War Manual*, para 2.3.

[35] ICRC, Interpretive Guidance, 82.

[36] In this regard, the ICRC favorably cites Pictet's statement that "[i]f we can put a soldier out of action by capturing him, we should not wound him; if we can obtain the same result by wounding him, we must not kill him. If there are two means to achieve the same military advantage, we must choose the one which causes the lesser evil" (Jean Pictet, *Development and Principles of International Humanitarian Law* (Martinus Nijhoff 1985) 75).

[37] ICRC, Interpretive Guidance, 80–1.

[38] Protocol I art 1(2). The Martens Clause first appeared in the Second Hague Convention. See Hague Convention (II) with Respect to the Laws and Customs of War on Land (opened for signature July 29, 1899, entered into force September 4, 1900), preamble.

There is no overarching, binding, norm of humanity, that tells us what we must do (or not do) in wartime. What we actually encounter are humanitarian considerations ... these considerations do not by themselves amount to law: they are meta-juridical in nature.[39]

Similarly, Michael Schmitt submits that "the principle of humanity is expressed through positive rules and not general application of the principle."[40] According to Schmitt, "[a]s only states make law, they alone can adjust the consensus balance."[41]

Importantly, the ICTY has suggested an intermediate position. On one hand, the Martens Clause

may not be taken to mean that the 'principles of humanity' and the 'dictates of public conscience' have been elevated to the rank of independent sources of international law, for this conclusion is belied by international practice.[42]

On the other hand:

In the light of the way States and courts have implemented it, this Clause clearly shows that principles of international humanitarian law may emerge through a customary process under the pressure of the demands of humanity or the dictates of public conscience, even where State practice is scant or inconsistent.

On this view, a rule of customary international law cannot emerge without both state practice and *opinio juris sive necessitatis* (an opinion of law or necessity). Normally, only a general practice among states, accepted as law, will suffice.[43] However, when a rule is strongly supported by the principles of humanity and the dictates of public conscience, as well as by *opinio necessitatis*, less state practice may be required.[44]

To my mind, all three views contain an important element of truth. The principle of humanity is a legal principle, not just a moral principle or meta-juridical consideration. To see this, consider that customary international law is formed by states performing or refraining from certain conduct out of a sense that the conduct is legally obligatory, permitted, or forbidden. The so-called "paradox of custom" is that, it seems, customary international law always begins with a *mistaken* opinion that certain conduct has a legal status that it does not yet have. If enough states make

---

[39] Yoram Dinstein, "The Principle of Proportionality," in Kjetil Mujezinovic Larsen, Camilla Guldahl Cooper, & Gro Nystuen (eds), *Searching for a 'Principle of Humanity' in International Humanitarian Law* (CUP 2013) 73.

[40] Schmitt, "Interpretive Guidance," 41.

[41] Michael N Schmitt, "Military Necessity and Humanity in International Humanitarian Law: Preserving the Delicate Balance" (2010) 50 Virginia Journal of International Law 795, 801.

[42] *Prosecutor v Kupreškić* (Judgment) IT-95-16-T (January 14, 2000), paras 525, 527.

[43] See Statute of the International Court of Justice, June 26, 1945, art 38.

[44] See also Frederic L Kirgis, "Custom on a Sliding Scale" (1987) 81 American Journal of International Law 146; John Tasioulas, "Custom, *Jus Cogens*, and Human Rights," in Curtis Bradley (ed), *Custom's Future: International Law in a Changing World* (CUP 2016).

the same mistake, then the conduct gains the legal status that it was mistakenly thought to have all along. This seems like an odd way to run a legal system.

The principle of humanity provides an escape from this paradox. If states refrain from specific conduct out of a sense that the conduct violates a general legal principle, then a specific rule prohibiting that conduct may arise without any such legal mistake. On this approach, for the customary law of armed conflict to escape the paradox of custom, the principle of humanity must impose legal obligations on states.

At the same time, it does not follow that the principle of humanity directly imposes legal obligations on individual combatants, prohibiting them from engaging in conduct that is not specifically prohibited by treaty or custom. While some conduct violates the principle of humanity under virtually any conditions (say, targeting civilians and torturing prisoners), much wartime conduct violates the principle of humanity only under certain conditions (say, killing opposing combatants whom one could safely capture). Perhaps the principle of humanity directly governs individual combatants in the former contexts. Certainly the principle of humanity only indirectly governs individual combatants in the latter contexts, namely by grounding specific rules that identify the conditions under which wartime conduct is unlawful.

On my view, the principle of humanity does not prohibit individual combatants from killing opposing combatants whom they could safely capture. Instead, the principle of humanity obligates states to adopt specific rules to that effect. As state practice converges around such a specific rule, out of a sense of legal obligation under the principle of humanity, that rule will become part of customary international law.

Importantly, "[w]here a rule of customary international law is logical, because it can be deduced from an existing underlying principle, the burden of proving the rule by way of inductive reasoning [from examples of state practice] is proportionally diminished."[45] Accordingly, less state practice may be required to generate a customary rule supported by the principle of humanity. It follows that legal restraints on the use of force against combatants may be more forthcoming than we might otherwise expect.

Finally, as we saw in Chapter 2, international human rights law continues to apply during armed conflict, is not displaced by the law of armed conflict, and may prohibit killings not prohibited by the law of armed conflict. Accordingly, killing an opposing fighter, or a civilian directly participating in hostilities, whom one could safely capture may violate human rights law even if it does not violate the law of armed conflict. Killing in such circumstances may be considered an

---

[45] Stefan Talmon, "Determining Customary International Law: The ICJ's Methodology between Induction, Deduction and Assertion" (2015) 26 EJIL 417, 427 ("In essence, a logical rule requires a smaller pool of state practice and *opinio juris*").

arbitrary deprivation of life, and derogating from human rights principles in such ways may not be strictly required by the exigencies of the situation. As the African Commission on Human and People's Rights concludes

Where military necessity does not require parties to an armed conflict to use lethal force in achieving a legitimate military objective against otherwise lawful targets, but allows the target for example to be captured rather than killed, the respect for the right to life can be best ensured by pursuing this option.[46]

Accordingly, where it applies, human rights law may fill the moral gap left open by the existing law of armed conflict.

Are Defenseless Combatants *Hors de Combat*?

Under both Protocol I and customary international law, a person is *hors de combat* and may not be the object of attack if:

a) he is in the power of an adverse Party;
b) he clearly expresses an intention to surrender; or
c) he has been rendered unconscious or is otherwise incapacitated by wounds or sickness, and therefore is incapable of defending himself; provided that in any of these cases he abstains from any hostile act and does not attempt to escape.[47]

In an important essay, Ryan Goodman argues that the drafters of Protocol I intended the phrase "in the power of an adverse Party" to extend beyond combatants already captured by the attacking force.[48] Tellingly, the broad language of Protocol I contrasts with the narrow language of the Hague Conventions of 1899 and 1907, which extend protections to combatants only "in the case of capture by the enemy."[49] In addition, the ICRC Commentary to Protocol I suggests that "[a] defenceless adversary is 'hors de combat' whether or not he has laid down arms."[50] According to the ICRC, the relevant phrase might include "cases [in which] land forces might have the adversary at their mercy by means of overwhelmingly superior firing power to the point where they can force the adversary to cease combat."[51] Goodman concludes that "the protection applies as long as the individual is defenceless or all

---

[46] African Commission on Human and Peoples' Rights, *General Comment No 3 on the African Charter on Human and Peoples' Rights: The Right to Life (Article 4)* (PULP 2015), para 34.

[47] Protocol I art 41; ICRC, *Customary IHL*, 164.

[48] Ryan Goodman, "The Power to Kill or Capture Enemy Combatants" (2013) 24 EJIL 819.

[49] Hague Convention (II) with Respect to the Laws and Customs of War on Land (opened for signature July 29, 1899, entered into force September 4, 1900), art 3; Hague Convention (IV) Respecting the Laws and Customs of War on Land (opened for signature October 18, 1907, entered into force January 26, 1910) 3 Martens Nouveau Recueil (ser 3) 461, art 3.

[50] ICRC, *Protocol I Commentary*, 1614.

[51] ICRC, *Protocol I Commentary*, 1612.

his means of defence have been exhausted"[52] and that "combatants who no longer have the means to defend themselves—who are at the mercy of their adversary—are [protected from direct attack]."[53]

Indeed, the ICRC Commentary takes an even stronger position than Goodman indicates. According to the ICRC Commentary, individuals are "[in] the power of the adverse Party . . . when the latter is able to impose its will upon them."[54] This broad standard "applies to any unarmed soldier, whether he is surprised in his sleep by the adversary, on leave or in any other similar situation."[55] Indeed, according to the ICRC Commentary, this standard applies to attacks "conducted by the airforce, which can certainly have enemy troops in its power without being able, or wishing, to take them into custody or accept a surrender (for example, in the case of an attack by helicopters)."[56] Since ground forces are often defenseless against air and artillery attack, the ICRC Commentary seems to entail that much air and artillery attack violates the prohibition on attacking persons *hors de combat*.

According to the ICRC Commentary, it seems that attackers may not kill a defenseless adversary even if they cannot capture him, just as they may not kill an adversary who is unconscious or incapacitated by wounds or sickness even if they cannot capture him. It is hard to believe that the states party to Protocol I understood its *hors de combat* provision to sweep so broadly. If they did, then presumably they would have expressed their understanding in clearer terms. Moreover, a prohibition on killing combatants who cannot effectively fight back but who also cannot be safely captured will not help attackers conform to their moral obligations. While combatants disabled by wounds or sickness are likely to remain so, combatants who are currently defenseless are unlikely to remain so for long. Indeed, combatants may be defenseless against air or artillery attack while deploying to attack opposing ground forces. It is hard to see the logic behind considering such combatants *hors de combat*.

Tellingly, the ICRC Commentary begins its discussion with the modest claim that "there *could be* a significant difference between 'being' in the power [of an adversary] and having 'fallen' into the power [of an adversary],"[57] that is, between the definition of persons *hors de combat* and the definition of prisoners of war. The Commentary's subsequent, categorical statements belie the tentativeness of its premise. Strikingly, the ICRC does not even mention the view expressed in the Commentary in its recent study of customary international humanitarian law or in its recent interpretive guidance—not even in the section in which it argues for

---

[52] Goodman, "Power to Kill or Capture Enemy Combatants," 834.
[53] Goodman, "Power to Kill or Capture Enemy Combatants," 836.
[54] ICRC, Protocol I Commentary, 1614.
[55] ICRC, Protocol I Commentary, 1614.
[56] ICRC, Protocol I Commentary, 1612.
[57] ICRC, Protocol I Commentary, 1612.

restraints on the use of force against combatants. I suspect that the ICRC itself has abandoned the view expressed in the Commentary.

In his response to Goodman, Michael Schmitt takes the position that a person is "in the power" of opposing forces only if that person has been "captured." Importantly, Schmitt submits that "capture ... does not necessarily require taking the [individual] into 'custody'" but only that the individual is "unambiguously in the captors' control, such that he poses no risk to the captors or civilians (e.g., a risk of suicide bombing) and taking custody would be operationally feasible in the attendant circumstances."[58] To illustrate, Schmitt invokes one of Goodman's hypothetical cases:

1. *No military advantage versus kill or capture:*

A Special Forces unit secures a house, and heads into the bedroom area where it discovers that the target of its operation – a military commander – is in the shower. His back is turned to it, and he is unaware of its presence. It could easily apprehend him. It fires a bullet into the back of his head.[59]

Schmitt concludes that, if "apprehension could be easily effected without risk to the team or civilians, [then] the commander is 'in their power.'"[60] However, Schmitt reaches the opposite conclusion regarding another of Goodman's hypotheticals:

5. *Militarily advantageous to capture rather than kill:*

High-level civilian leaders and military commanders meet to plan a kill or capture operation that will take place in a few weeks. They conclude that it will be more militarily feasible to capture the target than to kill him. . . . They decide, however, to try to kill the individual ... due to information ... that holding the individual in captivity would harm diplomatic relations.[61]

Schmitt concludes that the subsequent target killing operation would be lawful because the target's "capture has not been effectuated."[62]

To see the contrast in starker terms, consider the following variation of Goodman's first case:

1a. **Still** *no military advantage versus kill or capture:*

A Special Forces unit **approaches** a house, and **uses thermal imaging to determine** that the target of its operation – a military commander – is in the shower. His back is turned to **the door**, and he **would be** unaware **if they entered the house and surrounded him**. It could easily apprehend him. It fires a bullet into the back of his head **using a long-range rifle**.

---

[58] Michael N Schmitt, "Wound, Capture, or Kill: A Reply to Ryan Goodman's 'The Power to Kill or Capture Enemy Combatants'" (2013) 24 EJIL 860.
[59] Goodman, "Power to Kill or Capture Enemy Combatants," 821.
[60] Schmitt, "Wound, Capture, or Kill," 861.
[61] Goodman, "Power to Kill or Capture Enemy Combatants," 822.
[62] Schmitt, "Wound, Capture, or Kill," 861.

It seems that, on Schmitt's view, it is unlawful to kill the commander in Goodman's original case but lawful to kill the commander in the variation. Since there is no obvious moral difference between the two cases, Schmitt's view seems unsatisfying.

Of course, states could interpret "in the power" to mean "both defenseless and susceptible to capture," thereby combining elements of both Goodman's account and Schmitt's. Such an interpretation would yield morally desirable results and help combatants better conform to their moral obligations. Nevertheless, such an approach seems to miss the point. It is wrong to kill the commander not because he is defenseless and susceptible to capture but because killing him is unnecessary to prevent him from posing future threats. The fact that he is defenseless and susceptible to capture does not make killing him wrong; instead, this fact makes killing him unnecessary and the fact that killing him is unnecessary makes killing him wrong. Put another way, defenselessness and susceptibility to capture are not reasons not to kill but only conditions under which the true reason not to kill—the absence of necessity—obtains.[63]

In my view, the principle of humanity, rather than the prohibition on attacking individuals *hors de combat*, best reflects the moral reasons to legally prohibit the killing of combatants whom one could safely capture. Developing a new specific rule may prove more difficult than reinterpreting an existing specific rule. However, it is worth the effort to rest the desired legal prohibition on firmer moral and legal grounds.

Conclusion

It is objectively permissible to kill unjust combatants who perform combat functions. It is epistemically permissible to kill unjust combatants unless one has decisive reason to believe that they perform noncombat functions. However, since killing unjust combatants who perform noncombat functions is much less wrongful than killing civilians, one need not take risky precautions to avoid mistakenly killing such combatants. In addition, collateral harm to such combatants will seldom render acts of war—or the resort to war—disproportionate. It follows that international law should prohibit intentionally killing combatants if it becomes apparent that they perform noncombat functions. Such a prohibition will help just combatants avoid wrongful killing, and will help unjust combatants avoid particularly wrongful killings.

It is objectively impermissible to kill opposing combatants whom one could safely capture, not because they are defenseless or already effectively captured, but because killing them is unnecessary. The principle of humanity legally obligates

---

[63] On the distinction between reasons and enabling conditions, see Jonathan Dancy, *Ethics without Principles* (OUP 2004) ch 3.

states to order their armed forces to refrain from such killings, though that principle does not directly obligate individual combatants to refrain from such killings. Over time, convergent state practice and opinion will generate a specific rule of customary international law prohibiting such killings. Such a legal prohibition will help just and unjust combatants alike avoid wrongful killing.

5

Distinction

The "basic rule" crystallizing the "general protection from the effects of hostilities" that international law offers civilians provides that

> In order to ensure respect for and protection of the civilian population and civilian objects, the Parties to the conflict shall at all times distinguish between the civilian population and combatants and between civilian objects and military objectives and accordingly shall direct their operations only against military objectives.[1]

In my view, it is helpful to see this basic rule as containing two distinct principles. The *principle of distinction* provides that combatants "shall at all times distinguish between the civilian population and combatants" while the *principle of discrimination* provides that combatants "shall direct their operations only against military objectives."

Many experts view these two principles as one, but they seem to me conceptually and functionally distinct. Attacking forces may fail to distinguish between civilians and combatants and, as a result, use highly discriminate weapons and tactics to mistakenly attack civilians. Alternatively, attackers may distinguish between civilians and combatants but then launch indiscriminate attacks that are not directed at a specific military objective, use methods or means of combat which cannot be directed at a specific military objective, or use methods or means of combat the effects of which cannot be limited to military targets. Attackers who do not distinguish between civilians and combatants may not care to know whether a person is one or the other. Conversely, combatants who use indiscriminate weapons may know who is who but simply not care. I will use the terms *distinction* and *discrimination* accordingly, understanding that others may prefer to divide up the conceptual terrain differently.

In my view, it is also helpful to distinguish the principle of distinction from the principle that "[t]he civilian population as such, as well as individual civilians, shall not be the object of attack."[2] Attackers must distinguish between civilians and combatants not only to avoid mistakenly attacking civilians but also to avoid

---

[1] Protocol Additional to the Geneva Conventions of 12 August 1949, and relating to the Protection of Victims of International Armed Conflicts (Protocol I) (adopted June 8, 1977, entered into force December 7, 1978) 1125 UNTS 3, art 48. See also ICRC, *Customary International Humanitarian Law*, vol 1 (CUP 2009) 3.

[2] Protocol I art 51(2). See also ICRC, *Customary IHL Study*, 3.

Law and Morality at War. First Edition. Adil Haque. © Adil Haque 2017. Published 2017 by Oxford University Press

mistakenly disregarding collateral harm to civilians under the precautions rule and the proportionality rule. To borrow a phrase from Michael Walzer, attackers must both *not try* to kill civilians and *try not* to kill civilians.[3] Since I do not expect every reader to accept my conceptual scheme, I will simply stipulate that I will use the term *distinction* in this sense.

The principle of distinction exists "in order to ensure respect for and protection of the civilian population." Distinction is a means to avoid intentionally, unnecessarily, or disproportionately harming individuals who are in fact civilians. Respecting the moral rights of civilians requires more than not intentionally targeting or deliberately disregarding collateral harm to known civilians. Attackers must not intentionally target or disregard collateral harm to a person unless they are sufficiently certain that the individual is a combatant and not a civilian. The practical importance of this epistemic requirement is hard to overstate, particularly in irregular armed conflicts conducted in mixed battle spaces. Indeed, interviews with military personnel suggest that as many as seven out of ten civilian deaths caused by US forces in planned military operations in Iraq and Afghanistan resulted from misidentification of civilians as combatants.[4]

As we will see, international law does not identify the level of certainty required to lawfully attack a person. Some experts propose a *balancing approach*, according to which the required level of certainty varies with the relative risks of mistakenly killing a civilian or mistakenly sparing an opposing combatant. Unfortunately, this approach requires substantial modification if it is to avoid intolerable results.

Instead, I argue that it is epistemically permissible to intentionally kill another human being only if you reasonably believe, based on decisive evidence, that she is liable to defensive killing. In particular, combatants must presume that persons are civilians unless the behavior of those civilians provides decisive evidence that they are combatants. Above this *reasonable belief threshold*, the required level of certainty varies with the relative moral costs of mistakenly killing an innocent person or mistakenly allowing innocent people to be killed. This hybrid approach reflects the moral asymmetry between doing harm and allowing harm. I illustrate how this hybrid approach would operate in practice, proposing interpretations of existing rules as well as model rules of engagement. We should interpret the principle of distinction in line with the hybrid approach, thereby providing soldiers with superior moral guidance. If my arguments in the previous chapters were successful, then unjust combatants will also act less wrongfully if they avoid mistakenly targeting civilians.[5]

---

[3] Michael Walzer, *Just and Unjust Wars* (2nd edn Basic Books 1992) 155–6 (describing a principle of double intention).

[4] See Gregory S McNeal, "Are Targeted Killings Unlawful?: A Case Study in Empirical Claims without Empirical Evidence," in Claire Finkelstein, Jens David Ohlin, & Andrew Altman (eds), *Targeted Killings: Law and Morality in an Asymmetrical World* (OUP 2012) 326, 331.

[5] This chapter develops views first proposed in Adil Ahmad Haque, "Killing in the Fog of War" (2012) 86 Southern California Law Review 63.

To simplify the presentation, I will assume a non-international armed conflict involving *soldiers* pursuing a just cause, *combatants* pursuing an unjust cause, and *civilians* not directly participating in hostilities. Importantly, I will refer to members of organized armed groups as combatants, with the understanding that they are not entitled to lawful combatant immunity. Finally, unless otherwise noted, my claims regarding combatants also apply to civilians directly participating in hostilities, while my claims regarding civilians apply only to civilians not directly participating in hostilities.

Law of Doubt, Law in Doubt

As we have seen, the principle of distinction does not tell soldiers how certain they must be that they have successfully distinguished civilians from combatants. A number of supplementary legal rules similarly suggest or imply a legal requirement of sufficient certainty. Unfortunately, as the ICRC observes, "the various provisions are relatively imprecise and are open to a fairly broad margin of judgment."[6] In particular, none of these rules identifies the level of certainty required to lawfully attack a person.

First, Protocol I provides that "[i]n case of *doubt* whether a person is a civilian, that person shall be considered to be a civilian" and therefore may not be targeted.[7] However, there is no consensus regarding the degree of doubt sufficient to preclude lawful attack. The ICRC originally called for restraint in the face of "slight" doubt[8] but recently took a different position, as we will see. The United Kingdom and New Zealand require restraint in cases of "substantial doubt," while Israel requires restraint in cases of "significant doubt."[9] Australia says simply that "[i]n cases of doubt about civilian status, the benefit of the doubt must be given to the person concerned."[10]

As a matter of customary international law, one group of distinguished experts concluded, rather unhelpfully, that "[t]he degree of doubt necessary to preclude an attack is that which would cause a reasonable attacker in the same or similar circumstances to abstain from ordering or executing an attack."[11] Most dramatically,

---

[6] ICRC, Commentary on the Additional Protocols of 8 June 1977 to the Geneva Conventions of 12 August 1949 (ICRC/Martinus Nijhoff 1987) 679.

[7] Protocol I art 50 (emphasis added). See also ICRC, *Protocol I Commentary* 611 ("According to the ICRC draft there was [a] 'presumption' of civilian status, but this concept led to some problems and the Working Group decided to replace 'presumed' by 'considered'").

[8] ICRC, Protocol I Commentary, 680.   [9] ICRC, *Customary IHL Study*, 243–4.

[10] Australian Defence Force, Australian Defence Doctrine Publication 06.4—Law of Armed Conflict (2006) 5.33.

[11] Program on Humanitarian Policy and Conflict Research, *Commentary on the HPCR Manual on International Law Applicable to Air and Missile Warfare* (2010) 87. See also Michael N Schmitt, "Human Shields in International Humanitarian Law" (2008) 38 Israel Yearbook on

the US Department of Defense takes the view that "no legal presumption of civilian status exists for persons or objects, nor is there any rule inhibiting commanders or other military personnel from acting based on the information available to him or her in doubtful cases."[12]

Second, both treaty and custom direct that "[i]n the conduct of military operations, *constant care* shall be taken to spare the civilian population, civilians and civilian objects."[13] However, as APV Rogers concludes, "[t]he law is not clear as to the degree of care required of the attacker and the degree of risk that he must be prepared to take."[14] For his part, Matthew Waxman argues that soldiers should apply a flexible standard of "reasonable care" according to which "reasonableness is judged in terms of costs to the attacker of performing more rigorous analysis or expending scarce military resources."[15]

Third, the law instructs that "those who plan or decide upon an attack shall . . . do everything feasible to *verify* that the objectives to be attacked are neither civilians nor civilian objects and are not subject to special protection but are military objectives."[16] Unfortunately, the law identifies neither the level of certainty required to "verify" the legitimacy of a target nor the level of risk that it is "feasible" for soldiers to accept in pursuit of that level of certainty. This chapter examines the required level of certainty, while Chapter 7 examines the required level of risk.

Finally, international law commands that "an attack shall be cancelled or suspended if it becomes *apparent* that the objective is not a military one or is subject to special protection."[17] However, no one contends that the law requires merely that soldiers not target individuals who are *obviously* civilians. No doubt, "an airman who has received the order to machine-gun troops travelling along a road, and who finds only children going to school, must abstain from attack."[18] However, both law and morality require far more than this.

The Balancing Approach

In the absence of clear legal standards, a number of leading states, scholars, and practitioners embrace a *balancing approach*, according to which the required level

Human Rights 17, 56–7 ("In all cases of doubt, the appropriate international humanitarian law standard on the battlefield is whether a reasonable warfighter in the same or similar circumstances would hesitate to act based on the degree of doubt he harbored").

[12] US Dept of Defense, *Law of War Manual* (2015) 5.5.3.2.
[13] Protocol I art 57 (emphasis added).
[14] "Zero-Casualty Warfare" (2000) 82 International Review of the Red Cross 165, 177.
[15] Matthew C Waxman, "Detention as Targeting: Standards of Certainty and Detention of Suspected Terrorists" (2008) 108 Columbia Law Review 1365, 1387.
[16] Protocol I art 57(2)(a) (emphasis added). See also ICRC, *Customary IHL Study*, 55.
[17] Protocol I art 57(2)(b) (emphasis added). See also ICRC, *Customary IHL Study*, 60.
[18] ICRC, Protocol I Commentary, 2221.

of certainty varies with the balance of military and humanitarian considerations. As the balance tips in favor of humanitarian considerations, the required level of certainty rises. As the balance tips in favor of military considerations, the required level of certainty falls.

For example, the ICRC now maintains that the level of doubt that precludes attack is not fixed but rather varies with the possible consequences, for soldiers and civilians, of an erroneous decision:

> Obviously, the standard of doubt applicable to targeting decisions cannot be compared to the strict standard of doubt applicable in criminal proceedings but rather must reflect the level of certainty that can reasonably be achieved in the circumstances. In practice, this determination will have to take into account, inter alia, the intelligence available to the decision maker, the urgency of the situation, and the harm likely to result to the operating forces or to persons and objects protected against direct attack from an erroneous decision.[19]

Similarly, Ian Henderson writes that "the level of verification required to reduce doubt, and the degree of acceptable doubt, will vary depending upon the likely adverse consequences of a wrong decision."[20] APV Rogers takes the seemingly more demanding position that "[i]n the event of doubt about the nature of the target, an attack should not be carried out, with a possible exception where failure to prosecute the attack would put attacking forces in immediate danger."[21]

According to John Merriam, "[t]he *quantum* of evidence required must vary depending on the circumstances under which the targeting decision is being made."[22] For example,

> If the proposed target is simply one combat team among hundreds fielded by the enemy, and that group of fighters does not pose an immediate threat, reasonableness may require further information-gathering. On the other hand, if the proposed target is the opponent's battlefield commander, proceeding on 70% confidence may be entirely reasonable.[23]

In such cases, "the value of the target" and "the risk posed by the possibility of error" determine the required quantum of evidence.[24] For his part, Michael Schmitt

---

[19] ICRC, Interpretive Guidance on the Notion of Direct Participation in Hostilities Under International Humanitarian Law (ICRC 2009) 76.

[20] *The Contemporary Law of Targeting: Military Objectives, Proportionality, and Precautions in Attack under Additional Protocol I* (Martinus Nijhoff 2009) 165; 164. See also Waxman, "Detention as Targeting," 1388 (arguing that the law does not impose "a fixed and always highly exacting duty—like, say, the beyond reasonable doubt approach of criminal law—but a balancing one: Parties are obliged to balance humanitarian concerns for civilians with military needs").

[21] Rogers, "Zero-Casualty Warfare," 181.

[22] John J. Merriam, "Affirmative Target Identification: Operationalizing the Principle of Distinction for US Warfighters" (2016) 56 Virginia Journal of International Law 83, 129.

[23] Merriam, "Affirmative Target Identification," 129.

[24] Merriam, "Affirmative Target Identification," 130.

writes that "[j]ust as advantage offsets collateral damage and incidental injury to some degree, so it also acts as an offset to doubt (which risks collateral damage). The greater the military advantage, the more doubt will be justified."[25]

The logic of the balancing approach seems compelling. Soldiers acting under uncertainty must risk making one of two grave moral errors. They must either risk erroneously killing a civilian or risk erroneously sparing an opposing combatant and, in many cases, thereby allowing that combatant to kill them, their fellow soldiers, or civilians. It seems logical that the required level of certainty should vary with the possible costs of error from case to case. If no soldiers or civilians are vulnerable to attack, then the risks of attack may outweigh the risks of restraint and the required level of certainty may be quite high. However, as the number of vulnerable soldiers or civilians increases, the risk of restraint rises and the required level of certainty correspondingly falls. Perhaps for such reasons, France and the United Kingdom insist that even substantial doubt regarding the legal status of a person or object cannot override the duty of commanders to protect the safety of troops under their command or to preserve their military situation.[26]

To date, proponents of the balancing approach have not explained how to weigh military considerations against humanitarian considerations or how to derive the required level of certainty from the resulting balance. As Rogers observes, "[h]umanitarian considerations would require a pilot to get close to the target to identify it properly; military considerations would require the pilot to fly at a safe height to be at reduced risk from anti-aircraft fire. This is a conflict that cannot be resolved easily."[27] Since the balancing approach is the only serious approach in the field, we must try to make its content determinate and its implications clear. Only then will its merits or defects become apparent.

Balancing Risks

In this section, I attempt to formalize the logic of the balancing approach in decision-theoretic terms in order to facilitate its normative evaluation. In contemporary decision theory, the level of certainty sufficient for rational action is represented as a function of the values and disvalues of the possible outcomes. In the context of target verification, there are four possible outcomes: killing a combatant (true positive), killing a civilian (false positive), sparing a civilian (true negative), and sparing a combatant (false negative). However, in general the value of killing a combatant is just avoiding the disvalue of erroneously sparing a combatant and

---

[25] Michael N Schmitt, "Fault Lines in the Law of Attack," in Susan Breau & Agnieszka Jachec-Neale (eds), *Testing the Boundaries of International Humanitarian Law* (British Institute of International and Comparative Law 2006) 277, 304.
[26] See ICRC, *Customary IHL Study*, 24.
[27] Rogers, "Zero-Casualty Warfare," 175.

the value of sparing a civilian is just avoiding the disvalue of killing a civilian. We therefore may consider only the value of killing a combatant and the disvalue of killing a civilian, both to simplify matters and to bring the reasons against attack and the reasons in favor of attack into sharper focus.[28]

With this simplification in hand, we can represent the required level of certainty as a function of the disvalue of a false positive (FP) and the value of a true positive (TP):

$$p > \frac{FP}{FP - TP}$$

Let us assume that the disvalue of a false positive is the death of one erroneously targeted civilian and that the value of a true positive is the survival of at least one soldier or civilian. Let us also assume that the death of a civilian and the death of a soldier are equally bad outcomes. Civilians and soldiers are, after all, human beings whose lives and welfare are equally important from an impartial point of view.

These are no more than simplifying assumptions, intended to focus attention on the logical structure of the balancing approach as formalized in decision-theoretic terms. In practice, we would need to contend with several confounding variables. First, while every false positive involves the death of a civilian, not every false negative results in the death of a fellow soldier. Not every opposing combatant makes a necessary contribution to lethal operations such that killing her will prevent even one fellow soldier from being killed, and mistakenly spared combatants will often be killed in future operations before they can kill even one fellow soldier. Second, according to contemporary counterinsurgency theory, killing an insurgent may not yield a net military benefit because the insurgent's death may inspire friends and relatives to take up arms. Conversely, killing a civilian may yield a net military cost by turning the civilian population against one's forces.[29] Third, the death of a combatant not only eliminates the threat the combatant poses, but also may (perhaps temporarily) deplete the opposing force. Fourth, a combatant who is mistakenly spared at one time may become more dangerous or more difficult to kill or capture later. Finally, the deaths of soldiers at the hands of mistakenly spared combatants may place other soldiers at greater risk or jeopardize the success of a mission or, over time, the success of the war effort. Although these variables would certainly inform the practical implementation of the balancing approach, we should bracket these variables for the time being, since our immediate aim is to evaluate the balancing approach as a matter of principle.

---

[28] I used a different notation in "Killing in the Fog of War" and borrow the current notation from Seth Lazar, "In Dubious Battle: Uncertainty and the Ethics of Killing (unpublished ms).

[29] See US Dept of Defense, *The U.S. Army and Marine Corps Counterinsurgency Field Manual* (US Army Field Manual No 3-24, 2006).

Accordingly, it seems that even if the value of a true positive would be the survival of only one soldier, the required level of certainty would be fairly low:

$$p > \frac{-1}{(-1)-1} = .5$$

In other words, it seems that the balancing approach permits you to kill a person whom you believe is only slightly more likely a combatant than a civilian in order to prevent one soldier from being killed if the individual turns out to be a combatant. Moreover, it seems that if the value of a true positive is the survival of even two fellow soldiers, then the required level of certainty falls even lower:

$$p > \frac{-1}{(-1)-2} = .33$$

So, according to the balancing approach, it is permissible to kill a person whom you believe is at least twice as likely to be a civilian (66%) than to be a combatant (33%) and at most half as likely to pose a threat to two soldiers than to pose no threat at all. More broadly, on this view, it is permissible to kill a person whom you are reasonably confident is a civilian if by doing so you might (but very likely will not) save a small number of soldiers. These implications of the balancing approach are implausible in theory and dangerous in practice.

For example, consider the following scenario used to train US Marines deployed in Iraq:

You are in a five-vehicle convoy moving . . . at 60 mph. As you pass under an overpass you observe an adult male, with a grenade-sized object in his hand, looking over the pedestrian railing above your lane. You cannot tell what's in the man's hand. What do you do?[30]

The US Marine Corps correctly instructs its forces to "[s]tay ready, observe the man on the bridge and prepare to fire if you observe hostile intent or hostile act."[31] However, according to the balancing approach, if a substantial number of Marines would be killed if the man turns out to be an insurgent armed with a grenade, then it would be permissible to intentionally kill the man even if he is probably, much more likely, or almost certainly a civilian rather than an insurgent. If four Marines would be killed by a dropped grenade, then you may kill the man even if you are only 20% sure that he is an insurgent (and 80% sure he is a civilian); if nine Marines would be killed, then 10% certainty would be enough; and so on. These implications of the balancing approach seem morally indefensible. It is clearly wrong to intentionally kill someone who is probably, very likely, or almost certainly a civilian

---

[30] *Quiz: The Tough Choices*, PBS (February 19, 2008), http://www.pbs.org/wgbh/pages/frontline/haditha/etc/quiz.html.

[31] *Quiz Answers.*

except perhaps if a very large number of soldiers or civilians are vulnerable to a possible attack.

Expectabilism

Given its counterintuitive implications in the target verification context, it is worth pausing to ask why the decision-theoretic approach is widely accepted as a guide to rational decision-making in other domains. Let us call the philosophical view underlying the decision-theoretic approach *expectabilism*. According to expectabilists, "[w]hen the rightness of some act depends on the goodness of this act's effects or possible effects, we ought to act, or try to act, in the way whose outcome would be *expectably-best*."[32] An outcome is expectably-best if no alternative act has a higher *expected value*, where the expected value of an act is the average value of its possible outcomes discounted by the probability of their occurrence. For example, the number of people who will be *expectably-saved* by an act is the number of people who might be saved discounted by the probability that they will be saved.

Expectabilism is often motivated by cases in which it seems clear that we should do what is expectably-best rather than what has the best chance of bringing about the best outcome. Perhaps the most famous case is:

Mine Shafts: A hundred miners are trapped underground, with flood waters rising. We are rescuers on the surface who are trying to save the miners. We know that all of the miners are in one of two mine shafts, but we don't know which shaft. Given our evidence, it is equally likely that the miners are all in Shaft A or all in Shaft B. There are three flood-gates that we could close. The results would be these:

		The miners are in	
		Shaft A	Shaft B
	Gate 1	We save 100 lives	We save no lives
We close	Gate 2	We save no lives	We save 100 lives
	Gate 3	We save 90 lives	We save 90 lives[33]

If we close either Gate 1 or Gate 2, we have a 50% chance of doing what would be objectively best, namely saving all of the miners. If we close Gate 3, we have no chance of doing what would be objectively best. Yet clearly we should close Gate 3, since by closing Gate 3 we will certainly save almost all of the miners.

With some effort, we can construct a parallel wartime scenario:

---

[32] Derek Parfit, *On What Matters*, vol 1 (OUP 2011) 160. See also Frank Jackson, "Decision-Theoretic Consequentialism and the Nearest and Dearest Objection" (1991) 101 Ethics 467; Michael J Zimmerman, *Living with Uncertainty* (CUP 2009).

[33] Parfit, *On What Matters*, 159.

Rescue: Twenty soldiers are ambushed behind enemy lines. In such circumstances, they have instructions to make their way to one of two potential extraction points. However, their communications equipment is damaged and we have no way to know which extraction point they were able to reach. Given our evidence, it is equally likely that the soldiers are all at Location A or all at Location B. We have two helicopters, each of which can rescue 15 soldiers. We can send both helicopters to one location or one helicopter to each location. The results would be these:

		The soldiers are at	
		Location A	Location B
	Both to A	We save 20 soldiers	We save no soldiers
We send	Both to B	We save no soldiers	We save 20 soldiers
	One to A and B	We save 15 soldiers	We save 15 soldiers

If we send both helicopters to either Location A or Location B, we have a 50% chance of doing what would be objectively best, namely saving all of the soldiers. If we send one helicopter to each location, we have no chance of doing what would be objectively best. Yet clearly we should send one helicopter to each location, since by doing so we will certainly save fifteen soldiers.

What moral principles explain these intuitions? Why should we do what is expectably-best? There are two main possibilities. The first is that by maximizing the expected value of each of our acts taken individually we will maximize the actual value of all of our acts taken together. For example, if we know that we will conduct a large number of rescue operations, then we will save more people in the long run if we always do whatever will expectably-save the most people. More broadly, if we always do what is expectably-best rather than what is probably best then, over the long term, we will do what is actually best. If we always expectably-save the most people, then over time we will actually save the most people. We can call this the *rule consequentialist* interpretation of expectabilism.

The second possibility is that our reasons to perform an act are a function both of our reasons to bring about a certain outcome and of our reasons to believe that the act will bring about that outcome. Our reasons to believe that an act will have a good or bad result intensify, attenuate, or otherwise modify our reasons to perform that act.[34] For example, if our reasons to believe that act A will save ten people are twice as strong as our reasons to believe that act B will save the same ten people, then our reasons to perform act A are twice as strong as our reasons to perform act B. Similarly, if our reasons to believe that act C will save ten people are twice as

---

[34] See Joseph Raz, *From Normativity to Responsibility* (OUP 2011) 115 ("probability can be a so-called 'weight' or importance or force-influencing factor" such that "[t]he likelihood that [some means] will facilitate the end affects the force of the reason to [take that means]"). For a partially overlapping view, see Horacio Spector, "Decisional Nonconsequentialism and the Risk Sensitivity of Obligation" (2016) 32 Social Philosophy & Policy 91.

strong as our reasons to believe that act D will save twenty other people, then our reasons to perform act C are just as strong as our reasons to perform act D. Finally, if an act will expectably-save ten people, then our reasons to perform that act are as strong as our reasons to perform an act that will certainly save ten people. We can call this the *rational product* interpretation of expectabilism.

Often, we use *evidential probabilities* to represent the strength of our reasons for belief. For example, if we have conclusive reason to believe that an act will save ten people, then we can say that the act is 100% likely to save ten people. If our reasons to believe that an act will save ten people are as strong as our reasons to believe that the act will save no one, then we can say that the act has a 50% chance to save ten other people. If our reasons to believe that an act will save ten people are twice as strong as our reasons to believe that the act will save no one, then we can say that the act has a 67% chance to save ten other people. And so on. In what follows, I will refer to evidential probabilities, reasons for belief, or both as seems appropriate.

Of course, often we are not able to precisely quantify the strength of our reasons for belief in the form of exact evidential probabilities. I will have something to say about this problem later. For now, I will stipulate certain evidential probabilities for the narrow purpose of explicating and evaluating the logic of the balancing/expectabilist approach.

Cases like *Mineshaft* and *Rescue* suggest that, when all that matters is how many people you will save, you should not perform the act most likely to save the most people. Instead, you should perform the act that will expectably-save the most people. However, it does not follow that when what matters is whether to kill (and possibly save) or not kill (and possibly fail to save) you may kill some to expectably-save more.

Recall the Marine Corps training scenario described earlier, which we labeled *Overpass*. Suppose that, given the evidence, there is a 20% chance that the man is an insurgent with a grenade and an 80% chance that the man is a civilian with a soda can. Suppose also that if the man is an insurgent and is not killed, then he will kill ten Marines by a dropping a grenade onto their vehicle. On these facts, killing the man will expectably-save two Marines. Yet it seems clearly wrong to kill him given your evidence. Given your evidence, he is four times more likely to be an unarmed civilian than to be an armed insurgent. Your reasons to believe that he is an unarmed civilian are four times stronger than your reasons to believe that he is an armed insurgent. Something has gone awry.

In cases like *Mineshaft* and *Rescue*, we compare certainly saving some with possibly saving all. Importantly, the available means of saving (closing gates and directing helicopters) are themselves morally neutral. In such cases, only the (expectable) numbers count. In contrast, in *Overpass*, we compare certainly killing one with possibly saving more. Importantly, the available means of saving (intentionally killing another human being) is hardly morally neutral. In such cases, the intrinsic prop-erties of the contemplated act also count. Since killing is intrinsically worse than letting die, it is not permissible to intentionally kill one person who is probably not liable to defensive killing as a means of expectably-saving two people who are not liable to defensive killing.

Deontic Expectabilism

Perhaps expectabilism could avoid these implications by incorporating the deon-tic asymmetry between killing and letting die into its value function. Let us call this view *deontic expectabilism*. In *Overpass*, it seemed wrong to kill one person when there was only a 20% chance that he posed a lethal threat to ten other people. Perhaps the explanation for this result is that killing an innocent person is more than twice as bad as allowing an innocent person to be killed. This seems unlikely.

Suppose that killing is five times worse than letting die. According to deontic expectabilism, it would still be permissible to kill the man on the overpass if there is a 66% chance that he is an unarmed civilian and a 33% chance that he is an armed insurgent:

$$p > \frac{-5}{(-5)-10} = .33$$

Yet it seems wrong to kill a person when our reasons to believe that they retain their rights are twice as strong as our reasons to believe that they are liable to defensive killing.

Now suppose that killing is nine times worse than letting die. According to deontic expectabilism, it would still be permissible to kill the man on the overpass if there is a 53% chance that he is an unarmed civilian and a 47% chance that he is an armed insurgent:

$$p > \frac{-9}{(-9)-10} = .47$$

Yet it seems wrong to kill a person when our reasons to believe that they retain their rights are stronger than our reasons to believe that they are liable to defensive killing. These considerations suggest that more is at play than the moral asymmetry between killing and letting die.

Nor do our intuitive judgments waver when we consider the moral foundations of deontic expectabilism. It seems morally impermissible to target someone who is very likely a civilian simply because, if you do so in a large number of similar cases, you will save substantially more than you will kill. Moreover, when your reasons to believe that person is a civilian are stronger than your reasons to believe that person is a combatant it seems permissible to target that person only if your reasons to save are *far* stronger than your reasons not to kill. At a minimum, deontic expectabilism yields indefensible implications when the probability of targeting a civilian is high.

Perhaps the problem with deontic expectabilism is that, while incorporating the deontic asymmetry between killing and letting die, it ignores the deontic asymmetry between intentional killing and unintentional killing. While unintentionally killing an innocent person is substantially worse than allowing an innocent person to be killed, intentionally killing an innocent person is far worse than allowing an innocent person to be killed. Accordingly, a soldier may intentionally kill a possible civilian only to prevent far greater expected harm to others. Suppose that it is permissible to intentionally kill someone who is certainly a civilian if this will certainly save one hundred civilians from being killed. We can then say that intentionally killing civilians is as bad as allowing one hundred civilians to be killed. On this view, it is permissible to intentionally kill someone who is 80% likely to be a civilian only if there is a 20% chance that they are a combatant and will kill 400 people. Exact numbers aside, in practice it will hardly ever be permissible to kill someone that you are reasonably confident is a civilian. That general position seems correct. Let us call this view *restrictive expectabilism*.

Unfortunately, restrictive expectabilism seems too restrictive in other cases. For example, this view entails that it is impermissible to kill someone that you are 98% sure is a combatant and will otherwise kill one soldier or civilian. This view seems to rule out almost all killing in armed conflict as well as most killing in ordinary self-defense.

What we need, it seems, is a view on which intentionally killing a person whom you are reasonably confident is a civilian is morally comparable to intentionally killing a known civilian but intentionally killing a person whom you are reasonably confident is a combatant is morally comparable to unintentionally killing a civilian. In other words, we want a view that operates like restrictive expectabilism when the risk of targeting a civilian is high but that operates like deontic expectabilism when the risk of targeting a civilian is low. Moreover, such a view must not be ad hoc but must rest on a compelling moral foundation.

The Reasonable Belief Threshold

To frame such an alternative view, let us return to some distinctions drawn in Chapter 1. An act is *objectively* permissible if and only if it is permissible, given all the morally relevant facts. An act is *epistemically* permissible if and only if it is permissible, given the evidence available to the agent. An act is *subjectively* permissible if and only if it would be objectively permissible, were the agent's beliefs about the morally relevant facts true.[35]

We should understand objective and epistemic permissibility in terms of *moral reasons* for action and *epistemic reasons* for belief. An act is objectively permissible if and only if, given all the morally relevant facts, the moral reasons to perform that act are at least as strong as the moral reasons not to perform that act. In other words, an act is objectively morally permissible so long as it is supported by *undefeated* moral reasons. In contrast, a belief is epistemically permissible if and only if, given the evidence available to the agent, the epistemic reasons in favor of that belief are clearly stronger than the epistemic reasons against that belief. In other words, a belief is epistemically permissible only if it is supported by *decisive* epistemic reasons.

Why the contrast? If we have equally strong moral reasons to perform an act and to refrain from that act, then we *may* perform or refrain because we *must* perform or refrain. There is no third option, and both available options are equally reasonable. In contrast, if we have equally strong epistemic reasons to believe that something is the case or to believe that something is not the case, then we *may not* believe or disbelieve because we *need not* believe or disbelieve. There is a third option, namely to reserve judgment until we acquire decisive epistemic reasons one way or the other. Accordingly, a belief is epistemically permissible only if the epistemic reasons in favor of that belief (i) clearly outweigh any epistemic reasons against that belief and (ii) are sufficient to warrant belief rather than suspension of judgment.[36]

On my view, an act is epistemically permissible if and only if it is epistemically permissible to believe that the act is objectively permissible to perform. In other words, an act is epistemically permissible if and only if we have *decisive* epistemic reason to believe that we have *undefeated* moral reason to perform that act. For example, it is epistemically permissible for a soldier to attack a person only if that soldier has decisive epistemic reasons to believe that the person is a combatant and not a civilian. Conversely, if a soldier's reasons to believe that a person is a civilian are as strong as or stronger than her reasons to believe that the person is a combatant, then the soldier should refrain from attack. As we shall see, this is a necessary condition, but not a sufficient condition, for permissible killing in the fog of war.

In terms of evidential probabilities, it is epistemically impermissible to intentionally kill another human being if, given your evidence, there is a 50% chance or less that they are liable to be killed. As already noted, often we cannot precisely quantify our reasons for belief as exact evidential probabilities. However, if our

---

[35] cf Parfit, *On What Matters*, 150–1 (providing parallel accounts of wrongness in the "fact-relative" sense, the "evidence-relative" sense, and the "belief-relative" sense).
[36] cf Raz, *From Normativity to Responsibility*, 46.

reasons to believe that a person is liable to defensive killing are not clearly stronger than our reasons to believe that they retain their immunity from attack, then we should refrain from attack. In such cases, we know with certainty that a *wrong-making* fact obtains, namely that our act would kill another human being. In such circumstances, epistemic permissibility requires decisive reason to believe that a *wrong-justifying* fact obtains, namely that this particular person has done something to lose his ordinary right not to be killed.

On my view, the duty to distinguish civilians from combatants requires that attackers must believe that the individuals whom they attack are combatants and their beliefs must be supported by decisive epistemic reasons. In other words, an attack satisfies the principle of distinction only if the attacker *reasonably believes* that the individuals whom he attacks are combatants. For example, the Marines in the training scenario described earlier have stronger reasons to believe that the man on the overpass is a civilian than to believe that he is a combatant. It is epistemically impermissible, and would violate the principle of distinction, for them to kill the man in the "off chance" that he is in fact a combatant.

On this view, reasonable belief constitutes a *threshold* of epistemic permissibility. If soldiers have undefeated reasons to believe that a person is a civilian, then the soldiers must not kill that person even if the expected value of doing so substantially outweighs the expected disvalue of doing so. It is morally much worse to intentionally kill a person if one does not reasonably believe that he is morally liable to be killed than if one reasonably believes that he is morally liable to be killed. Intentional killing absent a reasonable belief in liability is almost never morally permissible.

This view of epistemic permissibility parallels a standard view of objective permissibility. The objective permissibility of intentionally killing another person generally turns on two distinct questions:

1. Has the person made herself (potentially) liable to intentional killing?
2. Will the good consequences of intentionally killing her justify the bad consequences of killing her (all things considered)?[37]

Except in extreme cases, the good consequences of intentionally killing another person cannot justify killing her unless she has made herself liable to intentional killing. In this sense, liability is not a reason to kill but rather an enabling condition that transforms the consequences of killing into reasons to kill.[38] Accordingly,

---

[37] The parentheticals are meant to keep the questions neutral with respect to certain issues, for example, whether necessity is internal or external to liability and whether it can be all-things-considered permissible to kill many liable attackers to save one innocent victim.

[38] In Razian terms, ordinarily we have exclusionary reasons not to treat the consequences of killing as first-order reasons to kill. Liability involves the cancellation of these exclusionary reasons.

liability and consequences do not stand on equal normative footing, such that one may be traded off against the other. Instead, liability must exist before consequences come into play.

On my view, the epistemic permissibility of intentionally killing another person generally turns on two, equally distinct questions:

1. What reason do we have to believe that this person has made herself (potentially) liable to intentional killing?
2. What reason do we have to believe that the good consequences of intentionally killing her will justify the bad consequences of killing her (all things considered)?

The basic mistake in the balancing/expectabilist approach is to conflate these two questions, trading off our epistemic reasons regarding liability with our epistemic reasons regarding consequences. On this approach, it may be epistemically permissible to intentionally kill another person whom we have very weak reason to believe is liable, so long as we have reason to believe that killing her might produce very good consequences. In my view, this approach puts the cart before the horse by considering the possible consequences of killing a person before establishing her liability to be killed.[39]

In contrast, on my view, we must first establish a person's liability by sufficient evidence before considering the possible consequences of killing her. Just as it is objectively impermissible to intentionally kill another person unless she is liable, it is epistemically impermissible to intentionally kill another person unless we have sufficient reason to believe that she is liable. Just as the actual consequences of killing another person cannot objectively justify killing her unless she is liable, the possible consequences of killing another person cannot epistemically justify killing her unless her liability has been established by sufficient evidence. Crucially, just as the standard of liability does not depend on the actual consequences of killing her, the standard of sufficient evidence should not depend on the possible consequences of killing her. Just as a person's "objective liability" depends on her voluntary conduct rather than on the actual consequences of killing her, a person's "epistemic liability" depends on evidence of her voluntary conduct rather than on the possible consequences of killing her.

We need a standard of sufficient evidence of liability that does not vary with the possible consequences of killing, since those consequences should only "count" once liability has been independently established. On my view, the appropriate standard of sufficient evidence of liability is the standard of reasonable belief, that is, belief based on decisive epistemic reasons. In other words, your reasons to believe that a person is liable to intentional killing must be clearly stronger than your

---

[39] The following argument is inspired by Alec Walen, "Proof Beyond a Reasonable Doubt: A Balanced Retributive Account" (2015) 76 Louisiana Law Review 355.

reasons to believe that they retain their ordinary protection from intentional killing. Since belief or action based on defeated reasons is clearly irrational, minimal
rationality requires decisive reasons for belief and undefeated reasons for action. As
we shall see, once this minimal epistemic threshold is reached, deontic expectabilist
considerations may come into play and require a still higher standard of certainty
that varies with the possible costs of error. However, until this minimal threshold is reached, expectabilist considerations have no place in determining epistemic
permissibility.

Before defending the reasonable belief threshold in the following sections, let me
add a theoretically important but practically irrelevant qualification. Like any other
deontic constraint, the reasonable belief threshold can be overridden in extreme
cases. In principle, it may be epistemically permissible to kill a person whom you
reasonably believe is innocent if the expected value of doing so is vastly greater
than the expected disvalue. In such cases, our reason to prevent vastly greater harm
to others may be so overwhelming that, even though we have only weak reason to
believe that our action will prevent such vastly greater harm, we may have decisive
reason to try. In addition, if we intentionally kill people in many such cases, then
over time we will save far more than we will intentionally kill. Although each
individual killing probably will prove unjustified, many such killings taken together
probably will prove justified. However, in armed conflict it is almost never the
case that by killing a person who is probably a civilian you will prevent far greater
expected harm to others. Moreover, such cases are so rare that killing in the few
cases that arise will probably not prevent far greater actual harm to others, since acts
that maximize expected value will only maximize actual value when performed
in large numbers. It follows that the reasonable belief threshold is, for all practical
purposes, absolute.

The Balance of Reasons

On the threshold approach, small evidential differences can produce large moral
differences. Suppose that, based on the evidence available to you, there is a 45%
chance that A is a civilian and a 55% chance that B is a civilian. How can it be that
killing B is many times harder to justify than killing A when B is only somewhat
more likely than A to be a civilian? Similarly, how can the moral difference between
killing A and killing B be so much greater than the moral difference between killing B and killing C, if there is a 65% chance that C is a civilian, or the difference
between killing A and killing D, if there is a 35% chance that D is a civilian? How
can a similar evidential difference make a far greater moral difference when it strad-
dles the reasonable belief threshold?

Of course, we are familiar with other deontic thresholds that generate large
moral differences from subtle mental or physical differences. For example, we attach

great moral importance to the distinctions between intentional killing and foresee-able killing; killing as a means and killing as a side effect; killing and letting die; or preventing comparable, substantially greater, much greater, or far greater harm to others. In each case, the moral permissibility of an action may depend on whether it falls on one side of a line or another. But even if we accept such sharp moral asymmetries elsewhere, why should we accept that reasonable belief has the same kind of dramatic moral importance?

As we have seen, epistemically justified acts are based on justified beliefs that the acts are objectively morally justified. In turn, both objectively justified actions and justified beliefs rest on a balance of reasons. An act is objectively morally justi-fied if and only if it supported by the balance of moral reasons, that is, by moral reasons to perform the act that are undefeated by any decisive moral reasons not to perform the act. Where there are strong moral reasons both to perform an act and not to perform an act, the objective permissibility of the act depends on the balance of reasons. The permissibility of the act will often depend, for example, on whether the reasons in favor of the act are 10% stronger or 10% weaker than the reasons against the act. In contrast, the permissibility (as opposed to the degree of wrongfulness) of the act never depends, for example, on whether the reasons in favor of the act are 10% or 20% stronger than the reasons against the act, or 10% or 20% weaker than the reasons against the act. So small differences in the strength of reasons can make all the difference to the objective permissibility of action when they affect the overall balance of reasons.

Similarly, a belief is justified if and only if it is supported by the balance of epis-temic reasons, that is, by epistemic reasons in favor of the belief that defeat any epistemic reasons against that belief. Where there are strong epistemic reasons both in favor of a belief and against that belief, the justification of that belief depends on the balance of reasons. It follows that a small change to the relative strength of the opposing epistemic reasons can render a belief justified or unjustified if that small change shifts the overall balance of reasons. Here, as elsewhere, a small difference can make all the difference.

On the threshold approach, an act is epistemically permissible only if it is sup-ported by a justified belief that the act is objectively justified. Conversely, an act is epistemically impermissible if it is supported by an unjustified belief that the act is objectively justified or by a justified belief that the act is objectively unjustified. Epistemic permissibility is sensitive to the balance of reasons because its constituent parts (justified beliefs and objectively justified acts) are sensitive to the balance of reasons.

In the context of armed conflict, killing a person is epistemically impermissible if it rests on a justified belief that the individual is a civilian, an unjustified belief that the individual is a combatant, or no belief either way. In contrast, the expectabilist approach endorses intentionally killing individuals whom one either reasonably believes are civilians, unreasonably believes are combatants, or about whom one has formed no belief regarding their moral or legal status. In other words, an act is supposed to derive some form of justification from an unjustified belief that the act is justified, a justified belief that the act is unjustified, or no belief one way or the other. This is not an attractive position.

We can now see where the rational product interpretation of expectabilism goes awry. The relationship between reasons for belief and reasons for action is not linear when the action involved is killing another human being. Whether our reasons to believe that a person is liable to be killed are decisive or defeated introduces a step change in the strength of our reasons not to kill that person. Perhaps our reasons to perform an act with a 20% chance of saving ten people are as strong as our reasons to perform an act that will certainly save two people. However, our reasons not to kill

(i) a person with a 20% evidential probability of being a combatant who poses a threat to ten people

are much stronger than our reasons not to kill

(ii) a person who is certainly a combatant who poses a threat to two people.

Our reasons not to kill the first individual decisively outweigh our reasons to kill him while our reasons not to kill the second individual are easily defeated.

Our reasons for action are a function not only of the relative strength of our reasons for belief but also of the overall balance of our reasons for belief. Our reasons not to kill a person whom we have undefeated reason to believe is a civilian are much stronger than our reasons not to kill a person whom we have decisive reason to believe is a combatant. When all that matters is saving the most or killing the fewest, then it is easy to justify proceeding on expectabilist grounds. In contrast, it is very hard to justify killing some to save others on even deontic expectabilist grounds. When we intentionally kill another human being we owe them a special kind of moral justification, in which a justified belief in liability plays an important and role.[40]

Respect and Reasonable Belief

There is another, perhaps more fundamental reason to embrace the threshold approach. Ordinarily, it is profoundly disrespectful to harm others as a means to our own ends. Every human being starts out with a moral right not to be treated as an opportunity to be exploited or as an obstacle to be eliminated. It is in part for this reason that, ordinarily, the most serious wrong we can commit is to intentionally

---

[40] For criticism of threshold views, see Frank Jackson & Michael Smith, "Absolutist Moral Theories and Uncertainty" (2006) 103 Journal of Philosophy 267. For an effective response, see Ron Aboodi, Adi Borer, & David Enoch, "Deontology, Individualism, and Uncertainty: A Reply to Jackson and Smith" (2008) 105 Journal of Philosophy 259.

kill another person, either to obtain a benefit or to avoid harm. Such killings inflict the greatest possible harm with the greatest possible disrespect.

Importantly, reasonable belief that a person is morally liable to intentional killing partly negates the disrespect that ordinarily attends intentional killing. In such cases, we examine the individual's voluntary conduct and reasonably conclude that he has voluntarily forfeited his moral right not to be harmed as a means. We believe that our treatment does not disrespect the individual but rather responds appropriately to his or her own voluntary choices. Moreover, our belief is formed reasonably, after due consideration of available evidence, rather than negligently, reflecting careless disregard for the individual's moral status.

Imagine for a moment that a soldier could address targeted individuals and defend each targeting decision to each targeted individual. On the threshold approach, a soldier could offer the following defense:

> I am about to intentionally kill you. I reasonably believe that you are liable to be killed, and that, if I kill you, I will prevent you from killing my fellow soldiers or civilians. Admittedly, I don't know for sure. But if I don't take a chance of possibly wrongfully killing you, then I will take a greater chance of allowing others to be wrongfully killed.

On the deontic expectabilist approach, often a soldier could only offer the following explanation:

> I am about to intentionally kill you. I do not believe that you are liable to be killed. Indeed, the evidence suggests that you are probably not liable. Nor do I believe that by killing you I will prevent others from being killed. Indeed, I will probably save no one. If I routinely kill people like you in situations like this, then most of the people I kill will be innocent. However, over time the innocent people that I save will substantially outnumber the innocent people that I kill.

The first defense seems much more compelling than the second. Ordinarily, we cannot justify or excuse wrongs committed against one person solely in terms of the aggregate consequences of acting similarly in apparently similar situations. Our treatment of each person should be justifiable to that person, based on our reasonable beliefs about his liability to be harmed and the likely consequences of not harming him.

Moreover, ordinarily we should not adopt a practice that violates rights more often than it justifiably infringes rights simply because some infringements will prove justified by a substantial margin. If killing is more likely to prove objectively unjustified than objectively justified, then ordinarily such killing cannot be redeemed by the average or total consequences of routinely killing in similar circumstances.

It is only in imaginary cases that killing someone who is probably innocent will prevent far greater expected harm to others, and that killing many such people will probably prevent far greater actual harm to others. The law can safely ignore such imaginary cases. As we shall see, reasonable belief that a person is liable is not always sufficient for respectful treatment but in all real cases it is necessary.

There is another sense in which applying the reasonable belief threshold is more respectful to civilians in mixed battle spaces. In general, each of us can easily avoid appearing *very* threatening to others. However, many civilians will find it very difficult to avoid appearing *somewhat* threatening to others. This is particularly true where combatants deliberately disguise themselves as civilians. Often, simply being a young man or wearing heavy clothing may be enough to appear slightly threatening. To permit attackers to target such civilians, as the expectabilist approach often will, denies such civilians an important measure of control over their fates. Conversely, the threshold approach guarantees each civilian substantial control over his or her own "epistemic liability."

Relatedly, while civilians generally have some degree of control over the epistemic *probability* that they pose a threat, they often have very limited control over the *gravity* of the threat that they may appear to pose. Certainly, the hypothetical Iraqi man on the overpass has *no* control over how many Marines are in the convoy. To rest the permissibility of targeting him on factors over which he has no control, as the expectabilist approach would, seems unjust. In contrast, the reasonable belief threshold ensures that attackers may only target individuals who appear likely to pose a threat, generally bracketing the gravity of the threat they appear to pose (more on this shortly). In this way, the reasonable belief threshold shows a measure of respect for the voluntary choices of individuals, even in the fog of war.

The Hybrid Approach

We have examined two approaches to killing under uncertainty. On the deontic expectabilist approach, a soldier may intentionally kill a person if, given the probability that the individual is a combatant and the threat the individual would pose if she is a combatant, killing her will prevent substantially greater expectable harm to others. On the threshold approach, except in rare cases, a soldier may intentionally kill a person only if the soldier reasonably believes that the individual is a combatant.

The virtues of each approach mirror the vices of the other. The virtue of the expectabilist approach is that the required level of certainty varies with the possible outcomes; the vice of the expectabilist approach is that it too readily endorses killing individuals who are probably, very likely, or almost certainly civilians. The virtue of the threshold approach is that it rejects killing individuals who are probably civilians except in rare cases; the vice of the threshold approach is that it too readily endorses killing individuals who are probably combatants even if the expected costs of doing so outweigh the expected benefits. For example, if a person is probably a combatant but poses no immediate threat to others, then it seems impermissible to take a substantial risk of erroneously killing a civilian for a small chance of preventing harm to others in the future.

It seems, then, that the most promising view is that the required level of certainty varies along deontic expectabilist lines but only above the reasonable belief threshold. On this hybrid approach, except in rare cases, intentionally killing a person is permissible if and only if the actor reasonably believes that the individual is morally liable to be killed *and* that killing the individual will prevent substantially greater expected harm to others. It is wrong to act on a level of certainty less than reasonable belief because it is profoundly disrespectful to intentionally kill someone when the balance of reasons indicates that he is not liable to be intentionally killed. It is wrong to act on a level of certainty lower than that required by the deontic expectabilist approach because over the course of your conflict the total harm that you will inflict will probably not prove justified by the total harm that you prevent.

Soldiers who follow this hybrid approach will both respect each individual they intentionally kill and prevent substantially greater harm than they inflict over the course of their conflict. In turn, civilians receive greater protection from erroneous targeting under the hybrid approach than under either the threshold approach or the expectabilist approach taken alone. Nor could civilians receive any greater protection from erroneous targeting by one party to the conflict without unfairly reducing the protection others receive from actions by the opposing party. Soldiers who act on a higher level of certainty than required by the deontic expectabilist approach will probably allow substantially greater harm than they will inflict over the course of their conflict. This is more than respect for the rights of targeted individuals demands.

We saw that reasonable belief that a person is morally liable to intentional killing negates the special disrespect that ordinarily attends intentional killing. The harm remains the same, but the degree of disrespect is reduced. For this reason, intentionally killing an innocent person whom you reasonably believe is liable to intentional killing is morally comparable to unintentionally killing an innocent person whom you know is innocent. Since it is permissible to unintentionally kill an innocent person to prevent substantially greater harm to others, it is permissible to risk unintentionally killing an innocent person to prevent substantially greater risk to others, that is, either a comparable risk of substantially greater harm or a substantially greater risk of comparable harm. In other words, it is permissible to risk unintentionally killing an innocent person to prevent substantially greater expected harm to others. It follows that it is permissible to intentionally kill someone whom you reasonably believe is liable in order to prevent substantially greater expected harm to others.

On the hybrid approach, you respect each individual by reasonably believing, first, that killing them is objectively justified and, second, that killing them is indirectly justified by a rule adherence to which is itself justified. By following this rule, the total wrongdoing that you erroneously commit over the course of your conflict will be morally justified by the substantially greater harm that you deliberately prevent. Here, as elsewhere, rule-consequentialist considerations can add to but cannot subtract from deontic constraints. Put another way, the hybrid approach permits soldiers to maximize expected moral value but not at the expense of respect for the individual targeted.

If they could defend their targeting decision to a targeted individual, soldiers following the hybrid approach could say something like the following:

> I am about to intentionally kill you. I reasonably believe that you are a combatant. Admittedly, I do not know for sure. But if I don't take a chance of possibly wrongfully killing you, then I will take a greater chance of allowing substantially greater wrongful harm to others. I realize that I am taking a risk with your life. However, the risk that you are a civilian is outweighed by a substantially greater risk that you will kill several of my fellow soldiers and civilians.

This defense, I submit, is one that the targeted individual could not reasonably reject. Since the hybrid approach combines a fixed deontic (reasonable belief) constraint with a variable deontically weighted (deontic expectabilist) constraint, we can call the hybrid approach to targeting in armed conflict *deontological targeting*.

Degrees of Belief

There is an alternative view, recently proposed by Seth Lazar, according to which the objective wrongfulness of killing an innocent person varies with the killer's subjective degree of belief that the person is innocent.[41] The more strongly one believes that a person is innocent the worse it will be to kill her if she is in fact innocent. As on the threshold view, killing an innocent person while subjectively believing that she is probably innocent is objectively worse than killing an innocent person while subjectively believing that she is probably liable to be killed. Accordingly, it will take more to justify killing someone whom you think is probably innocent than to justify killing someone whom you think is probably liable to be killed. Importantly, on Lazar's view, the relationship between objective wrongfulness and subjective belief is linear, or at least continuous, with no special importance attached to believing that a person is probably liable or probably not liable. Readers who remain skeptical of the reasonable belief threshold may therefore find Lazar's view attractive.

Lazar rests the moral importance of subjective degrees of belief on multiple grounds, but I will discuss only the grounds that I find most compelling. Lazar argues that the more strongly one believes that a person is innocent, the more disrespectful it would be to kill her despite the risk that she may be innocent. The more presumptively disrespectful an action, the more compelling a justification the action requires. Applying this view to armed conflict, the more strongly you believe that a person is a civilian, the more soldiers or civilians must be vulnerable to possible attack before you may kill the individual.

---

[41] "In Dubious Battle."

To evaluate Lazar's view, let us start with cases in which a soldier targets a person whom the soldier reasonably believes is a combatant. Certainly, the soldier would disrespect the individual if the soldier undervalues the individual's life relative to the lives the soldier seeks to protect. In addition, the soldier would disrespect the individual if the soldier ignores the moral asymmetry between doing and allowing harm. But it is hard to see any additional disrespect involved in targeting a person after her rights and welfare are given due consideration. It seems that generally a soldier treats a targeted individual respectfully if and only if she reasonably believes that the individual is a combatant and that killing the individual will prevent substantially greater expected harm to others. Above the reasonable belief threshold, Lazar's view seems on inspection to reduce to deontic expectabilism.

Now let us consider cases in which a soldier targets a person whom the soldier reasonably believes is a civilian but in which many others are vulnerable to attack. In these cases, it is indeed even harder to justify targeting a person who is almost certainly a civilian than to justify targeting a person who is probably or very likely a civilian. However, it is disrespectful to target a person whom one reasonably believes is a civilian if and only if doing so will not prevent far greater expected harm to others. As before, respectful treatment only requires due consideration of a person's rights and wellbeing. So below the reasonable belief threshold, Lazar's view seems on inspection to reduce to restrictive expectabilism.

Since the hybrid approach operates like deontic expectabilism above the reasonable belief threshold and operates like restrictive expectabilism below the reasonable belief threshold, it follows that soldiers who follow the hybrid approach will not disrespect the individuals they target. The hybrid approach captures what is best in Lazar's approach while leaving behind what seems dubious.

Presuming Civilian Status

To this point we have focused on when it is epistemically permissible for soldiers to intentionally kill other people given the information before them. We have left open the vitally important questions of when soldiers must seek additional information and how they should evaluate such additional information as it comes in.

Certainly, we should not accept a view on which soldiers who have just enough evidence to favor lethal action have no duty to seek additional evidence that might tip the balance in favor of restraint. In Chapter 7, I will argue that soldiers must take additional precautions in attack to avoid or reduce harm to civilians unless the marginal risks of doing so, to themselves or to their civilians, are substantially greater than the marginal risks of not doing so, for the civilians in harm's way. The duty to seek additional information regarding a person's civilian or combatant status is a special case of this general precautionary principle.

Of more immediate concern is the following problem. On a broadly Bayesian view, the rational weight of new information cannot be assessed except from the point of view of a person seeking to update his or her prior subjective estimate of the likelihood of an existing fact or future event in light of that new information. On this view, two soldiers with different prior estimates of the likelihood that a person is a combatant who rationally update their priors in light of the same new information will often rationally arrive at different updated estimates. Yet it seems unacceptable that the epistemic permissibility of intentionally killing another person could vary not with the available evidence but with the rationally arbitrary priors of the soldier pulling the trigger. It is therefore imperative either to show that the Bayesian view does not apply in the moral context or that soldiers should be morally or legally required to start from a uniform prior estimate. In this section I attempt the latter task.

One possibility is that soldiers should assume that the likelihood that a person is a combatant corresponds to the ratio of combatants to civilians in a well-constructed reference class. For example, if combatants make up 20% of the young men in a given town, then soldiers should first estimate that any given young man in that town is 20% likely to be a combatant and should update that prior estimate with new information as it comes in. Only if their updated estimate satisfies both the reasonable belief threshold and the deontic expectabilist standard may the soldiers use lethal force. This approach may seem attractive. Among other things, it mirrors how soldiers likely respond to different combat environments. The more combatants operate in a given area, the more alert soldiers will stay and the more closely they will inspect individual behavior for signs of hostile intent.

Unfortunately, this approach suffers from an obvious flaw. If a substantial majority of young men in a given area are combatants (for example, following a partial evacuation or a major incursion), then in many cases on this approach it would be epistemically permissible to kill a young man based solely on his age and gender, irrespective of his individual behavior. Indeed, if the prior estimate is sufficiently high, then it could be epistemically permissible to kill a young man even if all new information based on his individual behavior tends to show that the young man is a civilian. This seems both wrong and dangerous, especially considering that human beings tend to seek, interpret, and value information in ways that confirm their preexisting beliefs, while discounting contrary evidence.

An alternative view is that soldiers should assume that each individual is a civilian unless new information shows otherwise. In other words, soldiers should start with a prior estimate that each individual is 100% likely to be a civilian and update that prior estimate in light of new information. Only if their updated estimate satisfies both the reasonable belief threshold and the deontic expectabilist standard may the soldiers use lethal force. This is the view that I propose.

On this view, attackers must presume that persons are civilians unless their conduct gives attackers decisive reason to believe that they are combatants. In contrast, attackers may not presume that persons are combatants based on characteristics that they cannot change (such as age, race, or ethnicity) or that they may not be required to change on pain of death (such as religion). Just as we cannot *actually* lose our right not be killed involuntarily, we should not *effectively* lose our right not be killed involuntarily. Since we all act based on the evidence available to us, if the epistemic permissibility of intentionally killing us is out of our control, then it would be little comfort that the objective permissibility of intentionally killing us remains in our control.

This view is more demanding but also more attractive. First, it ensures a uniform level of protection for all civilians that does not depend on the presence or movements of combatants, almost always factors beyond the control of civilians. Second, it ensures that the epistemic permissibility of killing, like the objective permissibility of killing, depends to the greatest extent possible on the voluntary choices of each individual rather than on his or her membership in a social group or demographic category. Third, it may partially offset cognitive biases and heuristics that may distort a soldier's reasoning in irregular armed conflicts, frequently waged among foreign and hostile civilian populations. Finally, it gives substance to the important but contested principle that persons enjoy a legal presumption of civilian status that must be rebutted before they may be targeted.[42] For all these reasons, we should prefer this latter approach, which we may refer to as the *civilian presumption* view.

One way to express the civilian presumption view would be to say that soldiers should adopt a working hypothesis that every person they encounter is a civilian not directly participating in hostilities. Soldiers should abandon that hypothesis only if they acquire new evidence that is incompatible with that hypothesis or that makes the opposite hypothesis (that the person is a combatant or directly participating in hostilities) more reasonable.

Importantly, soldiers must carefully measure the true evidentiary weight of new information and resist cognitive heuristics and biases. For example, suppose that an occupying force experiences a series of suicide bombings by individuals concealing explosives beneath flowing robes. This information is quite vivid and available for easy recall. An occupying soldier may incorrectly think that the fact that a person is wearing flowing robes is strong evidence that they are a suicide bomber, since they seem representative of the population of suicide bombers. In doing so, the soldier would neglect the base rates of suicide bombers, persons wearing flowing robes, and total persons.

To illustrate the point, suppose there are 100 potential suicide bombers, 50 of whom wear flowing robes. These numbers tell us very little about the probability that a person wearing flowing robes is a suicide bomber. If one million people wear flowing robes in a population of 10 million, then the probability (P) that a person wearing flowing robes (R) is a suicide bomber (S) is 0.005%:

$$P(S \mid R) = P(R \mid S) \times P(S) / P(R)$$
$$P(S \mid R) = (1 / 2) \times (100 / 10,000,000) / (1,000,000 / 10,000,000)$$
$$= 0.00005$$

---

[42] Protocol I art 50; ICRC, *Interpretive Guidance*, 75–6. But see US Dept of Defense, *Law of War Manual*, 5.5.3.2.

Accordingly, the fact that someone is wearing flowing robes is very weak evidence that they are a suicide bomber, and would not do much to rebut the presumption of civilian protection. Commanders should instruct soldiers not to overvalue such salient but unreliable information.

Finally, attackers may not presume that persons are civilians but then seek and consider only information that might rebut that presumption. Instead, attackers must seek and consider all potentially relevant information available to them, both information that might confirm that the individuals are civilians and information that might indicate that the individuals are in fact combatants. As Protocol I states, attackers must

do everything feasible to verify that the objectives to be attacked are *neither* civilians *nor* civilian objects and are *not* subject to special protection but *are* military objectives ... and that it is *not* prohibited ... to attack them ....[43]

Attackers who consciously disregard or negligently fail to consider available information that indicates that their targets are civilian violate their precautionary obligations.

Deontological Targeting in Action

Imagine that you are remotely operating an unmanned aerial vehicle (UAV or "drone") and see several armed men on your monitor. The men's weapons, dress, and movements provide you with strong reasons to believe that they are insurgents but also with strong reasons to believe that they are civilians armed and organized to defend themselves and their community from insurgent attacks. Suppose that, even if the men are combatants, they pose no immediate threat to anyone and it is highly unlikely that they will kill a substantial number of soldiers or civilians before they are captured or killed in a future engagement.

In such a scenario, it would be wrong to kill the men even if your reasons to believe that they are opposing combatants are as strong, or slightly stronger, than your reasons to believe that they are civilians. As we have seen, soldiers who reasonably believe that a person is a combatant are not free to fire at will. Since a soldier's reasons not to erroneously kill a civilian are substantially stronger than her reasons not to allow a fellow soldier to be killed, generally a soldier may kill a person only if her reasons to believe that person is a combatant are considerably stronger than her reasons to believe that person is a civilian.

For example, if killing a civilian is at least twice as bad as allowing a fellow soldier to be killed, then a soldier may intentionally kill a person only if her reasons to believe that person is a combatant who will otherwise kill two soldiers are at least as strong as her reasons to believe that person is a civilian (50% evidential probability);

---

[43] Protocol I art 57(2)(a)(i) (emphasis added).

or if her reasons to believe that person is a combatant who will otherwise kill one soldier are at least twice as strong as her reasons to believe that person is a civilian (66% evidential probability); or if she has conclusive reason to believe that person is a combatant (100% evidential probability), even if that person poses no threat. Finally, as we have seen, it is practically never permissible for a soldier to kill a person if her reasons to believe that the individual is a civilian are stronger than her reasons to believe that person is a combatant.

What, then, should you do? If possible, you should track the men's movements and attack them only if new information provides you with conclusive reason to believe that they are combatants; with much stronger reason to believe that they pose an immediate threat to a comparable number of soldiers or civilians than reason to believe that they pose no such threat; or with decisive reason to believe that they pose an immediate threat to a substantially greater number of soldiers or civilians. Put another way, you should kill the men only if you are *reasonably convinced* that they are combatants; if you are *reasonably confident* that they are about to attack a comparable number of soldiers or civilians; or if you *reasonably believe* that they are about to attack a substantially greater number of soldiers or civilians. However, if such time and resources cannot be spared to obtain additional information and reduce the risk of mistakenly killing civilians, then you must disengage and accept the risk of mistakenly sparing combatants. These principles should guide all targeted killing operations conducted from relative safety, including through the use of drones.

Implementation

Let us distill the complex moral principles defended in the previous sections into new interpretations of existing legal rules that armed forces can incorporate into their targeting practices as well as model rules of engagement that soldiers can be trained to follow even under fire.

First, in 2003 the International Criminal Tribunal for the Former Yugoslavia (ICTY) articulated the following principle:

> **(I) A person shall not be made the object of attack when it is not reasonable to believe, in the circumstances of the person contemplating the attack, including the information available to the latter, that the potential target is a combatant.**[44]

Unfortunately, the Trial Chamber did not explain the legal basis of its position in treaty or custom and its actual holding was more limited. Nevertheless, states should embrace this dictum as legally valid, thereby incorporating the reasonable belief threshold into customary international law.

---

[44] *Prosecutor v Galić* (Judgment) IT-98-29-T (Dec 5, 2003), para 50 (bold added).

Second, Protocol I currently provides that, "[i]n case of doubt whether a person is a civilian, that person shall be considered to be a civilian." [45] To clarify the degree of doubt sufficient to preclude lawful attack, states and international courts should interpret this provision as follows:

> **(II) In case of doubt whether a person is a civilian, that person shall be considered to be a civilian unless there is decisive evidence that she is a combatant and the risk of sparing her is substantially greater than the risk that she is a civilian.**

Finally, both treaty and custom currently provides that "an attack shall be cancelled or suspended if it becomes apparent that the objective is not a military one or is subject to special protection." [46] To make it clear that subjective certainty that a target is civilian is not necessary to preclude lawful attack, this rule should be interpreted as follows:

> **(III) An attack shall be cancelled or suspended if decisive evidence becomes available that the objective is not a military one or is subject to special protection.**

These relatively modest efforts would give greater guidance to soldiers and greater protection to civilians.

Of course, we cannot expect soldiers under fire to calculate the expected moral value of every targeting decision. Instead, military commanders should issue Rules of Engagement (ROE), written in ordinary language, which soldiers can be trained to apply in combat. As a first cut, consider the following ROE:

Don't shoot anyone unless:

(i)   you believe that he poses an immediate threat to several members of your unit or to several civilians;

(ii) you are very confident that he poses an immediate threat to yourself, to another member of your unit, or to a civilian; or

(ii) you are absolutely convinced that he is a combatant, even though he poses no immediate threat to anyone.

Based on the information available to you, how sure are you that the possible target is a lawful target?

If you are absolutely convinced, then engage.

If you are very confident but not absolutely convinced, then engage only if he appears to pose an immediate threat to yourself, to another member of your unit, or to a civilian.

If you are not very confident, then only engage if he appears to pose an immediate threat to several members of your unit or to several civilians.

---

[45] Protocol I art 50 (emphasis added).

[46] Protocol I art 57(2)(b) (emphasis added); ICRC, *Customary IHL Study*, 60.

In the vast majority of ground operations, individual soldiers will make better decisions by following this ROE than by attempting to calculate the expected moral value of each targeting decision. Soldiers will better conform to their moral obligations indirectly—by following the ROE—than directly—by attempting to apply deep moral principles under adverse conditions. In contrast, the teams of military and intelligence personnel who plan and carry out drone strikes generally have the time, resources, personal safety, and direct access to legal advisors needed to make more precise judgments.

In some cases, mission-specific ROE permitting lethal action with a lower level of certainty may be appropriate. For example, soldiers guarding military barracks, civilian markets, or other densely populated locations from potential terrorist or insurgent attacks may require detailed ROE for dealing with approaching vehicles and individuals. These ROE may require giving visual and verbal warnings or creating physical obstacles and should give detailed escalation-of-force instructions (for example, requiring warning shots first, then shooting car tires or engines, before finally targeting individuals). In addition, "kill or capture" operations specifically targeting insurgent leaders may operate with more permissive ROE since killing such leaders will often prevent the opposing force from killing many soldiers or civilians.

The United States and its allies have issued ROE that substantially overlap with the ROE we proposed. For example, ROE issued to coalition forces in Iraq in 2005 provide that

Positive Identification (PID) is required prior to engagement. PID is a reasonable certainty that the proposed target is a legitimate military target.[47]

It is not clear, however, whether under current US ROE "a reasonable certainty" refers to a fixed, moderately high level of certainty or to whatever level of certainty soldiers deem reasonable under the circumstances.[48] On one hand, a fixed standard of "reasonable certainty" may prove too restrictive when the stakes are very high, too permissive when the stakes are very low, and too vague standing alone. On the other hand, a variable standard of certainty that does not identify the relevant variables provides poor guidance to soldiers. In contrast, my proposed ROE offers soldiers sound guidance in the vast majority of situations they will confront, without overwhelming soldiers with rules that are too fine-grained to apply under pressure.

Unfortunately, the US military has at times permitted soldiers to intentionally kill individuals without positively identifying them as legitimate targets, for

---

[47] Gary D Solis, *The Law of Armed Conflict* (CUP 2010) 516 (quoting MNC-I ROE Card issued to coalition forces in Iraq).

[48] For concerns that "a reasonable certainty" refers to a fixed, very high level of certainty, see Merriam, "Affirmative Target Identification."

example in "free-fire zones" from which civilians have been warned to leave as well as in buildings declared "hostile" prior to attack. Most dramatically, on November 19, 2005, US Marines killed twenty-four civilians in Haditha, Iraq, reportedly based on instructions by their platoon commander that once a dwelling is declared hostile they need not positively identify the individuals inside as combatants before using deadly force against them.[49] No morally sound ROE would permit such a practice.

Importantly, the proposed ROE is intended to guide—not replace—human judgment. That is why, like all ROE, the rule proposed must be incorporated into Situational Training Exercises in which soldiers apply their ROE in scores of realistic combat simulations. In addition, like all ROE, this rule can form the basis of real and hypothetical case studies through which soldiers learn to recognize scenarios in which the use of force is, or is not, appropriate. These exercises will clarify linguistic ambiguities in the wording of the ROE and convert rules into reflexes. Soldiers often must rely on pattern recognition as much as rule application, refined instinct as much as careful calculation. So long as their training is grounded in sound legal and moral norms, soldiers can trust themselves to make legally and morally sound decisions under fire.

Conclusion

Soldiers should presume that the individuals they confront are civilians unless new information provides them with decisive reasons to believe that these individuals are combatants and that killing these individuals will prevent substantially greater expectable harm to others. This view is quite demanding, and places significant constraints on the conduct of irregular armed conflicts waged in mixed battle spaces. This is a virtue of the view. It is partly because such conflicts are so difficult to wage in a morally and legally defensible manner that we should avoid such conflicts whenever possible.

---

[49] Associated Press, "Marine Accepts Plea Deal in Iraqi Civilian Deaths," Newsday, January 24, 2012, http://www.newsday.com/news/world/marine-accepts-plea-deal-in-iraqi-civilian-deaths-1.3474532.

6

Discrimination

Indiscriminate attacks—including attacks using highly inaccurate weapons—are prohibited by both conventional and customary international law.[1] The V2 rockets employed by German forces toward the end of World War II are often cited as the paradigm case of unlawfully indiscriminate weapons. In recent years, international lawyers have argued that anti-personnel landmines, SCUD missiles, cluster munitions, white phosphorous, and Katyusha rockets are also unlawfully indiscriminate.[2] Unfortunately, without a general account of what makes an inaccurate weapon unlawfully indiscriminate, such weapon-specific arguments remain inconclusive.

We might imagine that there are two questions here. First, how inaccurate must a weapon be before it should be considered unlawfully indiscriminate? Second, what is the moral justification of the legal prohibition of indiscriminate weapons? In fact, the first question cannot be answered independently of the second. When the content of a legal norm cannot be fixed by reference to positive legal materials alone, we should interpret that legal norm in its morally best light, thereby providing reliable guidance to combatants and meaningful protection to civilians. Since positive legal materials do not identify a required level of accuracy, we should consider a weapon unlawfully indiscriminate if its inaccuracy renders its use morally impermissible.

In this chapter, I explore two possible justifications for the legal prohibition on the use of indiscriminate weapons. The prohibition may be justified instrumentally, as an indirect strategy of implementing more fundamental prohibitions on inflicting intentional, unnecessary, and disproportionate harm on civilians. However, I argue that it is intrinsically morally wrong to use weapons that, either by their nature or by their use, are more likely to strike civilians or civilian objects than to strike combatants or military objectives. To interpret the law in its morally best light, we should consider the use of such weapons unlawfully indiscriminate.

---

[1] Protocol Additional to the Geneva Conventions of August 12, 1949, and relating to the Protection of Victims of International Armed Conflicts (Protocol I) (adopted June 8, 1977, entered into force December 7, 1978) 1125 UNTS 3, art 51(4); ICRC, *Customary International Humanitarian Law*, vol 1 (CUP 2009) 40.

[2] ICRC, *Customary IHL Study*, 249–50.

Law and Morality at War. First Edition. Adil Haque. © Adil Haque 2017. Published 2017 by Oxford University Press

Varieties of Indiscriminate Attack

Before examining the moral basis of the legal prohibition of indiscriminate weapons, we should first understand the nature of the legal prohibition itself. Indiscriminate attacks are

(a) those which are not directed at a specific military objective;
(b) those which employ a method or means of combat which cannot be directed at a specific military objective; or
(c) those which employ a method or means of combat the effects of which cannot be limited as required by international humanitarian law;

and consequently, in each such case, are of a nature to strike military objectives and civilians or civilian objects without distinction.[3]

The first and third kinds of indiscriminate attack are morally impermissible for obvious reasons. Attacks that are not directed at a specific military objective include firing blindly into enemy territory and randomly dropping bombs over enemy territory after hitting or missing the original target.[4] Such attacks violate the basic moral principle that soldiers must both *not try* to kill civilians and *try not* to kill civilians.[5] Similarly, methods (tactics) or means (weapons) of combat—such as biological weapons—whose effects cannot be technologically controlled cannot be ethically unleashed. There is no way to prevent such weapons and tactics from killing unnecessarily or disproportionately.[6]

It is only the second kind of indiscriminate attack—one that uses a tactic or weapon that cannot be directed at a specific military objective—that raises serious questions. For one thing, the text of the prohibition has not been and should not be read literally. Strictly speaking, a weapon *cannot* be directed at a specific military objective only if there is *nothing* that one can do to increase the likelihood that the weapon will strike that objective. If aiming the weapon makes it more likely to strike its intended target than, say, an equidistant point in the opposite direction, then in a limited sense it can be directed at a specific military target. Since such a narrow construction yields absurd results and defeats the purpose of the prohibition, a broader construction is required.

Generally speaking, a weapon or tactic is indiscriminate if it cannot be *accurately* or *precisely* directed at a specific military objective. For its part, the United Kingdom interprets the prohibition to bar the use of weapons "that lack[] the precision to

---

[3] ICRC, *Customary IHL Study* 40; Protocol I art 51(4) ("... as required by this Protocol").
[4] See Yoram Dinstein, *The Conduct of Hostilities under the Law of International Armed Conflict* (CUP 2010) 127–8.
[5] Michael Walzer, *Just and Unjust Wars* (Basic Books 2nd edn 1977) 155–6.
[6] Michael N Schmitt, "The Principle of Discrimination in 21st Century Warfare" (1999) 2 Yale Human Rights and Development Law Journal 143, 147.

ensure a reasonable probability that the targets under attack will be hit."[7] Similarly, the ICRC interprets the prohibition to bar "long-range missiles which cannot be aimed exactly at the objective."[8] This of course raises the question with which we began: how inaccurate does a weapon have to be before it becomes unlawfully indiscriminate? The law does not say.

In addition, article 51(5) of Protocol I goes on to stipulate that "the following types of attacks are to be considered as indiscriminate:

(a) an attack by bombardment by any methods or means which treats as a single military objective a number of clearly separated and distinct military objectives located in a city, town, village or other area containing a similar concentration of civilians or civilian objects;

and

(b) an attack which may be expected to cause incidental loss of civilian life, injury to civilians, damage to civilian objects, or a combination thereof, which would be excessive in relation to the concrete and direct military advantage anticipated.[9]

The prohibition on attacks which treat *clearly separated* and *distinct* military objectives as a single military objective—most notably through "area bombing"—seems like a logical extension of the prohibition on attacks which are *not* directed at a *specific* military objective. It seems natural to consider such attacks indiscriminate and to subject them to the general prohibition on indiscriminate attacks.

In contrast, the prohibition on attacks which may be expected to cause excessive incidental harm to civilians clearly reflects the proportionality principle. On most views, the proportionality principle is a fundamental principle of international humanitarian law. Yet, under Protocol I, disproportionate attacks are not subject to an independent prohibition. Instead, Protocol I stipulates that disproportionate attacks are to be considered indiscriminate and are prohibited on that basis.[10] Scholars have searched for a compelling rationale for this approach, but with little success.

Importantly, attacks that satisfy discrimination may violate proportionality. An attack might direct accurate means and methods of combat with limited effects at a specific military objective yet still might be expected to cause excessive harm to civilians. Conversely, attacks that violate discrimination do not necessarily violate proportionality. The proportionality principle clearly applies where an attacker *both*

[7] UK Ministry of Defense, *Law of Armed Conflict Manual* (OUP 2005) 5.23.3.
[8] ICRC, Commentary on the Additional Protocols of 8 June 1977 to the Geneva Conventions of 12 August 1949 (ICRC/Martinus Nijhoff 1987) 621 ("the V2 rockets used at the end of the Second World War are an example of this").
[9] Protocol I art 51(5).
[10] The proportionality principle reappears in article 57, under the heading of precautions in attack. Protocol I arts 57(2)(a)(iii) and 57(2)(b).

expects to cause harm to civilians *and* anticipates obtaining a military advantage. In contrast, many attacks that use indiscriminate weapons will *either* cause harm to civilians *or* obtain a military advantage. While the proportionality principle clearly applies to the use of cluster munitions that will strike both civilians and combatants, it does not clearly apply to the use of inaccurate rockets that will strike either civilians or combatants but not both. Finally, attacks that satisfy proportionality may violate discrimination. Most obviously, an attacker who treats clearly separated and distinct military objectives as a single military objective violates discrimination even if the military advantage that he reasonably anticipates outweighs the civilian losses that he reasonably expects.[11]

In moral theory, McMahan suggests that some indiscriminate attacks are morally permissible if their expected harms are proportionate to their expected benefits. McMahan presents the following hypothetical cases, from which I have removed some confounding variables:

(1) Suppose a pilot in a just war sees roughly 100 people concentrated in an open area. He sees that [some are] clearly [] civilian[s] but that the others are uniformed unjust combatants. . . . The pilot's only weapon is a bomb. If he drops it, it will kill all 100 . . . .

(2) Next suppose that [the pilot] circles back to drop his bomb, only to discover that the combatants have put [] uniform[s] on the civilian[s], so that [the former] cannot be distinguished from the[] [latter] . . .[12]

In 1, the pilot targets the combatants while foreseeing that the civilians will be collaterally killed. In contrast, "[i]n 2, . . . the agents intend to kill *each* of the 100." Rather than targeting specific military objectives, the pilot targets a group of individuals containing both civilians and combatants. However, McMahan argues that the pilot does not intend to kill the civilians as a causally necessary means of achieving his aims. The pilot neither seeks to benefit from their presence nor to prevent their presence from making others worse off. McMahan concludes that the attacks in 1 and 2 are morally on a par.

I disagree. It is true that, in one sense, the pilot in 2 *intends* only to kill the combatants. It also true that the pilot *plans* to kill the civilians. After all, the pilot plans to kill the combatants *by* killing each of the 100 individuals, including the civilians. To see this, consider that if some individuals were to survive a first bomb then the

---

[11] But see Dinstein, *Conduct of Hostilities*, 130 (inferring that "an attack giving rise to proportionate collateral damage can never be regarded as indiscriminate"). cf ICRC, *Protocol I Commentary* para 1979 (stating that "this theory is manifestly incorrect" and that an attack may be indiscriminate but not disproportionate).

[12] Jeff McMahan, "Who Is Morally Liable to Be Killed in War" (2011) 71 Analysis 544, 557–8. In the original example, McMahan stipulates ninety-nine combatants and one civilian but then asserts that his point would go through even if the numbers were reversed.

pilot, not knowing if they are civilians or combatants, will presumably drop more bombs until all are killed. Put another way, the pilot intends to involve the civilians in his plan for killing the combatants, foreseeing that the civilians will be killed. As Quinn argues, intentionally involving others in one's plans, foreseeing that they will be harmed, is morally closer to intentionally harming them than to unintentionally harming them as a side effect.[13] For this reason, despite apparent similarities, the attack in 2 is much harder to justify than the attack in 1.

Intention, Necessity, and Proportionality

The use of inaccurate weapons might be morally impermissible for at least three reasons. First, the attacking force may in fact *intend* to kill, harm, or terrorize civilians through the use of inaccurate weapons. Second, the use of such weapons may be *unnecessary* if the party using the weapon could have used more accurate weapons instead. Third, the use of such weapons may be *disproportionate*, if they may be expected to cause excessive incidental harm to civilians.

Indeed, most actual uses of inaccurate weapons inflict or risk inflicting intentional, unnecessary, or disproportionate harm on civilians and would be morally impermissible on those grounds. It is worth noting, however, that each concept (intent, necessity, and proportionality) contains certain ambiguities that would need to be resolved before they could be confidently applied in many cases.

For example, attacking forces clearly intend to harm civilians when they use inaccurate weapons *in order* to harm civilians, particularly when their "primary purpose . . . is to spread terror."[14] However, attacking forces might also have a disjunctive intention, to strike either specific military targets or nearby civilians, and use inaccurate weapons because they are indifferent between the two outcomes. In addition, attacking forces may use inaccurate weapons *in order* to strike specific military targets only *because*, or *on the condition* that, even if their weapons miss their military targets they will harm and terrorize civilians, which the attacking force takes to offset the military cost of the attack. In the latter cases, the attacking force does not consider the possibility of harming civilians as an affirmative reason to launch the attack, but rather as a "defeater of a defeater" which offsets reasons against launching the attack (such as expenditure of resources).[15] One might argue that the moral and legal prohibitions on intentionally attacking civilians do not apply to the latter cases. However, I believe that these prohibitions apply to these latter cases because in these cases attackers make opportunistic use of the presence of civilians to offset the potential opportunity costs of their attacks. On my view,

---

[13] See Warren Quinn, "Actions, Intentions, and Consequences: The Doctrine of Double Effect" (1989) 18 Philosophy & Public Affairs 334.

[14] Protocol I art 51(2).

[15] cf FM Kamm, *Intricate Ethics* ch 4 (OUP 2007).

attacks that make opportunistic use of the presence of civilians are morally and legally comparable to attacks that target civilians.

It seems clearly true that, other things equal, it is morally impermissible to use a less accurate weapon rather than a more accurate weapon when the former will place civilians at greater risk than the latter. Of course, other things are not always equal. For one thing, the use of more accurate weapons may place attacking forces at greater risk. For example, the alternative to using cluster munitions to render an area inaccessible to opposing forces may be to clear and hold that area with one's own ground forces. Yet the use of less accurate weapons cannot always be justified by reference to the risks to one's own forces of using more accurate weapons. As I argue in Chapter 7, combatants ought to use more discriminating means and methods of combat unless doing so will increase the marginal risk to those combatants to a substantially greater degree than using less discriminating means or methods would increase the marginal risk to civilians. Since I address these issues at length there I will not do so here.

Finally, some attacking forces may not have more accurate weapons that can achieve the desired effect. For example, organized armed groups that use primitive rockets against advanced militaries often do not have more accurate weapons that deliver comparable explosive payloads. However, as we shall see, the absence of accurate weapons does not necessarily render permissible the use of inaccurate weapons.

An Instrumentalist Account

If the use of inaccurate weapons is morally wrong only if it inflicts intentional, unnecessary, or disproportionate harm on civilians, then why have an independent legal prohibition on the use of inaccurate weapons? Why not rely on the distinct legal prohibitions on inflicting intentional, unnecessary, or disproportionate harm on civilians?

For one thing, combatants may better conform to those distinct prohibitions indirectly, by directly following the prohibition on using inaccurate weapons. While combatants necessarily know if they will inflict intentional harm on civilians, and generally know if they will inflict unnecessary harm on civilians, they do not always know if they will inflict disproportionate harm on civilians. Combatants might better avoid inflicting disproportionate harm on civilians by never using inaccurate weapons than by trying to evaluate the proportionality of using inaccurate weapons on a case-by-case basis. If so, then the legal prohibition on using inaccurate weapons would be instrumentally morally justified.

For another thing, third parties—including international organizations, international courts, military tribunals, the press, civil society organizations, and the general public—may find it easier to determine whether a weapon is unlawfully inaccurate than to determine that an attacker intended to attack civilians or predictably inflicted excessive collateral harm on civilians. In this way, the prohibition on intentionally or disproportionately harming civilians may be better enforced indirectly, by directly enforcing the prohibition on inaccurate weapons.

Of course, an instrumental rationale for the legal prohibition of indiscriminate weapons could succeed only if the content of the prohibition could be identified independently of its underlying rationale. If combatants have to determine whether the use of a weapon will likely cause disproportionate harm in order to determine whether it is unlawfully inaccurate, then they would be no better off following the prohibition on inaccurate weapons than directly following a prohibition on disproportionate attacks.

How might we identify the content of the prohibition of inaccurate weapons without simply applying a prohibition of disproportionate attacks? One approach would be to look to positive legal norms that specifically prohibit certain weapons, such as biological weapons, on the grounds of their inaccuracy. These legal norms could be followed directly, without reference to their underlying rationale.

We would, of course, want to know what leads states to recognize a weapon as unlawfully inaccurate. Presumably, states will reject a particular weapon only if the use of that weapon is very rarely proportionate and the proportionate uses of the weapon are very rarely necessary to military victory. When these conditions are satisfied, states will have much to gain and little to lose from agreeing with other states to abstain from using the weapon in future conflicts. Moreover, since states will accept or reject a ban on a particular weapon based on its military utility and its impact on civilians, such bans cannot be entirely dismissed as "merely conventional" or morally arbitrary.

One potential problem with relying on weapon-specific, categorical prohibitions is that such an approach prohibits only weapons that are indiscriminate *by their nature* but not weapons that are indiscriminate *by their use*. This approach might not allow us to say, for example, that it is unlawful to use cluster munitions against infantry units travelling through cities and towns but lawful to use cluster munitions against tank formations far from civilian areas. Similarly, some states might resist a categorical ban on cluster munitions while admitting that international law should regulate their use. We should therefore prefer an account that explains when it is unlawful to use an inaccurate weapon and when it is not.

There is another problem with the categorical approach, namely that it supports specific prohibitions of particular indiscriminate weapons rather than the general prohibition of all indiscriminate weapons. As we saw in Chapter 4, legal principles allow international law to escape from the "paradox of custom" by providing a legal basis for states to converge on specific rules that implement those principles out of a sense of legal obligation. For example, an international consensus that a weapon is unlawful due to its inaccuracy may generate a specific rule of customary international law prohibiting the use of that weapon. Yet the instrumental value of the specific rule seems disconnected from the intrinsic value expressed by the general principle from which the rule is derived. We should prefer an account that explains the moral force of the general principle.

While it is possible that a meaningful legal prohibition on inaccurate weapons can be morally justified on instrumentalist grounds, I will argue that this legal prohibition rests on an independent, non-instrumental moral foundation. On my view, it is inherently morally impermissible for combatants to use weapons that are more likely to strike civilians than opposing combatants or military objectives.[16] The use of such weapons is morally impermissible even if the attacking force does not intend to harm civilians, does not possess more accurate weapons, and even if the anticipated military advantage substantially outweighs the expected harm to civilians. The legal prohibition of indiscriminate attacks may therefore rest on the inherent moral wrongness of the legally prohibited conduct, rather than on the instrumental value of the legal prohibition itself.

Expectabilism (Again)

The use of inaccurate weapons may be disproportionate, not in the standard sense but in the following sense: the military advantage of striking the military target, discounted by the probability of striking the target, may be outweighed by the harm of striking civilians, discounted by the probability of striking civilians. We can refer to this probabilistic sense of proportionality as *e-proportionality*, for *expected value proportionality* or *expectable-proportionality*. Importantly, an attack may be e-disproportionate even if it will either harm civilians or obtain military advantage but not both, for example through the use of an inaccurate rocket or landmine.

Clearly, the e-disproportionate use of an inaccurate weapon should be legally prohibited even if it is not intended to harm civilians and even if it is the most accurate weapon available. While some attackers may get lucky and strike a lawful target while missing nearby civilians, most attackers will kill many civilians over the course of a conflict while failing to obtain military advantages sufficient to justify these deaths. It follows that each attacker will best conform to his moral obligations by avoiding the e-disproportionate use of inaccurate weapons.

To see that even an e-proportionate use of an inaccurate weapon can be morally impermissible, consider the following skeletal scenarios. The scenarios assume that all civilians who might be harmed or spared are members of the same political community and that the only relevant military advantage is the protection of

---

[16] For current purposes, "strike civilians" means either directly striking civilians or harming civilians as a direct side effect of striking civilian property.

civilians from the immoral and unlawful attacks of the other side.[17] Such a scenario might arise in internal armed conflict, in humanitarian interventions, or in attacks on invading forces. By describing military advantage solely in terms of civilian lives we are better able to recognize the effect of other moral considerations on our intuitive moral judgments.

Here is the first case:

30–70(i): If you strike the target, then you will save 100 civilians from being killed. However, there is only a 30% chance of hitting your target and a 70% chance of missing your target and killing 40 other civilians.

The expected number of deaths if you do not attack is 100. The expected number of deaths if you attack is ninety-eight (=.7(140)). Therefore, the expected value of the attack is two saved lives. Launching the attack would maximize expected value—in this case, the number of survivors discounted by the probability of their survival. Yet launching the strike seems intuitively impermissible. Why? One reason might be that we are not merely comparing possible outcomes but possible actions, and the permissibility of an action is affected by its causal structure as well as by its causal consequences.

Let us refer to the number of civilians that would be saved by a successful strike, discounted by the probability of success, as the number of civilians *expectably-saved*, and to the number of civilians that would be killed in a failed strike, discounted by the probability of failure, as the number of civilians *expectably-killed*.[18] If killing is substantially worse than letting die, then presumably expectably-killing N civilians is substantially worse than failing to expectably-save N civilians. Indeed, if killing is X times worse than letting die, then a permissible attack would have to expectably-save X times more civilians than it would expectably-kill. Let us call such an attack *de-proportionate*, since it remains e-proportionate even after its deontic properties are taken into account.

The attack in *30–70(i)* expectably-kills 28 and expectably-saves 30. It follows that if killing is even slightly worse than letting die, then the attack in *30–70(i)* is de-disproportionate. Nevertheless, we cannot explain the impermissibility of indiscriminate attacks solely in terms of de-disproportionality. Consider the following case:

30–70(ii): If you strike the target, then you will save 100 civilians from being killed. However, there is only a 30% chance of hitting your target and a 70% chance of missing your target and killing 10 other civilians.

The expected number of deaths if you do not attack is 100. The expected number of deaths if you attack is seventy-seven (=.7(110)). Therefore, the expected value of the

---

[17] Presumably, any relaxation of the final constraint may be offset by changing the number of civilian lives at stake.

[18] cf Derek Parfit, *On What Matters*, vol 1 (OUP 2011) 160.

attack is twenty-three saved lives, much greater than in *30–70(i)*. Moreover, the attack in *30–70(ii)* expectably-kills seven and expectably-saves thirty. It follows that killing would have to be more than four times worse than letting die to render the attack in *30–70(ii)* de-disproportionate. It is not clear that killing is four times worse than letting die, yet the attack in *30–70(ii)* seems clearly impermissible. Certainly, the attack in *30–70(ii)* does not seem four times less wrongful or easier to defend than the attack in *30–70(i)*. This suggests, at a minimum, that something other than de-proportionality is at play.

Now let us vary the probabilities but keep the expected value roughly the same as in *30–70(ii)*, and make the ratio of civilians expectably saved and expectably killed fall between those in *30–70(i)* and in *30–70(ii)*.

> *70–30*: If you strike the target, then you will save 50 civilians from being killed. There is a 70% chance of hitting your target and a 30% chance of missing your target and killing 50 other civilians.

The expected number of deaths if you do not attack is fifty. The expected number of deaths if you attack is thirty (=.3(100)). Therefore, the expected value of launching the attack is twenty saved lives, about the same as in *30–70(ii)*. Moreover, the attack in *70–30* expectably kills fifteen civilians and expectably saves thirty-five, a ratio between those in *30–70(i)* and *30–70(ii)*. Yet the attack in *70–30* intuitively seems much easier to defend. This intuitive judgment, in turn, seems to presuppose that the probability of killing civilians makes an independent contribution to the moral status of the attack, quite apart from its e-proportionality or de-proportionality. The following sections argue that both this intuitive judgment and its intriguing presupposition are in fact correct.

The Reasonable Belief Threshold (Again)

To understand why it is wrong to use inaccurate weapons, we should imagine trying to defend the killing or harming of civilians as a result of using such weapons.

Imagine that you are a pilot. You fire a highly accurate missile at a legitimate military target located in a civilian area. In mid-air, the missile's guidance system malfunctions. The missile veers off-course and strikes a group of civilians. You have killed these civilians, albeit unintentionally, and you must now explain why their deaths are not your fault. You cannot justify killing them, since they are not morally liable to be killed and their deaths did not prevent harm to others. But you might offer the following excuse: not only did you not intend to kill any civilians, you reasonably believed that you would not kill any civilians, since the probability that you would kill civilians was less than the probability that you would strike your target and kill no civilians. Of course, this is not a complete excuse. In addition, you might also have to show that the probability of killing civilians was so low, and the military value of your intended target so high, that the expected value of your launching the missile was not only positive but substantial enough to override the moral asymmetry between risking killing and risking letting die.

Now imagine that, instead, you are a member of an organized armed group. You fire a very inaccurate missile at a legitimate military target located in a civilian area. The missile misses its target and strikes a group of civilians. As before, you cannot justify killing the civilians. Moreover, you cannot offer the same excuse as before. You cannot say that you reasonably believed you would kill no civilians, because the probability of killing civilians was greater than the probability of striking your target and killing no civilians. Now, you may be able to say that the military value of your intended target was quite high and that the expected value of launching your missile was substantial. However, this latter claim is not enough to render your actions permissible.

As we have seen, an attack is objectively permissible only if it is supported by undefeated moral reasons and is epistemically permissible only if the actor has decisive epistemic reasons to believe that the act will prove objectively permissible. Conversely, an attack is epistemically impermissible if the actor has undefeated epistemic reasons to believe that the act will prove objectively impermissible. Accordingly, the use of a weapon is epistemically impermissible if the attacker has undefeated reasons to believe that the weapon will strike civilians or civilian objects. Expressed in terms of evidential probabilities, it is epistemically permissible to use a weapon only if—based on the information reasonably accessible to the attacker—the weapon will probably, or more likely than not, strike military targets rather than civilians.

This *reasonable belief threshold* explains the epistemic permissibility of the first attack and the epistemic impermissibility of the second attack. More broadly, this threshold sets a minimum standard of accuracy that every use of a weapon must satisfy. Weapon use that falls short of this threshold should be considered unlawfully indiscriminate.

To complicate matters, suppose that there is a 40% chance that a weapon will strike civilians, a 30% chance that the weapon will strike military targets, and a 30% chance that the weapon will hit empty spaces. On one hand, the weapon is more likely to strike civilians than to strike military targets. On the other hand, the weapon is less likely to strike civilians than to strike military targets or empty spaces. Which of these two facts should determine the permissibility of using the weapon?

In my view, *it is impermissible to use a weapon that is more likely to strike civilians than to strike military targets*, even if it is more likely to strike military targets or empty spaces than to strike civilians. When an act risks killing or injuring innocent people, the probability of a morally neutral result (striking empty spaces) seems morally irrelevant. What seems to matter is the relative probability of a wrong-making result (striking civilians) and a risk-justifying result (striking military targets). Accordingly, an act that risks killing or injuring innocent people is epistemically permissible only if there is decisive reason to believe that the act will produce a result capable of justifying the risk. Since the possibility of striking empty spaces cannot justify taking a risk of striking civilians, the probability of striking empty land should not affect the epistemic permissibility of using an imprecise weapon. The use of a weapon should be considered lawfully discriminate only if it is more likely to strike military targets than to strike civilians, disregarding the probability of striking empty spaces.

In general, statistical frequencies can give us reasons for belief and ground evidential probabilities. Other things equal, the more (statistically) frequently a weapon strikes within a given area in the past, the more (evidentially) likely that it will strike within that area in the future. For example, a weapon's circular error probable (CEP) describes the radius of a circle within which the weapon is expected to strike 50% of the time. If there are *no* civilians within a weapon's CEP, then the use of that weapon is not necessarily indiscriminate. Conversely, if there are *only* civilians within a weapon's CEP, then the use of that weapon is clearly indiscriminate. Finally, if there are *more* civilians than lawful targets within a weapon's CEP, then the use of that weapon is indiscriminate. Importantly, if a weapon has an elliptical or irregular confidence interval, then the weapon's CEP should be calculated conservatively, giving civilians the greatest possible protection while demonstrating the attacker's sincere intention to try not to kill civilians.[19]

As we saw in Chapter 5, the reasonable belief requirement is not absolute. For example, the use of an inaccurate weapon might be permissible if it would expectably-save 100 times as many civilians as it could possibly kill, even if it would probably or most likely kill some civilians and save none. Indeed, assuming that the use of the weapon is not intended to harm civilians, the deontological threshold for the permissible use of such a weapon will be lower than the deontological threshold for permissibly attacking civilians intentionally. For example, if it is permissible to intentionally harm N civilians to prevent comparable harm to $N(X)$ civilians, then it should be permissible to use an inaccurate weapon that could harm as many as N civilians if doing so will expectably-save $N(X-Y)$ civilians. How much lower the threshold should be (the value of Y relative to X) is a question that we need not resolve here because in practice the threshold will hardly ever be crossed.

Cluster Munitions

The principles laid out so far clearly govern the use of projectile weapons that strike a single target, such as Katyusha rockets and SCUD missiles, as well as landmines that trigger a single explosion. In contrast, cluster munitions release smaller "bomblets" in mid-air, some of which may strike civilians or civilian objects and some of which may strike combatants or military objectives.

It may be tempting to think that the reasonable belief threshold should not apply to such weapons and that only necessity and proportionality should constrain their use. One might reason in the following way. Compare two scenarios:

---

[19] cf Gregory S McNeal, "Targeted Killing and Accountability" (2014) 102 Georgetown Law Journal 681.

A: Civilians and military targets are located very close to each other. Your only weapon is a guided missile. You launch the missile, destroying the military targets and killing the civilians as an unintended side effect.

B: The same civilians and the same military targets are now located apart from each other. Your only weapon is a cluster bomb. You drop the cluster bomb, and the bomblets strike the same civilians and the same military targets.

In *A*, the strike is permissible if it is proportionate. The only obvious difference between *A* and *B* is that in *A* combatants and civilians are killed by the same weapon and in *B* they are killed by different bomblets. This difference may seem morally irrelevant, and one might conclude that in *B* the strike is also permissible if it is proportionate.

This reasoning, though superficially attractive, is mistaken. Compare *B* with:

C: Same as *B* except that you can only drop the bomblets individually. Each bomblet strikes the same thing as in *B*.

Clearly, the reasonable belief constraint governs the action in *C*. It is impermissible to drop a bomblet unless you reasonably believe that bomblet will not strike a civilian or civilian object. The only difference between *B* and *C* is that in *B* the bomblets are dropped together and in *C* the same bomblets are dropped separately. This difference is certainly morally irrelevant. It follows that the difference between *A* and *B* is morally relevant after all.

If you cannot reasonably believe that a bomblet will strike a lawful target while missing civilians and civilian objects, then you may not drop that bomblet *or a cluster bomb that contains it.* The use of cluster munitions is so difficult to justify because each cluster bomb is, in fact, not one weapon but many and the use of each weapon that it contains must be justified on its own terms. An attacker may use a cluster munition only if she reasonably believes, of each bomblet that it contains, that each bomblet will probably not strike a civilian or civilian object. In populated areas, this threshold will prove impossible to satisfy and the use of cluster munitions will therefore prove morally impermissible and unlawfully indiscriminate.

Expectabilism and Rule-Consequentialism

Derek Parfit defines *expectabilism* as the view that

When the rightness of some act depends on the goodness of the act's effects or possible effects, we ought to act, or try to act, in the way whose outcome would be *expectably-best.*[20]

---

[20] See Parfit, *On What Matters,* 160.

According to Parfit, the expectably-best outcome is the outcome with the highest expected value. Interestingly, Parfit later writes that

everyone ought always to do, or try to do, [i] whatever would be most likely to make things go best, or more precisely [ii] what would make things go expectably-best.[21]

However, as we have seen, [ii] is not a more precise formulation of [i] but is rather a quite different claim. In many cases, the act most likely to make things go best is not the act that would make things go expectably-best.

Parfit also claims that expectabilism is compatible with act-consequentialism so long as expectabilism is understood to use "ought" in the evidence-relative or belief-relative senses. This is incorrect. According to Parfit, an act is wrong in the evidence-relative sense if we have decisive reasons to believe that the act is wrong in the fact-relative sense.[22] It follows that, according to act-consequentialism, an act is wrong in the evidence-relative sense if we have decisive reason to believe that it will make things go worse. Yet, as we have seen, an act that will probably make things go worse may also make things go expectably-best, provided that the improbable good outcomes sufficiently outweigh the probable bad outcomes. It follows that an act that is required by expectabilism may be wrong in the evidence-relative sense according to act-consequentialism.

Of course, I have argued that the use of inaccurate weapons can be morally impermissible even if such use would be expectably-best. Is expectabilism false? How could it be morally impermissible to do what is expectably-best? Let me start by flipping the question around. Why ever seek the expectably-best outcome, rather than the probably-best outcome? Why ever do what will maximize expected value, rather than what will probably maximize actual value?

For example, imagine that you are offered a bet with a 30% chance of winning $100 and a 70% chance of losing $10. Why take such a bet, when the likely outcome is that you will lose $10? First, if you take the same bet a sufficiently large number of times, then over time your winnings will exceed your losses. Second, if you always take bets with positive expected value, then over time your winnings will exceed your losses. More generally, if you always do what maximizes expected value, then over time you will maximize actual value. In other words, by always doing what is expectably-best, you will perform a series of actions with greater actual value than the series of actions that you would perform by always doing what is probably-best.

It therefore seems that, although Parfit presents expectabilism as a component of act-consequentialism, expectabilism is better understood as a component of rule-consequentialism. Act consequentialists are committed to always choosing the action most likely to produce the best outcome. In contrast, rule consequentialists

---

[21] *On What Matters*, 374 (brackets are mine).
[22] *On What Matters*, 151.

are committed to always choosing the action that will produce the expectably-best outcome. Paraphrasing Parfit's definition of rule consequentialism, everyone ought to follow expectabilism because the universal acceptance of expectabilism would make things go best from an impartial point of view.[23]

It would seem that, according to expectabilism, the e-proportionate use of inaccurate weapons is permissible, even when the weapons will probably strike civilians, because the universal acceptance of a rule permitting the e-proportionate use of inaccurate weapons will make things go best—that is, result in substantially greater military advantage than civilian harm. Now, Parfit defines expectabilism such that we ought to do what is expectably-best only "[w]hen the rightness of some act depends on the goodness of the act's effects or possible effects."[24] This suggests that we need not show that expectabilism is false, but merely that the permissibility of the e-proportionate use of inaccurate weapons depends on more than the goodness of their actual or possible effects. If we can show this, then we can show that expectabilism simply does not apply to the issue at hand.

Indeed, we have already seen that the permissibility of using inaccurate weapons depends not only on their effects but also on how those effects are brought about. In particular, the most important bad effects of using inaccurate weapons involve doings (notably killings), while the most important bad effects of not using inaccurate weapons involve allowings (notably lettings die). These causal features of using inaccurate weapons give us additional, deontic reasons not to use such weapons over and above any non-deontic, impartial reasons that we might have to use or not use such weapons. It was for this reason that we introduced the concept of de-proportionality to describe an attack in which the expectable military advantage outweighs the expectable harm to civilians by a sufficient proportion to override the deontic asymmetry between killing and letting die. But of course we are now exploring a stronger position.

It is generally accepted that an action that intentionally wrongs another person cannot be defended on rule-consequentialist grounds alone. For example, it would be morally impermissible to punish all criminal defendants more than they deserve simply in order to deter more crime over the long term, even if doing so would reduce both the aggregate harm caused by crime and the aggregate harm inflicted through punishment. In general, we cannot justify infringing one person's rights solely in terms of the aggregate consequences of acting similarly in similar situations. We have to be able to defend our treatment of her to her, first citing her potential liability to some harm and only then adverting to the expectable consequences of so harming her. Put another way, only those potentially liable to instrumental harm may be subject either to act-consequentialist calculations or to rule-consequentialist calculations.

---

[23] *On What Matters*, 375.   [24] *On What Matters*, at 160.

For similar reasons, an action that we have most or decisive reason to believe will infringe someone's rights also cannot be defended on rule-consequentialist grounds alone. For example, it would be morally impermissible to dramatically lower the standard of proof in criminal cases simply in order to deter more crime over the long term. Each defendant's guilt must be established first, by an epistemic standard of sufficient evidence, before considering the aggregate consequences of punishing similarly situated defendants. Similarly, as we saw in Chapter 5, it would be morally impermissible to target individuals who are probably civilians on expectabilist grounds alone. Their potential liability to attack must be established first, by decisive evidence, before considering the aggregate consequences of targeting similarly situated individuals.

Indiscriminate weapons raise a distinct but related concern. The civilians in question retain their rights not to be harmed. It is therefore inappropriate to justify endangering them, or excuse killing them, solely by reference to the long-term aggregate consequences of using similar weapons in similar situations. The rights of these civilians are not subject to such rule-consequentialist considerations. Instead, attackers may not justify endangering these civilians, or excuse killing these civilians, without meeting an appropriate epistemic standard, namely reasonable belief that the weapons deployed will not strike these civilians. Only when this reasonable belief threshold is met may attackers consider the aggregate consequences of using similar weapons in similar situations, under the heading of de-proportionality.

Return to the two cases discussed earlier. The pilot can defend her attack by saying to any civilians killed "I reasonably believed that I would strike my intended (legitimate) target and thereby prevent harm to others." In contrast, the armed group member cannot defend her actions by saying "I reasonably believed that I would miss my intended target, harm civilians, and prevent no harm to others. However, I also reasonably believed that if I and others like me launch similar attacks in similar situations, then over time we will prevent substantially more harm than we inflict." Affected civilians could reasonably reject the latter defense but not the former.

There is another reason to prefer the reasonable belief threshold to the expectabilist approach, namely that the former gives each civilian more control over whether or not she will be struck than the latter. If a civilian does not directly participate in hostilities, then she should have some reasonable assurance that she will not be struck by a deadly weapon, either as the result of misidentification or as the result of an indiscriminate attack. The reasonable belief threshold reasonably assures each civilian that she probably will not be mistakenly targeted and that she probably will not be struck by an errant weapon. The expectabilist approach offers no comparable assurance, thereby denying civilians an important degree of control over their fate.

Conclusion

It is almost always morally impermissible to use weapons that are more likely to strike civilians and civilian objects than to strike combatants and military objectives. Such weapons should be considered unlawfully indiscriminate. In addition, the legal prohibition of such weapons should remain absolute, since the use of such weapons will hardly ever be morally permissible and even a narrow legal permission to use such weapons will be misused far more than it is properly used. Finally, the use of weapons that are not unlawfully indiscriminate in this sense is still unlawful if the weapons are used with the intent to harm civilians, or if they place civilians at unnecessary, e-disproportionate, or de-disproportionate risk.

This last point may seem surprising, given the conclusions of the previous section, but it should not. If prohibiting e-disproportionate and de-disproportionate attacks will help more combatants avoid inflicting disproportionate harm over the long term, then the law may do so without compromising the protection that it provides to each civilian or the guidance that it provides to each combatant.

7

Precautions

The precautions rule requires that, "[i]n the conduct of military operations, constant care shall be taken to spare the civilian population, civilians and civilian objects."[1] In more precise terms, "[a]ll feasible precautions must be taken to avoid, and in any event to minimise, incidental loss of civilian life, injury to civilians and damage to civilian objects."[2]

The precautions rule generates a number of specific sub-rules. Attacking forces must "do everything feasible to verify that targets are military objectives" in order to avoid mistakenly targeting civilians.[3] Similarly, attacking forces "must do everything feasible to assess whether the attack may be expected" to inflict excessive harm on civilians.[4] More distinctively, attacking forces must "take all feasible precautions in the choice of means and methods of attack with a view to avoiding, and in any event to minimizing, incidental loss of civilian life, injury to civilians and damage to civilian objects."[5] In particular, "effective advance warning shall be given of attacks which may affect the civilian population, unless circumstances do not permit."[6] Finally, "[w]hen a choice is possible between several military objectives for obtaining a similar military advantage, the objective to be selected shall be that the attack on which may be expected to cause the least danger to civilian lives and to civilian objects."[7]

The practical importance of the precautions rule is hard to overstate. While the proportionality rule sets an upper limit on the harm that attackers may inflict on civilians in pursuit of some military advantage, the precautions rule requires

[1] Protocol Additional to the Geneva Conventions of 12 August 1949, and relating to the Protection of Victims of International Armed Conflicts (Protocol I) (adopted June 8, 1977, entered into force December 7, 1978) 1125 UNTS 3, art 57(1); International Committee of the Red Cross, *Customary International Humanitarian Law*, vol 1 (CUP 2009) 51.

[2] ICRC, *Customary IHL Study*, 51.

[3] Protocol I art 57(2)(a) (emphasis added); ICRC, *Customary IHL Study*, 55.

[4] ICRC, *Customary IHL Study*, 58.

[5] Protocol I art 57(2)(a)(ii); ICRC, *Customary IHL Study*, 56. See also Protocol I art 57(4) ("In the conduct of military operations at sea or in the air, each Party to the conflict shall . . . take all reasonable precautions to avoid losses of civilian lives and damage to civilian objects").

[6] Protocol I art 57(2)(c); ICRC, *Customary IHL Study*, 62.

[7] Protocol I art 57(3); ICRC, *Customary IHL Study*, 65.

Law and Morality at War. First Edition. Adil Haque. © Adil Haque 2017. Published 2017 by Oxford University Press

attackers to inflict even less harm on civilians whenever feasible. Indeed, since proportionality is an imprecise standard, the precautions rule may promise civilians more effective protection.[8] For these reasons, the precautions rule should be recognized as a cardinal rule of the law of armed conflict, co-equal with distinction and proportionality.

Feasible precautions are "those precautions which are practicable or practically possible, taking into account all circumstances ruling at the time, including humanitarian and military considerations."[9] Presumably, "taking into account" both the humanitarian considerations in favor of taking a precaution and the military considerations against taking that precaution means balancing the former against the latter.[10] If the former outweigh the latter, then the precaution is required. Conversely, if the latter outweigh the former, then the precaution is not required. In particular, "[i]t is reasonable to require military forces to assume some degree of risk to avoid collateral damage and incidental injury. They do so regularly. By this analysis, the greater the anticipated collateral damage or incidental injury, the greater the risk they can reasonably be asked to shoulder."[11]

On one attractively simple approach, attacking forces should balance humanitarian and military considerations by placing equal weight on civilian and military lives and deaths and then choosing weapons, tactics, and targets so as to minimize overall expectable deaths, that is, possible deaths discounted by their respective probabilities. Unfortunately, this attractively simple approach ignores the fact that attacking forces risk killing civilians but only risk allowing their fellow soldiers to be killed. As Jeff McMahan writes

the kind of choice that is of most concern—the choice that combatants frequently have between causing greater harm to noncombatants as a side effect and exposing themselves to greater risk—is a choice between doing harm and allowing harm to occur. More specifically, it is often a choice between killing and letting die.[12]

As we have seen, there is a deontic moral asymmetry between doing harm and allowing harm. Ordinarily, we may not kill one innocent person—infringing her rights and making her much worse off—rather than allow another innocent person to be killed. It follows that we may not take a risk of killing one innocent person rather than accept a comparable risk of allowing another innocent person to be killed. If killing is substantially worse than letting die, then it is substantially worse to risk killing than to risk letting die. Similarly, if attacking forces may only

---

[8]   See, eg, Michael Walzer, *Just and Unjust Wars* (Basic Books 2nd edn 1977) 155–6.
[9]   ICRC, *Customary IHL Study*, 54, 70.
[10]   Michael N Schmitt, "Precision Attack and International Humanitarian Law" (2005) 87 International Review of the Red Cross 445, 462.
[11]   Schmitt, "Precision Attack" 462.
[12]   Jeff McMahan, "The Just Distribution of Harm between Combatants and Noncombatants" (2010) 38 Philosophy & Public Affairs 342, 369.

incidentally kill civilians in order to avoid allowing substantially more soldiers to be killed then attacking forces may only risk incidentally killing civilians in order to avoid accepting substantially greater risk to their own soldiers.

This, roughly, is the view that I will defend. A precaution should be considered feasible unless taking that precaution would increase the risk to soldiers substantially more than taking that precaution would decrease the risk to civilians. Similarly, "circumstances do not permit" effective advance warning only if advance warning would increase risk to soldiers substantially more than advance warning would reduce risk to civilians. Finally, it is "possible" to select a different target to obtain a similar military advantage while endangering fewer civilians unless selecting a different target would increase risk to soldiers substantially more than selecting a different target would reduce risk to civilians.

Three simplifications: Taking precautions may increase risk not only to soldiers but also to civilians whom the soldiers are trying to protect. My position treats such risks equally. However, for expository purposes, I generally refer only to the risks to soldiers of taking precautions and the risks to civilians of foregoing precautions.

Taking precautions may also increase operational risk, that is, risk of mission failure. On my view, operational risk is a function of the military advantage anticipated from the operation and the probability that the advantage will be lost or only partially obtained. In Chapter 8, I argue that the value of a military advantage lies in the prevention of future harm to attacking forces or to civilians. Accordingly, on my view, attackers must take a precaution unless doing so will increase future risk to attacking forces or civilians substantially more than doing so will reduce immediate risk to civilians. Since I defend my account of the value of a military advantage in the next chapter, I will leave this issue aside for now.

Finally, my view applies to target verification and assessment of the effects of attacks. On my view, the precautions rule requires attackers to pursue accessible information—both to verify that potential targets are lawful targets as well as to assess the effects of potential attacks on nearby civilians—unless the pursuit of such information would increase risk to attackers substantially more than doing so would reduce the risk of mistakenly targeting civilians or of disproportionately harming civilians. However, most of my examples involve the choice of means and methods of warfare—that is, weapons and tactics for carrying out attacks—since these cases illustrate the most distinctive contribution that the precautions rule makes to the law of armed conflict.

I argue that precautionary obligations apply equally to all armed conflicts, irrespective of the nationalities of the combatants and civilians involved, including to humanitarian military interventions that benefit the very civilian population that its constituent operations endanger. I conclude by applying a modified version of the same approach to the precautionary obligations of defending forces, "to the maximum extent feasible," to remove civilians from the vicinity of military objectives, to avoid locating military objectives within or near densely populated areas, and to take other necessary precautions to protect civilians under their control against the dangers resulting from military operations.[13]

First, however, we examine four leading positions on the law and ethics of humanitarian precaution and force protection.[14] According to the United States Department of Defense (DoD), attackers are not legally required to take *any* risks to themselves or to their mission in order to avoid harming civilians.[15] I will argue that the DoD's positions are both legally incorrect and morally unsound.

Interestingly, the legal positions taken by the DoD partly track moral arguments made by Asa Kasher and Amos Yadlin. According to Kasher and Yadlin, states are morally required to give the safety of their armed forces absolute priority over the safety of foreign civilians. In contrast, Michael Walzer and Avishai Margalit argue that all soldiers have a role-based moral duty to accept substantial risks to avoid harming any civilians. Finally, David Luban argues that, while ordinary morality permits individuals to impose significant risks on others to avoid equal or greater risks to themselves, soldiers assume a professional obligation not to impose significant risks on civilians rather than accept equal or somewhat greater risks to themselves. However, Luban argues that even soldiers have no natural or professional duty to accept a high absolute risk of being killed. I hope that the advantages of my view will be more apparent once the shortcomings of the leading alternatives are brought to light.

Humanitarian and Military Considerations

In 2013, the US Joint Chiefs of Staff took the position that "circumstances permit" effective advance warning of an attack when "any degradation in attack effectiveness is outweighed by the reduction in collateral damage [eg,] because advanced warning allowed the adversary to get civilians out of the target area."[16] On this sensible view, attackers must weigh the military reasons to attack without warning against the humanitarian reasons to give advance warning. If the latter outweigh the former, then advance warning must be given; if not, then not.

In a disturbing turn of events, the US Department of Defense *Law of War Manual* declares that "if a commander determines that taking a precaution would result in

---

[13] Protocol I art 58; ICRC, *Customary IHL Study*, 68–76.

[14] See also Mark Osiel & Ziv Bohrer, "Proportionality in Military Force at War's Multiple Levels: Averting Civilian Casualties vs. Safeguarding Soldiers" (2013) 46 Virginia Journal of International Law 747; Iddo Porat & Ziv Bohrer, "Preferring One's Own Civilians" (2015) 47 George Washington International Law Review 99.

[15] Indeed, according to the DoD, attackers are not legally required to select targets so as to endanger the fewest civilians. See Adil Ahmad Haque, "Off Target: Selection, Precaution, and Proportionality in the DoD Manual" (2016) 92 International Law Studies 31. I will not discuss this issue further here.

[16] United States Joint Chiefs of Staff, Joint Targeting (Joint Publication 3-60) (January 13, 2013) A-5.

operational risk (i.e., a risk of failing to accomplish the mission) or an increased risk of harm to their own forces, then the precaution would not be feasible and would not be required."[17] It seems that, according to the DoD, "feasible" means "risk-free." Far from "taking into account" both humanitarian and military considerations, the DoD seems to disregard or exclude the former when they conflict with the latter—as they almost always do.

To fix ideas, consider the following scenario:

> *Bomb or Raid*: Counterinsurgents use thermal imaging to determine that an insurgent lieutenant is asleep in his home with his four young children. The commander deter-mines that a missile strike on the house will certainly kill the lieutenant, as well as all four children, at no risk to attacking forces. The commander also determines that a night raid by special forces will certainly kill the lieutenant and kill none of the children, but that there is a small chance that the lieutenant will immediately wake up, spring into action, and either attack one of the soldiers or evade the soldiers and escape.[18]

Let us stipulate, for the sake of argument, that the deaths of four children, though horrific, would not be excessive in relation to the anticipated military advantage of killing the lieutenant. Importantly, the commander could almost certainly obtain the same military advantage without killing any of the children by accepting a small risk to his own forces. According to the DoD, it is lawful to bomb the home, kill-ing four children, rather than raid the home, killing no children but at some risk to attacking forces. These implications seem morally intolerable.

As a matter of law, the DoD is almost certainly wrong on both counts. As one international group of experts concluded, "whereas a particular course of action may be considered non-feasible due to military considerations (such as excessive risks to aircraft and their crews), some risks have to be accepted in light of humani-tarian considerations."[19] Similarly, APV Rogers writes "[m]ilitary necessity cannot always override humanity. In taking care to protect civilians, soldiers must accept some element of risk to themselves."[20] Rogers quotes British Defense Doctrine, which stated that "there may be occasions when a commander will have to accept a higher level of risk to his own forces in order to avoid or reduce collateral damage to the enemy's civil population."[21] Finally, as we have seen, Michael Schmitt writes that "[i]t is reasonable to require military forces to assume some degree of risk to avoid collateral damage and incidental injury. They do so regularly."[22] In particular,

---

[17] US Department of Defense, *Law of War Manual* (2015) 5.3.3.2.

[18] This example is adapted from one of David Luban's.

[19] Program on Humanitarian Policy and Conflict Research, Commentary on the HPCR Manual on International Law Applicable to Air and Missile Warfare (2010) 39.

[20] APV Rogers, "Conduct of Combat and Risks Run by the Civilian Population" (1982) Military Law & Law of War Review 310.

[21] British Ministry of Defence, *JWP 0-01 British Defence Doctrine* (1996).

[22] "Precision Attack," 462.

"the greater the anticipated collateral damage or incidental injury, the greater the risk [soldiers] can reasonably be asked to shoulder."[23]

To see the illogic of the Manual even more clearly, consider that often the military advantage anticipated from an attack lies precisely in its contribution to the success of future missions or to the future safety of the attacking force. Nevertheless, if the expected harm to civilians is excessive in relation to the anticipated reduction in future operational and personal risk, then the attack is flatly prohibited by the proportionality rule. Yet, according to the Manual, humanitarian considerations that can outweigh operational and personal risk under the proportionality rule count for nothing under the precautions rule. We might be forced to accept such an illogical result by strong evidence or argument that the result is compelled by treaty or custom. However, the Manual provides no such evidence or argument.

Nationality and Territory

Interestingly, the DoD's legal position on precaution and force protection closely tracks moral arguments put forward ten years earlier by Asa Kasher and Amos Yadlin. Kasher and Yadlin argue that soldiers may impose even great risks on foreign civilians not under their state's effective control rather than accept even small risks to themselves.[24] In contrast, soldiers may not impose even small risks on fellow citizens, or foreign civilians on territory under their effective control, even to avoid very great risks to themselves.[25] To see the implications of this view, return to *Bomb or Raid*. If the four children are foreign civilians not under the effective control of the attacking state, then Kasher and Yadlin's view entails that a bombardment that kills four children and risks no soldiers is not only permissible but required even if a raid would certainly kill no children but might result in harm to one soldier. In contrast, if the children are citizens of the attacking state, then a bombardment that kills four children is impermissible even if a raid would kill three children and result in the deaths of ten soldiers.

How do Kasher and Yadlin arrive at such a dramatically asymmetrical position? The authors begin with an account of the duties of states to minimize harm to different populations. They posit that each state has a very strong duty to minimize harm to its own citizens, a fairly strong duty to minimize harm to foreign civilians under its effective control, and a very weak duty to minimize harm to foreign

---

[23] For further discussion, see Haque, "Off Target."

[24] Asa Kasher & Amos Yadlin, "Military Ethics of Fighting Terror: An Israeli Perspective" (2005) 4 Journal of Military Ethics 3, 14–15, 18–21.

[25] The provision for non-citizen civilians under the effective control of the attacking state is telling because it tracks the legal protections afforded individuals living under military occupation.

civilians beyond its effective control. Soldiers, as agents of the state, are constrained by these duties in their military operations. At the same time, it seems morally problematic for the state to require its soldiers to risk their own lives to discharge the state's duties. Indeed, since soldiers are merely citizens in uniform, the state may not place them at risk without strong moral justification. However, Kasher and Yadlin insist that a state's duties to its own citizens, and to others under its effective control, are strong enough that a state may (indeed must) require soldiers to take risks and suffer harm rather than impose risks or inflict harm on these populations. In contrast, the duty of a state to minimize harm to foreign civilians beyond its effective control is too weak to justify placing its soldiers at avoidable risk. Kasher and Yadlin conclude that soldiers have no moral duty to take risks or suffer harm rather than impose risks or inflict harms on foreign civilians beyond their state's effective control.

Even if we accept Kasher and Yadlin's political premises, their moral conclusion seems like a *non sequitur*. At most, their political premises entail that a soldier has no role-based responsibility to accept rather than impose risks on foreign civilians. Their premises do not entail that a soldier has no natural duty to accept rather than impose risks on foreign civilians. If soldiers have such a natural duty, then states may enforce this natural duty without imposing any new role responsibilities upon their soldiers. In enforcing such a natural duty, states will not place their soldiers at greater risk than their soldiers are already morally required to bear. States will still need to justify placing their soldiers in situations in which they can only avoid imposing risks on foreign civilians by accepting risks to themselves. But states that are justified in placing their soldiers in such situations need no additional justification for demanding that their soldiers discharge their own natural duties.

For their conclusion to follow, Kasher and Yadlin must either show that human beings have no natural duty to accept even small risks rather than impose even great risks on others or show that a soldier's social role relieves her of her natural duties to foreign civilians. Kasher and Yadlin offer no argument for either claim. Nor is a compelling argument for either claim likely to materialize. It is easy to see how a soldier's social role could strengthen her natural duties to her fellow citizens. It is much harder to see how a soldier's social role could extinguish her natural duties to foreign civilians beyond her state's effective control. Perhaps Kasher and Yadlin will one day offer a compelling argument to this effect. Until they do so, there is no reason to discuss their views further.

Internalizing the Costs of War

In response to Kasher and Yadlin, Michael Walzer and Avishai Margalit took the opposing position that all soldiers have a role-based moral duty to accept substantial risks to avoid harming any civilians, irrespective of their nationality, location, or political allegiance.[26] In their view, the moral purpose of *jus in bello* norms is to limit war to the warriors as much as possible. It follows that soldiers may transfer risk from themselves onto opposing combatants but not onto civilians. As we have seen, it is not enough that soldiers *not intend* to harm civilians. In addition, soldiers must *intend not* to harm civilians. The strength of this latter intention is shown by their willingness to take risks rather than impose risks on civilians.

As elsewhere in his writing on the ethics of war, Walzer grounds his position not on abstract moral principles but rather on a constructive interpretation of what he calls "the war convention," that is, "the set of articulated norms, customs, professional codes, legal precepts, religious and philosophical principles, and reciprocal arrangements that shape our judgments of military conduct."[27] According to Walzer, "the task of the moral theorist is to study the pattern as a whole, reaching for its deepest reasons."[28] Walzer argues that if we interpret the war convention in light of its deepest reasons, then we will see that it requires soldiers to bear the costs of war to the greatest extent possible.

The moral justification for this requirement lies in the idea that violence is evil, and that we should limit the scope of violence as much as is realistically possible. As a soldier, you are asked to take an extra risk for the sake of limiting the scope of the war.[29]

Put another way, opposing combatants must jointly internalize the costs of war, rather than externalizing those costs onto civilians.

Margalit and Walzer do not attempt to precisely quantify the degree of risk that soldiers should assume rather than risk harming civilians. They write only that soldiers do not have to take suicidal risks or take risks that make their mission impossibly difficult. Importantly, they propose the following guideline:

Conduct your war in the presence of noncombatants on the other side with the same care as if your citizens were the noncombatants.[30]

As we saw in Chapter 1, soldiers have special duties to protect their fellow citizens and fellow soldiers but these special duties do not create special rights to harm foreign civilians. It follows that soldiers may not impose risks on foreign civilians that they may not impose on their fellow citizens. Since attacking forces too often take risks to foreign civilians much less seriously than they would take risks to fellow citizens, Margalit and Walzer's guidance serves a valuable corrective function in moral deliberation.

---

[26] Avishai Margalit & Michael Walzer, "Israel: Civilians and Combatants" New York Review of Books, May 14, 2009.

[27] Walzer, "Just and Unjust Wars," 44.   [28] "Just and Unjust Wars," 45.

[29] Margalit & Walzer, "Israel: Civilians and Combatants."

[30] "Israel: Civilians and Combatants."

We should all hope that Margalit and Walzer are right that the war convention requires soldiers to take substantial risks to reduce the risks they impose on civilians. However, since the war convention is a contingent social construct, the content of which is unclear and the proper interpretation of which is disputed, we should try to show that the war convention morally *should* require soldiers to take such risks. Indeed, the duty of combatants to take risky precautions does not rest on a contingent social practice but on necessary moral principles. This duty is not a positive duty to absorb the risks of war, but rather a negative duty not to impose risks on others except to avoid substantially greater risks to oneself.

Risk Egalitarianism and Vocational Soldiering

David Luban argues that ordinary morality forbids individuals from imposing greater risks on others to avoid smaller risks to themselves but permits individuals to impose significant risks on others to avoid equal or greater risks to themselves.[31] Luban refers to this position as *risk egalitarianism* since it assigns equal moral weight to risks of equal magnitude irrespective of who bears those risks. On this view, individuals are not permitted to prefer their own lesser good to the greater good of others, though they are permitted to prefer their own good to the equal or lesser good of others.

Luban argues that any more stringent duty must rest on the role-responsibilities inherent in what he calls the vocational core of soldiering. According to Luban, soldiers assume a professional obligation not to impose significant risks on civilians rather than accept equal or somewhat greater risks to themselves.

Finally, Luban argues that even soldiers have no natural or professional duty to accept a high absolute risk of being killed, that is, to select weapons, tactics, or targets that will probably result in their own deaths. Luban writes that morality cannot fairly demand so much of a soldier. Soldiers who accept such high absolute risks rather than impose risks on civilians act heroically and above the call of duty.

Notice first that risk egalitarianism is an impartial form of expectabilism. On this view, soldiers must take a precaution if and only if the expectable costs to civilians of foregoing the precaution outweigh the expectable costs to soldiers of taking the precaution. It follows that, like expectabilism, risk egalitarianism must be rejected as an account of our natural duties to others because it ignores the moral asymmetry between doing harm and allowing harm. If it is worse to inflict harm than to allow comparable harm, then it must be worse to risk inflicting harm than to allow comparable harm. From a soldier's perspective, the relevant risks are the risk of killing civilians and the risk of allowing fellow soldiers to be killed. The relevant

[31] David Luban, "Risk Taking and Force Protection," in Yitzhak Benbaji & Naomi Sussman (eds), *Reading Walzer* (Routledge 2014).

risks are not simply that an equivalent harm will befall either a civilian or a soldier, but rather that the soldier will commit a more serious moral wrong or a less serious moral wrong.

Luban rightly treats the death of a soldier and the death of a civilian as equally bad events, an equal loss of human life. However, killing a civilian is an action, not merely an event, and the moral significance of an action is a function not only of its outcome but also of its causal and intentional structure. Soldiers should accept greater risks to themselves in order to avoid imposing smaller risks on civilians, not because the lives of civilians are worth more than the lives of soldiers but because killing is worse than letting die. Unfortunately, Luban invokes the related asymmetry between imposing risks and avoiding risks only to defend risk egalitarianism from appeals to national partiality, not to move beyond risk egalitarianism toward the view that I favor.

In addition, professional obligation is an infirm point on which to balance risk to soldiers and risk to civilians. For one thing, the law of armed conflict regulates the conduct of civilians directly participating in hostilities, members of organized armed groups, contractors, mercenaries, irregular militia, and participants in a *levée en masse*. These individuals must also respect the rules of distinction, precautions, and proportionality. Yet these individuals do not occupy the institutional role of soldiers. Put the other way around, the law applies to soldiers and non-soldiers alike, so the content of the law cannot derive from the role-responsibilities of soldiers. To fix the content of indeterminate laws we should instead look to the general moral obligations of all persons who use lethal force.

Similarly, McMahan goes somewhat astray when he argues that "the reason why combatants are required to expose themselves to risk in the course of defending those who are threatened with wrongful harm is simply that it is their job to do that: it is what they have pledged to do and are paid to do. It is part of their professional role."[32] Evidently, the professional role of soldiers is partly defined by the law of armed conflict. If we seek to determine what level of risk the law should require combatants to accept, then it seems circular to rest this determination on the role-based duties of soldiers.

Professional obligations are created, sustained, and defined by social conventions including laws, codes of conduct, and custom. Yet the laws of armed conflict are indeterminate, rules of engagement vary with each armed force and each armed conflict, and state practice as a result remains unsettled. Moreover, armed forces and organized armed groups may opt out of whatever convention exists, rejecting the professional obligations associated with it, and construct their professional identity through a different set of norms, values, and ideals. Of course, defecting from a social convention can be a moral wrong in itself if the convention has a

---

[32] McMahan, "Just Distribution," 366.

compelling moral justification.[33] However, the most compelling moral justification for the social convention that Luban supports is the moral asymmetry between killing and letting die.

Finally, Luban is wrong to claim that law and morality may never demand that soldiers accept great risks to themselves rather than impose great risks on civilians. Clearly, both law and morality forbid a soldier from intentionally killing a civilian even to avoid his own certain death. In addition, it is morally impermissible for a soldier to unintentionally but certainly kill a civilian as a side effect of preventing her own certain death. Though someone will die either way, killing the civilian will also infringe her rights, affect her body in a way that harms her, and make her worse off than she would have been in the soldier's absence. It seems to follow that it is also morally impermissible for a soldier to take, say, an 80% chance of collaterally killing a particular civilian to avoid an 80% chance of being killed himself.

Luban is wrong to claim that there is an absolute level of risk that law and morality may never place on a soldier. As we shall see, the distribution of risks among soldiers and among civilians can sometimes make a moral difference. Perhaps this is what Luban had in mind. But first let me lay out my own approach in somewhat greater detail.

Deontic Precaution

Since my account of morally required precautions in attack is based on the deontic moral asymmetry between killing and letting die, I will label my account *deontic precaution*. As we have seen, even unintentional killing is substantially worse than letting die. When the counterinsurgents in *Bomb or Raid* consider the weapons and tactics available to them, they should consider not only the possible consequences of a given selection but also their own potential causal relationship with those consequences. If they bomb the compound, then they will kill four more civilians than if they raid the compound. Conversely, let us suppose that if they raid the compound then they may allow four more soldiers to be killed than if they bomb the compound. The total loss of life may be the same but neither the number of deaths nor the distribution of deaths exhausts the relevant moral considerations. The potential deaths are not simply bad events or states of affairs to be minimized or justly distributed. From the moral perspective of the soldiers, the potential deaths are either killings or lettings die. Since killing is substantially worse than letting die, the soldiers must raid rather than bomb.

More generally, a precaution should be considered "feasible" unless the additional losses that soldiers will suffer if they take the precaution are substantially greater than the additional losses civilians will suffer if they do not take the precaution.

---

[33] See Jeremy Waldron, *Torture, Terror, and Trade-offs* (OUP 2010) 80.

In particular, "circumstances" should be considered to "permit" effective advance warnings prior to attack unless the additional losses attackers will suffer if they issue such a warning are substantially greater than the additional losses that attackers will inflict on civilians if attackers strike without warning. Similarly, two targets should be considered to offer a "similar" military advantage unless the additional losses that attackers will suffer if they choose one target are substantially greater than the additional losses that civilians will suffer if attackers choose the other target.[34]

Of course, the consequences of taking a precaution are hardly ever certain. However, if killing is substantially worse than letting die, then it follows that it is substantially worse to take a given risk of killing than to take a comparable risk of letting die. The moral weight of a risk is determined not only by the gravity of the outcome that one risks producing or allowing but also by the wrongfulness of the action that one risks performing. It follows that it is worse to take a given risk of killing than to take an equal or slightly greater risk of letting die. However, it is permissible to take a given risk of killing rather than take a substantially greater risk of letting die. In such cases, it is permissible to take a smaller chance of performing a more serious wrong rather than a higher chance of performing a less serious wrong.

Since the gravity of a risk is the product of its magnitude and its likelihood, it is permissible to take a given risk of killing rather than take a substantially greater chance of letting an equal number die, an equal chance of letting substantially more many die, and so forth. For example, if killing is at least twice as serious a wrong as letting die, then it is permissible to risk killing only to avoid twice as great a risk of letting die—that is, twice as great a chance of letting the same number of individuals die, an equal chance of letting twice as many die, and so forth.

More generally, a precaution should be considered "feasible" unless the increased risk to soldiers if the precaution is taken is substantially greater than the increased risk to civilians if the precaution is not taken. In particular, "circumstances" should be considered to "permit" effective advance warning prior to attack unless the increased risk to soldiers if the warning is given is substantially greater than the increased risk to civilians if the warning is not given. Similarly, a choice of targets should be considered "possible" unless the increased risk to soldiers if they choose one target is substantially greater than the increased risk to civilians if they choose an alternative target.

Deontic precaution calls for a comparison between *marginal* risks to civilians—that is, the difference between the risks to civilians if a precaution is taken and the risks to civilians if a precaution is not taken—and *marginal* risks to soldiers—that

[34] cf Commentary on the HPCR Manual 129 ('there is no requirement to select among several objectives if doing so would be militarily unreasonable. As an example, if a choice has to be made between two alternative military objectives—one of which is more densely defended than the other—the attacker is not required to select the latter when heavy casualties are anticipated to the attacking force').

is, the difference between the risks to soldiers if a precaution is taken and the risks to soldiers if a precaution is not taken.[35] A precaution should be considered "feasible" unless the marginal risks to soldiers of taking the precaution are substantially greater than the marginal risks to civilians of not taking the precaution. Similarly, "circumstances" should be considered to "permit" effective advance warnings prior to attack unless the marginal risk to soldiers of giving advance warning are substantially greater than the marginal risk to civilians of attacking without warning. Finally, a choice of targets should be considered "possible" unless the marginal risks to soldiers of choosing one target are substantially greater than the marginal risks to civilians of choosing an alternative target.

One might think that deontic precaution is too complex to provide meaningful guidance to soldiers. However, the gist of deontic precaution can be neatly summarized in a single rule of engagement:

> *Careful*: Do not use weapons and tactics that will place civilians at significant risk unless the other weapons and tactics available to you will place your own forces at substantially greater risk.

Often, neither those who plan military operations nor those who carry them out will have enough information about existing facts to precisely estimate either the likelihood or the magnitude of possible harms to soldiers or civilians. Even so, it is reasonable to expect that armed forces following *Careful* will less often impose large risks on civilians in order to avoid small risks to themselves or impose significant risks on civilians to avoid comparable risks to themselves. Perhaps it is too much to expect armed forces to regularly follow *Careful* in close cases, for example by accepting slightly greater risks rather than imposing slightly smaller risks. Nevertheless, partial compliance with a morally justified rule generally is preferable to the absence of such a rule. Soldiers will better conform to their natural moral obligations by following *Careful* than by following their unguided moral judgment under the stress of combat.

Deontic precaution is a natural view, not in the sense that it is obvious or widely recognized, but rather in the sense that it is grounded on principles of natural morality rather than political or role morality. Since soldiers are first and foremost human beings, they bear the natural duties described above. As we have seen, Kasher and Yadlin argue that soldiers have no role-based duty to take even small risks rather than impose even large risks on foreign civilians not under their effective control. Conversely, Margalit, Walzer, and Luban argue that soldiers bear role-based duties not to impose risks on others even to avoid substantial risks to themselves.

---

[35] See Seth Lazar, "Necessity in Self-Defense and War" (2012) 40 Philosophy & Public Affairs 3, 43 ("When comparing options that involve different degrees of risk to civilians and to friendly combatants, we must ask whether the additional marginal risk imposed on civilians is justified by the marginal reduction in risk to combatants"). As elsewhere, I broadly agree with Lazar's approach, but on my view the relevant marginal risks reflect the moral asymmetry between doing harm and allowing harm.

Since role-based duties depend on contingent social conventions, different armed forces at different times may aspire to the higher professional standards articulated by Luban, Margalit, and Walzer or accept only the lower professional standards defended by Kasher and Yadlin. However, all armed forces must conform to the minimum moral standards of deontic precaution.

Before moving on, let me address one additional issue. From the perspective of a commander, the decision to order an attack that places troops at risk may seem like a decision to actively *occasion* harm to those troops rather than to passively *allow* harm to those troops. Generally, actively occasioning harm to others is somewhat harder to justify than passively allowing harm to others, since the former but not the latter makes others worse off than they would be in our absence. In contrast, occasioning harm to *ourselves* seems morally comparable to allowing harm to ourselves, particularly when we choose to engage in the activity that would occasion harm to ourselves. It is therefore understandable that some commanders may hesitate to order their forces to take risky precautions that the commanders would be willing to take themselves were their positions reversed. However, the precautionary obligations of the attacking forces must be determined by the moral reasons that apply to them, and those moral reasons reflect the moral asymmetry between doing harm to civilians and allowing harm to themselves. Commanders should consider the moral significance of occasioning harm to their troops when they decide whether or not to order an attack. However, once the decision to attack is made, the attack should be carried out in accordance with deontic precaution.

Taking and Distributing Risks

Many soldiers place themselves at risk repeatedly throughout a military campaign, while many civilians will only be placed at risk once or a few times. It might seem that we should therefore compare the cumulative marginal risk to a particular soldier of consistently taking a precaution with the cumulative marginal risk to a particular civilian if that precaution is never taken.[36]

To fix ideas, suppose that Tactic A involves a 10% risk that an attacking soldier will be killed and a 0% risk that the soldier will kill a civilian, while Tactic B involves a 0% risk that the soldier will be killed and a 30% risk that the soldier will kill a civilian. It seems that the soldier must use Tactic A. Now suppose that the soldier expects to use either Tactic A or Tactic B in at least twenty future operations, repeatedly placing herself in danger but never endangering any *particular* civilian

---

[36] See Elad Uzan, "Soldiers, Civilians, and in Bello Proportionality: A Proposed Revision" (2016) 99 The Monist 87. Infelicitously, Uzan compares the cumulative risk to soldiers of adopting Tactic A with the cumulative risk to civilians of adopting Tactic A. However, as we have seen, the precautions rule compares the *marginal* risk to soldiers of adopting Tactic A *as opposed to* Tactic B with the *marginal* risk to civilians of adopting Tactic B *as opposed to* Tactic A.

more than once. Is it now permissible for the soldier to adopt Tactic B, since the cumulative risk to the soldier is greater than the cumulative risk to any particular civilian? No. For one thing, if the soldier takes a 30% risk of killing at least one civilian twenty times, then the soldier should expect to kill around six civilians. Yet a soldier may not kill around six civilians even to avoid her own certain death. Clearly, something has gone wrong.

Instead, we should compare the cumulative marginal risk to a particular soldier of repeatedly taking a precaution with the cumulative marginal risk that the soldier will kill *any* civilian if that precaution is repeatedly not taken. Obviously, this is equivalent to comparing the marginal risk to a particular soldier of taking a precaution on a particular occasion with the marginal risk that the soldier will kill a civilian if the precaution is not taken on that particular occasion. The soldier owes each civilian a justification for not taking a precaution that might spare his life, and that justification must be that the increased marginal risk to that civilian on this occasion is outweighed by the decreased marginal risk to the soldier on this occasion.

So far, we have tacitly assumed that the risks of military operations are evenly distributed among attacking soldiers on one hand and civilians on the other. On this assumption, we need only compare the risk that one or more additional soldiers will be killed if a precaution is taken with the risk that one or more additional civilians will be killed if a precaution is not taken. However, the risks of military operations are often unevenly distributed. For example, in the raid of a residential compound, the first soldier through the door may be much more likely to be killed on entry than the last. At the same time, civilians located near doors and windows may be at much greater risk than civilians in interior rooms. How, if at all, should the distribution of risk affect soldiers' precautionary obligations?[37]

Return to *Raid or Bomb*. Assume that the attacking force consists of four soldiers and the home contains four children. There are two ways of carrying out the raid:

A: 50% chance some soldier will die in raid, 12.5% chance each

B: 50% chance soldier S will die in raid

In raid A, the risks to the attacking force are evenly distributed. In raid B, the risks are concentrated on soldier S (who perhaps will be the first to enter the compound). Now consider two ways in which bombardment might unfold:

C: 50% chance some civilian will die in bombardment, 12.5% chance each

D: 50% chance civilian N will die in bombardment

In bombardment C, the risks to the civilians are evenly distributed. In bombardment D, the risks are concentrated on civilian N (who perhaps is sleeping on the roof).

---

[37] Thanks to Frances Kamm and Seth Lazar for raising the general issue of individualized risk, though in different contexts.

Clearly, the soldiers must choose raid A over bombardment C. The unit is not at substantially greater overall risk than the civilians, and no soldier is at substantially greater risk than any civilian. Similarly, the soldiers must choose raid B over bombardment D. The overall risks are the same, and soldier S is not at substantially greater risk than civilian N. Finally, the soldiers must choose raid A over bombardment D, since the overall risk is the same and no soldier is at substantially greater risk than civilian N.

Must the soldiers choose raid B over bombardment C? The overall marginal risks are the same but the marginal risk to S is substantially greater than the marginal risk to any individual civilian. Nevertheless, soldier S should be primarily concerned with the risk that he or she will kill (individually or jointly) a civilian and only secondarily with the risk that he or she will kill any particular civilian. If, as I believe, it is wrong for S to take a 50% risk of killing N rather than take a 50% risk of being killed, then it is also wrong for S to take a 50% risk of killing *any* civilian rather than take a 50% risk of being killed.

Forced to choose a weapon or tactic that will certainly kill civilian N and an alternative weapon or tactic that will certainly kill two of ten civilians (each with a 20% chance of being killed) one ought to choose the former. Similarly, given a choice between taking a 25% risk of killing civilian N or a 50% risk of killing one of four civilians (12.5% each) a soldier ought to take the lower overall risk rather than the lower risk to each individual. It is only when the overall risks to the same group are close to equal that the distribution of risk makes a difference. Forced to choose between bombardment C and bombardment D, the attacking force should choose C. However, forced to choose between raid B and bombardment C, soldier S and the attacking force must choose raid B.

The distribution of risks among soldiers affects the best option for soldiers; the distribution of risks among civilians affects the best option for civilians; but only the overall risks to civilians affects whether the best option for soldiers may be chosen over the best option for civilians. Similarly, only the overall risks to soldiers affects whether the best option for soldiers may be chosen over the best option for civilians.

Consider these two ways in which a raid might unfold:

E: 100% chance one of eight soldiers will die in raid, 12.5% chance each

F: 100% chance that soldier S will die in the raid

The soldiers may choose C or D over E because the overall marginal risk to the soldiers (100%) in E is substantially greater than the overall marginal risk to the civilians (50%) in C or D. It is true that the marginal risk to each soldier in E (12.5%) is equal to the marginal risk to each civilian in C and substantially less than the marginal risk to N in D (50%). However, the soldiers may "pool" their individual risks, just as they must "pool" the risks to each civilian in C. The number of soldiers at risk must matter morally, because the risk that this or that soldier will be killed affects the risk that some soldier will be killed.

Finally, S may choose C or D over F, not because the absolute risk to S is too high but because the marginal risk to S (100%) is substantially greater than the overall marginal risk to civilians (50%). Perhaps this is what Luban had in mind when he wrote that there is an absolute level of risk that no soldier is required to accept. As we have seen, this view is false. However, it is often true that if the absolute risk to a particular soldier is very high then the overall marginal risk to soldiers is substantially greater than the overall marginal risk to civilians.

In short, soldiers must take extra precautions unless doing so will increase their overall marginal risk substantially more than doing so will decrease the overall marginal risk to civilians. Soldiers should be concerned with the overall risks they impose and may pool the individual risks they face.

Humanitarian Intervention

Suppose that a state will militarily intervene to stop ongoing atrocities occurring on the territory of another state only if intervention will result in the deaths of very few intervening soldiers. In order to minimize its own losses, the state contemplating intervention will not take precautions in attack that place its own forces at any additional risk. For example, the state will intervene only if it can rely entirely on air power unguided by real-time intelligence from ground forces. In other words, the state will only intervene if it is permitted to ignore deontic precaution.

If the ongoing atrocities are sufficiently widespread and systematic, then more potential victims may be saved than killed by intervention and each potential victim's *ex ante* risk of death may be lower than it would be without intervention. It therefore may seem desirable for international law to exempt potential interveners from deontic precaution. Indeed, Jeff McMahan argues that principles like deontic precaution do not apply as a matter of morality in contexts of humanitarian intervention, since the civilians placed at risk by the interveners are already at risk and the intervention actually lowers their overall risk of being killed.[38]

One threshold problem with such arguments is that it is not clear how or when to determine a potential victim's *ex ante* risk. The initial decision to intervene may lower a person's *ex ante* risk, if he or she was more likely to be killed in the atrocities than to be killed in the intervention. However, a specific operation may raise his or her *ex ante* risk, if he or she is more likely to be killed in the operation than to be killed in the atrocities. It seems arbitrary to determine *ex ante* risk at the start of the intervention rather than at the start of each specific operation. Moreover, it seems untenable to defend killing a person on the grounds that the intervention that kills her reduces her *ex ante* risk of being killed. That seems like poor consolation.

---

[38] McMahan, "Just Distribution."

McMahan anticipates this objection, but his response is somewhat unclear. McMahan argues that, at the time the decision is made to intervene militarily, the endangered civilians "all have reason, at that time, to want the war to be fought" even though some may have the bad luck of being endangered more by the war than by the atrocities the war seeks to prevent.[39] This may be true, but it seems irrelevant. These endangered civilians have *most* reason to want the war to be fought in accordance with applicable moral and legal rules, including the obligation to take reasonably risky precautions. It is true that, if potential interveners refuse to take risky precautions, then endangered civilians may have no choice but to take whatever they can get. But it is hard to believe that actual acceptance (let alone hypothetical acceptance) of such a coercive offer would actually change the moral and legal obligations of the potential intervener.[40] On the contrary, it is wrong for potential interveners to exploit the plight of the endangered civilians in order to extract such concessions, and any concessions so obtained should be without moral or legal effect.

As a general matter, few would argue that we should strip individual civilians of legal protection whenever doing so will reduce aggregate harm to the civilian population and, with it, *ex ante* risk to each individual civilian. Indeed, civilians in any armed conflict would be impartially best off, and individuals better off *ex ante*, if attacking forces chose to minimize overall civilian casualties rather than obey deontological constraints. Yet no one suggests that attacking forces should be legally permitted to intentionally kill civilians when this will result in less overall harm to civilians.

To see this clearly, consider an admittedly extreme case. Suppose that a genocidal force threatens to randomly kill one in ten members of a civilian population. Another armed force is willing to intervene and protect the civilian population from this genocidal force. However, in return for its largess, this intervening force demands the right to randomly kill one in twenty members of the civilian population. More civilians will be saved, and each member's *ex ante* risk of death will be cut in half, if the intervention occurs than if it does not. Yet no one suggests that international law should permit the intervening force to randomly kill one in twenty civilians.

Some readers might wonder whether deontic precaution does not apply to humanitarian interveners for a different reason. Generally, it is substantially worse to kill members of one group as a side effect of preventing harm to members of another group. However, in humanitarian intervention cases, attacking forces kill members of a group as a side effect of preventing harm to members of the same group. Rather than killing some to save others, attacking forces kill fewer to save

[39] "Just Distribution of Harm," 363.
[40] On coercive offers, see Joel Feinberg, *The Moral Limits of the Criminal Law Vol 3: Harm to Self* (OUP 1989).

more. In such cases, the moral asymmetry between doing harm and allowing harm narrows.

Indeed, there may be cases in which it is permissible to unintentionally kill some to prevent harm to an equal or even smaller number when the alternative is that all will be killed. For example, suppose that a genocidal force will massacre a village of one hundred civilians unless an intervener bombards the genocidal force, collaterally killing fifty (or even ninety) civilians. Since the fifty (or ninety) civilians will be killed whether or not the attack is carried out, such an attack might be proportionate even though it kills as many civilians as it saves (or perhaps even more). True, the attack would directly harm the fifty (or ninety) civilians, infringing their rights and affecting their bodies. However, the attack would not make these civilians much worse off than they would have otherwise been, since these civilians would otherwise have been killed by the genocidal force. In such cases, perhaps intervening forces ought to save as many as they can.

Cases like these suggest that proportionality may operate differently in the context of humanitarian intervention, at least when only civilian lives are at stake. However, cases like these suggest nothing about the precautionary obligations of an intervening force. These precautionary obligations do not regulate inflicting harm on some members of a civilian population in order to prevent harm to other members of the same civilian population. Instead, these precautionary obligations regulate inflicting harm on civilians in order to avoid harm to the attacking force. The harms inflicted and the harms avoided threaten members of different groups. In such cases, intervening forces ought to kill as few as they can without exposing themselves to substantially greater risk than they impose.

Put another way, it is irrelevant that attacking without taking feasible precautions may leave some civilians better off, and leave other civilians not much worse off, than they would have been had you not attacked at all. What matters is that attacking without taking feasible precautions will make civilians worse off than they would have been had you attacked while taking feasible precautions. It is the latter, marginal detriment that must be justified.

Finally, some readers may reason as follows. In humanitarian interventions, the intervening force is voluntarily placing its members at risk for the sake of the civilian population. The civilians have no right that the interveners take these risks, yet benefit from their taking these risks. Therefore, when risk can be borne either by the interveners or by the civilians it ought in fairness to fall on the civilians. This argument, too, is hard to understand. No one thinks that it is permissible for an intervening force to intentionally kill civilians to prevent equal or somewhat greater harm to its own members. Why then would it be permissible for an intervening force to unintentionally kill civilians to avoid equal or lesser harm to its own members?

As we have seen, the proper moral function of the law of armed conflict is not to incentivize soldiers to produce the impartially best outcomes, but rather to help soldiers to better conform to their deontic obligations. If soldiers kill more civilians than is strictly necessary to achieve a military advantage, then this choice must be justified. A plausible justification is that any other means of preventing such harm to others would occasion substantially greater harm to soldiers. But it is no justification at all that the soldiers are unwilling to take risks themselves rather than impose risks on civilians. Nor is it sufficient that the civilians themselves will benefit from the intervention, either collectively *ex post* or individually *ex ante*.

Conclusion

The precautions rule requires attackers to take into account both the humanitarian considerations in favor of taking some precaution and the military considerations against taking that precaution. These considerations, in turn, should be understood in light of the moral risks of taking or foregoing that precaution. For attackers, these moral risks reflect the general moral asymmetry between doing harm and allowing harm. It follows that attacking forces must select weapons, tactics, and targets that reduce the marginal risk they pose to civilians unless doing so will increase the marginal risk to themselves to a substantially greater degree. In particular, effective advance warnings must be given prior to attack unless such warnings would increase marginal risk to soldiers substantially more than such warnings would reduce marginal risk to civilians. Finally, attackers must select one target rather than another unless the marginal risk to attackers of attacking the former rather than the latter is substantially greater than the marginal risk to civilians of attacking the former rather than the latter.

Importantly, defending forces have precautionary obligations of their own, namely, "to the maximum extent feasible," to remove civilians from the vicinity of military objectives, to avoid locating military objectives within or near densely populated areas, and to take other necessary precautions to protect civilians under their control against the dangers resulting from military operations.[41] Evidently, this obligation is not absolute. Defenders may be justified in operating near civilians in order to protect those civilians, to attack opposing forces operating near civilians, or even to avoid detection by opposing forces. Defenders are only categorically prohibited from locating themselves near civilians for the purpose of using those civilians to shield themselves from attack.

Like attackers, defenders must weigh the moral risks of operating among civilians against the moral risks of operating elsewhere. Unlike attackers, these moral risks reflect the general moral asymmetry between *occasioning* harm and allowing harm. Occasioning harm makes those harmed worse off than they would be in your absence but does not directly infringe their rights that you not kill or injure them.

---

[41] Protocol I art 58; ICRC, *Customary IHL Study*, 68–76.

It follows that occasioning harm is worse than allowing harm but not as hard to justify as doing harm. Defending forces must therefore avoid operating near civilians unless the marginal risk to them or to other civilians of operating elsewhere is significantly greater than the marginal risk to civilians of operating near those civilians. If defending forces are morally required to take greater risks to avoid occasioning harm to civilians, then these moral duties rest on their professional duties as soldiers rather than on their natural duties as human beings. Such professional duties may raise the ceiling on their moral obligations so long as their natural duties secure the floor to their moral obligations.

8

Proportionality

The proportionality rule prohibits attacks "which may be expected to cause incidental loss of civilian life, injury to civilians, damage to civilian objects, or a combination thereof, which would be excessive in relation to the concrete and direct
military advantage anticipated."[1] The importance of this prohibition is difficult to
overstate. While the precautions rule regulates *how* armed forces may pursue a particular military advantage, the proportionality rule regulates *whether* a particular
military advantage may be pursued or must be abandoned. Even if attacking forces
select weapons, tactics, and targets that best avoid or most reduce harm to civilians,
even at their own risk, they must forego one path to victory if the expected civilian
losses are too great. Rather than inflict disproportionate harm on civilians, attacking
forces must find another way to win.

An account of *jus in bello* proportionality must satisfy two apparently conflict-
ing demands. First, such an account must explain how we can rationally compare
civilian losses with military advantages. At the same time, such an account must
apply symmetrically to all parties to every conflict independently of the *jus ad bellum* status of their war effort. Existing accounts of *jus in bello* proportionality satisfy
either one demand or the other. In this chapter, I offer a new account that satisfies
both demands. In addition, I offer an account of how combatants should cope with
predictive uncertainty regarding the likely humanitarian costs and likely military
benefits of their actions as well as moral uncertainty regarding their relative weight.

I argue that an attack that inflicts incidental harm on civilians is objectively proportionate only if it prevents opposing forces from inflicting substantially greater
harm on attacking forces or civilians in current or future military operations. This
account reflects the moral asymmetry between doing harm and allowing harm
while looking beyond particular tactical engagements to the broader operational
context. I argue that an attack is epistemically proportionate only if the attacker
reasonably believes—on the basis of decisive epistemic reasons—that the attack
will prove objectively proportionate. Put another way, an attacker must reasonably

---

[1] Protocol Additional to the Geneva Conventions of August 12, 1949, and relating to the
Protection of Victims of International Armed Conflicts (Protocol I) (adopted June 8, 1977,
entered into force December 7, 1978) 1125 UNTS 3, art 51(5). See also ICRC, *Customary
International Humanitarian Law*, vol 1 (CUP 2009) 46.

Law and Morality at War. First Edition. Adil Haque. © Adil Haque 2017. Published 2017 by Oxford
University Press

believe that, of all the possible outcomes of the attack, it is probable that the outcome of the attack will be objectively proportionate.

My account of *jus in bello* proportionality is in one way more determinate than existing accounts—for example, it does not compare incommensurable values but instead compares immediate losses to civilians with future losses to civilians and to attacking forces. At the same time, my account must still grapple with the predictive uncertainty inherent in determining whether immediate losses inflicted will be redeemed by future losses avoided. Accordingly, I explore a number of decision procedures and rules of engagement that combatants may use to make the best possible decision given the limited information available to them.

Elements of the Proportionality Rule

Let us begin by briefly reviewing key elements of the proportionality rule. First, civilian losses are *excessive in relation to* military advantage just in case the former *exceed, outweigh,* or are *unjustified by* the latter.[2] Strangely, it is sometimes suggested that civilian losses are not excessive in relation to military advantage unless the former significantly outweigh the latter.[3] This suggestion has no obvious basis in language or logic. In ordinary language, "excessive" simply means "exceeding" or "going beyond" some normative standard.[4] Moreover, it seems bizarre to concede that the humanitarian considerations against an attack outweigh the military considerations in favor of the attack yet insist that the attack is nevertheless justified.

Second, international law prohibits attacks which *may be expected* to cause civilian losses which *would be* excessive in relation to the military advantage *anticipated*. In other words, the lawfulness of an attack depends not on its actual consequences but on its reasonably foreseeable consequences.[5] Attackers must do everything feasible

---

[2] See US Dept of Defense, *Law of War Manual* 2.4.1.2 ("*Proportionality* generally weighs the justification for acting against the expected harms to determine whether the latter are disproportionate in comparison to the former").

[3] See, eg, Israel Ministry of Foreign Affairs, *The 2014 Gaza Conflict: Factual and Legal Aspects* (2015) 185 ("As long as there is no significant imbalance between the expected collateral damage and the anticipated military advantage, no excessiveness exists"); Geoffrey S Corn, Laurie R Blank, Chris Jenks, & Eric Talbot Jensen, "Belligerent Targeting and the Invalidity of a Least Harmful Means Rule" (2013) 89 International Law Studies 536 ("an attack does not become unlawful when the expected collateral damage or incidental injury is slightly greater than the military advantage anticipated (as is suggested by the term 'disproportionate'), but only when those effects are 'excessive'").

[4] See, eg, *Merriam-Webster's Dictionary* (defining "excessive" as "exceeding what is usual, proper, necessary, or normal"); *Oxford English Dictionary* ("More than is necessary, normal, or desirable").

[5] cf Program on Humanitarian Policy and Conflict Research, *Commentary on the HPCR Manual on International Law Applicable to Air and Missile Warfare* (2010) 91 ("the standard is objective in that expectations must be reasonable").

to assess whether an attack will cause excessive civilian losses and to cancel or suspend an attack if it becomes apparent that it will do so.[6] It follows that

In determining whether an attack was proportionate it is necessary to examine whether a reasonably well-informed person in the circumstances of the actual perpetrator, making reasonable use of the information available to him or her, could have expected excessive civilian casualties to result from the attack.[7]

Put another way, international law does not prohibit objectively disproportionate attacks but instead prohibits epistemically disproportionate attacks. Much more on this below.

Third, only *military* advantages that are *concrete and direct* can legally justify civilian losses. A *military* advantage is "any consequence of an attack which directly enhances friendly military operations or hinders those of the enemy" such as disabling opposing combatants, destroying their equipment, denying them opportunities to attack, and creating opportunities to attack them.[8] By contrast, "forcing a change in the negotiating position of the enemy only by affecting civilian morale does not qualify as military advantage."[9] A military advantage is *concrete* only if it is substantial and clearly identifiable. A military advantage is *direct* only if it is proximately caused, either without further intervening agency (as with the destruction of weapons to prevent their future use) or with reasonably foreseeable intervening agency (as with strikes intended to lead an adversary to divert troops or resources away from one's true objective).

It has been claimed that military advantages are concrete and direct only if they are "relatively close" to the attack in space and time, and that advantages "which would only appear in the long term should be disregarded."[10] However, it seems clear that the destruction of weapons in a factory or armory would yield a concrete and direct advantage even if the weapons would not have been sent to the front lines for many weeks. Accordingly, a concrete and direct advantage "may or may not be temporally or geographically related to the object of the attack" so long as it is "foreseeable by the [attacker] at the relevant time."[11]

When the achievement of a military advantage requires coordinated attacks, the proportionality rule compares the harm expected and the military advantage anticipated from the operation as a whole.[12] Paradigmatically, it may be necessary

---

[6] Protocol I arts 57(2)(a)(iii) and 57(2)(b); ICRC, *Customary IHL Study*, 58 and 60.

[7] *Prosecutor v Galić* (Judgment) IT-98-29-T (December 5, 2003), para 58.

[8] *Commentary on the HPCR Manual*, 45.

[9] *Commentary on the HPCR Manual*, 45.

[10] ICRC, Commentary on the Additional Protocols of 8 June 1977 to the Geneva Conventions of 12 August 1949 (ICRC/Martinus Nijhoff 1987) para 2209.

[11] See, eg, International Criminal Court, *Elements of Crimes* (2011) n 36.

[12] See, eg, UK Ministry of Defense, *Law of Armed Conflict Manual* (OUP 2005) 5.33.5; ICRC, *Protocol I Commentary*, para 2218.

to destroy several bridges in order to prevent the movement of troops or supplies. The military advantage of destroying any one bridge may be trivial if the opposing force could simply use one of the other bridges. Accordingly, we should compare the advantage anticipated and the harm expected from destroying all the bridges.

Fourth, it is sometimes claimed that "[r]emote harms resulting from [an] attack do not need to be considered in a proportionality analysis."[13] On the contrary, unlike military advantages, civilian losses need not be concrete and direct to fall under the proportionality rule. Moreover, it is hard to believe that temporally remote harms foreseeably resulting from placing a mine or improvised explosive device in a civilian area do not need to be considered in a proportionality analysis. Similarly, destroying bridges or roads necessary to bring food or medicine to a civilian population may predictably result in civilian deaths when existing supplies run out.[14] It seems that such foreseeable remote harms also need to be considered in a proportionality analysis.

Fifth, an attack may be rendered disproportionate by loss of civilian life, injury to civilians, or damage to civilian property.[15] Other bad consequences of an attack may render the attack morally impermissible all things considered, but will not render an attack legally disproportionate.

My account of *jus in bello* proportionality compares *harms* inflicted with *harms* prevented, and is compatible with different accounts of how to compare death, injury, and property damage to one person or across persons. To take but one example, nothing in my account precludes measuring the harmfulness of death, injury,

---

[13] US Dept of Defense, *Law of War Manual* 5.12.3.

[14] See *Prosecutor v Prlić* (Judgment) IT-04-74, Trial Chamber, May 29, 2013, paras 1582–4.

[15] Environmental damage raises interesting issues. For example, Protocol I prohibits methods or means of warfare which may be expected to cause widespread, long-term and severe damage to the natural environment. Protocol I, art 55(1). Accordingly, environmental damage is prohibited if it is severe even if it is not excessive, but is not prohibited if it is excessive but not severe.

In contrast, the Rome Statute of the International Criminal Court recognizes a war crime of knowingly inflicting "widespread, long-term and severe damage to the natural environment which would be clearly excessive in relation to the concrete and direct overall military advantage anticipated." Rome Statute of the International Criminal Court (opened for signature July 17, 1998, entered into force July 1, 2002) 2187 UNTS 3, art 8(2)(b)(iv). Accordingly, environmental damage is punishable only if it is both severe and clearly excessive.

Finally, the ICRC takes the view that customary international law prohibits attacks "which may be expected to cause incidental damage to the environment which would be excessive in relation to the concrete and direct military advantage anticipated." ICRC, *Customary IHL Study*, 143. Accordingly, environmental damage is prohibited if it is excessive even if it is not severe. I will not attempt to reconcile these approaches here.

See also Eliav Lieblich, "Beyond Life and Limb: Exploring Incidental Mental Harm under International Humanitarian Law," in Derek Jinks, Jackson Nyamuya Maogoto, & Solon Solomon (eds), *Applying International Humanitarian Law in Judicial and Quasi-Judicial Bodies: International and Domestic Aspects* (TMC Asser 2014) 185.

and property damage in terms of quality-adjusted life years or "QALYs" and simply aggregating such QALYs across persons. Although my account prominently includes a deontic asymmetry between doing and allowing harm, it is compatible with broadly utilitarian accounts of measuring and aggregating harms.

As it happens, I believe that it would be impermissible to collaterally kill one innocent person as a side effect of preventing small harms to many people, even if the total harm prevented (however measured) would be substantially greater than the total harm inflicted. On this roughly prioritarian view, we should consider not only total harm inflicted or prevented but also distributions of harm that leave some much worse off than others.[16]

Accordingly, it may be impermissible to collaterally kill or injure civilians merely to prevent a great deal of damage to military or civilian property. Conversely, it may be permissible to collaterally damage a great deal of civilian property if necessary to prevent soldiers or civilians from being killed or injured. In principle, those who would be killed or injured would be made far worse off than those who would lose only their property. Of course, in practice, damage to military or civilian property often leads to death, injury, destitution, or illness. Accordingly, proportionality may depend not on property damage as such but instead on its predictable downstream consequences.

Similarly, it may be objectively impermissible to kill civilians to prevent several more civilians or soldiers from being injured. Conversely, it may be objectively permissible to prevent soldiers or civilians from being killed even if it means collaterally injuring several more civilians. In principle, those who would be killed would be made far worse off than those who would be injured. Of course, in practice, it is often very hard to predict whether an act will kill or injure. Accordingly, often it will be epistemically permissible to launch attacks that will (in fact) collaterally kill civilians in order to prevent attacks that would (in fact) have only injured many others. In any event, my account of *jus in bello* proportionality does not depend on any particular resolution of these difficult issues of measurement and comparison.

Finally, civilian losses may be legally justified only by advantages that that are causally downstream from disabling opposing combatants and destroying, capturing, or neutralizing military objectives. In contrast, the proportionality rule excludes advantages that are causally downstream from collateral harm to civilians. As we saw in Chapter 1, attackers may not opportunistically take advantage of the presence of civilians to obtain military advantages. Accordingly, the fact that collateral harm to civilians would spread terror or damage morale may not render an otherwise disproportionate attack proportionate.

---

[16] For more on prioritarianism, see Derek Parfit, "Equality and Priority" (1997) 10 Ratio 202–21.

Incommensurable and Incomparable Values

On its face, *jus in bello* proportionality seems to call for a comparison between two incommensurable values—civilian losses and military advantage—irreducible to any more basic value.[17] Civilian losses may be ranked according to their relative moral gravity, military advantages according to their relative contribution to military victory, but there appears to be no single standard according to which both may be ranked by their relative value.

Although civilian losses and military advantages seem incommensurable, they are not entirely incomparable.[18] Certainly, we often make confident proportionality judgments in extreme cases. As Henry Shue observes, "[i]t is undeniably excessive to inflict very large civilian losses for the sake of a very small military advantage."[19]

For example, the ICRC writes that "the presence of a soldier on leave obviously cannot justify the destruction of a village. Conversely, if the destruction of a bridge is of paramount importance for the occupation or non-occupation of a strategic zone, it is understood that some houses may be hit, but not that a whole urban area be leveled."[20] Similarly, the Israeli High Court writes that "shooting at [a sniper firing on soldiers or civilians] is proportional even if as a result, an innocent civilian neighbor or passerby is harmed. That is not the case if the building is bombed from the air and scores of its residents and passersby are harmed."[21] However, our less confident judgments in close and intermediate cases suggest that military advantages and civilian losses are at most imprecisely or roughly comparable.

If civilian losses and military advantages are only imprecisely comparable, we should not expect *jus in bello* proportionality to provide clear guidance in the vast majority of tactical situations that attacking forces confront. Nevertheless,

---

[17]   See, eg, APV Rogers, *Law on the Battlefield* (1996) 17 ("some delegations at the diplomatic conference at which Protocol I was negotiated . . . were reluctant to include any reference to the proportionality rule because of the difficulty of comparing things that were not comparable (i.e. military advantage and civilian losses)"); Michael N Schmitt, "The Principle of Discrimination in 21st Century Warfare" (1999) 2 Yale Human Rights and Development Law Journal 143, 151 ("Optimally, balancing tests compare like values. However, proportionality calculations are heterogeneous, because dissimilar value genres—military and humanitarian—are being weighed against each other. How, for example, does one objectively calculate the relative weight of an aircraft, tank, ship, or vantage point in terms of human casualties?").

[18]   See Ruth Chang, "Introduction" in Ruth Chang (ed), *Incommensurability, Incomparability, and Practical Reason* (Harvard University Press 1997) 14 (noting that incommensurable values often permit "nominal–notable" comparisons in extreme cases).

[19]   Henry Shue, "Proportionality in War" in Gordon Martel (ed), *The Encyclopedia of War* (Wiley 2012) 6.

[20]   ICRC, *Protocol I Commentary*, para 2214.

[21]   *Public Committee Against Torture in Israel v Israel* (Judgment) HCJ 769/02, December 11, 2005, para 46. See also *Beit Sourik Village Council v Israel* (Judgment) HCJ 2056/04, June 30, 2004, para 41.

Shue proposes that we can improve our proportionality judgments by sorting particular military advantages and civilian losses into rough categories along the following lines:

	Military Advantage	Civilian Losses
Level 1	Important	Moderate
Level 2	Compelling	Severe
Level 3	Decisive	Catastrophic

According to Shue, "it is excessive to inflict civilian losses of a category higher than the category of military advantage anticipated."[22] On this view, an attacking force may inflict moderate civilian losses in pursuit of an important, compelling, or decisive military advantage; severe civilian losses in pursuit of a compelling or decisive advantage; and catastrophic civilian losses only in pursuit of a decisive military advantage.

Shue does not attempt to fix the boundaries of each category, but he imagines that the task of doing so would proceed along parallel tracks, with military experts categorizing military advantages according to military standards and "morally sensitive" individuals categorizing civilian losses according to moral standards. Independent moral judgment would then be exercised to sort the categories created by the two groups into three (or more) levels. Each level would then contain categories of losses and advantages that are roughly equal in moral weight.

The virtue of Shue's approach is that it can apply symmetrically to all sides of a conflict independently of the justice of their respective war aims. The basic shortcoming of Shue's approach is that it leaves our intuitive judgments opaque. Since it does not identify the moral principles or empirical assumptions underlying our judgments, it cannot tell us when those principles are inapplicable or those assumptions are unsound. Since it does not illuminate the basis of our intuitive proportionality judgments in extreme cases, it cannot help us make inferential proportionality judgments in non-extreme cases. This approach cannot tell us what to consider or ignore when we make such judgments, or what circumstances might render our intuitive judgments more or less reliable.

On a practical level, Shue's approach organizes our intuitive moral judgments but cannot replace or improve upon them. Certainly, we can rank civilian losses by their moral gravity and military advantages by their military utility, but we lack a common standard of value through which the two rankings can be integrated. True,

---

[22] Shue, "Proportionality in War," 7. For a similar approach, see Jason D Wright, "'Excessive' Ambiguity: Analysing and Refining the Proportionality Standard" (2012) 94 International Review of the Red Cross 819, 852.

we could directly judge one item in the first ranking comparable to one item in the second ranking, and use this direct comparison as an anchor for integrating the remainder of the two rankings. However, simply ranking two items does not reveal the degree of difference between them. It is not enough to know that a "compelling" military advantage is greater than an "important" military advantage and that "severe" civilian losses are greater than "moderate" civilian losses. We also need to know *how much* greater advantages or losses in one category are than advantages or losses in another category. Only then can we use our anchor point to generate parallel rankings of imprecisely comparable values. It seems unlikely that Shue's approach could generate such a complete ranking.

Intrinsic and Instrumental Values

Thomas Hurka and Jeff McMahan reject the view that civilian losses and military advantages are incommensurable values on the grounds that military advantages have no intrinsic value at all.[23] Indeed, soldiers ought not harm opposing combatants, capture strategic territory, or destroy military equipment for its own sake. Such military advantages have instrumental or derivative value only if they contribute to some further, intrinsically valuable state of affairs. Importantly, the defeat of an opposing armed force has intrinsic value only if one fights for a just cause—such as national self-defense or humanitarian intervention—that morally justifies resorting to or continuing the use of military force.

Hurka and McMahan conclude that the value of a military advantage, if any, lies in the contribution that it makes to the achievement of a just cause. Conversely, a military advantage that contributes to an unjust cause has no moral value. Hurka and McMahan therefore reject the independence of *jus ad bellum* just cause and *jus in bello* proportionality and with it the symmetrical application of *jus in bello* proportionality. Put another way, *jus in bello* proportionality is just a special application of *jus ad bellum* proportionality. Just as *jus ad bellum* proportionality compares civilian losses inflicted by the war as a whole with the importance of a just cause, *jus in bello* proportionality compares civilian losses inflicted by a particular military operation with the contribution of that operation to the achievement of the same just cause.

For just combatants, this moral standard makes for an impossible decision procedure. Soldiers would first have to measure the moral importance of their war aims, since a similar contribution to a more important war aim would justify more extensive civilian losses. Soldiers would then have to measure the degree to which the achievement of a particular military advantage would increase the probability

---

[23] See Thomas Hurka, "Proportionality in the Morality of War," *Philosophy & Public Affairs* 33 (2005) 34; Jeff McMahan, "Proportionality and Necessity in *Jus in Bello*," in Helen Frowe & Seth Lazar (eds), *The Oxford Handbook of the Ethics of War* (OUP 2016); McMahan, "Proportionate Defense" (2013–14) 23 Journal of Transnational Law and Policy 1, 20–1.

of achieving their war aims, discount the value of their war aims by this marginal increase in probability, and compare the resulting expected value with the civilian losses that they expect to inflict. Finally, if their just cause depends on collective values such as national self-determination then soldiers will have to somehow compare incommensurable (individual and collective) values. Nor is it clear how a more manageable decision procedure could be derived from the moral standard proposed.

Importantly, on this view, unjust combatants cannot conform to *jus in bello* proportionality. A military advantage cannot inherit moral value from a war aim that has no moral value to pass on, and a military advantage with no moral value cannot morally justify inflicting civilian losses. On this view, every harm that unjust combatants inflict on civilians is morally disproportionate. It follows that, on this view, proportionality prohibits but cannot regulate the conduct of unjust combatants. This view provides no moral guidance to combatants who are forced to fight without a just cause. To be sure, unjust combatants can still choose to minimize the harm that they inflict on civilians in pursuit of their war aims and even to place themselves at greater risk to reduce the risks that they impose on civilians. But since unjust combatants cannot pursue their unjust war aims by *proportionate* means it is useless for them to try. Nor can observers judge a particular military operation proportionate or disproportionate simply by comparing the military advantage that it aims to achieve with the civilian losses that it predictably inflicts. Except in extreme cases, observers must first judge the war as a whole. If this view prevails, then proportionality judgments will become even more politicized than they are already.

Hurka and McMahan offer an account of *jus in bello* proportionality that is morally intelligible but applies asymmetrically and yields an impractical decision procedure. Shue offers an account that applies symmetrically but is morally inexplicable and of limited practical use. In the following sections I will try to do better.

Inflicting and Preventing Harm

As we saw in Chapter 1, killing and injuring other human beings presumptively infringes their basic moral rights. In some cases, these others may, by their voluntary conduct, make themselves morally liable to be killed or injured. In such cases, the relevant moral rights are forfeited and not infringed. Alternatively, killing or injuring some may be the lesser of two evils, necessary to prevent greater harm to others. More precisely, killing or injuring some may be morally permissible as a necessary means of preventing far greater harm to others or as an unavoidable side effect of preventing substantially greater harm to others. This qualification reflects the view that, other things equal, intentionally doing harm is morally much worse—that is, harder to justify—than unintentionally doing harm which is, in turn, morally substantially worse than allowing harm. In such cases, the relevant moral rights are overridden and therefore justifiably infringed.

I propose that it is *jus in bello* proportionate to collaterally harm civilians as an unintended side effect of achieving a military advantage that will prevent or enable one to prevent opposing forces from inflicting substantially greater harm to one's own forces or civilians in current or future military operations. The last qualification ("in current or future military operations") is important because, while attacks on opposing forces sometimes prevent imminent harm to attacking forces or to civilians, most attacks on military equipment or strategic locations prevent or avoid such harm only over the medium- or long-term.

If the proposed standard is satisfied, then the moral rights of the civilians harmed may be permissibly overridden to protect the moral rights of others. On this view, the moral value of a military advantage lies in the harm to soldiers and civilians that it prevents. This standard applies symmetrically to all sides of a conflict, independently of their war aims, yet identifies a morally compelling explanation for when military advantage justifies civilian losses.

While my account may seem unfamiliar to readers steeped in military practice, it should not. Targeting decisions are often driven by considering the *criticality* of a target, including the target's importance to the adversary's ability to conduct operations (*value*), the time interval between a strike on the target and a measurable impact on the adversary's ability to conduct operations (*depth*), and the time and cost required for the adversary to regain its functional capability (*recuperation*).[24] My account simply focuses targeting decisions on the adversary's capacity to inflict serious harm.

Let me illustrate the account by applying it to a series of skeletal cases. To keep things simple, these cases will assume an international armed conflict between state armed forces. At the end of the chapter I will apply the account to targeted killing operations within a non-international armed conflict between state armed forces and organized armed groups.

The first case is the simplest:

> *Simple Prevention*: State A is at war with State B. If State A destroys State B's long-range missiles, then some of State B's civilians will be killed as a side effect. However, if State A does not destroy State B's long-range missiles, then State B will use those missiles to kill many more of State A's soldiers and civilians in future military operations.

A strike on the long-range missiles directly prevents State B from harming State A's soldiers and civilians (hence *Simple Prevention*). On my view, this operation seems proportionate since the immediate harm that it inflicts is substantially less than the future harm that it prevents. Importantly, we can judge the operation without reference to the war aims of either State A or State B. More on this below.

It might seem that the preceding case calls for a simple comparison between the consequences of action and the consequences of inaction but that is not quite

---

[24] US Joint Chiefs of Staff, *Joint Publication 3-60: Joint Targeting* (2007) D-2–D-4.

correct. The harm that an attack will prevent depends not only on what the opposing party will do if the attack is not carried out but also on what the attacking party
will do if the attack is not carried out and how the opposing force will respond. The
preceding scenario assumes that if the operation is not launched, then State A will
not simply surrender but will continue to fight State B by other means. However,
State A's alternative means of fighting will not prevent State B from launching its
long-range missiles. In this sense, my view assumes that parties will pursue victory
until they either win or lose. My view compares only the harms inflicted and prevented by intervening military operations.

Now let us add some facts to the first case:

> *Triple Prevention*: If State A destroys State B's anti-aircraft missiles, then some of State B's
> civilians will be killed as a side effect. However, if State A does not first destroy State B's
> anti-aircraft missiles, then State A's air forces will be shot down before they can destroy
> State B's long-range missiles.

A strike on the anti-aircraft missiles will not directly prevent State B from harming
State A's soldiers and civilians. Instead, the strike will prevent State B from preventing State A from preventing State B from harming State A's soldiers and civilians
(hence *Triple Prevention*).

On my view, *jus in bello* proportionality is satisfied only if the losses inflicted
on State B's civilians by *both* the strike on the anti-aircraft missiles *and* the subsequent strike on the long-range missiles are substantially less than the losses that the
long-range missiles would inflict on State A's soldiers and civilians. Cases like *Triple
Prevention* illustrate the general truth that the proportionality of an attack depends
not only on the harm that it prevents but also on the harm that it enables additional attacks to prevent. For example, "[i]f, in order to prevent the enemy's army
from advancing, planners decide to destroy all the bridges that span a river, ... each
driver or pilot may judge that his own action is disproportionate, [but] the operation as a whole may meet the proportionality requirement."[25]

Now let us change the facts of the second case slightly:

> *Timely Prevention*: If State A destroys State B's anti-aircraft missiles, then some of State
> B's civilians will be killed as a side effect. However, if State A does not first destroy State
> B's anti-aircraft missiles, then it will take longer for State A's air forces to destroy State
> B's long-range missiles and the long-range missiles will kill many of State A's civilians
> before they are destroyed.

In this case, State A can prevent State B from using its long-range missiles to kill
State A's soldiers and civilians without first destroying State B's anti-aircraft mis-
siles. However, if State A first destroys State B's anti-aircraft missiles, then fewer of
State A's civilians will be killed. Evidently, *Timely Prevention* is just a special case

---

[25] Jean-François Quéguiner, "Precautions under the Law Governing the Conduct of
Hostilities" (2006) 88 International Review of the Red Cross 804.

of *Triple Prevention*, in which we compare the losses inflicted by the attack on the anti-aircraft missiles with the losses prevented by destroying the long-range missiles sooner rather than later.

Now consider the following variation on the previous cases:

> *Costly Triple Prevention*: If State A destroys State B's anti-aircraft missiles, then some of State B's civilians will be killed as a side effect. However, if State A does not first destroy State B's anti-aircraft missiles, then State A's air forces will suffer substantial losses before destroying State B's long-range missiles.

In this case, State A can prevent State B from using its long-range missiles to kill State A's soldiers and civilians without first destroying State B's anti-aircraft missiles. However, if State A first destroys State B's anti-aircraft missiles, then fewer of State A's soldiers will be killed trying to prevent State B from using its long-range missiles. It follows that an attack on the anti-aircraft missiles is justified only if the losses that *those* missiles would inflict on attacking forces are substantially greater than the civilian losses that the attack itself would inflict.

Arguably, cases like *Costly Triple Prevention* are not governed by the proportionality rule but by the precautions rule. On this interpretation, the true targets are the long-range missiles and attacking forces must choose between one method of attacking those targets that involves greater harm to civilians but less harm to attacking forces and another method of attacking the same targets that involves greater harm to attacking forces but less harm to civilians. As we saw in Chapter 7, the precautions rule should be interpreted to prohibit the method more harmful to civilians unless alternative methods would be substantially more harmful to attacking forces.

On an alternative interpretation, there are two distinct targets in such cases, each of which offers distinct though related military advantages. The advantage of destroying the long-range missiles lies in the losses that this will prevent, assuming that the attacking force will not surrender and would otherwise pursue victory by other means. The advantage of destroying the anti-aircraft missiles lies in the losses that this will prevent, assuming that the attacking force will, and could proportionately, attack the long-range missiles. On this view, *Costly Triple Prevention* simply combines two cases of *Simple Prevention*, one nested within the other. An attack on the anti-aircraft missiles will prevent substantially greater harm than it will inflict because it will enable an attack on the long-range missiles that will in turn prevent substantially greater harm than it will inflict.

The proper classification of such cases is conceptually interesting but makes no practical difference. Both the precautions rule and the proportionality rule are best understood in terms of the moral asymmetry between doing harm and allowing harm and will prohibit the same conduct. However, as a matter of legal interpretation, it seems better to classify such cases under the proportionality rule. The precautions rule governs the choice of alternative means and methods of carrying out a single attack on a single target, or a choice between targets. However, attacking a secondary target does not seem like a *method* of attacking a primary target. Instead, we should view these as distinct attacks on distinct targets.

As a general matter, attacks on opposing combatants, military equipment, and military facilities will share the same causal structure as the four preceding cases. Such attacks either prevent the object of attack from inflicting future harm, prevent the object of attack from preventing the attacking force from preventing some further object of attack from inflicting future harm, prevent the object of attack from delaying the attacking force from preventing some further object of attack from inflicting future harm, or prevent the object of attack from inflicting harm on the attacking force or its civilian population as it seeks to prevent some further object of attack from inflicting future harm. Such attacks are proportionate if they (or the sequence of attacks of which they are a necessary part) prevent (or enable the prevention of) substantially greater harm than they inflict.

Attacks that aim to capture strategic locations introduce an additional causal step between the initial attack and the prevention of harm. Such attacks either indirectly prevent harm by denying such locations to the opposing force or enable the attacking force to prevent harm in subsequent operations. Though the causal structure of such cases is more complex, their moral structure is the same. Such attacks are proportionate only if they indirectly prevent (or indirectly enable the prevention of) substantially greater harm than they (or the sequence of attacks of which they are a necessary part) inflict.

The Value of Military Advantage

We can now see where, on my account, the value of a military advantage lies. Let X represent the total losses that one's own forces and civilians will suffer in current or future military operations if a military advantage—say, destroying a munitions factory or killing an insurgent leader—is not achieved. Let Y represent the total losses that one's own forces and civilians will suffer in current or future military operations if that military advantage is achieved. The value of the military advantage is the difference between X and Y, that is, the total overall losses prevented by achieving the advantage. Let Z be the losses that one would unintentionally inflict on opposing civilians in pursuit of the advantage. On my view, an attack is proportionate just in case the difference between X and Y is substantially greater than Z.

In more familiar terms, collateral harm to civilians is proportionate only if it is outweighed by *military necessity*. According to one influential formulation:

Military necessity permits a belligerent, subject to the laws of war, to apply any amount and kind of force to compel the complete submission of the enemy with the least possible expenditure of time, life, and money.[26]

---

[26] *US v List*, at 1253.

Since the complete submission of the enemy seldom depends on a single attack, almost all attacks are supported by military necessity only to the extent that their execution will reduce the expenditure of time, life, and money in pursuit of military victory, relative to their non-execution. Evidently, the conservation of time and money cannot justify collateral harm to civilians, except insofar as shortening the conflict or conserving resources would avoid or enable the avoidance of comparable harm to others. It follows that attacks that collaterally harm civilians are supported by military necessity only if their execution reduces the expenditure of life and serious injury in pursuit of military victory, relative to their non-execution.

Put another way, the value of a military advantage is the *difference* between the harm that attacking forces and their civilians will suffer during a given military campaign if that advantage is obtained and the harm they will suffer during the same military campaign if that advantage is not obtained or, if the advantage is necessary to the success of the campaign, any otherwise permissible alternative campaign that does not require that advantage to succeed. Harm to civilians inflicted in pursuit of a military advantage satisfies *jus in bello* proportionality only if the same campaign without that advantage, or any otherwise permissible alternative campaign, would involve substantially greater harm to civilians and to the attacking force. Advanced militaries already compare possible courses of action when planning operations, typically in terms of effectiveness, risks to attackers, and costs.[27] On my view, they should also compare possible courses of action in terms of the harms they will inflict on civilians and the harms they will allow their adversary to inflict on attackers or on civilians.

Why should the proportionality of an attack depend on a comparison between possible campaigns? Such a comparison is unavoidable because the harms that an attack will prevent are just the harms that the opposing party will inflict if the attack is not carried out, which in turn depend on what the attacking force will do instead of carrying out that attack: retreat, surrender, or (more likely) design and carry out a modified or alternative military campaign. Again, *jus in bello* proportionality assumes that parties will pursue military victory, by otherwise permissible means, at the lowest cost to their forces and civilian population. The harm that a particular attack prevents is just the harm that the attacking force would suffer if it pursued the next-least costly and otherwise permissible campaign.[28]

---

[27] See, eg, Allied Joint Publication AJP-5, Allied Joint Doctrine for Operational-Level Planning (2013) 3–37; US Naval War College, Workbook on Joint Operations Planning Process, NWC 4111H, January 21, 2008.

[28] Note that full moral justification requires a comparison between campaigns that each satisfies the *jus ad bellum* as well as other *jus in bello* norms. Certainly, an attack cannot be morally justified on the grounds that if the attack is not carried out then the attackers will pursue a campaign that violates other moral or legal standards.

Of course, it is often the case that a series of attacks overdetermines the success of a military campaign. In such cases, each attack is causally connected to success even though success is not counterfactually dependent on any individual attack. In my view, an act that infringes rights can only be justified by its results if those results are counterfactually dependent on the act. It follows that attacks that harm civilians and make no difference to the success or cost of a military campaign may be objectively impermissible. However, since the results of an attack are always difficult to predict, it may be epistemically permissible to launch a series of attacks some of which will prove superfluous and therefore objectively impermissible. Only such a view seems to capture the moral reality that war inevitably involves pointless suffering that is recognizable as such only in retrospect.

In rare cases, securing a particular military advantage is strictly necessary for military victory. In such cases, there is no campaign sufficient for military victory that does not require securing this advantage. As we have seen, *jus in bello* proportionality compares the costs of pursuing victory by first securing a particular military advantage with the costs of pursuing victory without first securing that advantage. It follows that an attack violates *jus in bello* proportionality only if victory can be achieved without first securing that advantage. We may say that attacks necessary to secure advantages that are necessary for victory necessarily satisfy *jus in bello* proportionality.[29]

Jus in bello proportionality can foreclose many ways to win, but cannot foreclose the only way to win. Of course, "the rules of international law must be followed even if it results in the loss of a battle or even a war."[30] However, following the rule of *jus in bello* proportionality may result in the loss of a battle but may not result in the loss of a war. While the *jus in bello* categorically prohibits attacking civilians irrespective of anticipated military advantage, the *jus in bello* only prohibits collaterally harming civilians out of proportion to anticipated military advantage. Accordingly, civilian losses cannot outweigh the military advantage of winning a war under the *jus in bello*. However, as we shall see, civilian losses can outweigh the aims of the war under the *jus ad bellum*.

Crucially, to say that attacks necessary for victory do not violate *jus in bello* proportionality is not to say that such attacks are lawful let alone morally permissible. In particular, if an attack necessary for victory would cause more harm than victory itself would justify, then the war effort as a whole would violate *jus ad bellum* proportionality. Properly understood, *jus ad bellum* proportionality compares the harm inflicted by an overall military strategy, including by all of its constituent attacks,

---

[29] Seth Lazar suggested to me that attacks that secure such necessary advantages necessarily satisfy *jus in bello* proportionality because if the war aim is achieved, then the war will end, thereby avoiding all the harm that would have occurred had the war continued. Unfortunately, wars do not always end when one party achieves its aims.

[30] *US v List* (American Military Tribunal, Nuremberg, 1948), 11 NMT 1230, at 1272 para 128.

with the aims of the war as a whole. Accordingly, attacks necessary to the success of the overall strategy may satisfy *jus in bello* proportionality while the broader strategy violates *jus ad bellum* proportionality. If an attack necessary for victory would cause more harm than victory itself would justify, then the problem lies not at the *jus in bello* level but at the *jus ad bellum* level, not with the attack as such but with the overall strategy of which it is a necessary part. In other words, to say that an attack necessary for victory is disproportionate is just to say that the pursuit of victory is disproportionate, and is best understood as a *jus ad bellum* claim rather than as a *jus in bello* claim.

The legal standard of *jus ad bellum* proportionality is not found in any treaty but resides instead in customary international law. Unfortunately, state practice and *opinio juris* remains confused and fractured, with substantial support for three very different approaches. On one approach, proportionality requires that defensive force must be comparable in its scale and effects to that of the armed attack to which it responds. On a second approach, proportionality requires that defensive force must be no greater than necessary to prevent or repel the armed attack to which it responds. Finally, on a third approach, proportionality requires that the harm prevented by defensive force must outweigh the harm inflicted by defensive force.[31]

Many scholars favor the second, "instrumental" or "functional" approach, often adopting a state-centric view of the *jus ad bellum* while relegating humanitarian considerations to the *jus in bello*.[32] This rationale is somewhat surprising, since the object and purpose of the modern *jus ad bellum* regime is "to save succeeding generations from the scourge of war."[33]

Suppose that a non-state armed group G launches a series of armed attacks against State A from the territory of State T. Each attack harms a small number of persons in State A, but any defensive response sufficient to stop these attacks would collaterally kill hundreds of civilians in State T. Under the instrumental approach, such a defensive response by State A would be 'proportionate'. This seems hard to accept.

Now suppose that State T does not support group G and is in no way responsible for group G's actions. Perhaps State T is trying its best to prevent future attacks from group G but has thus far been unable to do so. However, State T also does not consent to State A's use of force on its territory out of concern for its civilians. If State

---

[31]   See, eg, US Dept of Defense, Law of War Manual 3.5.1 ("in *jus ad bellum*, proportionality refers to the principle that the overall goal of the State in resorting to war should not be outweighed by the harm that the war is expected to produce"); Dapo Akande & Thomas Liefländer, "Clarifying Necessity, Imminence, and Proportionality in the Law of Self-Defense" (2013) 107 AJIL 563, 566; David Kretzmer, "The Inherent Right to Self-Defence and Proportionality in *Jus Ad Bellum*" (2013) 24 EJIL 235, 278–9. See also Tom Ruys, '*Armed Attack' and Article 51 of the UN Charter* (CUP 2010) 121–2.

[32]   See, eg, Yoram Dinstein, *War, Aggression and Self-Defence* (CUP 2005) 237–42.

[33]   United Nations Charter, preamble.

A attacks group G in State T, killing hundreds of State T's civilians, then it seems that international law should permit State T to use force against State A, in defense of its territory and civilian population. Yet, under international law, "there can be no self-defense against self-defense."[34] In my view, we should avoid this conflict of rights by rejecting the instrumental approach and finding State A's use of defensive force disproportionate.

When states disagree over the content of a customary rule, which interpretation should prevail, at least provisionally, until general consensus is reached? If states disagree over the content of a *prohibition*, then arguably the prohibition should be construed narrowly, on the grounds that international law presumptively permits (in the weak sense) what it does not clearly prohibit.[35] In contrast, if states agree regarding the content of a prohibition but disagree over the content of an *exception* to that prohibition, then generally the exception should be construed narrowly, since the prohibition presumptively applies absent an agreed-upon exception. Importantly, international law generally prohibits the use of military force, with a limited exception for self-defense. Accordingly, if states disagree over the limits of self-defense, then we should favor the more restrictive position, namely that the resort to force, even if commensurate with and necessary to prevent the armed attack to which it responds, may be rendered disproportionate if the total harm it inflicts is out of proportion to the defensive aim it seeks to achieve.

Before moving on, let me take a moment to distinguish my view from one that McMahan effectively criticizes, namely the view that *jus in bello* proportionality compares harms inflicted on civilians with harms avoided to combatants *in the very same engagement*.[36] On this view, just combatants may inflict harm on civilians if such harm is a necessary and proportionate side effect of using defensive force against unjust combatants. This view could at most explain the permissibility of *unit self-defense*, that is, of force used to repel a direct attack on particular combatants. However, as McMahan observes, this view would preclude all offensive operations, since if a party refrains from offensive operations, then the necessity to use defensive force on behalf of its members often will not arise. In particular, McMahan argues that this view would preclude humanitarian military interventions. Since attacking forces could simply not intervene, attacking forces will inflict losses on civilians that are not strictly necessary to protect their members. In addition, it is not clear how this view would apply to targeted killing operations in which the attacking force is never in danger.

My view is not subject to these objections. On my view, we hold constant the war aim of the attacking force and ask whether an attack is a necessary part

---

[34] *US v Von Weizsaecker* et al (Ministries Case) (Nuremberg, 1949), 14 NMT 314, 329.
[35] See *SS "Lotus"* (*France v Turkey*) (Judgment) [1927] ICGJ 248.
[36] Jeff McMahan, "War Crimes and Wrongdoing in War," in RA Duff et al (eds), *The Constitution of Criminal Law* (OUP 2013).

of a broader campaign for achieving military victory. Attacks are proportionate, including as part of a humanitarian intervention, only if the immediate losses that they (or the sequence of attacks of which they are a necessary part) inflict are substantially less than the future losses that they will prevent in current or future military operations, assuming always that the attacking force will pursue military victory.

According to McMahan, "[w]hereas necessity requires comparisons between an act of defense and alternative means of avoiding a threatened harm, proportionality requires a comparison between an act of defense and *doing nothing* to prevent the threatened harm."[37] On this view, it might seem that, by tying the harm prevented by an attack to what the attacking force would permissibly do if it does not carry out the attack, I am conflating proportionality and necessity. Not so. It is just that, in war, there are two threats to consider: the micro-threats posed by particular military targets (such as infantry units or artillery positions) and the macro-threat posed by the opposing armed force as a whole. Accordingly, if the *jus ad bellum* permits a strategic response to the macro-threat posed by the opposing force, then the micro-threats posed by particular targets depend on which otherwise permissible strategy is chosen.

For example, suppose that State A launches an unjust war against State V. To end State A's aggression, State V plans a land invasion of State A, in full conformity with the *jus ad bellum*. Before and during the invasion, State V attacks military targets deep inside State A that would otherwise pose micro-threats to State V's invasion force. Surely such attacks are governed by the proportionality rule rather than by the necessity or precautions rule. Yet the alternative to destroying the targets and preventing the micro-threats they pose is hardly "doing nothing." If the targets are not destroyed, then the invasion force will still invade, but will take heavier losses in the process. Accordingly, the micro-threats posed by the targets depend on what the invading force would permissibly do if the targets are not destroyed.

Indeed, if the proportionality rule applied only to micro-threats that cannot be avoided through non-forcible means, as McMahan seems to suggest, then it would apply only to cases of unit self-defense, and perhaps to cases like *Simple Prevention*, but not to offensive military campaigns that make up much of war. Such a view seems open to many of the objections that McMahan offered to the simple view discussed above.

---

[37] McMahan, "Proportionate Defense," 3. McMahan also writes that "necessity compares the expected consequences of an act of defense with those of other means of defense, negotiation, or retreat, while proportionality compares the consequences of an act of defense with those of submission" (at 3). This view seems plausible with respect to the *jus ad bellum*. If force is necessary to prevent or repel an armed attack, then the only remaining decision is to resist or submit. However, assuming that the *jus ad bellum* is satisfied, the remaining decision under the *jus in bello* is *how* to resist.

Symmetry and Independence

On my view, *jus in bello* proportionality assumes that all parties to a conflict will pursue military victory and asks whether particular attacks prevent substantially greater harm to the soldiers and civilians of one side than they inflict on the civilian population of another. One virtue of my approach, then, is that it allows both participants and observers to evaluate the proportionality of particular military operations without reference to the justice or legality of the broader conflict. A party that violates the *jus ad bellum* may still conform to *jus in bello* proportionality. Conversely, a party that conforms to the *jus ad bellum* may systematically violate *jus in bello* proportionality.

The law assumes that warring parties will seek to pursue military victory at the least possible cost to their own soldiers and civilians. *Jus ad bellum* proportionality constrains each party's pursuit of military victory by comparing the value of their war aims with the total cost of their pursuit. In contrast, *jus in bello* proportionality constrains a party's attempts to reduce its own losses by comparing the future harm that an attack prevents with the immediate harm that it inflicts. Accordingly, a military strategy may satisfy *jus ad bellum* proportionality while many of its constituent attacks violate *jus in bello* proportionality. Alternatively, a military strategy may violate *jus ad bellum* proportionality while many of its constituent attacks satisfy *jus in bello* proportionality.

Certainly, the law requires both the independence of *jus in bello* proportionality from *jus ad bellum* considerations and the symmetrical application of *jus in bello* proportionality to all sides of a conflict. Presumably, a legal rule that flatly prohibits harming civilians in pursuit of an unjust cause will be ignored both by combatants who believe that their cause is just and by combatants who feel compelled to fight for a cause that they recognize is unjust.

Not everyone will see the symmetrical application of my approach as a virtue. Recall that Hurka and McMahan argue that a military advantage that does not contribute to the achievement of a just cause has no moral value that could justify the moral disvalue of harm to civilians. They conclude that any harm inflicted on civilians by unjust combatants in pursuit of an unjust cause is disproportionate from a moral point of view.

Hurka and McMahan are clearly right that attacks by unjust combatants are seldom fully morally justified, since they generally kill and injure just combatants, make the achievement of unjust causes more likely, and are in one sense unnecessary if the opposing party would agree to a ceasefire and ultimately to a just peace. However, attacks by unjust combatants may be less wrongful to the extent that they prevent harm to others. Since almost all civilians retain their moral right not to be harmed, there are almost always strong moral reasons to prevent civilians from being harmed. Similarly, since even unjust combatants do not deserve death or dismemberment, there is almost always some moral reason to prevent them from being harmed. An attack is less wrongful to the extent that it is supported by such reasons and more wrongful to the extent that it is not. Since proportionality is in part a function of such reasons, it is almost always morally worse for unjust combatants to harm civilians in violation of *jus in bello* proportionality than for them to harm civilians without violating *jus in bello* proportionality. It follows that even combatants who knowingly fight without a just cause (perhaps under duress) have significant moral reasons to comply with *jus in bello* proportionality. In doing so they will seldom act permissibly, but they will almost always act less wrongfully than they would otherwise.

There is an obvious objection to this argument. Suppose that State A is an unjust aggressor, that State B is fighting solely in national self-defense, and that if State A stops fighting, then State B will stop fighting as well. On these facts, State A could prevent all future harm to its own soldiers and civilians without harming any of State B's civilians simply by ending its aggression. It follows that State A is not even partially morally justified in harming any of State B's civilians. This argument succeeds subject to an important qualification. State A's political and military leaders are indeed responsible for all the harm inflicted by their armed forces, including in operations that do not violate the law of armed conflict. If they are prosecuted for the crime of aggression, then their sentences should reflect the total number of civilians *and combatants* harmed in pursuit of their unjust cause. These leaders may not claim *jus in bello* proportionality in defense of their conduct or in mitigation of their moral fault.

However, it is hardly ever in the power of operational and tactical commanders, let alone ordinary soldiers, to end an unjust war. They cannot do so on their own and are unlikely to succeed in mounting an effective joint or collective effort. As a result, unjust combatants often must choose between harming just combatants and foreign civilians or allowing just combatants to harm their fellow soldiers and their own civilians. In many such cases, individual unjust combatants are partially morally justified in defending their fellow soldiers and their own civilians.[38] Often, unjust combatants should refuse to fight *on balance*, that is, often their reasons to refuse are even stronger than their reasons to fight. However, their reasons to fight are powerful—even if defeated by even more powerful opposing reasons—and it is in this sense that they are partially justified in fighting.[39]

It is true that, on my view, *jus in bello* proportionality does not prohibit unjust combatants from collaterally harming just combatants or civilians in order to prevent harm to unjust combatants (themselves included). Yet many just combatants

---

[38] In rare cases, unjust combatants may be fully justified in participating in an unjust war. See Uwe Steinhoff, "When May Soldiers Participate in War?" (2016) 8 International Theory 236.

[39] cf Vera Bergelson, "Rights, Wrongs, and Comparative Justifications" (2007) 28 Cardozo Law Review 2481, 2493 ("A partially justified act is, therefore, a wrongful act that, due to certain mitigating circumstances, is less wrongful than that required by the charged offense").

do not pose unjust threats and therefore are not liable to defensive harm. Moreover, many unjust combatants pose unjust threats and therefore are liable to defensive harm. It follows that it is often objectively impermissible for unjust combatants to collaterally harm either just combatants or civilians in defense of unjust combatants. This inescapable fact seems to favor an asymmetrical standard.

At the same time, as we saw in Chapter 3, many just combatants pose unjust threats to civilians who retain their rights not to be harmed. These just combatants may be liable to defensive harm—perhaps even if the unjust threats they pose to civilians are themselves justified under the proportionality rule. Accordingly, it may be permissible for unjust combatants to collaterally harm such just combatants in defense of such civilians—perhaps even if doing so would prevent the prevention of substantially greater harm to others. Moreover, it may be permissible for unjust combatants to collaterally harm such just combatants, as well as civilians, in defense of unjust combatants, if only so that these unjust combatants may defend innocent civilians from unjust threats in the future.

Of course, not all just combatants will pose unjust threats to civilians, and not all unjust combatants will defend civilians from unjust threats. It follows that a gap will remain between symmetrical law and asymmetrical morality. This gap may be justifiable, or at least tolerable, for pragmatic and epistemic reasons. After all, most combatants *believe* that they are just combatants and that their opponents are unjust combatants. Accordingly, in practice, most combatants would simply ignore an asymmetric standard.

As a final plea in mitigation, we should recall that the law of armed conflict is prohibitive rather than permissive. Accordingly, the law of armed conflict prohibits acts that violate *jus in bello* proportionality, but does not permit, authorize, or condone acts that conform to *jus in bello* proportionality. Acts not prohibited by the proportionality rule may be prohibited by other legal or moral norms.

As we saw in Chapter 2, the moral function of the law of armed conflict is to help all combatants, just and unjust alike, more closely conform to the moral reasons that apply to them. For unjust combatants, full conformity is generally impossible and partial conformity is the most that they can achieve so long as they continue to fight at all. However, given the moral stakes of armed conflict, even partial conformity is most welcome. If unjust combatants stop harming civilians except as a side effect of preventing substantially greater harm to civilians or combatants, then armed conflict will be much less unjust than if they are not so constrained.

Expected Losses and Anticipated Advantages

As we have seen, the proportionality rule requires attacking forces to predict the harm that an attack may inflict on civilians, typically in the form of collateral damage estimates (CDEs). On my view, attacking forces must also predict the harm that their attacks will prevent in current or future military operations. Such predictions may seem impractical but in fact are ubiquitous in warfare and reflect a basic skill of responsible command. Most notably, commanders regularly make such predictions when deciding to carry out attacks that place their own forces in danger. Commanders seek to achieve military victory at the least possible cost to their own forces and civilians. Commanders will therefore place their own forces at risk only if they believe that doing so will prevent greater harm to their own forces and civilians in current or future military operations. My view simply requires commanders to bring together these two predictions in order to determine the epistemic permissibility of an attack.

In general, an action is epistemically permissible only if the actor has decisive reason to believe (a) that the action will infringe no rights, (b) that a justifying circumstance exists, or (c) that a justifying result will occur. Conversely, an action is epistemically impermissible if the actor has undefeated reason to believe (a) that the action will infringe rights, (b) that no justifying circumstance exists, and (c) that no justifying result will occur. It follows that an attack is epistemically impermissible if the attacker has undefeated reason to believe that the attack will harm civilians (an infringement of unforfeited rights) unless the agent has decisive reason to believe that the attack will prevent substantially greater harm to friendly forces or to friendly civilians (a justifying result). In other words,

> *Probably Proportionate*: An attack may be carried out only if, based on the information reasonably accessible to the attacker, the attack will probably prevent opposing forces from inflicting substantially greater harm on attacking forces and civilians in current or future military operations than the attack will inflict on civilians.

In this formulation, the degree of evidential probability reflects the strength of the attacker's epistemic reasons for belief. An attack is probably proportionate if the attacker's reasons to believe that it will prove objectively proportionate are stronger than the attacker's reasons to believe that it will prove objectively disproportionate.[40]

In many cases, there will be an amount of harm that an attack will probably inflict—for example, using a missile that will probably kill everyone in its blast radius—and an amount of harm that the attack will probably prevent—for example, by providing close air support to infantry units under fire. However, often there will be no single number that an attack will probably kill or that an attack will probably save. For example, suppose that there is a 40% chance that an attack will kill 10, a 30% chance that it will kill 20, and a 30% chance that it will kill 30. Similarly, suppose there is a 40% chance that the attack will save 20, a 30% chance that it will save 40, and a 30% chance that it will save 60. Assume that these probabilities are independent of each other, such that the number who will be killed is unrelated to the number that will be

---

[40] cf *Commentary on the HPCR Manual* ("'Expected' collateral damage and 'anticipated' military advantage, for these purposes, mean that that outcome is probable, i.e. more likely than not").

saved. There is no exact harm that the attack will probably prevent and no exact harm that the attack will probably inflict. Instead, there are nine possible outcomes, none of which is very likely to occur. We can illustrate this by adapting the Risk Assessment/ Tolerance Matrix used in NATO operational planning doctrine:[41]

	.4 harm 10	.3 harm 20	.3 harm 30
.4 save 20	.16 (20:10)	.12 (20:20)	.12 (20:30)
.3 save 40	.12 (40:10)	.09 (40:20)	.09 (40:30)
.3 save 60	.12 (60:10)	.09 (60:20)	.09 (60:30)

Nevertheless, we can still determine whether or not the attack will probably result in a proportionate outcome. For example, there is only a 33% chance that the attack will prevent at least three times more harm than it will inflict. These additional outcomes are indicated in bold. It follows that if harming is at least three times worse than allowing harm, then the attack will probably not prove proportionate and is therefore epistemically impermissible. Alternatively, there is an additional 34% chance that the attack will prevent twice the harm that it will inflict. These possible outcomes are indicated in italics. It follows that if harming is less than twice as bad as allowing harm, then there is a 67% chance that the attack will prove proportionate and is therefore epistemically permissible. If the possible harm inflicted and the possible harm prevented are not independent in this way, then the attacking force would have to determine the likelihood of each possible outcome and then determine whether the attack will probably result in one of the proportionate outcomes.

Any serious account of *jus in bello* proportionality will require attackers to make similar probabilistic judgments with respect to both civilian losses and military advantages, however the latter are understood. Nevertheless, such probabilistic judgments may seem too complicated for attacking forces to perform in many situations. Often the probabilities themselves are uncertain or the possible outcomes too numerous to carefully examine. In such cases, attacking forces may be unable to determine the epistemic permissibility—let alone the objective permissibility—of their actions. Attacking forces will have no choice but to base their decisions on presumptions, heuristics, and other mental shortcuts.

Since attacking forces tend to underestimate the harm that they will inflict and overestimate the harm that they will prevent, they should adopt a decision procedure that skews in the opposite direction. I propose the following:

Max–Min: If an attacker cannot determine whether or not an attack will probably prevent substantially more harm than it will inflict, then the attack may be carried out only if the minimum harm that the attack might plausibly prevent is substantially greater than the maximum harm that the attack might plausibly inflict.

[41] Allied Joint Doctrine for Operational-Level Planning, 3–39.

To exclude very unlikely outcomes, the term "plausibly" stands in for a rough probability threshold, around 20%, above which possible harm becomes operative. For example, if there is a 20%-or-greater chance that an attack will harm as many as 30 civilians and a 20%-or-greater chance that the attack will save as few as 20 soldiers or civilians, then the attack should not be carried out. If attackers cannot determine that an attack will probably prove proportionate, then they should assume the worst—within limits—and act accordingly.

One might think that an attack is permissible if the *expectable* harm to civilians—that is, the average of the possible harms to civilians discounted by their respective probabilities—is substantially less than the *expectable* military advantage—that is, the average of the possible military advantages discounted by their respective probabilities. In Chapter 6, we described this concept as *expectable proportionality*. The attack described above would expectably-harm around six and expectably-save around twelve. The attack is therefore expectably proportionate if doing harm is at most twice as bad as allowing harm but expectably disproportionate otherwise. In this case, my approach and the expectabilist approach yield the same result. However, in other cases the two approaches diverge.

For example, suppose that a targeted killing operation directed at a particular low-level insurgent will almost certainly harm several civilians and prevent little or no harm to soldiers because such fighters are seldom effective and so easily replaced. However, there is a small chance that this low-level insurgent will one day develop into a senior leader who will make a necessary contribution to the harming of many soldiers. Even if the harm that the attack will expectably prevent is substantially greater than the harm that the attack will expectably inflict, the attack is epistemically impermissible because it will almost certainly inflict far greater harm than it will prevent. If the attack ultimately harms civilians and saves no one, then the attacker could not possibly defend the attack to those civilians.

Here, as elsewhere, reasonable belief—that is, belief supported by decisive epistemic reasons—sets a minimum threshold of epistemic permissibility. However, we can endorse more restrictive standards on expectabilist grounds. For example, even an attack that will probably prevent substantially greater harm than it will inflict is expectably impermissible if it will inflict greater expectable harm than it will prevent. For example, if an attack carries a low probability (say, 10%) of inflicting very great harm (say, 1,000 civilian deaths) and no probability of preventing very great harm, then it may be expectably impermissible even if it will probably prevent greater harm (say, 30 combatant deaths) than it will inflict (say, 10 civilian deaths). Thus, an attack should be prohibited if it is *either* probably disproportionate *or* expectably disproportionate.

Finally, the reasonable belief threshold is no more absolute than other deontological constraints. For example, even an attack that will probably not prevent substantially greater harm than it will inflict is permissible if it will prevent far greater expected harm than it will inflict. For example, if an attack carries a low probability (say 10%) of preventing very great harm (say, 1,000 civilian deaths) and inflicting much less harm (say, 10 civilian deaths), then it may be epistemically permissible even if it will *probably* prevent only slightly more harm (say, 20 civilian deaths) than it will inflict (say, 10 civilian deaths). Thus, an attack is permissible only if it is *either* probably proportionate *or* expectedly overriding.

Moral Uncertainty

On my view, proportionality incorporates the moral asymmetry between doing harm and allowing harm. Expected harm to civilians is excessive in relation to anticipated military advantage when the former exceeds what the latter would justify. The value of a military advantage lies in the harm to combatants and civilians that its achievement will prevent in current or future military operations. Since doing harm is substantially worse than allowing harm, it follows that expected harm to civilians exceeds what anticipated military advantage would justify when the latter will not prevent substantially greater harm to others.

As we saw at the beginning of this chapter, proportionality judgments are somewhat imprecise. For example, we rarely judge that an attack would be proportionate if it will likely harm N civilians but would be disproportionate if it will likely harm $N + 1$ civilians. Most scholars suppose that proportionality judgments are imprecise because they compare incommensurable values, namely civilian losses and military advantage. Of course, I have argued that the value of a military advantage lies in the losses prevented by its achievement. Thus, on my account, proportionality judgments compare fully commensurable values, namely harms to some and harms to others.

On my view, proportionality judgments are imprecise because the moral asymmetry between doing and allowing harm is imprecise. When we say that killing is substantially worse than letting die, we do not mean that killing is *precisely* X or Y times worse than letting die, where X and Y are exact numbers like 3.14. Rather, we mean that killing is *at least* X times worse and *at most* Y times worse than letting die, where X and Y are substantial figures. Put another way, we mean that collaterally killing one innocent person would be a disproportionate side effect of preventing *fewer than* X innocent people from being killed but a proportionate side effect of preventing *more than* Y innocent people from being killed. At the same time, the permissibility of collaterally killing one innocent person as a side effect of saving between X and Y innocent people may be impossible to determine.

Importantly, on my view, the imprecision of our proportionality judgments is significant but hardly debilitating. Certainly, it would be disproportionate to collaterally harm one innocent person as a side effect of preventing comparable harm to only one other innocent person. This much seems to follow from any nontrivial asymmetry between doing harm and allowing harm. Yet even requiring a 1:2 ratio of harm inflicted to harm prevented would transform military practice. After all, the imprecision of the proportionality rule is thought by many to render it either fairly permissive or very permissive. In contrast, on my account, the imprecision of the proportionality rule renders it either fairly restrictive or very restrictive.

With respect to the upper bound (*Y*), responses to the famous Trolley Problem suggest that it would be proportionate to collaterally harm one innocent person as a side effect of preventing comparable harm to five other innocent people.[42] It is true that the Trolley Problem involves redirecting an existing threat, while collateral harming in war involves creating new threats as a side effect of eliminating existing threats. Arguably, it is harder to justify creating new threats than to justify redirecting existing threats. At the same time, it is possible that most people would think it permissible to redirect a threat away from two or three innocents toward one innocent. Accordingly, most people might think it permissible to create a new threat that would collaterally harm one innocent to prevent comparable harm to five innocent persons from an existing threat. Empirical studies of lay and expert judgments on these matters would be most illuminating.

Since proportionality judgments are necessarily somewhat imprecise, we should ask whether the law of armed conflict should prohibit attacks that are neither clearly proportionate nor clearly disproportionate. First, we should distinguish how attacking forces should act and how reviewing tribunals should judge. Obviously, reviewing tribunals should only punish individuals if the legal element of excessiveness is established beyond reasonable doubt. As we shall see in Chapter 10, this is the truth contained in the view that criminal liability should only attach to attacks that are *clearly* excessive.[43]

However, if attacking forces cannot determine whether the military advantage anticipated from an attack would justify the expected civilian losses, then they should refrain from attack. As the ICRC comments

the disproportion between losses and damages caused and the military advantages anticipated raises a delicate problem; in some situations there will be no room for doubt, while in other situations there may be reason for hesitation. In such situations [of doubt] the interests of the civilian population should prevail.[44]

---

[42] See, eg, Helen Frowe, "Claims Rights, Duties and Lesser Evil Obligations" (2015) 89 Proceedings of the Aristotelian Society, Supplementary Volume, 267, 277; McMahan, "Proportionality and Necessity in *Jus in Bello*."

[43] See Rome Statute, art 8(2)(b)(iv).

[44] ICRC, *Protocol I Commentary*, para 1979.

Harming civilians is not wrong because it is disproportionate. On the contrary, harming civilians is wrong unless it is proportionate. Attacking forces should presume that collaterally harming civilians is wrong unless they acquire decisive reason to believe that they are justified in doing so. Accordingly, combatants should refrain from attacks that are not clearly proportionate.

Moral Standards and Decision Procedures

In war, as elsewhere, often the surest way to miss a target is to aim at it directly, ignoring both adverse conditions as well as our own imperfections. Instead, we may be more likely to hit our target by aiming a bit above or below, to the left or to the right. Similarly, we may be more likely to satisfy a moral standard not by trying to apply it directly but by applying a decision procedure that anticipates and corrects for potentially distorting factors. The standard of *jus in bello* proportionality that I propose is a complex one. Attackers may better conform to that standard indirectly, by following a decision procedure that relies as much on intuition as on calculation.

In the regulation of armed conflict, the distinction between moral standards and decision procedures corresponds to the distinction between legal rules and rules of engagement (ROE). ROE do not directly track applicable legal rules in all of their complexity but instead provide clear and straightforward instructions to combatants of varying ages and education levels that, if followed, will more often succeed in eliciting lawful conduct.

To help combatants conform to *jus in bello* proportionality, I propose two ROE. First, consider

> *Us = Them*: Do not carry out an attack that will endanger civilians unless you would accept the same risk to your own unit to achieve the same goal.
>
> Ask yourself: Will the attack harm civilians? If so, would you carry out the attack even if your unit would suffer the same amount of harm? If you would not, then DO NOT carry out the attack.

To illustrate, *Us = Them* would direct an officer not to order a missile strike against an insurgent that would collaterally kill three civilians unless the officer would be willing to lose three soldiers in order to kill the insurgent. The officer might consider whether he would order a ground assault that would claim the lives of three soldiers, or whether he would order the strike even if three soldiers, held hostage by the insurgent, would be collaterally killed in the strike. In general, officers will endanger their own troops now only to substantially reduce danger to their own troops or civilians later. It follows that most officers who directly follow *Us = Them* will indirectly conform to *jus in bello* proportionality.

Next, consider the following ROE:

Ours = Theirs: Do not carry out an attack that will endanger foreign civilians unless you would accept the same risk to your own civilians.

Ask yourself: Will the attack harm civilians? If so, would you carry out the attack even if they were your own civilians? If you would not, then DO NOT carry out the attack.

To illustrate using the same scenario, *Ours = Theirs* would direct a commander not to order a missile strike against an insurgent that will collaterally kill three foreign civilians unless the commander would order the strike even if it would instead collaterally kill three of his own civilians. In general, officers will endanger their own civilians now only to substantially reduce danger to their own troops or civilians later. It follows that most officers who directly follow *Ours = Theirs* will indirectly conform to *jus in bello* proportionality.

As we saw in Chapter 1, soldiers have special duties to protect their fellow soldiers and fellow citizens even at grave risk and at great cost to themselves. However, these special duties do not give soldiers special rights to harm foreign civilians as a means or as a side effect of protecting their fellow soldiers or fellow citizens. Soldiers must bear the costs of their own special duties and may not impose costs on foreign civilians that the latter have no duty to accept. It follows that soldiers may not impose costs on foreign civilians that they may not impose on their fellow soldiers or fellow citizens. Accordingly, my proposed ROE require that attacking forces take losses to foreign civilians just as seriously as they take losses to their fellow soldiers and fellow citizens. Since attacking forces too often take the former much less seriously than the latter, these ROE serve a valuable corrective function in moral deliberation.

Importantly, military officers routinely decide how many soldiers under their command they are willing to risk or lose in order to obtain a given military advantage. *Us = Them* simply prohibits these officers from imposing greater risks or losses on civilians in order to obtain the same military advantage. With respect to *Ours = Theirs*, Ian Henderson reports that

I have used this simple concept [that collateral harm to foreign civilians is proportionate only if comparable harm to fellow civilians would be proportionate] in lectures, exercises and operations and can attest to its usefulness in helping military members "grasp" the concept of applying proportionality rather than merely thinking about it in abstract terms.[45]

Hopefully, these proposed ROE will provide military officers with practical decision procedures that are simpler and more direct than the proportionality rule itself.

Of course, these ROE are only decision procedures and not moral or legal standards. For one thing, much like the Golden Rule, these ROE depend for their application on the subjective values of the applicant. The less value an officer places on

---

[45] Henderson, Ian, *The Contemporary Law of Targeting: Military Objectives, Proportionality, and Precautions in Attack under Additional Protocol I* (Martinus Nijhoff 2009) 229.

the lives of his own forces, the less value these ROE require him to place on the lives of civilians. These ROE only tell us to place equal value on the lives of our own forces and the lives of civilians. They do not tell us how much absolute value to place on the lives of anyone. At the same time, since most attackers—consciously or subconsciously—place as much or more value on their troops than on foreign civilians, most attackers will act less wrongfully if they follow these ROE than if they allow their implicit biases to affect their targeting decisions.

Superiors and Subordinates

Until now we have discussed the duties of attacking forces as collective agents without attending to the moral division of labor within such collectives. However, the moral and legal duties of superiors and subordinates differ in potentially significant ways. One obvious difference is that operational commanders must ensure the proportionality of entire military campaigns, while tactical commanders must ensure the proportionality of particular attacks. More interesting differences arise between those who order attacks and those who carry them out.

For example, Protocol I requires "those who plan or decide upon an attack . . . [to] refrain from deciding to launch any attack" that would inflict disproportionate harm on civilians.[46] This norm clearly applies only to those who design and order military operations. However, Protocol I also directs that "an attack shall be cancelled or suspended if it becomes apparent" that the attack will inflict excessive harm on civilians.[47] The use of the passive voice suggests that this norm applies to all soldiers at all levels, including those who only carry out attacks. According to the ICRC, "[t]he rule set out here . . . applies not only to those planning or deciding upon attacks, but also and primarily, to those executing them."[48] Indeed, if it is apparent to a subordinate that an attack would be disproportionate then the attack is manifestly unlawful and any order by a superior to carry out the attack must be refused.[49]

True, subordinates will not always know the value of the military advantage that an attack would yield and therefore cannot always know when new information regarding possible harm to civilians reveals the attack to be disproportionate. In many cases, subordinates will better conform to their moral obligations by deferring to their superiors, whose access to information, analysis, and legal counsel better positions

---

[46] Protocol I art 57(2)(a)(iii).
[47] Protocol I art 57(2)(b); ICRC, *Customary IHL Study*, 60.
[48] ICRC, *Protocol I Commentary*, para 2220. See also Quéguiner, "Precautions under the Law Governing the Conduct of Hostilities," 803.
[49] See Rome Statute of the International Criminal Court, art 33(1)(c) (superior orders are not a defense to war crimes if the defendant did not believe that the orders were lawful or if the orders were manifestly unlawful).

them to make reliable proportionality judgments. If the attack is in fact disproportionate, then responsibility lies with the superiors and not with the subordinates.

Importantly, however, there are at least three situations in which subordinates should
not defer to their superiors.[50] First, subordinates may learn that the possible harm to
civilians is much greater than their superiors anticipated. Presumably, a judgment based
on false factual assumptions warrants little deference. Accordingly, such subordinates
should not carry out the attack unless they relay the new information to their superiors and then receive orders to proceed with the attack. Second, subordinates may have
reason to doubt that their superiors are applying the proportionality standard reasonably and in good faith. Accordingly, such subordinates should not carry out attacks
unless the information provided by their superiors convinces the subordinates themselves of their lawfulness. Finally, subordinates may conclude, based on the information
available to them, that an attack appears so grossly disproportionate as to be manifestly
unlawful.[51] In such extreme cases, it is so unlikely that additional evidence, available
only to their superiors, would support the contrary conclusion that subordinates may
not defer but must insist on additional information before carrying out an attack.

For example, suppose that a drone pilot is ordered to launch a missile at an
unnamed, low-level insurgent away from an active battlefield. Before launching
the missile, the pilot sees a dozen civilians pass into the expected blast radius of the
missile. Presumably, the potential harm to civilians is much greater than the pilot's
superiors anticipated. Moreover, the attack now appears so grossly disproportionate
that it is highly unlikely that the pilot's superiors have specific information regarding the targeted individual that would support a judgment of proportionality. It is
very unlikely that the targeted individual will otherwise kill substantially more than
a dozen soldiers or civilians, as would be required to render the attack proportionate. In this case, the pilot legally must and morally should suspend the attack.[52]

Targeted Killings Revisited

Thus far, I have illustrated my account of *jus in bello* proportionality mostly using
skeletal cases involving international armed conflict. While the US–Iraq war shows

---

[50] cf Raz, *The Morality of Freedom* (OUP 1986) 42–6.

[51] Raz, *Morality of Freedom.*

[52] cf *Commentary on the HPCR Manual*, 94 ("Anyone with the ability and authority to suspend,
abort or cancel an attack, must do so once he reaches the conclusion that the expected collateral
damage would be excessive in relation to the anticipated military advantage. For instance, a pilot
who has the target in view and unexpectedly observes civilians in the target area—who were
not supposed to be there, based on the information provided to him during the briefing preceding the attack—must assess the collateral damage expected to befall them and cancel the attack
if he concludes that the principle of proportionality will be violated"); Quéguiner, "Precautions
under the Law Governing the Conduct of Hostilities," 805 ("[I]f, before launching a first salvo
against a bridge, a tank driver notices that a crowd of fleeing civilians have taken refuge under
the targeted bridge, the driver cannot assume that the planners have correctly considered the

that state-to-state conflict is hardly a thing of the past, it is worth pausing to apply my account to non-international armed conflicts between states and non-state actors.

For over a decade, the United States has pursued a strategy of targeted killing of individual adversaries using unmanned aerial vehicles (UAVs) or "drones." One of the supposed virtues of drones is that they can hover over a target for an extended period and strike when few or no civilians are in harm's way. Indeed, the ratio of civilians killed to combatants killed by drone strikes has fallen from almost 1:1 under the Bush administration to under 1:4 under the Obama administration and continues to fall.[53] However, the Obama administration also expanded the drone campaign from targeting mostly high-level terrorists and insurgents to targeting primarily mid-level and low-level Taliban fighters. As a result, the number of drone strikes increased dramatically in 2010, and the annual number of civilian deaths remained very high for several years. These changes in the design and execution of the drone program make it both more difficult and more important to evaluate its morality and legality.

To evaluate the proportionality of a particular drone strike, we must compare the losses that the strike will inflict on civilians to the losses that the strike will prevent from befalling soldiers or civilians in current or future military operations. It therefore seems that drone strikes against low-level insurgents and terrorists that unintentionally kill civilians will seldom prove proportionate. Many low-level insurgents will never kill anyone, and many are so easily replaceable that killing them will not prevent substantially greater future harm. Such insurgents may be *liable* to be killed even if they will be replaced if killed. However, attacks that inflict losses on civilians can be *proportionate* only if the attacks also prevent substantially greater harm to others. It follows that if killing a low-level insurgent will not prevent substantially greater harm to others, then it would be disproportionate to harm any civilians in the process.[54]

In contrast, a high-level insurgent commander might make a necessary contribution to the deaths of many soldiers or civilians in current or future military operations. High-level insurgents may be difficult to quickly replace, or may be replaced by others with less skill or charisma. In principle, it could be proportionate to

principle of proportionality and continue his mission in wilful blindness and impunity. He must, at the very least, suspend his attack in order to allow the civilians to evacuate, or to request that his orders be confirmed in the light of these new circumstances").

[53]   See Bureau of Investigative Journalism, "Covert Drone War," http://www.thebureauinvestigates.com/category/projects/drones/.

[54]   For a similar conclusion reached on strategic rather than moral or legal grounds, see United States Department of Defense, *The U.S. Army and Marine Corps Counterinsurgency Field Manual*, para 7-32 (US Army Field Manual No 3-24, 2006) ("In COIN environments, the number of civilian lives lost and property destroyed needs to be measured against how much harm the targeted insurgent could do if allowed to escape. If the target in question is relatively inconsequential, then proportionality requires combatants to forego severe action, or seek non-combative means of engagement").

collaterally kill some civilians as a side effect of killing such a high-level insurgent.[55] Importantly, even if a particular drone strike satisfies *jus in bello* proportionality, the overall strategy of using drones to achieve broader war aims may violate the *jus ad bellum*.

Conclusion

An attack that inflicts incidental harm on civilians is proportionate only if it prevents opposing forces from inflicting substantially greater harm on attacking force or civilians in current or future military operations. This account of *jus in bello* proportionality does not compare incommensurable values, only immediate losses to civilians and future losses to civilians and to attacking forces. In addition, this account applies symmetrically to all parties to an armed conflict, independently of the *jus ad bellum* morality and legality of their use of military force. Attacks that are disproportionate under this account are morally impermissible when carried out by just combatants, and disproportionate attacks carried out by unjust combatants are morally worse than proportionate attacks carried out by unjust combatants. It follows that both just and unjust combatants have decisive moral reasons to avoid attacks that are disproportionate under this account, and the law would guide soldiers well by prohibiting such attacks.

---

[55] cf Michael N Schmitt, "Unmanned Combat Aircraft Systems and International Humanitarian Law: Simplifying the Oft Benighted Debate" (2012) 30 BU Int'l LJ 595, 616 ("Multiple civilian casualties may not be excessive when attacking a senior leader of the enemy forces, but even a single civilian casualty may be excessive if the enemy soldiers killed are of little importance or pose no threat").

9

Human Shields

International law categorically prohibits using civilians as human shields. As a matter of customary international law, "the use of human shields requires an intentional co-location of military objectives and civilians or persons *hors de combat* with the specific intent of trying to prevent the targeting of those military objectives."[1] As Protocol I puts it

The presence or movements of the civilian population or individual civilians shall not be used to render certain points or areas immune from military operations, in particular in attempts to shield military objectives from attacks or to shield, favour or impede military operations. The Parties to the conflict shall not direct the movement of the civilian population or individual civilians in order to attempt to shield military objectives from attacks or to shield military operations.[2]

Simply put, it is unlawful either to move civilians near military targets—"active" shielding—or to move military targets near civilians—"passive" shielding—for the specific purpose of preventing or dissuading attacks on those targets. Indeed, using civilians as human shields is a war crime.[3]

The moral bases of this legal prohibition are not hard to find. Combatants who use human shields opportunistically take advantage of the presence of civilians; place those civilians at grave risk; and often occasion foreseeable harm to those civilians. In addition, the use of involuntary human shields involves coercing civilians to serve an end they need not share. As far as I know, no one argues that it is legally permissible to use human shields and only Cécile Fabre argues that it is morally permissible to use human shields outside of extreme cases.[4] Since I respond to Fabre's arguments elsewhere, I will leave them aside here.[5] Instead, I will focus on the legal and moral permissibility of killing human shields.

---

[1] International Committee of the Red Cross, *Customary International Humanitarian Law*, vol 1 (CUP 2009) 340.

[2] Protocol Additional to the Geneva Conventions of August 12, 1949, and relating to the Protection of Victims of International Armed Conflicts (Protocol I) (adopted June 8, 1977, entered into force December 7, 1978) 1125 UNTS 3, art 51(7).

[3] Rome Statute of the International Criminal Court (opened for signature July 17, 1998, entered into force July 1, 2002) 2187 UNTS 3, art 8(2)(b)(xxiii).

[4] Cécile Fabre, *Cosmopolitan War* (OUP 2012) 256–67.

[5] Adil Ahmad Haque, "Human Shields" in Helen Frowe & Seth Lazar (eds), *The Oxford Handbook of the Ethics of War* (OUP 2015).

Law and Morality at War. First Edition. Adil Haque. © Adil Haque 2017. Published 2017 by Oxford University Press

Combatants use civilians as *involuntary shields* by co-locating those civilians with military targets by force, without their knowledge, or without their consent, for the purpose of preventing or discouraging attacks on those targets. I will defend the view that involuntary shields retain their legal and moral protection from intentional, unnecessary, and disproportionate harm. In contrast, the United Kingdom as well as a few scholars suggest that attackers may lawfully *discount* collateral harm to involuntary shields in determining proportionality. More dramatically, the United States Department of Defense now takes the position that attackers may lawfully *disregard* collateral harm to involuntary shields in determining proportionality. On either view, an attack that would be disproportionate if some number of civilians is near the target by chance will be proportionate if the same number of civilians—or even a greater number of civilians—is near the target by force. I will argue that both views are legally baseless and morally unsound. In my view, the law is clear and needs at most a moral defense. For readers who find the law unclear, my moral arguments indicate how any legal indeterminacy should be resolved.

Voluntary shields are civilians who freely choose to co-locate with military targets for the purpose of preventing or dissuading attacks on those targets. The legal status of voluntary shields remains controversial. Some experts argue that all voluntary shields directly participate in hostilities and thereby forfeit their civilian immunity. The ICRC insists that voluntary shields directly participate in hostilities only if their presence creates a physically obstacle to military operations but not if their presence creates a legal obstacle to military operations. Against both these views, I will argue that voluntary shields directly participate in hostilities only when their physical shielding is an integral part of a coordinated military operation likely to directly cause serious harm. However, I will also argue that collateral harm to other voluntary shields may be discounted—though not disregarded—when determining the proportionality of an attack. Since neither treaty nor custom definitively settles the question, I rely more heavily on moral arguments to show that my interpretation of the law offers combatants the best possible moral guidance.

A few preliminaries. First, I will refer to civilians who find themselves near military targets but who do not intend to shield military targets and are not intended by the defending force to shield military targets as *passersby*.

Second, one might distinguish between *contra-voluntary* shields—civilians whom defenders forcibly use to shield themselves—and *non-voluntary* shields—civilians whose presence defenders non-forcibly exploit to shield themselves. For example, a fleeing combatant may take refuge in a hospital or an apartment building, intending to use its civilian occupants as passive human shields, while the civilian occupants remain where they are not under duress but instead due to ignorance (they may be unaware of his presence), incapacity (they may be physically unable to leave), or for purposes other than shielding (they may have no safe place to go or no safe way to get there). However, legal scholars generally treat both contra-voluntary shields and non-voluntary shields as involuntary shields. This seems appropriate.

After all, non-voluntary shields differ from civilian passersby only in the defending force's specific purpose in locating military targets near them. If, as I argue below, the conduct and purposes of the defending force should not deprive civilians of their moral and legal protection, then non-voluntary shields are indeed morally and legally comparable to contra-voluntary shields in relevant respects.

Finally, my moral arguments assume tactical encounters between attacking forces pursuing a just cause and defending forces that use human shields while pursuing an unjust cause. However, if my legal and moral arguments succeed, then attacking forces pursuing an unjust cause will act less wrongfully if they obey the law than if they violate the law and discount or disregard collateral harm to all human shields.

Involuntary Shields

As noted above, Protocol I prohibits using civilians as human shields.[6] In its very next provision, Protocol I states that "any violation of these prohibitions shall not release the [other] Parties to the conflict from their legal obligations with respect to the civilian population."[7] It follows that, under Protocol I, the use of human shields by one party does not release other parties from their legal obligations not to launch attacks "which may be expected to cause incidental loss of civilian life . . . which would be excessive in relation to the concrete and direct military advantage anticipated."[8]

The "no-release" provision of Protocol I—as I will call it— reflects the general principle of customary international law that "[t]he obligation to respect and ensure respect for international humanitarian law does not depend on reciprocity."[9] On the contrary, each party's legal obligations with respect to the civilian population apply categorically, unconditionally, and independently of the conduct of the opposing party. These legal obligations are not owed to the opposing party but to the civilian population, and rest not on considerations of fairness or reciprocity but on considerations of humanity.

The legal obligations of combatants correspond to the legal rights of civilians. As we have seen, "[t]he civilian population and individual civilians shall enjoy general protection against dangers arising from military operations . . . unless and for such time as they take a direct part in hostilities."[10] It follows that civilians can lose their own rights through their own conduct, but they cannot lose their rights through the unlawful conduct of others. While civilian *objects* can lose their protected status as a result of the conduct of opposing forces—for example, when a civilian object

---

[6] Protocol I art 51(7).   [7] Protocol I art 51(8).
[8] Protocol I art 51(5)(b) and 57(2)(a)(iii).   [9] ICRC, *Customary IHL Study*, 498.
[10] Protocol I arts 51(1) and 51(3). See also ICRC, *Customary IHL Study*, 19 ("Civilians are protected against attack unless and for such time as they take a direct part in hostilities").

is used to make an effective contribution to military action[11]—civilian *persons* can lose their protected status only as a result of their own voluntary conduct.

To test the moral soundness of this position, consider the following scenario:

> *One Target*: You can strike a legitimate military target from the North or from the South. If you strike from the North, then you will kill 19 civilians who are unwittingly passing by. If you strike from the South, then you will kill 20 civilians forced to serve as involuntary human shields.

Presumptively, it is worse for you to kill 20 civilians than for you to kill 19 civilians. Moreover, it is hard to see why it should matter to you which civilians are near the target by chance and which are there by force. You know that none are there by choice or to fight. That should be enough.

No doubt, your adversary has acted wrongfully, even criminally. But now the choice is yours: to kill fewer or to kill more. In my view, you ought to strike from the North or not at all. Moreover, if it is disproportionate to strike from the North, killing 19, then it is disproportionate to strike from the South, killing 20. If the military advantage of striking the target cannot justify killing 19 civilians who have done nothing to forfeit their rights, then it cannot justify killing 20 civilians who have done nothing to forfeit their rights.

Indeed, if a strike from the North would kill 20 passersby, then you still have no obvious moral reason to strike from the South. The wrongful conduct of the defending force is not even a moral "tie-breaker." If anything, it might be slightly worse to kill 20 involuntary shields than to kill 20 passersby. As we shall see, the moral wrongfulness of harming a person can vary somewhat in degree depending on how easily the individual could have avoided being in harm's way. As hard as it is for passersby to avoid military targets, particularly in dense urban environments, it is even harder for involuntary shields to avoid military targets. At a minimum, it is equally hard to justify killing 20 involuntary shields as it is to justify killing 20 passersby. If the anticipated military advantage would not justify killing the latter, then it does not justify killing the former.[12]

Discounting Harm to Involuntary Shields

Into this sea of unconditional obligations, some seek to establish an island of conditional obligation. Most notably, the UK *Manual of the Law of Armed Conflict* states that

---

[11] See Protocol I art 52(2); ICRC, *Customary IHL Study*, 29.

[12] Killing involuntary shields might also be slightly worse than killing passersby on roughly prioritarian grounds. In general, it is better to confer a benefit on the potential recipient who is comparatively worse off; similarly, it is worse to impose a cost on the potential victim who is comparatively worse off. Since involuntary shields have been threatened and coerced by the defending force, they are in some respects worse off than passersby. For more on prioritarianism, see Derek Parfit, "Equality and Priority" (1997) 10 Ratio 202–21.

Even where human shields are being used, the proportionality rule must be considered. However, if the defenders put civilians or civilian objects at risk ... this is a factor to be taken into account in favour of the attackers in considering the legality of attacks [that harm those civilians].[13]

Similarly, the UK *Manual* states that

Any violation by the enemy of this rule [prohibiting the use of human shields] would not relieve an attacker of his responsibility to take precautions to protect the civilians affected, but the enemy's unlawful activity may be taken into account in considering whether the incidental loss or damage was proportionate to the military advantage expected.[14]

The use of the passive voice, as well as the past tense, leaves the meaning of these passages somewhat unclear. These passages do not say that *attackers* may take a defender's conduct into account in considering the legality of their own future attacks. Instead, the passage seems to address a third party considering the legality of an attacker's past attacks.

The peculiar phrasing of the UK *Manual* tracks the following passage from Rogers:

Those carrying out attacks in such circumstances [including the use of human shields] are not relieved of their obligation to attack military objectives only and reduce incidental damage as much as possible, but in considering the rule of proportionality, any tribunal dealing with the matter would be obliged to weigh in the balance in favour of the attackers any such illegal activity by the defenders.[15]

This passage suggests that the parallel language of the UK *Manual* is addressed to tribunals considering past attacks and not to attackers considering future attacks. The passage from Rogers invites additional questions. Does Rogers mean that tribunals should consider an attack disproportionate if the civilians in danger are there by chance but proportionate if the same civilians are there by force? Or does Rogers mean only that tribunals should remember that even a high degree of expected incidental harm may turn out to have been proportionate because there were important military targets nearby? It is hard to say. Certainly, if Rogers and the UK *Manual* mean that attackers may discount expected harm to human shields when determining the proportionality of an attack, then they chose an odd way of saying so.

In any event, Rogers and the UK *Manual* are often cited for the proposition that collateral harm to involuntary shields may be discounted—though not entirely disregarded—in determining the legal proportionality of an attack.[16] This view flies

---

[13] UK Ministry of Defence, *The Manual of the Law of Armed Conflict* (OUP 2005) 2.7.2.
[14] UK Ministry of Defence, *Manual of the Law of Armed Conflict*, 5.22.1.
[15] Rogers, "Zero-Casualty Warfare" (2000) 82 International Review of the Red Cross 179.
[16] See, eg, Yoram Dinstein, *The Conduct of Hostilities under the Law of International Conflict* (2nd edn CUP 2010), 155 (internal cross-reference omitted); Schmitt, "Human Shields," 51.

in the face of the unconditional structure and humanitarian purpose of the law of armed conflict. Importantly, if this less extreme position is legally unsound, then the US Department of Defense's more extreme position must be legally unsound as well.

We should first distinguish between two legal positions. The first legal position concedes that Protocol I forbids its 174 signatories (including the United Kingdom) from attacks "which may be expected to cause incidental loss of civilian life ... which would be excessive in relation to the concrete and direct military advantage anticipated"[17] and clearly states that the use of civilians as involuntary human shields "shall not release the Parties to the conflict from their legal obligations with respect to the civilian population."[18] However, according to this first position, civilian losses that would be excessive if the civilians are mere passersby may not be excessive if the civilians are involuntary shields. On this view, "even if the principle [of proportionality] as such endures—the test of what amounts to 'excessive injury to civilians must be relaxed.'"[19] On this view, Protocol I permits attackers to discount—though not entirely disregard—expected collateral harm to civilians used as involuntary shields.

Put simply, this first position seeks to circumvent the "no-release" provision of Protocol I by reinterpreting the prohibition on excessive civilian losses. Such a reinterpretation seems impossible to accept. Under Protocol I, the excessiveness of expected civilian losses is determined "in relation to the concrete and direct military advantage anticipated" from killing opposing combatants, destroying enemy equipment or facilities, capturing or denying territory, and so forth. Yet neither the moral gravity of expected civilian losses nor the military value of the anticipated advantage depends on whether the civilians harmed are involuntary shields or mere passersby. If attacking forces seek to justify expected civilian losses not by reference to anticipated military advantage but by reference to the opposing party's legal violations, then they seek, in effect, to be released from their legal obligation under Protocol I.

One might think that there is an extra military advantage in denying one's adversary the ability to prevent attacks through the use of involuntary human shields. This is incorrect. The advantage anticipated from preventing one's adversary from preventing an attack is just the advantage anticipated from the attack itself. To see this, consider the following scenario:

> *Metal Shield*: State A wants to destroy a military target in State B. State B erects a metal shield to physically block attacks on the target. If State A destroys the metal shield, then this will collaterally kill 10 civilians as a side effect.

---

[17] Protocol I art 51(5)(b) and 57(2)(a)(iii).   [18] Protocol I art 51(8).
[19] See Dinstein, *Conduct of Hostilities*, 155.

Clearly, it cannot be more important to destroy the shield than to destroy the target that it shields. It is permissible to collaterally kill 10 civilians as a side effect of destroying the metal shield only if it would be permissible to collaterally kill 10 civilians as a side effect of destroying the original target. It follows that if the advantage anticipated from an attack would not justify killing some number of civilians, then preventing an adversary from preventing that attack cannot justify killing the same number of civilians.

The second legal position is that the 19 *non*-signatories to Protocol I (including the United States, Israel, and Iran) are released from their duty under *customary* international law not to inflict excessive civilian losses if the defending force is using the civilians in question as involuntary human shields. On this view, the no-release provision of Protocol I does not reflect customary international law and may be ignored by countries that have not ratified Protocol I.[20]

This second legal position rests on a mistake. The no-release provision of Protocol I is not a substantive norm independent of distinction, precautions, and proportionality that may be rejected while the others are accepted. Instead, the non-release provision merely clarifies and underscores the unconditional nature of the substantive norms themselves, whose customary status is undisputed. One cannot endorse the principles of distinction, precautions, and proportionality only on the condition that the opposing party fulfills its legal obligations because it is part of the principles of distinction, precautions, and proportionality that they apply unconditionally. As we have seen, the unconditional application of the law of armed conflict is itself a principle of customary international law.

Disregarding Harm to Involuntary Shields

Not long ago, Michael Schmitt wrote that the view that "treats involuntary shields as civilians entitled to the full benefits of their international humanitarian law protections," "seems to dominate among international humanitarian law experts."[21] Schmitt elsewhere described the opposing view, that harm to involuntary shields may be entirely disregarded in determining the proportionality of an attack, as "an extreme view that has, fortunately, gained little traction."[22]

Indeed, as recently as 2013, the United States Joint Chiefs of Staff took the view that when civilians are intermingled in the target area or are used as human shields

---

[20] See, eg, W Hays Parks, "Air War and the Law of War" (1990) 32 Air Force Law Review 1, 163.

[21] Michael N Schmitt, "Human Shields in International Humanitarian Law" (2008) 38 Israel Yearbook on Human Rights 17, 50–1. See also Program on Humanitarian Policy and Conflict Research, *Commentary on the HPCR Manual on International Law Applicable to Air and Missile Warfare* (2010) 93.

[22] Michael N Schmitt, "Fault Lines in the Law of Attack," in Susan Breau & Agnieszka Jachec-Neale (eds), *Testing the Boundaries of International Humanitarian Law* (British Institute of International and Comparative Law 2006) 277, 300.

Joint force targeting ... is driven by the principle of proportionality, so that otherwise lawful targets involuntarily shielded with protected civilians may be attacked ... provided that the collateral damage is not excessive compared to the concrete and direct military advantage anticipated by the attack.[23]

On this sensible view, if the expected harm to civilians used as involuntary shields is not justified by the anticipated military advantage, then the attack is disproportionate and therefore unlawful. Collateral harm to involuntary shields may not be discounted, let alone disregarded, when determining the proportionality of an attack.

Unfortunately, in 2015, the United States Department of Defense (DoD) departed from the sensible view of the Joint Chiefs and embraced the extreme view that Schmitt and others hoped would gain little traction. The DoD's *Law of War Manual* takes the following position:

Harm to the following categories of persons and objects would be understood not to prohibit attacks under the proportionality rule: (1) military objectives [that is, enemy combatants, civilians taking a direct part in hostilities, and military equipment]; (2) certain categories of individuals who may be employed in or on military objectives; and (3) human shields.[24]

Evidently, these categories differ from one another in a number of legally and morally relevant respects. Combatants and direct participants in hostilities forfeit their civilian immunity from both direct attack and collateral harm. In contrast, civilians who work in or on military objectives retain their civilian immunity from direct attack. However, according to the DoD, such employees "are deemed to have assumed the risk of incidental harm from military operations."[25] Perhaps the same can be said of voluntary shields. Certainly, the same cannot be said of involuntary shields. Remarkably, the DoD draws no distinction between civilians who freely choose to serve as voluntary shields and civilians forced to serve as involuntary shields. According to the DoD, all of these civilians count for nothing in determining proportionality.

Since the United States is not a party to Protocol I, the DoD must be claiming that, under customary international law, the general prohibition on disproportionate harm to civilians contains a specific exception for civilians used as human

---

[23] United States Joint Chiefs of Staff, Joint Targeting (Joint Publication 3-60) (January 13, 2013) A-2. See also United States Joint Chiefs of Staff, Joint Targeting (Joint Publication 3-60) (Apr. 13, 2007) E-2–E-3 ("[A] defender may not use civilians as human shields . . . . In these cases, the civilians have not lost their protected status and joint force responsibilities during such situations are driven by the principle of proportionality").

[24] US Department of Defense, *Law of War Manual* (2015) 5.12.3.

[25] US Department of Defense, *Law of War Manual*, 244. This appears to be a minority view. See, eg, UK *Manual*, para 2.5.2 (stating that "munitions factories are legitimate military targets and civilians working there, though not themselves legitimate targets, are at risk if those targets are attacked. Such incidental damage is controlled by the principle of proportionality"); *Commentary on the HPCR Manual*, 93–4 ("The majority of the Group of Experts felt that the principle of proportionality applies to such civilians as in all other cases").

shields. In general, the burden of proof should fall on the party claiming an exception to a general prohibition. Strikingly, the DoD cites no state practice or *opinio juris* reflecting this claimed exception other than that of the United States which, as we have seen, only recently seemed to reject such an exception.

On the contrary, according to the ICRC, state practice indicates that, while the presence of human shields does not automatically prohibit an attack, an attacker "must respect the principle of proportionality ... even though the defender violates international humanitarian law."[26] For example, the Israeli Supreme Court holds that when "civilians are forced to serve as 'human shields' ... the rule is that the harm to the innocent civilians must fulfill, *inter alia*, the requirements of the principle of proportionality."[27] Since Israel is not a party to Protocol I, and has extensive experience with adversaries that use civilians as human shields, its practice is particularly significant in determining the content of customary international law.

The absence of an affirmative legal argument is even more remarkable when we consider the implications of the DoD's position. Consider the following case:

> *Apartment*: An ordinary combatant takes refuge in an apartment building, intending to use the patients as passive, involuntary human shields. Since the attacking force has no troops on the ground, the most discriminate weapons and tactics available to attackers will destroy half of the building, killing half of the residents.

For most experts, attacking a building and killing half of its residents to kill one ordinary combatant is a paradigm case of a disproportionate attack.[28] In contrast, according to the DoD, such an attack would be as proportionate as an attack that would kill no civilians. On the DoD's view, as far as proportionality is concerned, these resident-shields may as well not exist.

The DoD's position generates other bizarre results. Consider the following scenario:

> *Two Targets*: Military targets A and B are weapons caches containing the same number of rifles. 10 civilians are unwittingly passing by target A. 20 civilians are forced to serve as involuntary human shields for target B.

If the military advantage anticipated by destroying the weapons in each cache is fairly small, then it might be disproportionate to strike target A, killing 10 civilians. However, according to the DoD, it is necessarily proportionate to strike from the south, killing 20 civilians, because those civilians are being used as involuntary

[26] ICRC, *Customary IHL Study*, 71.
[27] HC [High Court of Justice] 796/02, *Public Committee against Torture in Israel et al v Government of Israel et al*, Judgment, December 13, 2006, para 42. This remains the official position of the Israeli Defense Forces. See Michael N Schmitt & John J Merriam, "The Tyranny of Context: Israeli Targeting Practices in Legal Perspective" (2015) 53 University of Pennsylvania Journal of International Law 118.
[28] See, eg, *Public Committee against Torture in Israel et al*, para 46.

human shields. This result seems illogical. If a military advantage cannot justify killing ten civilians who have done nothing to forfeit their legal rights, then an equivalent military advantage cannot justify killing twenty civilians who also have done nothing to forfeit their legal rights.

To see a subtler problem with the DOD's position, compare the following scenarios:

> *Shortcut*: An ordinary combatant runs through a crowded market because that is the fastest route to his destination. Attacking him will kill many nearby civilians.

On any plausible view, the proportionality rule would prohibit attacking the combatant in *Shortcut*, because the expected collateral harm is great and the anticipated military advantage is small. Now consider the following variation:

> *Cover*: The same combatant runs through the same market because he hopes that he will not be attacked with so many civilians nearby. Attacking him will kill the same number of nearby civilians.

According to the DoD, the proportionality rule would permit attacking the combatant in *Cover* because he is using the nearby civilians as human shields. Yet it seems illogical that the lawfulness of killing the nearby civilians should turn on the combatant's mental state—his purpose or motive for co-locating with civilians—rather than on the expected harm to the civilians and the anticipated military advantage of killing the combatant.

Rather than offer a legal argument that its position reflects customary law, the DoD offers three inchoate moral arguments that customary law should reflect its position:

Use of human shields violates the rule that civilians may not be used to shield, favor, or impede military operations. The party that employs human shields in an attempt to shield military objectives from attack assumes responsibility for their injury, provided that the attacker takes feasible precautions in conducting its attack.

If the proportionality rule were interpreted to permit the use of human shields to prohibit attacks, such an interpretation would perversely encourage the use of human shields and allow violations by the defending force to increase the legal obligations on the attacking force.[29]

I address these inchoate moral arguments below.

Responsibility

The DoD claims that "[t]he party that employs human shields ... assumes responsibility for their injury" and concludes that an attacker who expects to kill many human shields in pursuit of a small military advantage does not violate the

---

[29] US Dept of Defense, *Law of War Manual*, 5.12.3.3. This passage seems to reflect the views of the *Manual*'s principal architect. See Parks, "Air War and the Law of War," 163.

proportionality rule.[30] Simply put, the DoD's conclusion is a *non sequitur*. Of course, defenders who use human shields are responsible for the foreseeable harm that they occasion. It simply does not follow that attackers who kill human shields are not responsible for the foreseeable harm that they inflict and may therefore inflict foreseeable harm out of all proportion to the military advantage they anticipate. In the context of war, attributing responsibility is not a zero-sum game.

Recall the scenario in *Apartment*. No doubt, the combatant has acted wrongfully, even criminally, by using the residents as involuntary shields. But now the choice is yours: to kill the residents or to spare them. If you choose to kill the residents, then you cannot deny responsibility for your choice. The combatant is responsible for his choice and you are responsible for yours. The combatant is wrong to use the residents as involuntary shields and you would be wrong to kill the residents simply to eliminate the combatant.

Suppose that a bank robber takes a bank teller hostage and uses her to shield his escape. You are a police officer and may lawfully kill the bank robber to prevent his escape. However, if you shoot at the bank robber, then you will almost certainly kill the hostage as well. If you shoot at the bank robber and kill the hostage, then no doubt the robber (assuming he survives) will be held criminally responsible for her death. After all, he put her in harm's way. But surely you may also be held criminally responsible for her death. After all, you shot her. Perhaps you can convince a court that you did not act recklessly, that the risk of killing the hostage, though substantial, was justifiable in light of the danger posed by the bank robber. But surely you will convince no one that, so long as you tried your best not to shoot the hostage, you had no obligation to weigh the risk of killing her against the need to stop the robber. The robber put her in harm's way but, ultimately, her life was in your hands.

When defending forces use civilians as human shields it is the attacking force that would kill these civilians, directly causing their deaths without further intervening agency. Moreover, the attacking force generally chooses to attack knowing that civilians are in or near the targets. Importantly, the bases of the attacking force's responsibility (knowledge, ultimate control, and direct causation) are exactly the same whether the civilians are being used as involuntary shields or are simply in the wrong place at the wrong time. Ultimately, it is up to the attacking force to either kill the civilians or spare them.

To see the moral significance of direct causation and ultimate control more clearly, compare the following cases:

Collateral: If you attack a legitimate military target, then you will kill some number of nearby civilians.

---

[30] US Dept of Defense, *Law of War Manual*, 5.12.3.3. cf Thomas Hurka, "Proportionality in the Morality of War" (2005) 33 Philosophy & Public Affairs 47–50; Michael Walzer, "Responsibility and Proportionality in State and Nonstate Wars" (2009) Parameters 40–52.

Threat: The defending force threatens that, if you attack a legitimate military target, killing no civilians, then the defending force will kill the same number of civilians as you would kill in *Collateral*.[31]

There may very well be some number of civilians such that it would be permissible to attack in *Threat* but not in *Collateral*. Though the same number of civilians will die, in *Collateral* you would ultimately choose to directly kill them while in *Threat* the defending force would ultimately choose to directly kill them. Importantly, cases of "mediated harm" like *Threat* do not support disregarding or even discounting the lives of involuntary shields. When attacking forces collaterally kill involuntary shields it is the attacking force and not the defending force that ultimately chooses to directly kill those civilians.

Alternatively, the DoD's position may trade on an equivocation. If an attacking force inflicts proportionate harm on involuntary shields, then the defending force has violated the rights of those civilians but the attacking force has not. In one sense, then, the defending force is morally responsible—that is, responsible for moral wrongdoing—and the attacking force is not. However, if an attacking force inflicts disproportionate harm on involuntary shields, then both the defending force and the attacking force violate the rights of those civilians. Both are therefore morally responsible and, in principle, criminally responsible as well. In this sense, proportionality determines moral and legal responsibility, not the other way around.

From an attacker's perspective, it does not matter that the defending force is responsible for the presence of involuntary shields but not for the presence of civilian passersby. What matters is that involuntary shields are not responsible for their presence near the target. They have done nothing to lose or compromise their rights against you that you not kill them. Your corresponding duty not to kill them remains as strong as ever. You may breach your duty and thereby infringe their rights only to prevent a greater evil. You may not justify collaterally killing civilians to prevent a lesser evil on the grounds that you are not responsible for the greater evil that you inflict.

Discouraging the Use of Human Shields

The DoD also claims that "[i]f the proportionality rule were interpreted to permit the use of human shields to prohibit attacks, such an interpretation would perversely encourage the use of human shields."[32] Put the other way around, if the proportionality rule is interpreted to exclude expected harm to human shields, such an interpretation would discourage the use of human shields. This view rests on a series of legal, factual, and logical mistakes.

---

[31] I adapt these cases from Seth Lazar, "On Human Shields" (Aug 5, 2014) Boston Review, http://www.bostonreview.net/world/seth-lazar-human-shields.

[32] US Dept of Defense, *Law of War Manual*, 5.12.3.3.

First, this argument falsely assumes that individual civilians enjoy specific legal protections unless and for such time as stripping them of some legal protections might yield desirable consequences. On the contrary, individual civilians enjoy general legal protection unless and for such time as they take a direct part in hostilities.[33] It is a truism that the law of war seeks to "alleviat[e] as much as possible the calamities of war."[34] It hardly follows that the law of war is some crude exercise in rule-consequentialism. Parties should always strive to reduce overall suffering, but never at the expense of individual civilians entitled to legal protection.

Civilians lose their legal protection only when they choose to directly participate in hostilities, not whenever dictated by some utilitarian calculus. For example, the law of war does not permit terroristic attacks directed against civilians even when such terror would hasten the end of the war. Nor does the law of war permit attacking civilians in order to leave irregular combatants nowhere to hide. Suppose that attacking forces could discourage the use of human shields by deliberately killing the elderly parents and young children of defending forces who use human shields. It hardly follows that international law should permit attackers to instrumentally harm these civilians, who have done nothing to lose their moral and legal protection. Similarly, even if excluding expected harm to involuntary shields from the proportionality rule would discourage the future use of involuntary shields, it simply does not follow that the law of war should deny those civilians who are used as involuntary shields legal protection under the proportionality rule.

Importantly, it is a state's conduct, not its interpretation of the proportionality rule as such, that affects a defender's incentives to use human shields. In order to discourage the use of human shields in the way the DoD suggests, the United States would have to order its forces to knowingly kill civilian men, women, and children—forced against their will or used without their consent as involuntary human shields—whose deaths would ordinarily be considered excessive in relation to the concrete and direct military advantage anticipated. In blunt terms, the DoD proposes that we kill more civilians now so we will have to kill fewer civilians later.

As far as I am aware, there is no empirical evidence that if we exclude civilians used as human shields from the proportionality rule, then we will end up killing fewer civilians overall. True, if attackers disregard harm to human shields, then defenders may use fewer civilians as human shields; on the other hand, attackers will kill almost all of those civilians whom defenders nevertheless use as human shields. The number used may be smaller, but the proportion killed will be greater. Conversely, if attackers apply the proportionality rule to human shields, then defenders may use more civilians as human shields; on the other hand, attackers

---

[33] ICRC, *Customary IHL Study*, 19; Protocol I, art 51.
[34] Declaration Renouncing the Use, in Time of War, of Explosive Projectiles Under 400 Grammes Weight [St Petersburg Declaration], Nov 29/Dec 11, 1868, 138 Consol TS 297, 18 Martens Nouveau Recueil (ser 1) 474.

will only kill some of the civilians who are in fact used as human shields. The number used may be greater, but the proportion killed will be smaller. Absent empirical evidence that the difference in the number used will offset the difference in the proportion killed, the DoD's position seems to rest entirely on a priori speculation.

Of course, the proportionality rule prohibits attacks expected to kill civilians that are based on mere speculation that the long-term benefits will outweigh the short-term costs. Instead, the proportionality rule compares expected harm to civilians only to the *concrete and direct* military advantage anticipated. According to the ICRC, "the advantage concerned should be substantial and relatively close, and . . . advantages which are hardly perceptible and those which would only appear in the long term should be disregarded."[35] The *Manual* takes a more expansive view (a topic for another day), but concedes that, under the proportionality rule, "the military advantage may not be merely hypothetical or speculative."[36] It seems illogical to deny civilians protection under the proportionality rule based on the very kind of speculation that the rule itself rejects.

Indeed, the DoD's a priori prediction that disregarding expected harm to involuntary shields will dramatically reduce the use of involuntary shields is highly implausible. Presumably, defenders heedless of law and morality will use involuntary shields if and only if the expected benefits to defenders outweigh the expected costs to defenders. By disregarding harm to involuntary shields, attackers deprive defenders of one potential benefit of using human shields, namely temporary avoidance of attack. The question then becomes whether the other expected benefits of using involuntary shields outweigh the expected costs of using involuntary shields.

Importantly, it is not ordinarily costly for a combatant to take refuge in a residential building, for a group to establish a command center in a hospital, or for a unit to fire rockets from a schoolyard. In each such case, defenders use civilians as involuntary shields at little cost to themselves. It follows that if ruthless defenders expect any significant benefit from using civilians as involuntary shields, then they will do so irrespective of the legal position of the attacking force. For example, if such defenders expect that the killing of involuntary shields by attackers will redound to the defenders' broader strategic advantage—for example, by gaining them new recruits or by politically isolating their adversary—then defenders will continue to use involuntary shields when it is not costly to do so. Significantly, since only the defenders' subjective expectations affect their behavior, it does not matter whether they are in fact likely to gain the advantage that they expect.

It is true that taking and maintaining hostages is often quite costly.[37] Of course, most involuntary shields are not hostages who need to be fed, clothed, washed, hidden, and regularly moved (think again of the apartment residents, the hospital

---

[35] *Protocol I Commentary*, para 2209.   [36] DoD, *Manual*, para 5.12.5.
[37] See Charles J Dunlap Jr, "The DoD Law of War Manual and Its Critics: Some Observations" (2106) 92 International Law Studies 85.

patients, and the school children in the previous examples). In addition, many hostages are held for ransom rather than for use as human shields. Finally, many hostages are taken from the attacker's political community; attackers may therefore refrain from attack not for legal reasons but for emotional, political or ethical reasons. It is therefore doubtful that excluding harm to hostages from the proportionality rule will reduce the number of hostages taken by defenders enough to offset the number of hostages killed by attackers.

In any event, as we have seen, such utilitarian considerations are legally beside the point. The law of armed conflict protects each individual civilian unless and for such time as he or she directly participates in hostilities. There is no legal basis for stripping individuals of their protection under the proportionality rule in the hope that the long-term benefits to others may outweigh the immediate costs to them. Nor, as we have seen, is there any factual or logical basis for doing so.

It is hard to see why any US service member would think that, by following the DoD's position, they will better conform to her own moral obligations. By disregarding collateral harm to involuntary shields, most attackers will kill innocent people and produce no good sufficient to justify these killings. My prediction, and my hope, is that US service members will ignore the DoD's position and exercise their independent moral judgment. They have no reason to defer to directives that are so clearly morally incorrect on their face.

On a related view, in determining the proportionality of an attack that kills involuntary shields, we should consider not only the immediate benefit of, say, destroying a legitimate target but also discouraging the future use of involuntary shields.[38] On this view, the use of involuntary shields is discouraged not by a *rule* permitting attackers to disregard their presence in determining proportionality but by the *act* of collaterally killing them. This broadly act-consequentialist view fails. As noted in Chapter 1 as well as in Chapter 8, the proportionality of an attack that kills innocent civilians generally excludes good consequences of the attack that are causally downstream from the civilian deaths. By denying justificatory weight to the downstream consequences of civilian deaths, morality gives substance to the inviolability of every human being.

It might be objected that, while it would be wrong to *intentionally* kill involuntary shields *in order to* discourage the future use of involuntary shields, it is not wrong to attack a legitimate military target, *foreseeably* killing involuntary shields, *on the condition* that killing them will discourage the future use of involuntary shields.[39] However, either way, the attacker kills the involuntary shields *instrumentally*,

[38] See, eg, Michael Walzer, "Can the Good Guys Win?" (2013) 24 EJIL 438; Noam Zohar, "Risking and Protecting Lives: Soldiers and Opposing Civilians," in Helen Frowe & Gerald Lang (eds), *How We Fight: Ethics in War* (OUP 2014) 168.

[39] On the distinction between acting in order to bring about an outcome and acting on the condition that an outcome will occur, see FM Kamm, *Intricate Ethics* (OUP 2007) 101–2.

regarding their deaths as acceptable causal means of producing good outcomes. On my view, morality excludes the downstream consequences of the deaths of innocent people from justifying the acts that kill them. Accordingly, if an attack that kills civilians would be disproportionate but for the good consequences of the civilian deaths, then that attack *is* disproportionate and therefore impermissible.

On my view, it does not matter whether an attacker intentionally kills innocent people as a causal means of producing good consequences or knowingly kills innocent people on the condition that killing them will be an effective causal means of produce good consequences. The deaths of innocent people are morally inappropriate causal means of producing good consequences, and for that reason such good consequences cannot justify their deaths. Accordingly, the attacker's precise motivating reasons are irrelevant because, either way, the attacker fails to act on justifying reasons.

Alternatively, it might be objected that such killing of involuntary shields is not *opportunistic* if the attack would still be carried out in their absence. This objection fails because the counterfactual test that it deploys is too crude. A killing may be opportunistic if it seeks a benefit that could not be obtained in the victim's absence, even if, in the victim's absence, a different benefit might have been sought. If you attack a legitimate military target surrounded by involuntary shields only on the condition that doing so will discourage the future use of involuntary shields, then you seek to obtain a benefit from their deaths that could not be obtained in their absence. Such killing remains opportunistic even if, absent the involuntary shields, you would seek the distinct benefit of destroying the target.

To see the opportunistic nature of such killing more clearly, return to an earlier scenario:

> *Another Target*: You can strike a legitimate military target from the North or from the South. If you strike from the North, then you will kill 10 civilians who are unwittingly passing by. If you strike from the South, then you will kill 20 civilians forced to serve as involuntary human shields.

If you choose to strike from the South rather than from the North, because doing so will discourage the future use of human shields, then you clearly kill the 20 involuntary shields opportunistically, to obtain a benefit that you could not obtain in their absence.

Now assume that it would be disproportionate to strike from the South unless both destroying the target and discouraging the future use of human shields are considered. An attack from the South remains opportunistic, so long as it seeks to benefit from the deaths of the involuntary shields. The fact that you might still attack from the South if, counter-factually, the involuntary shields were absent is neither here nor there. What matters is that you would not attack from the South, killing the involuntary shields, if killing the involuntary shields would not produce good consequences. Perhaps you would prefer that the shields were absent.

However, given that they are present, it would be impermissibly opportunistic to take advantage of the consequences of their deaths to justify killing them.

Finally, it might be objected that it is not the deaths of the involuntary shields that discourage but rather the demonstrated willingness of the attacking force to attack despite their presence. If, by luck, the involuntary shields survive the attack, then the discouraging effect of the attack will still be sufficient to render the attack proportionate.[40] Even on these facts, the attacking force opportunistically uses the presence of the involuntary shields to achieve a benefit that the attacking force could not achieve in their absence. After all, the attack can only discourage the future use of involuntary shields if some involuntary shields are present. Moreover, opportunistic use that foreseeably results in harm is morally comparable to intentional harming.[41] Since it is wrong to intentionally kill involuntary shields, it is also wrong to opportunistically use the presence of involuntary shields, foreseeably killing them, to render an attack proportionate. We should discourage the use of involuntary shields by criminally punishing those who so use them, imposing costs on wrongdoers rather than on their victims.

Fairness

Finally, the DoD claims that "[i]f the proportionality rule were interpreted to permit the use of human shields to prohibit attacks, such an interpretation would ... allow violations by the defending force to increase the legal obligations on the attacking force."[42] To be clear, defending forces that use human shields do not thereby "increase" the legal obligations on the attacking force but instead trigger the ordinary legal obligation not to inflict excessive incidental harm on civilians. Evidently, defending forces trigger this obligation whenever they locate their personnel and equipment near civilians, whether or not they intend to thereby shield their personnel and equipment from attack.

More precisely, the DoD suggests that it is *unfair* for defending forces to intentionally trigger the legal obligations of the attacking force, through unlawful conduct, as a means of obtaining tactical advantage. Put more simply, it seems unfair for defenders to profit from their wrongdoing. Indeed it is. However, it does not

---

[40] Thanks to Seth Lazar for raising this objection, which resembles the "closeness" objection to the traditional doctrine of double effect.

[41] See Warren Quinn, "Actions, Intentions, and Consequences: The Doctrine of Double Effect" (1989) 18 Philosophy & Public Affairs 334. For example, Quinn considers a terror bomber who narrowly intends to create a large explosion over a civilian area that will convince the adversary's political leaders that the civilians below have been killed. This terror bomber does not strictly intend the deaths of the civilians but instead "strictly intends to involve them in something (to make his bombs explode over them) in order to further his purpose precisely by way of their being involved" (at 343 fn 16). Quinn rightly concludes that this terror bomber commits a moral wrong much closer to intentionally killing civilians than to unintentionally killing civilians.

[42] DoD, *Manual*, 5.12.3.3.

follow that attacking forces may deprive defending forces of such unfair advantages by killing involuntary shields without limit.

War, like other parts of life, is often unfair. Killing involuntary shields shifts the unfair burdens imposed on the attacking force, not onto the defending force that imposed them, but onto the latter's civilian victims. We cannot correct but can only compound the unfairness of war by killing civilians who have done nothing to forfeit their legal rights. Instead, we should annul the unfair advantages gained through the use of involuntary shields by prosecuting those who use them for war crimes. We should not, in effect, punish civilians for war crimes committed against them.[43]

Shields and Conscripts

One party's use of civilians as involuntary shields does not and should not strip those civilians of their rights or release the opposing party from its corresponding obligations. In particular, expected collateral harm to involuntary shields rightly affects the proportionality of an attack to exactly the same extent as harm to civilian passersby. Before moving on to discuss the status of voluntary shields, there is one remaining issue to address.

Most legal experts and moral philosophers agree that civilians forced to serve as involuntary shields retain their basic rights. Some involuntary shields are physically unable to avoid military targets, while others are not morally responsible agents. At the same time, many involuntary shields consciously choose to go or remain in or near military targets, albeit under duress. This point is significant because most commentators agree that conscripts who will be killed if they refuse to fight for an unjust cause are morally liable to defensive force if they choose to fight.[44] Why, then, are civilians who will be killed if they refuse to serve as involuntary shields not morally liable if they choose to serve rather than die?

The answer must turn on the different kinds of contributions that conscripts and shields make to the unjust threats posed by defending forces. Many conscripts who fight on behalf of an unjust cause kill innocent people, either individually, jointly with other combatants, or through other combatants under their effective control.[45] It is wrong for them to do so, even to save their own lives. Other things equal, it is permissible for you to save your own life rather than save someone else's life. In contrast, it is wrong for you to kill an innocent person to avoid your own death because doing harm is worse than allowing harm. It follows that generally it is not wrong to kill you to prevent you from killing an innocent person.

---

[43] cf Schmitt, "Fault Lines," 301 (observing that "equalizing the fighting position of belligerents is not an underlying purpose of LOIAC").

[44] See, eg, McMahan, *Killing in War*, 183.

[45] Of course, many conscripts do not harm innocent people in any of these ways or even enable other combatants to do so. See Chapter 4.

Unlike conscripts, shields do not kill or otherwise harm innocent people. At the same time, shields do not simply allow innocent people to be killed. Shields make it harder for attacking forces to prevent defending forces from killing innocent people. Ordinarily, when we fail to save another person we leave that other person no worse off than he would have been in our absence. In contrast, shields make innocent people worse off than they would have been in the shields' absence.[46] However, it does not follow that shields are morally liable to intentional or collateral harm. To see this, consider the following scenario:

> *Freeze*: Terrorist enters a government building and yells "I'm only here to kill Official, but if anyone else moves, then I'll kill them too." Counter-terrorist cannot shoot Terrorist because Employee is standing in the way. Counter-terrorist discretely motions to Employee to get out of the way. If Employee moves, then Terrorist will kill him before Counter-terrorist kills Terrorist. If Counter-terrorist kills Employee, then Counter-terrorist will have a clear shot at Terrorist.

In this case, Employee's presence makes Official worse off than Official would be in Employee's absence. Nevertheless, Employee's duty not to prevent Counter-terrorist from saving Official is not so stringent that Employee is morally required to get out of the way at the cost of Employee's own life. It follows that it would be wrong for Counter-terrorist to (intentionally though eliminatively) kill Employee in order to get a clear shot at Terrorist.[47]

In general, shielding an unjust threat to an innocent person is morally close enough to allowing harm to an innocent person that both are permissible to avoid one's own death and neither render one morally liable to be killed to save that innocent person.[48] It follows that most involuntary shields are not morally liable to be killed because they do not pose unjust threats and they are morally justified in shielding unjust threats.

Voluntary Shields

The legal status of voluntary shields presents a much closer question. As we have seen, civilians retain their protected legal status unless and for such time as they take a direct part in hostilities. The critical question is therefore whether voluntary shields satisfy the legal standard for direct participation in hostilities.

---

[46] For similar reasons, Helen Frowe argues that involuntary shields should be considered innocent threats rather than innocent bystanders (*Defensive Killing*).

[47] cf Frowe, *Defensive Killing*, 24; Tadros, "Wrongful Intentions," 72–4.

[48] See Matthew Hanser, "Killing, Letting Die, and Preventing People from Being Saved" (1999) 11 Utilitas 277–95; Samuel C Rickless, "The Moral Status of Enabling Harm" (2011) 92 Pacific Philosophical Quarterly 66.

As we saw in Chapter 3, direct participation in hostilities requires the commission of specific acts or participation in military operations likely to directly cause harm in support of one party to the conflict and in opposition to another. The ICRC takes the view that voluntary *physical* shields—those who voluntarily create physical obstacles to attacks on lawful targets—directly participate in hostilities.[49] For example, a civilian who stands in front of or moves along with combatants firing from behind her may be directly targeted or collaterally harmed as if she were firing weapons herself.

However, the ICRC also takes the view that voluntary *legal* shields—those whose voluntary presence in or near lawful targets might render an attack disproportionate—do not directly participate in hostilities. For example, a civilian who stands in or near a military target creates no physical obstacle to attack by air or artillery although, depending on the stakes, her presence might render an attack on the target disproportionate.

According to the ICRC, voluntary legal shields *directly* cause a change in the lawfulness of a potential attack, which is the wrong kind of harm to satisfy the legal standard. At the same time, if voluntary legal shields cause an attacking force to cancel an attack, then they cause the right kind of harm but do so too indirectly to satisfy the legal standard. It follows that voluntary legal shields do not directly cause the right kind of harm necessary to directly participate in hostilities.[50] The ICRC notes that, although voluntary legal shields "abuse their legal entitlement," the price of this abuse is not the loss of legal protection but rather "an increased risk of suffering incidental death or injury during attacks against [military] objectives."[51]

Indeed, the view that voluntary legal shields directly participate in hostilities seems self-defeating. Consider the following sequence of events:

t_1: Civilian enjoys general legal protection

t_2: Civilian voluntarily co-locates with a military objective

t_3: Civilian thereby creates a legal obstacle to attack

t_4: Civilian thereby directly participates in hostilities

---

[49] ICRC, *Interpretive Guidance*, 41–64. See also Ian Henderson, *The Contemporary Law of Targeting* (Brill 2009) 217–18. In ethics, Fabre draws a parallel distinction, between "shields-as-targets" and "shields-as-deterrents" (*Cosmopolitan War*, 258).

[50] See Nils Melzer, "Keeping the Balance Between Military Necessity and Humanity: A Response to Four Critiques of the ICRC's Interpretive Guidance on the Notion of Direct Participation in Hostilities" (2010) 42 New York University Journal of International Law & Politics 869 (writing that "the decisive question must be whether the presence of human shields directly adversely affects the enemy's capability, and not merely his willingness, to attack and destroy the shielded objective"). Perhaps more precisely, a civilian whose presence affects the legality of an attack but not its feasibility does not cause the kind of harm necessary to qualify as a direct participant in hostilities.

[51] ICRC, *Interpretive Guidance*, 57.

t_5: Civilian thereby loses her general legal protection

t_6: Civilian does not create a legal obstacle to attack

t_7: Civilian does not directly participate in hostilities

t_8: Civilian enjoys general legal protection

Simply put, a civilian cannot directly participate in hostilities and create a legal obstacle to attack at the same time. It follows that creating legal obstacles to attack cannot amount to direct participation in hostilities.

Many states and scholars reject the ICRC position and insist that both voluntary physical shields and voluntary legal shields directly participate in hostilities.[52] The main objection to the ICRC position seems to be that it generates unacceptable results. In particular, "unless voluntary shields are characterized as direct participants excluded from the proportionality equation, a sufficient number of them can absolutely immunize a target from attack."[53]

We might blunt the impact of this objection with two observations. First, even on the ICRC's view, voluntary legal shielding remains very risky. After all, the presence of voluntary shields will not prevent an attack on a military target when

(i)   the attacking force does not know how many shields are present,

(ii) the attacking force reasonably determines that the shields whom it knows are present are too few to render an attack disproportionate,

(iii) the attacking force *un*reasonably determines that the shields whom it knows are present are too few to render an attack disproportionate, or

(iv) the attacking force determines that an attack would be disproportionate but chooses to attack anyway.

It seems likely that most civilians will be deterred from serving as voluntary shields by the risk that their presence will not, in fact, dissuade an attack.

Second, the presence of voluntary legal shields will only immunize a target from attack when the expected collateral harm to those shields outweighs the military advantage anticipated from attacking the target. The more important the target, the more voluntary shields it will take to render an attack disproportionate. It follows that it would take many voluntary shields, systematically deployed, to simultaneously immunize important military targets across the battle space. Although such systematic, coordinated placement of voluntary shields is certainly possible,

---

[52] See, eg, United States Joint Chiefs of Staff, *Joint Targeting* (Joint Publication 3-60) (January 13, 2013) A-2; *Public Committee against Torture in Israel et al v Government of Israel et al*, para 36. Interestingly, the DoD's *Manual* does not identify voluntary shields as direct participants or as military objectives. Instead, the *Manual* indicates that all human shields are protected by the precautions rule but not by the proportionality rule.

[53] Schmitt, "Human Shields," 42.

defending forces will have a very hard time exploiting the ICRC's position to gain a decisive military advantage.

Understandably, some argue that since physical shields and legal shields share the same intent and have the same practical effect—to prevent attacks on lawful targets—they should suffer the same loss of legal rights.[54] This argument suppresses a false premise, namely that the loss of rights turns on the intended consequences of our actions. Instead, in law and morality, the loss of rights turns on *how* our actions would bring about those intended consequences. To take a fanciful example, an international lawyer who persuasively argues that certain military operations are unlawful, intending to prevent or discourage such operations, might succeed in doing so if not eliminated. Hopefully, all will agree that such a lawyer does not directly participate in hostilities and is not a lawful target.

Importantly, the view that all voluntary shields directly participate in hostilities generates unacceptable results of its own.

First, recall that direct participants in hostilities may be lawfully targeted at any time during their participation, even if doing so is unnecessary to prevent any harm to others. It follows that, on this view, if a group of civilians surrounds a single combatant in an attempt to prevent or dissuade an attack on that combatant, then a sniper may shoot the civilians one by one before (or even instead of) simply shooting the combatant.[55]

Second, recall that attacking forces need not take feasible precautions to avoid or minimize harm to direct participants in hostilities. It follows that, on this view, attacking forces may use weapons or tactics that will kill some number of voluntary shields even if using different weapons or tactics would kill fewer voluntary shields at no additional risk to the attacking force.

Third, recall that attacking forces need not consider harm to direct participants in hostilities when they select their targets. It follows that, on this view, combatants may attack a military objective surrounded by voluntary shields when they could obtain a similar military advantage by attacking a different military objective surrounded by fewer voluntary shields or by no voluntary shields.

Fourth, recall that collateral harm to direct participants in hostilities cannot render an attack disproportionate. It follows that, on this view, attackers may kill 20, 50, or 100 civilians as a foreseeable side effect of killing an ordinary combatant if the civilians are attempting to shield that combatant. Indeed, under current law, members of state armed forces are lawful targets even if they pose no immediate threat

---

[54] See Schmitt, "Human Shields," 41–2.

[55] cf Schmitt, "Human Shields," 48 (conceding that "the approach opens the possibility of directly targeting voluntary shields. While accurate as a matter of law, doing so would serve little practical purpose"). Since IHL exists in large part to prohibit the infliction of unnecessary suffering, Schmitt's appeal to "economy of force" considerations to prevent such conduct seems unsatisfying.

and even if they perform a noncombat function. It follows that, on this view, attackers may kill scores of civilians attempting to shield one unarmed soldier whose job is to cook or wash clothes.

Finally, recall that civilians directly participating in hostilities lose their legal protections against both attacking forces and defending forces, including their legal protection from being used as human shields. It follows that, on this view, defenders are legally permitted to use willing civilians as voluntary shields and will face no criminal liability for doing so.

While the ICRC's position seems somewhat too restrictive, the opposing position seems much too permissive. I will therefore propose an alternative view according to which some voluntary shields entirely lose their general protection while most voluntary shields partly compromise their specific protection under the proportionality rule.

Participant Shields, Shielding Participants

My own view is that voluntary shields directly participate in hostilities only for such time as they physically shield others who are directly participating in hostilities. Paradigmatically, civilians directly participate in hostilities by physically shielding individuals carrying out attacks, that is, "acts of violence against the adversary, whether in offence or in defence."[56] Such civilians play an integral part in coordinated military operations likely to directly cause serious harm and thereby forfeit their civilian immunity.

In contrast, civilians do not directly participate in hostilities by physically or legally shielding individuals who are not currently engaged in military operations. Of course, combatants are lawful targets even if they are not directly participating in hostilities. However, civilians who shield combatants are lawful targets only while the combatants they shield are directly participating in hostilities.[57]

The main legal objection to my view is that voluntarily shielding military targets—as opposed to military operations—directly causes "military harm," that is, "any consequence adversely affecting the military operations or military capacity of a party to the conflict."[58] However, as we saw in Chapter 3, direct causation of "military harm" should be rejected as a free-standing basis for loss of civilian immunity. No one who causes such "military harm" is, without more, morally liable to defensive killing on any plausible view. Combatants who kill civilians simply for threatening to directly cause "military harm" are much more likely to kill wrongfully than to prevent wrongful killing. The law of armed conflict will

---

[56] Protocol I art 49(1).

[57] Obviously, an individual whose continuous function is to shield military operations loses their civilian status and may be targeted when they are not performing that function. See Chapter 4.

[58] ICRC, *Interpretive Guidance*, 47.

best achieve its constitutive aim of providing moral guidance to combatants if it accepts my view that only those who directly cause "military harm" as an integral part of a coordinated military operation—thereby jointly posing threats of serious harm—directly participate in hostilities. It follows that voluntary shields who only directly cause "military harm" should not be considered direct participants in hostilities.

To see the moral appeal of my position, compare the following cases:

Shield Attack: A combatant is firing on opposing soldiers. A group of civilians, who support the party for whom the combatant fights, voluntarily move in front of the combatant, enabling the combatant to fire over and between them while shielding the combatant from return fire.

Shield Escape: A group of civilians stroll down the street, chatting among themselves. An unarmed combatant runs over to them and explains that opposing forces are close behind. The combatant begs the civilians to stand still and thereby shield his escape. The civilians, who support the party for whom the combatant fights, agree.

In *Shield Attack*, the civilians do not merely shield a threat posed by the combatant but jointly pose a threat together with the combatant, each performing their respective roles within a common—though perhaps spontaneous—plan. In contrast, in *Shield Escape*, the civilians passively shield a combatant who poses no immediate threat. The fact that they may thereby contribute to the combatant posing future threats does not render them morally liable to defensive killing, as we saw in Chapter 3.

At the same time, it is hard to believe that collateral harm to voluntary shields is morally equivalent to collateral harm to civilian passersby. To see this, consider the following scenario:

Voluntary Shields: You can strike a legitimate military target from the North or from the South. If you strike from the North, you will kill 20 civilians voluntarily serving as human shields. If you strike from the South, then you will kill 19 civilians who are merely passing by.

In this case, it seems worse to kill the 19 passersby than to kill the 20 voluntary shields. If either strike would be proportionate, then you ought to strike from the North. Moreover, depending on the importance of the target, it might be proportionate to strike from the North but not from the South.

On the other hand, it seems that harm to voluntary human shields can render an attack disproportionate. For example, in *Shield Escape*, it would seem disproportionate to kill, say, twenty civilians voluntarily shielding an ordinary combatant who is both unarmed and fleeing. Alternatively, consider the following scenario:

Voluntary Shields 2: You can strike a legitimate military target from the North or from the South. If you strike from the North, you will kill 20 civilians voluntarily serving as human shields. If you strike from the South, then you will kill two civilians who are merely passing by.

In this case, it seems worse to kill the 20 voluntary shields than to kill the two passersby. If either strike would be proportionate, then you ought to strike from the South. Moreover, depending on the importance of the target, it might be proportionate to strike from the South but not from the North.

On my view, an attack that would be disproportionate if it predictably harms civilian passersby may be proportionate if it similarly harms voluntary shields. In other words, voluntary shields who do not directly participate in hostilities do not entirely lose but instead partly compromise their protection under the proportionality rule.

The first legal objection to this view is that the proportionality rule compares only two variables, namely expected harm to civilians and anticipated military advantage. As we have seen, the proportionality rule excludes exogenous considerations such as defender responsibility, deterrence, and fairness that do not affect the normative weight of either variable. In contrast, on my view, the proportionality rule does not exclude voluntary conduct of civilians that directly affects the normative weight of expected harm to those very civilians. After all, if civilians directly participate in hostilities, then they lose their protection under the proportionality rule.

The second legal objection to my view is that, under existing law, civilians either retain their legal protections in full or lose them entirely. On this view, civilians who do not directly participate in hostilities enjoy general legal protection, while civilians who directly participate in hostilities enjoy no such general legal protection. Indeed, there is little evidence in positive legal materials that voluntary conduct short of direct participation in hostilities may result in reduced legal protection short of total loss. For example, while the United States takes the position that civilians who work in military targets lose their protection under the proportionality rule, this view is rejected by the United Kingdom as well as by a majority of experts.[59] Accordingly, voluntary shields who do not directly participate in hostilities retain the full protection of the proportionality rule.[60]

I wrote earlier that voluntary shields "compromise" their protection under the proportionality rule, and it is time to clarify that formulation. On my view, voluntary shields retain their protection from disproportionate harm. However, what counts as disproportionate harm depends, in part, on the voluntary conduct of the

---

[59] Compare DoD's *Manual*, para 5.12.3.2 with the UK's *Manual*, para 2.5.2 and *Commentary on the HPCR Manual*, 93–4.

[60] See, eg, Henderson, *Contemporary Law of Targeting*, 218 ("as there is no gradation amongst civilians, each civilian is 'worth' the same as every other civilian, and where they are counted as collateral damage voluntary human shields are given the normal weighting of any other civilian in the proportionality equation").

civilians harmed. The same amount of harm may be disproportionate if inflicted on ordinary civilians but proportionate if inflicted on voluntary shields. On my view, harm to civilians is disproportionate only if it is morally unjustified by military advantage, and the same advantage may justify harm to voluntary shields but not to ordinary civilians. Harming voluntary shields is less wrongful, or easier to justify, than harming ordinary civilians, for reasons discussed below.

Avoidability and Liability

In most cases, voluntary shields can avoid being harmed in attacks on military targets more easily than can civilian passersby or involuntary shields. To be sure, at the moment of attack, voluntary shields are just as vulnerable as any other unarmed civilian. However, before an attack voluntary shields can more easily reduce their future vulnerability. Voluntary shields know that they are near a military target; know that an attack may be imminent; and typically have no other compelling reason to be there. Passersby and non-voluntary shields presumably lack this knowledge or have other compelling reasons for being where they are, while contra-voluntary shields are physically prevented from leaving.

Now, the fact that you can easily avoid some harm does not entail that you are morally liable to suffer that harm, let alone that you deserve to suffer that harm, only that inflicting that harm upon you is less wrongful (that is, easier to justify) than it would be if you could not easily avoid that harm. Ordinarily, if some action will prevent some harm to one person but inflict a comparable harm on another person, then that action is impermissible. However, if the person whom your action will harm can easily avoid being harmed—or could have easily avoided a situation in which she or the other person will be harmed—then harming her may be permissible.

Similarly, on my view, voluntary shields do not forfeit their rights not to be killed, nor do they deserve to die. Nevertheless, it is less wrongful to kill voluntary shields than to kill passersby because the former could more easily avoid being killed than the latter. Put the other way around, it is more wrongful to kill passersby because they have less control than voluntary shields over whether or not they will be killed. Since the moral gravity of losses to voluntary shields is reduced by their ability to avoid these losses, military advantages that would not justify given losses to civilian passersby may justify similar losses to voluntary shields. It is for this reason that collateral harm that would be disproportionate if inflicted on civilian passersby may be proportionate if inflicted on voluntary shields.[61]

---

[61] Comparative avoidability explains why it is worse for unjust combatants to kill civilian passersby than to kill voluntary shields. To the extent that combatants kill in furtherance of an unjust cause, it is impermissible for them to kill anyone. However, as we have seen, some impermissible killings are worse than others.

As we have seen, the comparative avoidability of harm is morally relevant but is not morally dispositive. Although it is worse to kill one passerby than to kill one voluntary shield, it is not ten times worse to kill one passerby than to kill one voluntary shield. Of course, it is hard to say precisely how much worse it is to kill passersby than to kill voluntary shields. A conservative view is that avoidability offsets the general moral asymmetry between doing harm and allowing harm. On this view, an attack that collaterally kills some number of voluntary shields is proportionate if it saves a comparable number of innocent civilians. A more permissive view is that avoidability inverts this asymmetry. On this view, an attack that collaterally kills some number of voluntary shields is proportionate if it saves a substantially smaller number of innocent civilians. It is hard to determine which view is correct. However, the view that avoidability obliterates this asymmetry, rendering it proportionate to collaterally kill a very large number of voluntary shields to save a very small number of innocent civilians, seems far too strong.

Objections

Some readers may feel that many voluntary shields choose to create a situation in which either attacking forces will kill them or—at some point—those they shield will kill either innocent civilians or combatants fighting for a just cause. On this view, voluntary shields are morally liable to be killed in order to resolve a moral dilemma of their own making. However, if the innocent civilians or combatants fighting for a just cause could easily avoid being killed by the defending force, then it seems wrong to kill the voluntary shields. So, on this view, it is permissible to kill the voluntary shields to the extent that they could have avoided the situation comparatively more easily than the innocent civilians and combatants.

This view resembles Jeff McMahan's view that it is permissible to kill A to save B if A is comparatively more responsible than B for the fact that B will be killed unless A is killed. However, as I argue in the Appendix, just as the possession of basic rights depends on non-comparative properties of our moral status, the loss of basic rights depends on our non-comparative degree of moral responsibility. No doubt, voluntary shields generally bear greater moral responsibility than innocent civilians for the fact that either the former or the latter will be killed. Similarly, generally it is easier for voluntary shields than for innocent civilians to avoid situations in which either voluntary shields will be killed or innocent civilians will be killed. As we shall see, it does not follow that the voluntary shields are morally liable to be killed. Instead, comparative responsibility and comparative avoidability entail only that it is comparatively easier to justify killing voluntary shields than to justify killing innocent civilians.[62]

---

[62] cf Hurka, "Proportionality in the Morality of War," 47 ("[B]y placing themselves near [military targets, voluntary] shields arguably take upon themselves some responsibility for their deaths and remove it from us, so their deaths countless against our attack's proportionality"). Obviously, counting less is better than not counting at all.

Other readers may feel that civilians have moral duties not to aid combatants fighting for an unjust cause and not to interfere with combatants fighting for a just cause. These readers may feel that voluntary shields violate these moral duties and thereby forfeit their basic rights.

However, if civilians have a moral duty not to shield military targets from combatants fighting for a just cause, then this duty is not very stringent. After all, civilians are not morally required to die or suffer serious injury rather than serve as involuntary shields. Since civilians need not risk death or serious injury to avoid shielding military objectives it is presumptively wrong to kill or seriously injure civilians who do so.

It may be objected that, although civilians are not required to die rather than shield military targets, voluntary shields do not, in fact, shield military targets under threat of death. True enough. As we saw in Chapter 3, moral liability to defensive killing does not turn on our motivations but instead on the stringency of the moral duty that we violate. For example, an adult who fails to save a drowning child for a trivial or wicked reason is not morally liable to be killed to save that child. True, the adult does not fail to save the child in order to avoid being killed. However, the moral duty that the adult violates is insufficiently stringent to result, when violated, in moral liability to be killed.

In most cases, voluntary shields, involuntary shields, and civilian passersby perform similar actions: they go or remain near military targets. They differ primarily in their motivation. On my view, the duty not to shield military targets is insufficiently stringent to result, when violated, in moral liability to be killed. The fact that voluntary shields breach that duty for reasons other than fear of death does not make them morally liable to be killed.

It may be further objected that voluntary shields *culpably* breach their duty not to shield military targets—they intend to shield military targets and are free from duress—and that the moral blameworthiness of the breach combines with the stringency of the duty to yield moral liability. Indeed, since involuntary shields retain their basic rights, some form of moral fault must be necessary for shielding to result in moral liability. Of course, it does not follow that culpability is sufficient for shielding to result in liability to be killed. But I will pursue a different point.

Presumably, almost all civilians willing to serve as voluntary shields subjectively believe that the defending force that they aid fights for a just cause. Often, their belief is reasonable, that is, epistemically justified by the evidence available to them. Civilians who serve as voluntary shields in support of what they reasonably believe is a just cause are not morally blameworthy even if they intend to shield and are not coerced. Indeed, it is remarkable that defenseless civilians would make themselves vulnerable to death and dismemberment for the sake of what they believe to be a just cause. Certainly, such civilians are not so morally blameworthy that by merely shielding military targets they forfeit their basic rights.

As we have seen, some argue that the law must regard voluntary shields as direct participants because otherwise voluntary shields will systematically frustrate the conduct of military operations. We saw above that most civilians will be deterred from voluntary shielding by the serious risks involved and that deploying a sufficient number of voluntary shields to simultaneously render attacks on many important military targets disproportionate would prove enormously complex and difficult.

We now see that collateral harm to voluntary shields may be discounted—though not entirely disregarded—in determining the proportionality of an attack. As before, the more important the target, the more voluntary shields it will take to render an attack disproportionate. It follows that it will take *very* many voluntary shields, systematically deployed, to decisively frustrate the pursuit of a just cause. For example, if a military campaign is necessary to repel an unjust invasion or to stop a genocide, then it may take hundreds of thousands of carefully placed voluntary shields to render the entire campaign disproportionate. The theoretical possibility of such systematic use of voluntary shields should not drive us to the view that the lives of civilians who actually serve as voluntary shields in the real world should count for little or nothing.

The position that I defend may seem to tie the hands of attacking forces. However, the truth is that the objective legal status of voluntary shields will often make no practical difference. After all, as we saw in Chapter 5, attacking forces are legally required to presume that civilians retain their legal protection in cases of doubt. Even if voluntary shields lose their legal protection, attacking forces would need decisive evidence that a civilian is near a military target voluntarily and with the specific intent to prevent or dissuade an attack on that target before treating that civilian as a voluntary shield.[63] Since attacking forces hardly ever possess such decisive evidence of voluntariness and intent, they will be obliged to treat such civilians as involuntary shields or as passersby entitled to full protection by the proportionality rule. In practice, attackers will hardly ever be disadvantaged if, as I argue, voluntary shields retain their legal protections.

Conclusion

Civilians who are used as involuntary shields retain their legal and moral rights not to be harmed intentionally, unnecessarily, or disproportionately. In particular, collateral harm to involuntary shields may not be discounted or disregarded in determining the proportionality of an attack. Here, as elsewhere, attackers must weigh the collateral harm they expect to inflict on civilians—who have done nothing to lose their rights—against the concrete and direct military advantage they anticipate from their attack.

Civilians who voluntarily serve as human shields directly participate in hostilities—and thereby lose their civilian immunity—only when their physical presence is an integral part of a coordinated military operation that is likely to directly cause serious harm. Collateral harm to other voluntary shields may be discounted—but not entirely disregarded—in determining the proportionality of an attack.

---

[63] See *Commentary on the HPCR Manual*, 93; Schmitt, "Human Shields," 56.

10

War Crimes

War crimes are serious violations of the law of armed conflict for which international law imposes individual criminal liability. As we have seen, attacking forces may violate the law of armed conflict by failing to distinguish between civilians and combatants; by launching indiscriminate attacks; by failing to take feasible precautions to avoid harming civilians; and by launching attacks that foreseeably inflict excessive harm on civilians. These violations are undoubtedly "serious" since they breach "rules protecting important values" and "involve grave consequences" for their victims.[1] These violations express a culpable lack of respect and concern for civilian lives and likely account for the majority of civilian deaths in contemporary armed conflict. If international law is to offer meaningful legal protection for civilians in armed conflict, then the prevention and punishment of such violations is of the utmost importance.

It may surprise readers that many combatants who violate these fundamental legal rule and thereby kill civilians will escape criminal liability before the International Criminal Court (ICC). Under the Rome Statute—the treaty that establishes the ICC and defines its jurisdiction—the ICC may hold combatants legally accountable for the war crime of attacking civilians, defined as

Intentionally directing attacks against the civilian population as such or against individual civilians not taking direct part in hostilities[2]

as well as for the war crime of causing excessive incidental death, injury, or damage, defined as

Intentionally launching an attack *in the knowledge* that such attack will cause incidental loss of life or injury to civilians . . . which would be *clearly* excessive in relation to the concrete and direct overall military advantage anticipated.[3]

Importantly, the war crime of attacking civilians falls within the ICC's subject matter jurisdiction whether committed in international armed conflict or

---

[1] *Prosecutor v Tadić*, Decision on the Defence Motion for Interlocutory Appeal on Jurisdiction, IT-94-1-AR72, Appeals Chamber, Oct 2, 1995, para 94.

[2] Rome Statute of the International Criminal Court (opened for signature July 17, 1998, entered into force July 1, 2002) 2187 UNTS 3, arts 8(2)(b)(i) and 8(2)(e)(i) (emphasis added).

[3] Rome Statute art 8(2)(b)(iv) (emphasis added).

Law and Morality at War. First Edition. Adil Haque. © Adil Haque 2017. Published 2017 by Oxford University Press

in non-international armed conflict.[4] Disturbingly, the war crime of causing excessive incidental death, injury, or damage falls within the ICC's jurisdiction only when committed in international armed conflict. Since many contemporary armed conflicts are non-international, this disparity seems hard to accept. Presumably, the drafters of the Rome Statute meant to track the provisions of Protocol I, which prohibits disproportionate attacks in international armed conflict, and Protocol II, which does not prohibit disproportionate attacks in non-international armed conflict. However, since customary international law prohibits disproportionate attacks in both international and non-international armed conflict, the Rome Statute leaves an unfortunate gap in the ICC's jurisdiction.[5]

In any event, my focus lies elsewhere. The Elements of Crimes—a separate document which "shall assist the Court in the interpretation and application of" the substantive offenses identified in the Rome Statute[6]—underscores the requirements that

The perpetrator *intended* the civilian population as such or individual civilians not taking direct part in hostilities to be the object of the attack[7]

or that

The perpetrator *knew* that the attack would cause incidental death or injury to civilians ... and that such death [or] injury ... would be of such an extent as to be *clearly* excessive in relation to the concrete and direct overall military advantage anticipated.[8]

As we shall see, attacking forces may violate the principles of distinction, discrimination, precautions, and proportionality without thereby violating these provisions of the Rome Statute.

The resulting gap between the law of armed conflict and the Rome Statute seems hard to defend. The ICC was created out of a sense that "the most serious crimes of concern to the international community as a whole must not go unpunished" and in order "to put an end to impunity for the perpetrators of these crimes and thus to contribute to the prevention of such crimes."[9] Admittedly, since the ICC cannot punish most perpetrators of international crimes, the ICC can neither achieve perfect retributive justice nor effectively deter future international crimes. Since the deterrent effect of punishment is a product of the severity of possible punishment and the probability of its imposition, the small chance of prosecution

---

[4] Roughly, armed conflicts between states are international while armed conflicts between states and organized armed groups or between such groups are non-international.

[5] ICRC, *Customary IHL Study*, 48–9.   [6] Rome Statute art 9(1).

[7] Rome Statute of the International Criminal Court, Elements of Crimes (2012) art 8(2)(b)(i) (emphasis added).

[8] Elements of Crimes art 8(2)(b)(iv) (emphasis added).

[9] Rome Statute, preamble.

before the ICC will seldom deter potential perpetrators from committing international crimes when they stand to personally benefit from doing so.[10]

At the same time, by recognizing serious violations of the law of armed conflict as international crimes and punishing some of those who perpetrate them the ICC can achieve partial retributive justice. Moreover, the ICC can "contribute to the prevention of such crimes," not through deterrence but instead through *positive general prevention*.[11] The ICC can express moral condemnation of these crimes on behalf of the international community, thereby underscoring their moral wrongfulness. If combatants internalize this moral message, then they may refrain from committing such crimes not out of fear of punishment but out of a sense of obligation.

International criminal law in general, and the ICC in particular, should underscore the moral legitimacy of the law of armed conflict and thereby reinforce the moral guidance that the law of armed conflict aims to provide. Unfortunately, combatants who learn that the ICC considers violations of distinction, discrimination, precaution, and proportionality insufficiently serious to constitute war crimes may come to doubt the moral importance of these fundamental principles. Such combatants may then disregard these fundamental principles when obeying them might prove costly or dangerous—as is often the case.

Fortunately, the Rome Statute neither exhausts nor limits customary international criminal law.[12] Unfortunately, the Court is already the world's preeminent international tribunal and may soon become the world's only international tribunal as the ad hoc tribunals for Rwanda, the former Yugoslavia, and elsewhere complete their work. It seems unlikely that the United Nations Security Council will establish many more ad hoc tribunals in the future, given their considerable startup and overhead costs, rather than refer future conflicts to the ICC. Although new hybrid and regional bodies may emerge to compete with the ICC for jurisdiction, these bodies may very well accept the substantive law of the Rome Statute. As a result, customary international criminal law that is not reflected in the Rome Statute may quickly fall into practical desuetude.

Of course, customary international criminal law may live on in the national courts and military tribunals of states. However, we should not expect states to impose more demanding legal standards on their own soldiers than the ICC imposes on the defendants before it. In particular, states party to the ICC may well draw on

---

[10] But see Hyeran Jo & Beth A Simmons, "Can the International Criminal Court Deter Atrocity?" (unpublished manuscript).

[11] See Adil Ahmad Haque, "Legitimacy as Strategy" in Paul H. Robinson, Stephen Garvey, & Kimberly Ferzan (eds), *Criminal Law Conversations* (OUP 2009) 57.

[12] See Rome Statute art 10 ("Nothing in this Part shall be interpreted as limiting or prejudicing in any way existing or developing rules of international law for purposes other than this Statute").

the Rome Statute when defining war crimes under their own national and military law.[13] The shortcomings of the Rome Statute should therefore concern us all.

In this chapter, I first show how the Rome Statute fails to enforce the principles of distinction, discrimination, precautions, and proportionality. I then consider and reject possible justifications for this failure. Along the way, I compare the Rome Statute with customary international criminal law, drawing on the case law of the International Criminal Tribunal for the former Yugoslavia (ICTY), showing both the promise and limits of the latter. Finally, I propose two ways to close the gap between the Rome Statute and the law of armed conflict.

It is not by accident that this chapter is dominated by legal analysis rather than by moral argument. If the previous chapters were successful, then the moral importance of these fundamental principles has already been established. It is therefore fitting to close this book by turning to the enforcement of these principles. For the sake of the non-lawyers reading this book, I will try to keep my legal analysis direct and concise, leaving some technical issues for discussion elsewhere.[14]

Distinction

As we saw in Chapter 5, attackers must distinguish between civilians and combatants, do everything feasible to verify that potential targets are military and not civilian, and presume that persons are civilians in case of doubt. Attackers must take these steps in order to "ensure respect for and protection of the civilian population"—in particular, in order to avoid mistakenly attacking individuals who are in fact civilians.

Remarkably, the Rome Statute does not effectively enforce the principle of distinction. The root of the problem is that the Rome Statute prohibits *intentionally* directing attacks against civilians. The Elements of Crimes underscores that the Rome Statute requires that the perpetrator *intends* civilians to be the object of the attack.

However, a combatant cannot *intend* for civilians to be the object of an attack unless the combatant *believes* that civilians will be the object of the attack. Under the Rome Statute, "a person has intent where . . . [i]n relation to conduct, that person means to engage in the conduct" or "[i]n relation to a consequence, that person means to cause that consequence or is aware that it will occur in the ordinary course of events."[15] A combatant who does not *believe* that those he attacks are civilians

---

[13] Thanks to David Luban for raising the latter point.

[14] See, eg, Adil Ahmad Haque, "War Crimes and the Law of War" in Kevin Jon Heller, Frédéric Mégret, Sarah Nouwen, Jens Ohlin, & Darryl Robinson (eds), *The Oxford Handbook of International Criminal Law* (OUP, forthcoming 2017); Haque, "Protecting and Respecting Civilians: Correcting the Substantive and Structural Defects of the Rome Statute" (2011) 14 New Criminal Law Review 519.

[15] Rome Statute art 30(2).

cannot *mean* to attack civilians, cannot *mean* to kill civilians, and is not *aware* that those who will be killed in the ordinary course of events are civilians.

It follows that if an attacker *unreasonably* believes that those he attacks are not civilians, then he commits no crime recognized by the Rome Statute. It does not matter if this mistake is made *despite* doing everything feasible to verify that the target is military rather than civilian or is made *because* the attacker does not even attempt to distinguish civilians from combatants.

Indeed, even if attackers kill individuals without bothering to form *any* affirmative belief regarding their legal status—neither believing that they are civilians nor believing that they are combatants—then the attackers do not intentionally direct an attack against civilians. Simply put, the Rome Statute fails to prohibit attacking civilians *recklessly, negligently*, or with *willful blindness*. At one time, some hoped that the ICC might recognize the related mental state of *dolus eventualis*, perhaps as a component of intention, but that door now seems firmly closed.[16]

In contrast, under Protocol I, "making the civilian population or individual civilians the object of attack" "shall be regarded as [a] war crime[]" "when committed *wilfully*" and "causing death or serious injury."[17] According to the International Criminal Tribunal for the former Yugoslavia (ICTY), willfully making civilians the object of attack is also a war crime under customary international law. More precisely, according to the ICTY, "the crime of attack on civilians" has the following material and mental elements:

1. Acts of violence directed against the civilian population or individual civilians not taking direct part in hostilities causing death or serious injury to body or health within the civilian population.
2. The offender wilfully made the civilian population or individual civilians not taking direct part in hostilities the object of those acts of violence.[18]

Importantly, the ICTY has now repeatedly held that "the notion of 'wilfully' incorporates the concept of recklessness, whilst excluding mere negligence." It follows that, according to the ICTY, "[t]he perpetrator who recklessly attacks civilians acts 'wilfully.'"[19]

---

[16] See *Prosecutor v Bemba*, Decision on the Confirmation of Charges, ICC-01/05-01/08, Pre-Trial Chamber II, June 15, 2009, para 369 ("the text of article 30 of the Statute does not encompass *dolus eventualis*, recklessness or any lower form of culpability").

[17] Protocol Additional to the Geneva Conventions of August 12, 1949, and relating to the Protection of Victims of International Armed Conflicts (Protocol I) (adopted June 8, 1977, entered into force December 7, 1978) 1125 UNTS 3, art 85(3) (emphasis added). I reorder the quoted text for concision.

[18] *Prosecutor v Galić* (Judgment) IT-98-29-T (December 5, 2003), para 56.

[19] *Galić* para 54. See also *Prosecutor v Strugar* (Judgment) IT-01-42-A, Appeals Chamber, July 17, 2008, para 270; *Prosecutor v Perišić* (Judgment) IT-04-81-T, Trial Chamber, September 6, 2011, para 100. In contrast, courts in the United States typically interpret willfulness to require consciousness of wrongdoing. See George P Fletcher & Jens David Ohlin, "Reclaiming Fundamental Principles of Criminal Law in the Darfur Case" (2005) 3 Journal of International Criminal Justice 539, 555.

According to the ICTY, to prove such recklessness "the Prosecution must show that the perpetrator was aware or should have been aware of the civilian status of the persons attacked."[20] Put the other way around, "the Prosecution must show that in the given circumstances a reasonable person could not have believed that the individual he or she attacked was a combatant."[21] Perhaps more precisely, if a defendant directs an attack, aware of a grave risk that the object of attack is a civilian but consciously disregarding that grave risk, then the defendant commits a war crime if the object of attack turns out to be a civilian who is killed or injured by the attack.

Surprisingly, Jens Ohlin criticizes the ICTY's position, arguing that that it threatens to erase the distinction between attacking civilians and causing excessive civilian harm.[22] According to Ohlin, if it is a war crime to recklessly attack civilians, then it is always a war crime to launch an attack that one expects to kill civilians, even when such an attack would be proportionate given the likely military advantage. On this view, the ICTY position effectively criminalizes war itself, since war necessarily involves attacks that one expects to kill civilians.

Ohlin's argument seems misdirected. According to the ICTY, it is a war crime to recklessly make civilians the object of attack, that is, to direct attacks against individuals while consciously disregarding the risk that they are civilians. On this view, the mental element of recklessness modifies a circumstance element of the crime, namely the fact that those attacked are civilians. In contrast, the ICTY does not claim that it is a war crime to recklessly kill civilians. The mental element of recklessness does not modify a result element of the crime, such as the ensuing deaths of civilians, because under the Rome Statute the war crime of attacking civilians has no result element.[23] The war crime of attacking civilians is a conduct crime, not a result crime, the material elements of which are directing an attack (conduct) at persons who are civilians (circumstance). Accordingly, a war crime of recklessly attacking civilians would not collapse into a war crime of recklessly causing incidental harm to civilians. The failure of the Rome Statute to follow the ICTY and to recognize a war crime of recklessly directing attacks against civilians is an occasion for nothing but regret.

Indiscriminate Attacks

As we saw in Chapter 6, the law of armed conflict categorically prohibits indiscriminate attacks. Strikingly, indiscriminate attacks as such do not constitute war

---

[20] *Galić*, para 55.   [21] *Galić*, para 55.
[22] Jens David Ohlin, "Targeting and the Concept of Intent" (2013) 35 Michigan Journal of International Law 79.
[23] In contrast, attacking civilians is a grave breach of Protocol I only if the attack causes death or serious injury. See Protocol I art 85(3).

crimes under the Rome Statute.[24] The Rome Statute prohibits intentionally directing attacks against civilians but does not prohibit all attacks not directed at specific military objectives. Logically, attacks not directed at specific military objectives
encompass attacks directed at civilians, but the latter do not encompass the former. Similarly, the Rome Statute does not prohibit indiscriminate attacks that the
attacker does not expect to cause clearly excessive incidental harm to civilians.
The Rome Statute recognizes the criminality of using certain traditionally prohibited weapons such as poisons, gases, and expanding bullets.[25] However, the Rome
Statute does nothing to protect civilians from new indiscriminate weapons such as
cluster munitions.[26]

Understandably, some commentators argue that the Rome Statute's war crime
of attacking civilians "encompasses attacks that are not directed against a specific
military objective or combatants or attacks employing indiscriminate weapons."[27]
The most obvious difficulty with such an interpretation is that Protocol I contains
separate prohibitions of attacks with civilians as their objects[28] and indiscriminate
attacks.[29] The drafters of the Rome Statute used the former prohibition as the basis
for the war crime of attacking civilians[30] but recognized no war crime corresponding to the latter prohibition. Ordinary principles of legal interpretation suggest that
the two Protocol I prohibitions are not redundant but distinct, and that the drafters
of the Rome Statute adopted the former and rejected the latter. Similarly, Protocol
I lists disproportionate attacks as a special case of indiscriminate attacks.[31] Ordinary
interpretive principles suggest that the Rome Statute's inclusion of the narrower
prohibition entails its exclusion of the broader prohibition.

These commentators may have been misled by statements from the ICTY that
"indiscriminate attacks ... may qualify as direct attacks against civilians."[32] Of
course, the use of indiscriminate weapons may *indicate* that its users intended to
direct attacks against civilians. For example, in one case the ICTY "*inferred* from
the arms used in an attack ... that the perpetrators of the attack had wanted to
target Muslim civilians, since these arms were difficult to guide accurately, their

---

[24] See Antonio Cassese, *International Criminal Law* (2nd edn OUP 2008) 95 ("The use
in international conflict of modern weapons which ... are inherently indiscriminate, is
not banned per se and therefore does not amount to a war crime under the ICC Statute—
whereas arguably such use constitutes a war crime under customary international law").

[25] See Rome Statute arts 8(2)(b)(xvii)–8(2)(b)(xx).

[26] See Memorandum from Luis Moreno-Ocampo, Chief Prosecutor, Int'l Criminal
Court, to the International Criminal Court, February 9, 2006, 5 ("Cluster munitions are not
included in the list and therefore their use per se does not constitute a war crime under the
Rome Statute").

[27] Knut Dormann, *Elements of War Crimes under the Rome Statute of the International Criminal
Court: Sources and Commentary* (CUP 2003) 132.

[28] Protocol I art 51(2).   [29] Protocol I art 51(4).

[30] See, eg, Dormann, *Elements of War Crimes*, 131.

[31] Protocol I art 51(5)(b).   [32] *Galić*, para 57.

trajectory was 'irregular' and non-linear, thus being likely to hit non-military targets."[33] Similarly, in a different case, the ICTY "regarded the use of an Orkan rocket with a cluster bomb warhead as *evidence* of the intent of the accused to deliberately attack the civilian population."[34] However, it does not follow that the use of indiscriminate weapons, without more, *constitutes* a direct attack against civilians. A combatant may launch an indiscriminate attack, not intending to strike civilians, but simply not caring that civilians may be struck. Such indiscriminate attacks occupy the conceptual space between *not trying* to kill civilians and *trying not* to kill civilians. Unfortunately, the Rome Statute requires the former but not the latter.

Precautions

As we saw in Chapter 7, the law of armed conflict requires attacking forces to take feasible precautions in the selection of weapons, tactics, and targets to avoid unnecessary harm to civilians. Strikingly, the Rome Statute simply contains no corresponding provision.

It is tempting to interpret the Rome Statute's war crime of causing excessive incidental death to incorporate precautionary obligations. On this interpretation, civilian losses that are clearly *unnecessary* to achieve a military advantage are also clearly *excessive* in relation to that advantage. Since one meaning of "excessive" is "unnecessary," this interpretation is both linguistically and morally attractive. Unfortunately, this interpretation is not sustainable. As the Elements of Crimes makes clear, the war crime of causing excessive incidental death only reflects the proportionality principle.[35] Since both Protocol I and customary international law distinguish between the proportionality principle and the precautions principle, the incorporation of the former but not the latter strongly indicates a deliberate choice to exclude the latter from the scope of the Rome Statute.

The Rome Statute fails to recognize the criminality of incidental killing of civilians that is proportionate but unnecessary. This omission is particularly upsetting because violations of the precautions principle are often more blameworthy than violations of the proportionality principle. Defendants who disproportionately kill civilians may assign some weight—though not enough weight—to civilian life in their deliberations. In contrast, defendants who unnecessarily kill civilians

---

[33] *Galić*, para 57 fn 101 (emphasis added) (citing *Prosecutor v Blaškić* (Judgment) IT-95-14-T, Trial Chamber, March 3, 2000, paras 501, 512).
[34] *Galić*, para 57 fn 101 (emphasis added) (citing *Prosecutor v Martić*, Review of the Indictment under Rule 61, IT-95-11, Trial Chamber, March 8, 1996, paras 23–31).
[35] Elements of Crimes art 8(2)(b)(iv) fn 36. See also Memorandum from Luis Moreno-Ocampo 5 ("Article 8(2)(b)(iv) [of the Rome Statute] draws on the principles in Article 51(4)(b)" of Protocol I).

apparently assign no weight to civilian life. The latter defendants apparently do not view the avoidance of civilian deaths as a reason to select alternative weapons, tactics, or targets for obtaining similar military advantages.

It is true that proving a violation of the precautions principle requires a counterfactual analysis of the tactical options available but not taken at the time the decision was made to attack. It is indeed important for courts not to convict defendants based on mere speculation that an alternative weapon, tactic, or target would have proven superior to the one that the defendants chose. But the requirement of proof beyond reasonable doubt exists precisely to ensure that courts convict only on the basis of sufficient evidence of an actual violation. Moreover, violations of the precautions principle include clear cases: bridges, roads, and railroad tracks can be targeted in more or less populated areas; weapons caches hidden in civilian buildings can be targeted at more or less busy times of day. The fact that violations of the precautions principle are sometimes difficult to prove does not entail that those violations that can be proven should not be punished.

Proportionality

Finally, as we saw in Chapter 8, an attack violates the law of armed conflict if the civilian losses that a reasonable attacker would expect are objectively excessive in relation to the military advantage that a reasonable attacker would anticipate. Just as attackers have a duty to verify their targets, attackers also have a duty to assess whether their attacks would result in excessive collateral harm to civilians. Put simply, proportionality depends not on what the attacker believed but on what the attacker should have believed.

Accordingly, the ICTY takes the position that an attacker commits a war crime if "the attack was launched wilfully and in knowledge of circumstances giving rise to the expectation of excessive civilian casualties."[36] The ICTY explains that

In determining whether an attack was proportionate it is necessary to examine whether a reasonably well-informed person in the circumstances of the actual perpetrator, making reasonable use of the information available to him or her, could have expected excessive civilian casualties to result from the attack.[37]

In particular, "the determination of relative values must be" an objective one, namely "that of the 'reasonable military commander.'"[38]

---

[36] *Galić*, para 59.   [37] *Galić*, para 58.
[38] ICTY, Final Report to the Prosecutor by the Committee Established to Review the NATO Bombing Campaign Against the Federal Republic of Yugoslavia, June 8, 2000 (2000) 38 ILM 1257, para 50.

In contrast, under the Rome Statute, criminal liability attaches only to launching attacks *in the knowledge* that the attack will cause civilian losses that would be *clearly* excessive in relation to the anticipated military advantage. The requirement of knowledge raises the subjective threshold for criminal liability, while the requirement of clear excessiveness raises the objective threshold for criminal liability. Under the Rome Statute, knowledge "means awareness that a circumstance exists or a consequence will occur in the ordinary course of events."[39] A combatant who does not believe that persons near a military target are civilians is not "aware" that those individuals are civilians and is not "aware" that civilians will be killed in the ordinary course of events. Similarly, a combatant who does not believe that the expected losses would be clearly excessive in relation to the anticipated advantage is not aware of that circumstance.

It follows that, under the Rome Statute, no criminal liability will attach if the perpetrator unreasonably expects very few civilian losses, unreasonably anticipates very great military advantage, or unreasonably judges that the losses that he expects are not clearly excessive in relation to the advantage that he anticipates. Each of the Rome Statute's deviations from customary international law warrants some discussion.

As the former ICC Prosecutor underscored, the Rome Statute draws on Protocol I's formulation of the proportionality principle but "restricts the criminal prohibition to cases that are 'clearly' excessive."[40] The word "clearly" might refer to the objective magnitude of the excessiveness that is prohibited. The Rome Statute might recognize the criminality of incidental civilian killing that is *very* or *grossly* excessive but not of incidental civilian killing that is only somewhat excessive. This is not an attractive position. As one leading commentator observes, "[t]o the best of my knowledge, in no war crime trial has the defendant ever asserted that he enjoyed immunity on account of the scarce gravity of his war crime."[41]

International criminal law should punish the unjustified killing of civilians and not merely the grossly unjustified killing of civilians. Of course, the grossly excessive incidental killing of civilians is an especially serious crime. However, any excessive incidental killing of civilians should rank among "the most serious crimes of concern to the international community as a whole." Certainly, the excessive incidental killing of civilians is, in general, a more serious crime than many other war crimes prohibited by the Rome Statute.[42] Such killings warrant international

---

[39] Rome Statute art 30(3).

[40] See Memorandum from Luis Moreno-Ocampo, 5.

[41] Antonio Cassese, "The Italian Court of Cassation Misapprehends the Notion of War Crimes" (2008) 6 J Int'l Crim Just 1077, 1087–8 (noting that "the [willful or disproportionate] killing of one or more civilians, as well the other 'minor' war crimes mentioned above, whatever their criminal magnitude, remain acts utterly contrary to international IHL and consequently to international criminal law").

[42] For example, the Rome Statute recognizes war crimes involving destruction of civilian property. See Rome Statute art 2(2)(a)(iv) and art 8(2)(b)(xiii).

prosecution, "in particular when committed as part of a plan or policy or as part of a large-scale commission of such crimes."[43]

Alternatively, the Rome Statute may prohibit incidental civilian death that is *obviously* or *manifestly* excessive. According to the Office of the Prosecutor (OTP), the insertion of the term "clearly" "reflects the drafters' intent to emphasize that a value judgment within a reasonable margin of appreciation should not be criminalized, nor second guessed by the Court from hindsight."[44] The OTP goes on to explain that

This approach represents a deliberate deviation from Protocol I, and reflects the consideration that the difficulties of calculating anticipated civilian loses and anticipated military advantage and the lack of a common unit of measurement with which to compare the two make this assessment difficult to apply, both in military decision making and in any *ex post facto* assessment of the legality of that action.[45]

Such a narrow prohibition is also difficult to defend. The addition of "clearly" to the material elements of the crime is unnecessary to direct acquittal in close cases. After all, the prosecution must prove every material element of every charged offense beyond reasonable doubt.[46] Accordingly, if there is any reasonable doubt that the losses a defendant expected were excessive in relation to the advantage the defendant anticipated, then the defendant must be acquitted.

Put another way, if it is a war crime to knowingly cause *excessive* harm to civilians, then the standard of proof ensures that soldiers will be punished only if it is *clear* that the expected losses were *excessive*. In contrast, if it is only a war crime to knowingly cause *clearly excessive* harm to civilians, then the standard of proof ensures that soldiers will be punished only if it is *clear* that the expected losses were *clearly excessive*. Such a narrowing of international criminal law is itself clearly excessive.[47]

It might be argued that a limited prohibition on clearly excessive harm is appropriate given the inherent imprecision of the proportionality rule. In fact, the amendment simply introduces an additional layer of imprecision. Under the traditional rule, attackers must distinguish between excessive harm and non-excessive harm. Under the Rome Statute, attackers must distinguish between *clearly* excessive harm, *merely* excessive harm, and *non*-excessive harm. It is not clear how this amendment improves the situation.

---

[43] Rome Statute art 8(1).

[44] Office of the Prosecutor, Article 53(1) Report on the situation on Registered Vessels of Comoros, Greece and Cambodia, November 6, 2014, para 103.

[45] OTP, Article 53(1) Report on the situation on Registered Vessels, fn 175.

[46] Rome Statute art 66(3).

[47] cf Robert Cryer, "Of Custom, Treaties, Scholars, and the Gavel: The Influence of the International Criminal Tribunals on the ICRC Customary Law Study" (2006) 11 J Conflict & Security L 239, 260 ("The term does not fulfill its ostensible purpose, which was to clarify

Under the Rome Statute, a defendant commits the war crime of causing excessive incidental death only if the civilian losses that the defendant subjectively expected were, in the defendant's subjective judgment, clearly excessive in relation to the military advantage that the defendant subjectively anticipated. According to the Elements of Crimes, conviction requires that the defendant knew that the attack would cause incidental harm to civilians and knew that such harm "would be of such an extent as to be clearly excessive in relation to the concrete and direct overall military advantage anticipated."[48] Importantly, conviction requires that the defendant "make the value judgment" that the harm the defendant expects to cause would be clearly excessive in relation to the military advantage the defendant anticipates.[49] It follows that a defendant may be exonerated either by mistaken factual beliefs or by deviant moral values.

If the defendant unreasonably underestimates the extent of the incidental civilian deaths that the attack would cause, or unreasonably overestimates the likelihood of achieving the anticipated military advantage, then his unreasonable belief is exculpatory rather than inculpatory. Moreover, if the defendant unreasonably overvalues the military advantage sought or undervalues the importance of civilian life, then his unreasonable value judgment negates the required mental element. Indeed, a defendant who does not even pause to consider whether an attack will likely cause incidental harm to civilians, or whether the incidental harm it would cause is clearly excessive, lacks the required mental state and must therefore be acquitted.[50]

The requirement that the defendant make the value judgment that the harm he expects would be clearly excessive is virtually without precedent in either international or domestic criminal law. This requirement represents an explicit exception to the general rule of the Elements of Crimes that "[w]ith respect to mental elements associated with elements involving value judgment, such as those using the terms 'inhumane' or 'severe,' it is not necessary that the perpetrator personally completed a particular value judgment."[51] The subjective evaluation requirement seems particularly objectionable in the context of armed conflict. Combatants may overvalue the lives of their comrades and the importance of their mission. Alternatively, combatants may undervalue the lives of civilians, particularly civilians of a different nationality, ethnicity, or religion. Yet, under the Rome Statute, such distorted and self-serving value judgments are grounds for acquittal.

---

the crime, but simply raises the threshold and introduces greater uncertainty into the law in this area").

[48] Elements of Crimes art 8 (2)(b)(iv) element 3.

[49] Elements of Crimes art 8(2)(b)(iv) fn 37.

[50] But see Dormann, *Elements of War Crimes*, 165 (arguing that "an unreasonable judgment or an allegation that no judgment was made . . . would simply not be credible").

[51] Elements of Crimes General, Chapter 1, para 4.

The subjective evaluation provision was inserted as a poorly worded footnote "[w]ithout intensive discussions in the formal Working Group or informal consultations as to its rationale"[52] and it is tempting to hope that the judges of the ICC will simply decline to follow it. Unfortunately, the footnote simply makes explicit what is already implicit in the text of the Elements of Crimes. If the drafters wanted to make "clearly excessive" an entirely objective evaluation to be performed by the court, then they would have restricted "clear excessiveness" to the material elements of the crime and left it out of the mental elements of the crime. For example, the drafters could have modeled the mental element related to clear excessiveness on provisions requiring that "[t]he perpetrator was aware of the factual circumstances that established the gravity of the conduct."[53] Instead, the Elements of Crimes requires that the defendant make the value judgment that the losses he expects are clearly excessive in relation to the advantage he anticipates.

Finally, the subjective evaluation requirement casts further doubt on the requirement that the defendant must expect to cause *clearly* excessive civilian losses. If the defendant himself judged the expected harm to civilians excessive, then his decision to launch the attack is highly culpable, indeed reprehensible. There is no reason to require that the defendant judged the expected harm to civilians *clearly* excessive. Deliberately inflicting unjustified harm on the innocent should be more than enough for criminal liability. Indeed, the notion that a defendant could defend her conduct by arguing that she expected to cause excessive harm on civilians—but not clearly excessive harm on civilians—seems hard to accept.[54]

While the law of armed conflict requires combatants faced with "close calls" to err on the side of sparing civilians, the Rome Statute frees combatants to err on the side of killing civilians. This dilution of the principle of proportionality is not as dramatic as the total exclusion of the principles of distinction, discrimination, and precautions, but it is a serious failing nonetheless.[55]

Explaining the Gap

The fact that the Rome Statute requires intention or knowledge with respect to every element of the war crimes of attacking civilians and causing excessive

---

[52] Dormann, *Elements of War Crimes*, 164. See also Roy S Lee (ed), *The International Criminal Court: Elements of Crimes and Rules of Procedure and Evidence* (Transnational 2001) 150 ("Time did not allow for a plenary or even informal discussion of this issue. It was negotiated in the corridors between a few particularly interested delegations and approved of by the others only as part of the final package").

[53] See, eg, Rome Statute art 7(1)(e)(3), 7(1)(g)-6(3), 8(2)(b)(xxii)-6(3), 8(2)(e)(vi)-6(3).

[54] Relatedly, consider the spectacle of an expert witness testifying, on behalf of the defendant, that in their judgment the expected harm was excessive but not clearly excessive.

[55] Some scholars also object to the inclusion of the term "overall." However, as long as this term is understood to refer to the military advantage anticipated from a coordinated

incidental death might be tolerable if it reflected a principled judgment that the ICC should only concern itself with crimes committed with the highest levels of subjective culpability. Such a policy would require intention or knowledge even with respect to circumstance elements, such as the civilian status of the individuals attacked.

In fact, the Elements of Crimes identifies six offenses of which defendants may be found guilty if they knew *or should have known* that a relevant circumstance existed.[56] The Elements of Crimes thereby accepts recklessness—perhaps even negligence—regarding circumstance elements as sufficient for criminal liability. All six offenses, though serious in their own right, are certainly not more serious than the offense of attacking civilians. It makes no sense for less serious offenses committed recklessly to rank among "the most serious crimes of concern to the international community" while more serious offenses must be committed intentionally or knowingly to cross the gravity threshold.

One delegation to the Rome conference specifically proposed that conviction for the war crime of attacking civilians should be able to rest on a finding that that the defendant "recklessly fail[ed] to take the necessary precautions to protect the civilian population" but this proposal was passed over without recorded discussion.[57] It appears that the drafters simply did not give this issue the attention that it deserves.[58]

Similarly, the fact that the Rome Statute does not punish violations of distinction, discrimination, and precautions might be tolerable if it reflected a consistent policy of prohibiting only "grave breaches" of Protocol I. Such a policy would have some basis in the law of armed conflict, since signatories to Protocol I are obligated to repress grave breaches and to regard them as war crimes. Importantly, attacking civilians and causing excessive incidental harm to civilians constitute grave breaches of Protocol I while violations of distinction, discrimination, and precautions do not.[59] In addition, while Protocol I prohibits

> any attack which *may be* expected to cause incidental loss of civilian life, injury to civilians, damage to civilian objects, or a combination thereof, which *would be* excessive in relation to the concrete and direct military advantage anticipated[60]

military operation involving multiple acts of violence (sometimes referred to as an "attack as a whole"), then it likely tracks customary law and is adequately limited in scope.

[56] See Elements of Crimes arts 6(e), 8(2)(b)(vii)-1, -2, and -4, 8(2)(b)(xxvi), 8(2)(e)(vii).

[57] See Lee (ed), *International Criminal Court*, 142.

[58] See Roger S Clark, "The Mental Element in International Criminal Law: The Rome Statute of the International Criminal Court and the Elements of Offences" (2002) 12 Crim LF 291, 300–1 ("*dolus eventualis* fell out of the written discourse before Rome. Recklessness, in the sense of subjectively taking a risk to which the actor's mind has been directed, was ultimately to vanish also from the Statute at Rome, with again only an implicit decision as to whether it was appropriate for assessing responsibility").

[59] See Protocol I arts 85(3)(a) and 85(3)(b).   [60] Protocol I art 57(2)(a)(iii).

Protocol I only lists as a grave breach

launching an indiscriminate attack affecting the civilian population or civilian objects *in the knowledge* that such attack will cause excessive loss of life, injury to civilians or damage to civilian objects, as defined in Article 57.[61]

According to the ICRC, "there is only a grave breach if the person committing the act knew with certainty that the described results would ensue, and this would not cover recklessness."[62]

However, the Rome Statute itself "reflects the fact that not all war crimes are grave breaches."[63] For example, at least three war crimes under the Rome Statute—prohibiting the use of human shields, starvation, and child soldiers, respectively—are derived from Protocol I but are not grave breaches. Conversely, the Rome Statute does not recognize at least one grave breach of Protocol I—relating to unjustifiable delay in the repatriation of civilians and prisoners of war—"on the basis that a violation of the norm was not serious enough to warrant consideration by the Court."[64] Finally, grave breaches of Protocol I must cause death or serious injury, while the Rome Statute prohibits attacking civilians even if no death or injury results.[65] In other words, whether or not a violation of the law of armed conflict constitutes a war crime turns on the moral seriousness of the violation, not on its formal classification as a grave breach.

Nor is the Rome Statute limited by the precedents of prior international criminal tribunals. The three war crimes mentioned above—relating to the use of human shields, starvation, and child soldiers, respectively—were included in the Rome Statute despite never having been the subject of international criminal prosecution.[66] Indeed, the Rome Statute recognizes at least one war crime—prohibiting attacks on humanitarian and peacekeeping personnel—that had neither appeared in previous international treaties nor been the subject of international prosecution.[67]

In my view, it is entirely appropriate that the war crimes recognized under the Rome Statute are not drawn exclusively from the grave breach provisions of

---

[61] Protocol I arts 85(3)(b). It is not entirely clear whether article 57 defines the term "excessive" or the entire prohibition. For present purposes, I will assume the former.

[62] ICRC, *Protocol I Commentary*, para 3479. Neither the provision nor the commentary state whether a grave breach only requires factual knowledge of the consequences or also requires a subjective judgment that the consequences will be excessive.

[63] Dormann, *Elements of War Crimes*, 131. See also Cassese, "Italian Court of Cassation," 1084 (arguing that the Italian Court "clearly confuses war crimes with grave breaches of the Geneva Conventions and the First Additional Protocol. It is well established that the latter are simply a sub-category of the former").

[64] Herman von Hebel & Darryl Robinson, "Crimes within the Jurisdiction of the Court" in Roy S Lee (ed), *The International Criminal Court: The Making of the Rome Statute—Issues, Negotiations, Results* (Springer 1999) 104.

[65] Compare Protocol I art 85(3) with Elements of Crimes, art 8(2)(b)(i).

[66] Dormann, *Elements of War Crimes*, 344–5, 363–74, 375–81.

[67] Dormann, *Elements of War Crimes*, 154.

Protocol I or from the precedents of past international tribunals. The three war crimes mentioned above—involving the use of human shields, starvation, and child soldiers—are rightly prohibited under the Rome Statute because they are among the most serious moral wrongs prohibited by the law of armed conflict. Similarly, killings of civilians that violate the principles of distinction, discrimination, precautions, or proportionality constitute serious moral wrongs that are, in fact, more serious than many other war crimes included in the Rome Statute. Such killings should therefore rank among the most serious international crimes, and should be prohibited and punished at both the international and the national levels.

Finally, it is worth noting that the Rome Statute grants the ICC jurisdiction over war crimes "in particular when committed as part of a plan or policy or as part of a large-scale commission of such crimes."[68] Certainly, a plan or policy of indiscriminate attacks or careless attacks, or the large-scale commission of reckless targeting or disproportionate attacks "must not go unpunished."[69]

Closing the Gap

There are several ways in which we might narrow the gaps between the Rome Statute and the law of armed conflict. The simplest but least complete is to expand the mental elements of the war crime of attacking civilians, to define it as

> Intentionally[, knowingly, or recklessly] directing attacks against the civilian population as such or against individual civilians not taking direct part in hostilities

as well as the mental elements of the war crime of causing excessive incidental death, injury, or damage, to define it as

> Intentionally launching an attack in the knowledge [or aware of a substantial and unjustifiable risk] that such attack will cause incidental loss of life or injury to civilians … which would be clearly excessive in relation to the concrete and direct overall military advantage [reasonably] anticipated.

The modifier "clearly" could then be deleted from the latter offense, and the Elements of Crimes could be amended to emphasize that the court rather than the defendant must make the ultimate value judgment that the civilian losses reasonably expected would be excessive in relation to the military advantage reasonably anticipated.

With these simple amendments, the Rome Statute would largely implement the principles of distinction and proportionality. However, these amendments would not implement the principles of discrimination and precaution. To recklessly direct an attack against civilians is to direct an attack against individuals while culpably

---

[68] Rome Statute art 8(1).   [69] Rome Statute, preamble.

disregarding the risk that those individuals are civilians. In contrast, indiscriminate attacks are, by definition, not directed at anyone. Evidently, failing to lawfully direct an attack is not the same as unlawfully directing an attack; the former includes the latter but the latter does not include the former. Finally, as we have seen, proportionality and precautions are distinct principles. Even the perfect implementation of the former would not implement the latter.

We could therefore further amend the Rome Statute to include a new war crime of indiscriminate attack, defined as

> Launching an attack which is not directed at a specific military objective; which employs a method or means of combat which cannot be directed at a specific military objective; or which employs a method or means of combat the effects of which cannot be limited as required by international humanitarian law

as well as a new war crime of careless attack,[70] defined as

> Launching an attack without taking feasible precautions in the choice of means or methods of attack, or selecting alternative military objectives for obtaining a similar military advantage when possible, to avoid or minimize incidental loss of civilian life or injury to civilians.

With these further amendments, the Rome Statute would largely implement the principles of discrimination and precaution as well.

My main misgiving with this approach is that it understands the relevant war crimes as *conduct offenses* rather than as *result offenses*. While some conduct is inherently wrongful irrespective of its results, causing some results is inherently wrongful irrespective of how one causes them. For example, it may be wrong to drive over the applicable speed limit even if this results in no harm. In contrast, it is wrong to cause death irrespective of how one causes death—with a gun, a knife, a car, or by any other means. Intuitively, the wrongfulness of launching attacks (conduct) in violation of the law of armed conflict derives from the basic wrongfulness of killing civilians (result) in violation of the law of armed conflict. We should therefore start with a basic result offense of killing civilians in violation of the law of armed conflict. We can then add derivative offenses of launching attacks in violation of the law of armed conflict, attempting to kill civilians, and recklessly endangering civilians.

In my view, the best way to close the gaps between the Rome Statute and the law of armed conflict would be to expand the mental elements and material scope of the war crimes of Willful Killing and Murder.[71] Both offenses involve intentionally

---

[70] I take the name of this proposed offense from the general precautionary principle that "[i]n the conduct of military operations, constant care shall be taken to spare the civilian population, civilians and civilian objects." Protocol I art 57(1); International Committee of the Red Cross, *Customary International Humanitarian Law*, vol 1 (CUP 2009) 51.

[71] Rome Statute art 8(2)(a)(i) and 8(2)(c)(i). Willful killing and murder have similar material elements. The former applies in international armed conflict while the latter applies in non-international armed conflict.

or knowingly killing protected persons while subjectively aware of the factual circumstances that establish their protected status.[72] Importantly, although not imme-
diately apparent from the Elements of Crimes, both offenses involve violations of
the Geneva Conventions of 1949, which primarily regulate the treatment of persons
in the power of an adversary rather than the conduct of hostilities.[73] Accordingly,
these provisions may be held inapplicable to reckless targeting and careless attack.

We should amend these offenses—or, if necessary, introduce new offenses—to
apply to the conduct of hostilities and to contain the following elements:

1. The perpetrator intentionally, knowingly, or recklessly killed one or more persons.
2. Such person or persons were either *hors de combat*, or were civilians, medical personnel,
   or religious personnel taking no active part in the hostilities.
3. The perpetrator was aware of the factual circumstances that established this status or
   should have been aware of such factual circumstances.

Defendants who kill protected persons in violation of the principle of distinction
are or should be aware of the factual circumstances that established their protected
status. Defendants who kill protected persons in violation of the principle of discrimination recklessly kill one or more protected persons.

To reflect the principles of precautions and proportionality, defendants who satisfy the elements of the revised offenses would then have the opportunity to raise a
new affirmative defense, defined as follows:

[Proposed] Article 31(i)(e):

In an attack directed at a specific military objective, the incidental loss of civilian life or
injury to civilians that the defendant reasonably expected would not have been excessive in relation to the concrete and direct overall military advantage that the defendant
reasonably anticipated. The defendant also reasonably believed that it was not feasible
to avoid or minimize such incidental loss of civilian life or injury to civilians through
the choice of alternative means or methods of attack or possible to do so through the
selection of alternative military objectives for obtaining a similar military advantage.

This affirmative defense protects defendants who took feasible precautions in their
choice of weapons, tactics, and targets and who reasonably believed that their
attacks would prove objectively proportionate.

Importantly, criminal recklessness requires more than consciously disregarding a
substantial and unjustifiable risk to others, just as criminal negligence requires more
than failing to perceive a substantial and unjustifiable risk to others. It is often difficult to predict the possible consequences of our actions, to calculate the probability
that such consequences will occur, and to weigh these risks against one's reasons

---

[72] See Elements of Crimes art 8(2)(a)(i) and art 8(2)(c)(i).
[73] See Rome Statute art 8(2)(a) and 8(2)(c).

for action. Small miscalculations along these lines do not reflect the degree of moral blameworthiness necessary for criminal punishment. Instead, criminal liability requires a moral judgment that a defendant's conscious disregard or failure to perceive a risk fell so far short of minimum standards of conduct that she deserves moral condemnation and punitive deprivation.[74] Combatants who take slightly unreasonable risks should be retrained, or perhaps reassigned to noncombat functions, but not criminally punished.

If recklessly killing civilians is accepted as a war crime, then international law should require a degree of recklessness that is morally comparable to intention or knowledge. Arguably, reckless killing is morally comparable to purposeful killing only when the defendant displays not only flawed reasoning but also flawed values. In these cases, the defendant's culpability is not merely cognitive but also conative or affective, and therefore more deeply expressive of his or her moral agency. For this reason, liability for the war crime of attacking or killing civilians might be limited to defendants whose "conscious disregard of the risk, under the circumstances, manifests extreme indifference to the value of human life."[75] Alternatively, the law might require the mental element of *dolus eventualis*, which requires both advertence to risk and an attitude of approval, reconciliation, or identification with the result.[76]

At one time, I argued that international criminal law should recognize the negligent killing of civilians as a war crime.[77] As a practical matter, it seems unlikely that a judge will believe that an attacker simply failed to perceive a grave risk that her attack might kill civilians, despite the availability of adequate information. Nevertheless, there may be expressive value to declaring that negligent killing of civilians ranks among the most serious crimes of international concern.

Understandably, many of the ICC's member states do not punish criminal negligence under their domestic criminal law. Indeed, occasional carelessness by ordinary people in everyday life may be unavoidable and therefore excusable. None of us remain constantly alert to remote possibilities that generally safe activities may unexpectedly endanger others. However, combatants engage in uniquely hazardous activities and operate under a specific legal duty to take constant care to spare civilians from harm. It hardly seems unfair to demand that combatants remain alert to the risks that they may pose to others.

---

[74] See, eg, American Law Institute, Model Penal Code and Commentaries §2.02 (1985) ("The risk must be of such a nature and degree that, considering the nature and purpose of the actor's conduct and the circumstances known to him, its disregard involves a gross deviation from the standard of conduct that a law-abiding person would observe in the actor's situation").

[75] American Law Institute, Model Penal Code and Commentaries §210.2(1)(b) (distinguishing reckless murder from reckless manslaughter).

[76] See, eg, *Prosecutor v Stakić* (Judgment) IT-97-24-T, July 31, 2003, para 587.

[77] See Haque, "Protecting and Respecting Civilians."

At the same time, the mere failure to perceive a risk is a cognitive failing, not necessarily a moral failing. If a combatant who fails to perceive a risk to civilians would not attack had she perceived that risk to civilians, then she may not be sufficiently morally blameworthy to deserve criminal conviction and punishment. Accordingly, we might limit criminal liability to those combatants whose negligent killing of civilians manifests insufficient concern for civilian life rather than, say, poor training or fatigue. On this approach, soldiers who fail to verify their targets or assess likely collateral harm may deserve demotion, discipline, or even discharge, but only those whose failure reveals morally defective agency deserve punishment.[78]

No doubt there are others ways to close the gap between the Rome Statute and the law of armed conflict. What matters most is not *how* we close the gap but *that* we close the gap. Attacks that kill civilians in violation of distinction, discrimination, precautions, and proportionality are serious moral wrongs. When committed with a high degree of moral culpability, without justification or excuse, such violations warrant criminal punishment if anything does. Although the ICC cannot punish all or even most violations, it can at least prohibit all such violations and punish some such violations, "in particular when committed as part of a plan or policy or as part of a large-scale commission of such crimes."[79]

Conclusion

The Rome Statute recognizes the criminality of intentionally directing attacks against civilians and knowingly inflicting clearly excessive harm on civilians. However, the Rome Statute does not recognize the criminality of directing attacks against individuals without first doing everything feasible to verify that they are not civilians; launching indiscriminate attacks; carrying out attacks without taking feasible precautions to avoid harming civilians; or launching attacks that reasonable attackers would expect to inflict excessive harm on civilians. The Rome Statute therefore fails to enforce the principles of distinction, discrimination, precaution, and proportionality.

We should revise the Rome Statute, bringing it into alignment with the law of armed conflict. We should recognize violations of these fundamental legal principles as war crimes, thereby underscoring the moral seriousness of these violations, affirming the moral legitimacy of the law of armed conflict, and reinforcing the moral guidance that the law of armed conflict aims to provide.

---

[78] cf ICRC, Protocol I Commentary, para 3474 ("failing to take the necessary precautions, particularly failing to seek precise information, constitutes culpable negligence punishable at least by disciplinary sanctions").
[79] Rome Statute art 8(1).

Appendix

Revisionism

One might expect a legal principle as fundamental as civilian immunity to enjoy universal acceptance. On the contrary, the principle of civilian immunity is under pressure as seldom before. Across the globe, many non-state armed groups reject civilian immunity entirely: they target civilians, seek to inflict the gravest possible civilian losses, and expect little military advantage in return. At the same time, a number of state armed forces target civilians who only indirectly contribute to hostilities, take few precautions to avoid collateral harm to certain civilian populations, and inflict far greater harm on civilians who support their adversaries than they seek to prevent from befalling their own citizens.

Distressingly, several leading moral philosophers have launched a simultaneous attack on the moral foundations of civilian immunity. These revisionists argue that many civilians who do not directly participate in hostilities are morally liable to intentional or collateral killing. On their views, contributing civilians lose their moral right not to be killed by making political, material, strategic, and financial contributions to an unjust war.

Revisionists often add that, for pragmatic and epistemic reasons, the legal immunity of civilians should remain absolute. For one thing, combatants often falsely believe that they fight for a just cause and may falsely conclude that civilians who support the opposing party forfeit their basic rights.[1] In addition, combatants who try to target morally liable civilians will often mistakenly target or collaterally harm morally protected civilians, including young children.[2] Finally, killing civilians is hardly ever effective in achieving a just cause or preventing harm to others, and pointless killing is always morally impermissible.[3]

Indeed, soldiers who refrain from intentionally killing contributing civilians are much more likely to avoid wrongful killing than to allow wrongful killing. Soldiers will best conform to their moral obligations by following the law protecting all civilians rather than by trying to identify and target morally liable contributing civilians. Unfortunately, in an increasing number of cases, a purely instrumentalist account of civilian immunity may prove inadequate. States are often convinced that they fight for a just cause, such as preventing terrorist attacks or stopping mass atrocities. In addition, some states use advanced surveillance technology and

---

[1] Jeff McMahan, *Killing in War* (OUP 2009) 235.
[2] Helen Frowe, *Defensive Killing* (OUP 2014) 195–7.
[3] McMahan, *Killing in War*, 225–6.

precision weapons in lethal operations against specific individuals, reducing the risks of misidentification and collateral harm. Finally, the strategic advantage expected from killing certain contributing civilians (say, a charismatic spokesperson for an organized armed group) can be considerable.

More fundamentally, the pragmatic and epistemic arguments favored by revisionist scholars seem largely (though not entirely) beside the point. The primary justification for the legal immunity of civilians is that almost all civilians retain their moral rights not to be killed or injured. It is only in rare cases that civilian immunity rests on instrumentalist considerations alone. In what follows I will consider and reject the leading revisionist arguments against the moral immunity of contributing civilians.

Preventive Justice and the Responsibility Account

Famously, Jeff McMahan argues that if a situation arises in which one of several people will suffer an indivisible harm, then it is fair for that harm to befall the person who bears the greatest *comparative* responsibility for that situation, even if that person bears only slight *absolute* responsibility for that situation. According to McMahan, "[j]ust as we may think of liability in torts as a matter of corrective justice, or justice in the distribution of harm ex post, so we may think of liability to defensive action as a matter of preventive justice, or justice in the distribution of harm ex ante."[4]

McMahan illustrates his principle of preventive justice with the following case:

Conscientious Driver: A person keeps his car well maintained and always drives cautiously and alertly. On one occasion, however, freak circumstances cause the car to go out of control. It has veered in the direction of a pedestrian whom it will kill unless the pedestrian blows it up by using one of the explosive devices with which pedestrians in philosophical examples are typically equipped.[5]

McMahan argues that it is morally permissible for the pedestrian to kill the driver. Although the driver bears only slight responsibility for the threat that his car poses to the pedestrian, the driver bears more responsibility than the pedestrian for the fact that one of them must die.

Similarly, McMahan argues that just combatants may intentionally kill contributing civilians as a means of preventing harm to themselves or to their own civilians. Although contributing civilians bear only slight responsibility for the unjust threats posed by their armed forces, contributing civilians bear more responsibility than either just combatants or their civilians for those unjust threats.

---

[4] Jeff McMahan, "The Basis of Moral Liability to Defensive Killing" (2005) Philosophical Issues 386, 39.
[5] McMahan, "Moral Liability to Defensive Killing," 393.

On the basis of his principle of preventive justice, McMahan argues that minimal moral responsibility for an unjust threat generates liability to defensive killing. According to McMahan's *responsibility account*, minimal moral responsibility requires foreseeably contributing to an unjust threat. Since contributing civilians foreseeably contribute to unjust threats posed by their armed forces, McMahan concludes that contributing civilians may be morally liable to defensive killing.

Strikingly, McMahan argues that "many civilians in Hiroshima bore more than a negligible degree of responsibility for their country's acts of unjust aggression that had made the defeat of Japan a moral necessity. It was, after all, *their* government, expressing the beliefs and values of their culture, and acting with their support."[6] Although McMahan insists that these civilians were not, in fact, morally liable to defensive killing, McMahan suggests that these civilians would have been liable to killing if, contrary to fact, the United States had been forced to choose between

three options: (1) sacrificing a large number of American men, torn from their peaceful lives by Japanese aggression, (2) intentionally killing a comparable number of Japanese civilians, many of whom bore some responsibility for that aggression, and (3) allowing the aggression to go undefeated.[7]

McMahan recognizes that "[m]any of us will still feel intuitive unease" about this counterfactual on the "appealing" grounds that "it takes more than a modicum of responsibility to override" the moral presumption against intentional killing. However, McMahan feels compelled to reject the idea of a threshold of responsibility below which liability will not arise. After all, "[i]f there were such a threshold for liability, it seems that the conscientious driver would have to be below it."[8] Since McMahan feels sure that the conscientious driver is morally liable to defensive killing, McMahan concludes that "we should not accept the idea of a threshold of responsibility."

McMahan elsewhere writes that *Conscientious Driver* "is not the kind of case against which we can usefully test a theory's implications. It is a case about which most of us have only weak or doubtful intuitions."[9] In contrast, the conclusion that many civilians in Hiroshima would have been morally liable to killing on the counterfactual grounds that McMahan posits seems like a *reductio ad absurdum* of the responsibility account. Something has gone very wrong. Let us therefore examine the responsibility account as well as the principle of preventive justice on which it rests on their own terms.

I suspect that McMahan's principle of preventive justice rests on a kind of moral category error. Simply put, defensive killing does not distribute harm. Defensive killing does not channel some fixed amount of inevitable harm falling from the sky. Defensive killing does not even redirect a pre-existing threat away from one

---

[6] McMahan, *Killing in War*, 228–9.   [7] *Killing in War*, 228–9.
[8] *Killing in War*, 230–1.   [9] "Moral Liability to Defensive Killing," 403.

person toward another person, except in hypothetical cases. On the contrary, defensive killing intentionally inflicts harm on one person as a means of preventing a different harm to a different person. In cases of defensive killing, someone will be killed no matter what you do. But you will not kill no matter what you do. Your moral problem is not a problem of distributing benefits and burdens but a problem of respecting basic rights.

The moral question to ask about defensive killing is not "is it better for A to die or for B to die?" but rather "would I wrong A by intentionally killing A to save B"? Neither question resolves the other. Intentionally killing A to save B may wrong A yet bring about a morally desirable distribution of harm. Alternatively, intentionally killing A to save B may not wrong A yet bring about a morally objectionable distribution of harm. One thing may have little to do with the other. In general, we have a right not to be intentionally killed as a means of producing a morally preferable state of affairs.[10] If we lose that right, then the explanation cannot be that stripping us of that right will facilitate the production of morally preferable states of affairs. It follows that the principle of preventive justice cannot explain the permissibility of defensive force. Indeed, no distributive principle can do so.

If we reject McMahan's principle of preventive justice, then we must reject the responsibility account that rests upon it. To see this, consider the following variations of *Conscientious Driver*:

> *Conscientious Seller*: A car seller keeps all the cars that she sells well maintained and always implores her customers to drive cautiously and alertly. On one occasion, however, freak circumstances cause a car that the seller sold to go out of control. It has veered in the direction of a pedestrian whom it will kill unless the pedestrian kills the seller through a complex but reliable causal chain typical in philosophical examples.

The seller is at least as responsible as the driver, and comparatively more responsible than the pedestrian, for the threat to the pedestrian. Yet, it seems clear that the seller is not sufficiently responsible for that threat in absolute terms to make herself morally liable to defensive killing.

It follows that *Conscientious Driver* at most shows that minimal responsibility for posing an unjust threat—directly infringing someone's rights without intervening agency—generates moral liability to defensive killing. However, *Conscientious Seller* shows that minimal responsibility for contributing to an unjust threat posed by someone else does not generate moral liability to defensive killing. Since civilians who do not directly participate in hostilities do not pose unjust threats but at most contribute to unjust threats posed by others it follows that cases like

---

[10] As Seth Lazar observes, every person has a "moral status, which protects her against marginal interpersonal trade-offs" (*Sparing Civilians* (OUP 2016) 4).

Conscientious Driver do not show that contributing civilians are morally liable to defensive killing.

McMahan writes that, unlike the driver, "civilians who actively support an unjust war do often act culpably, even if their causal influence is negligible."[11] On this view, liability to defensive killing results either from high causal influence and minimal responsibility (the driver) or from high culpability and low causal influence (contributing civilians). This view seems unlikely. Culpability does not exist in a vacuum. On the contrary, culpability is always culpability with respect to something: typically some act, occasionally some attitude. If one is not culpable with respect to some act, then this fact might render one non-liable to treatment that one's act might otherwise warrant. In contrast, if one is culpable with respect to some act then this fact cannot render one liable to treatment that one's act would not otherwise warrant. Put another way, culpability can be an enabling condition for liability but culpability cannot be a ground of liability. If superfluous contribution to an unjust threat is not the kind of thing that can ground liability to defensive killing, then culpably making a superfluous contribution to an unjust threat does not ground liability to defensive killing.

To see one final problem generated by the responsibility account, consider the following variation:

> *Conscientious Passenger.* Two people keep their car well maintained and always drive cautiously and alertly. On one occasion, however, freak circumstances cause the car to go out of control. It has veered in the direction of a pedestrian whom it will kill unless the pedestrian kills the passenger, who co-owns the car with the driver, through a complex but reliable causal chain typical in philosophical examples.

In this variation, the choice is not between one person dying and another person dying but between one person dying and two people dying. It is very hard to believe that the minimal moral responsibility of the driver and the passenger is sufficient to overturn the moral asymmetry between killing two people and allowing one person to be killed. Yet, ordinarily, if two people are *each* morally liable to defensive killing, then they are *both* morally liable to defensive killing. Conversely, if the driver and passenger are not both liable, then it seems that neither is liable. McMahan is well aware of this problem, and continues to refine his response.[12] In my view, this problem reveals the impossibility of basing moral liability to defensive killing on the just distribution of harm.

More generally, there is a compound moral asymmetry between intentionally killing one person and unintentionally allowing another person to be killed. It follows that only a large difference in moral responsibility could offset this compound

[11] *Killing in War*, 230.
[12] See Jeff McMahan, "Liability, Proportionality, and the Number of Aggressors," in Saba Bazargan & Samuel Rickless (eds), *The Ethics of War* (OUP, forthcoming).

moral asymmetry and render it permissible to intentionally kill a more responsible person to save a less responsible person.[13] Put another way, ordinarily it is impermissible to intentionally kill one person except perhaps to prevent many others from being comparably harmed. In sharp contrast, it is permissible to intentionally kill someone liable to defensive killing to prevent only one other person from being comparably harmed. Only a very large difference in moral responsibility could explain this very large difference in moral permissibility.

In fact, *differences* in *comparative* moral responsibility cannot explain moral liability to defensive killing. Whether you retain or lose your right not to be killed should depend on what you do, not on how what you do compares to what I do. Since you possess moral rights in virtue of your non-comparative properties as a human being, you should retain or lose moral rights in virtue of the non-comparative properties of your actions. In particular, the loss of moral rights should require moral wrongdoing of a degree commensurate with the importance of the rights lost.[14]

To see this, consider a variation of *Conscientious Seller* in which the seller is slightly more responsible than the driver for the loss of control and that the pedestrian can save herself by killing either the driver or the seller. On McMahan's view, the seller is liable to defensive killing and the driver is not, even though the driver's conduct is exactly the same as in the original case. This seems wrong. Either the driver is sufficiently responsible for the threat to the victim that the driver forfeits his right not to be killed or he is not. Either way, the driver's moral status should depend on his own conduct, not on the independent conduct of others. Of course, if several people are liable to defensive killing then it may be morally preferable to defensively kill the liable person who is most responsible for the unjust threat. But such comparative considerations come into play only after the liable individuals are identified on non-comparative grounds.

What, then, should we say about McMahan's conscientious driver? It is certainly possible that the driver is not morally liable to be killed.[15] Perhaps the pedestrian must not kill the driver even if this means allowing himself to be killed.[16] Or perhaps third parties may not kill the non-liable driver to save the pedestrian but the pedestrian has an agent-centered prerogative to eliminatively kill the non-liable

[13] In contrast, there may be only a small moral asymmetry between allowing one person to be killed and redirecting a lethal threat away from that person toward another person. If so, then it is at least plausible that a small difference in moral responsibility could offset this small moral asymmetry and render it permissible to redirect a threat away from a less responsible person toward a more responsible person.

[14] See Lazar, *Sparing Civilians*, 16 (arguing that "we think there should be some degree of 'fit' between what the target has done and the fate of losing her right to life").

[15] See Seth Lazar, "Responsibility, Risk, and Killing in Self-Defense" (2009) 119 Ethics 699–728.

[16] See Frowe, *Defensive Killing*, 82.

driver to save himself.[17] On either view, minimal moral responsibility for directly posing an unjust threat does not generate moral liability to defensive killing. Both views recognize a responsibility threshold for moral liability to defensive killing. There is no reason to believe that contributing civilians cross that threshold.

The Complicity Analogy

On my view, one becomes morally liable to defensive killing by threatening to unjustly kill directly, jointly with others, or indirectly through others one controls. My view maps both onto modes of direct participation in hostilities under international humanitarian law and modes of perpetration under international criminal law. One directly participates in hostilities by performing an act likely to directly cause harm, by performing an integral part of a coordinated military operation likely to directly cause harm, or by commanding subordinates to directly cause harm. Similarly, one perpetrates an international crime through direct perpetration, co-perpetration, or indirect perpetration by means of another whom one controls.

In contrast, McMahan suggests that contributing civilians are morally liable to defensive killing because they are *complicit* in the unjust threats posed by unjust combatants.[18] Under international criminal law, a defendant is complicit in crimes perpetrated by others only if the defendant makes a substantial contribution to their commission. Importantly, criminal complicity does not require counterfactual dependence; superfluous encouragement and facilitation, for example, may be sufficient.[19] While the International Criminal Court requires that the defendant act for the purpose of facilitating the commission of the crimes, other international tribunals require only that the defendant is aware of a substantial likelihood that his or her acts will facilitate the commission of the crimes.[20]

There are many problems with *the complicity analogy*. To begin with, current legal doctrine is very likely too broad. Many scholars argue that only necessary contributors should be convicted of the same crime as perpetrators, while superfluous contributors should be convicted of some lesser offense such as criminal facilitation.[21] Similarly, many scholars argue that accomplices should be convicted of the same crime as perpetrators only if they intend that the perpetrators engage in prohibited

---

[17] See Jonathan Quong, "Liability to Defensive Harm" (2012) 40 Philosophy & Public Affairs 46.

[18] See McMahan, *Killing in War*, 208–9, 214–15, 218.

[19] *Prosecutor v Blaškić* (Judgment) IT-95-14-A, Appeals Chamber, July 29, 2004, para 48.

[20] Rome Statute art 25; *Prosecutor v Taylor* (Judgment) SCSL-01-01-A, Appeals Chamber, September 26, 2013.

[21] See, eg, Joshua Dressler, "Reforming Complicity Law: Trivial Assistance as a Lesser Offense?" (2008) 5 Ohio St J Crim L 427, 435–7.

conduct (such as rape or torture) or intend that the perpetrator engage in conduct (such as firing a gun) that causes a prohibited result (such as death). Since the law requires that perpetrators intend their conduct (under some description), the law should require that accomplices intend the perpetrator's conduct (under some description). Only then will the agency of the accomplice fully map onto the agency of the perpetrator for whose crimes the accomplice is to be convicted.[22]

Another problem with the complicity analogy is that, while accomplices are convicted of the same crime as perpetrators, it is unjust to punish a superfluous or reckless accomplice as severely as a direct, indirect, or joint perpetrator. In general, the punishment to which accomplices are justly liable varies with the significance of their individual contribution. It follows that the complicity analogy does not support holding contributing civilians derivatively liable *to* defensive killing *for* the unjust threats posed by their armed forces.

More fundamentally, criminal liability is liability to moral condemnation and humane punishment, while defensive liability is liability to death and dismemberment. Of course, most scholars now reject the moral permissibility of capital punishment and almost all reject the moral permissibility of corporal punishment. Certainly, it seems morally impermissible to execute or maim accomplices as punishment for superfluous contributions to the crimes of others. Moreover, since the basis of killing and harming in war is preventive rather than retributive, the relevant wrongs to which civilians might contribute are inchoate wrongs such as incomplete attempts. Certainly, it seems morally impermissible to execute or maim marginal accomplices to punish merely inchoate crimes. So even if some civilians are complicit in the unjust threats posed by unjust combatants it does not follow that they are liable to killing and maiming.

Finally, liability to harm is always liability to be harmed for certain reasons.[23] It follows that liability to be harmed for punitive reasons does not entail liability to be harmed for preventive reasons. For example, if retributivism is true, then criminal liability is liability to be punished as a response to past wrongdoing, not as a means to prevent future wrongdoing. Although I will not argue here for the truth of retributivism,[24] it would be surprising if the correct theory of justified defensive force depends on the falsity of retributivism.

---

[22] See American Law Institute, Model Penal Code and Commentaries §2.06 (1980 and 1985); Adil Ahmad Haque, "The U.S. Model Penal Code's Significance for Complicity in the ICC Statute, December 13, 2014," http://jamesgstewart.com/the-u-s-model-penal-codes-significance-for-complicity-in-the-icc-statute-an-american-view/. Note that criminal perpetration requires voluntary conduct, that is, conduct that executes an intention of the actor. The actor need not intend his or her conduct under the description that renders it criminal, but must intend his or her conduct under some description.

[23] See McMahan, *Killing in War*, 10.

[24] I do so in Haque, "Retributivism: The Right and the Good" (2013) 32 Law & Philosophy 59.

Intentional but superfluous contributions to unjust threats posed by others may render one criminally complicit but will not render one morally liable to defensive killing. To test the implications of my view, consider the following cases:

> *Abettor*: Attacker is determined to stab Victim to death with a knife. Abettor, who does not know Attacker but who dislikes Victim, yells to Attacker "Good for you, I hate that guy." Victim cannot kill Attacker but can kill Abettor and thereby frighten off Attacker.
>
> *Seller*: Attacker is determined to stab Victim to death with a knife when he notices that Seller is offering an identical knife for its regular market price. Attacker quickly purchases the identical knife and resumes his attack on Victim. Victim cannot kill Attacker but can kill Seller and thereby frighten off Attacker.

In these cases, Abettor and Seller make Victim no worse off than Victim would have been in their respective absences. On the contrary, killing Abettor or Seller will make Victim better off than Victim would be in their respective absences. Abettor and Seller contribute to the direct threat posed by Attacker to Victim but do not jointly threaten Victim with Attacker. It follows that, on my view, only Attacker is morally liable to defensive killing. Abettor and Seller may be wrongdoers and criminals but they are not killers and may not be killed. Some courts may find Abettor and Seller criminally complicit in Attacker's attempt to kill Victim, but Abettor and Seller are not morally liable to defensive killing.

Contributing Civilians as Indirect Threats

Helen Frowe argues that contributing civilians are *indirect threats*, by which she means that they make causal contributions to the direct threats posed by their armed forces.[25] Frowe argues that contributing civilians are morally liable to defensive killing if they contribute to direct, unjust, and lethal threats posed by their armed forces—for example through political advocacy, the design and manufacture of weapons, and even the provision of medical care—despite reasonable opportunities to avoid doing so.

Considering the dramatic implications of Frowe's account, the brevity of her affirmative argument is striking. Frowe's claim that freely contributing to unjust threats posed by others makes one liable to defensive killing appears to rest entirely on one case:

> *Drive-By*: Terrorist holds a gun to Driver's head, and orders him to drive the car for a drive-by shooting, in which Terrorist will kill Victim.[26]

---

[25] *Defensive Killing*, 7, 15–16.

[26] *Defensive Killing*, 80. Frowe later offers a variation of this case in which Driver mistakenly believes that Victim poses an unjust threat and that the drive-by shooting is a permissible exercise of defensive force (at 84).

Frowe submits that Driver must not drive the car, even to avoid his own death, and is morally liable to defensive killing if he does so.

On my view, if Driver drives the car for the drive-by shooting, then he does not merely help Terrorist kill Victim but jointly kills Victim with Terrorist, performing an integral role in a common plan in which each will mutually respond to the other's efforts to perform their respective roles. If Terrorist and Driver together kill Victim through such a coordinated joint action, then Driver kills Victim even if Terrorist pulls the trigger. On my view, Driver may not jointly kill Victim to avoid being killed by Terrorist. It follows that *Drive-By* does not show that contributing to an unjust threat generates liability to defensive killing, only that jointly posing an unjust threat generates liability to defensive killing. Since contributing civilians do not jointly pose threats with their armed forces, this case does not support the liability of contributing civilians to defensive killing.

Some readers may reject the distinction between jointly acting with another person and contributing to the action of another person. To these readers, Frowe's case may show that *some* contributions to direct threats generate liability to defensive killing. However, it is not clear whether Driver makes a necessary contribution or a superfluous contribution to the direct threat Terrorist poses to Victim. If Terrorist could not kill Victim without Driver, then it is at least plausible that Driver may not *enable* Terrorist to kill Victim even to avoid his own death. In contrast, if Terrorist could kill Victim just as easily without Driver then it is hard to believe that Driver may not superfluously contribute to the direct threat posed by Terrorist to avoid his own death. It is one thing to say, as I do, that we may not jointly pose direct threats even if our participation will not make the victim worse off and our non-participation will make us worse off. It is quite another thing to say that we may not contribute to direct threats posed by others even if our contribution will not make the victim worse off and our non-contribution will make us much worse off. Since almost all contributing civilians make superfluous contributions to the direct threats posed by their armed forces, *Drive-By* fails to show that contributing civilians are liable to defensive killing.

Since Frowe thinks that *Drive-By* establishes a *prima facie* case that contributing civilians are liable to defensive killing she provides no further affirmative argument but instead considers possible counter-arguments.[27] For example, Frowe rejects the view that causal proximity is relevant to liability, citing the following case:

> *Coercion*: The German army capture[s] a town. Nazi forces Mayor to shoot Citizen, on pain of Nazi shooting a much greater number of citizens.[28]

---

[27] *Defensive Killing*, 162 ("Much of the argumentative work for this claim—that those who are morally responsible for indirect unjust threats are liable to defensive killing—has been done already. My focus in this chapter is therefore on defending the plausibility of extending this argument to non-combatants").

[28] *Defensive Killing*, 168.

Frowe submits that "[i]f Citizen has a gun with which he can lethally defend himself, both Nazi and Mayor seem like potentially legitimate targets."[29] Frowe concludes that "intervening agency … doesn't give us a plausible way to sustain non-combatant immunity."[30]

On my view, Nazi will not merely contribute to Mayor killing Citizen or merely enable Mayor to kill Citizen. Instead, Nazi will kill Citizen through or by means of Mayor. In criminal law terms, Nazi is not a mere accomplice but an indirect perpetrator. It is not as if Mayor conditionally intends to kill Citizen and Nazi merely helps Mayor by fulfilling the relevant condition. Instead, it is up to Nazi to tell Mayor what to intend. Of course, Mayor is a moral agent who could choose to defy Nazi and spare Victim. However, so long as Mayor remains committed to saving the much greater number of citizens, Nazi can manipulate Mayor's commitment as if it is a causal mechanism, rationally requiring Mayor to kill on Nazi's command. It follows that, on my view, *Coercion* does not show that causal proximity and intervening agency are irrelevant to liability. Instead, *Coercion* shows that when one person effectively controls another, the controller is causally proximate to harms inflicted by the controlled and the agency of the controlled does not intervene in the morally relevant sense.

Some readers may reject the distinction between indirectly acting through another person and contributing to the action of another person. To these readers, *Coercion* may show that some contributions to direct threats generate liability to defensive killing. However, if Mayor would not kill Citizen but for the command of Nazi then *Coercion* only shows that necessary contributions to direct threats generate liability to defensive killing. Since almost all contributing civilians make superfluous contributions to the direct threats posed by their armed forces, *Coercion* does not support the liability of contributing civilians to defensive killing.

Frowe also rejects the view that "individual contributions" to an unjust threat "must pass a threshold of causal significance," citing the following case:

> *Hit*: Mafia Boss wants to take Victim out, but he cannot afford to hire Assassin, who is extremely skilled and thus extremely expensive. Mafia Boss has a whip-round amongst all the members of his mob, none of whom really like Victim. Everyone coughs up a few pounds for the assassination fund.[31]

Frowe submits that "Victim would be permitted to kill any individual member of the mob (or even all of them)" to defend himself.[32]

On my view, *Hit* suggests what international criminal lawyers call *indirect co-perpetration*, which combines joint and indirect perpetration.[33] It seems that the members of the mob are working together to kill Victim and that Mafia Boss's role

[29] *Defensive Killing*, 168.   [30] *Defensive Killing*, 169.
[31] *Defensive Killing*, 176.   [32] *Defensive Killing*, 176.
[33] See Stefano Manacorda & Chantal Meloni, "Indirect Perpetration versus Joint Criminal Enterprise" (2011) 9 Journal of International Criminal Justice 159.

in the common plan is to hire Assassin and order Assassin to kill Victim. On this interpretation, the members jointly threaten to kill Victim through Assassin and are therefore morally liable to defensive killing.

Perhaps this is not what Frowe intends and shared membership in the mob is a red herring. Let us therefore consider the following variation, which in any event more closely resembles the relationship between contributing civilians, their governments, and their armed forces:

> *Another Hit*: Mafia Boss wants Victim dead, but he cannot afford to hire Assassin, who is extremely skilled and thus extremely expensive. Mafia Boss demands money from local business owners. Some owners pay to avoid retaliation by Mafia Boss; some pay in return for Mafia Boss's protection from other gangs; and some pay because they dislike Victim. Everyone pays a few pounds for the assassination fund.

In this variation, the business owners merely contribute to Mafia Boss killing Victim through Assassin. Presumably, no business owner makes a necessary contribution, since Mafia Boss could compensate for the non-payment of any owner by asking more from others or by paying more himself. In my view, the business owners who superfluously contribute in order to avoid harm to themselves are justified in doing so. It follows that the business owners who superfluously contribute for other reasons do not breach a sufficiently stringent duty to render themselves liable to defensive killing. Since contributing civilians almost always make superfluous contributions to threats directly posed by their armed forces (and indirectly posed by their governments), *Another Hit* does not support the liability of contributing civilians to defensive killing.

Importantly, Frowe argues that the unjustified breach of a moral duty can ground liability to defensive killing even if one could justifiably breach that duty in order to avoid one's own death. Frowe invites us to consider the following case:

> *Selfish Bridge*: Victim is fleeing Murderer, who wants to kill him. Victim's only escape route is across a narrow bridge that can hold only one person. Selfish Pedestrian is out for a walk on the bridge. Selfish Pedestrian could easily get off the bridge, but doing so will involve getting her feet wet and she has on her lovely new shoes. She decides, with a certain amount of regret, to stay on the bridge, realizing that her doing so impedes Victim's escape.[34]

According to Frowe:

even though Selfish Pedestrian is not initially required to bear a lethal cost to avoid posing a threat to Victim ... Selfish Pedestrian's initial refusal to bear a *reasonable* cost [] makes her liable to bear a much higher cost as part of Victim's defence of his life.

Frowe argues that, "by getting off the bridge at the cost of wet shoes, Selfish Pedestrian could have ensured that neither she nor Victim needed to bear a serious

---

[34] Frowe, *Defensive Killing*, 76.

harm. In refusing to bear this reasonable cost, she becomes morally responsible for endangering Victim's life."

Of course, unlike Frowe's Selfish Pedestrian, contributing civilians do not pose threats to others—even in Frowe's sense—since their presence makes no one worse off than would their absence. Relatedly, contributing civilians generally cannot ensure that neither they nor others will suffer serious harm. Except in rare cases, there is nothing that contributing civilians can do to avoid being seriously harmed or to prevent others from being seriously harmed. In any event, as we have seen, moral responsibility for the fact that someone else will be harmed if you are not harmed first does not, without more, make you morally liable to defensive killing.

Nevertheless, it might be all-things-considered permissible for Victim to kill Selfish Pedestrian. Killing Selfish Pedestrian would be eliminative rather than opportunistic. Selfish Pedestrian could easily avoid making Victim worse off due to her presence. Finally, Selfish Pedestrian could easily avoid being harmed at all. These considerations might combine to make it permissible for Victim to kill Selfish Pedestrian in order to save herself. None of these considerations apply to the killing of contributing civilians.

Finally, Frowe rejects the view that intentionally killing contributing civilians is impermissibly opportunistic or exploitative, based on the following case:

> *Mob*: Victim is being chased by an angry racist mob who[se members] are trying to kill him. They corner him in a dead-end street. One of the mob [members] throws a knife to the ringleader, who advances menacingly towards Victim. Unbeknown to the mob, Victim has a concealed gun. But he also has terrible eyesight: his short-distance vision is just awful. He cannot hope to accurately aim at the ringleader at such close range. His only hope of saving his life is to shoot the guy who threw the ringleader the knife, who is standing further away. When the rest of the mob [members] realize that he has a gun and he's not afraid to use it, they will be scared off.

Frowe submits that "[i]t does not seem impermissible for Victim to kill the knife-thrower if this is the only way in which he can save himself."[35] In particular, Frowe writes that "[s]uch *merely opportunistic* harming lacks the moral repugnance that attaches to the *exploitative* harming of bystanders to make oneself better off than one would have been in their absence."[36]

I disagree with Frowe's analysis of *Mob*. If the ringleader needs the knife to kill Victim, then the knife-thrower makes Victim worse off than Victim would be in the knife-thrower's absence. On these facts, the knife-thrower can be eliminatively killed before he throws the knife or merely opportunistically killed after he throws the knife. Either way, killing the knife-thrower prevents him from making Victim worse off than Victim would be in his absence. In contrast, if the ringleader does not need the knife to kill Victim then the knife-thrower does not make Victim

---

[35] *Defensive Killing*, 178–9.   [36] *Defensive Killing*, 179 (italics added).

worse off than Victim would be in the knife-thrower's absence. On the contrary, killing the knife-thrower as a means of scaring off the rest of the mob will make Victim better off than Victim would be in the knife-thrower's absence. Killing the knife-thrower is therefore "exploitative" as Frowe defines that term.

As we have seen, the contributions of contributing civilians generally do not make anyone worse off. It follows that contributing civilians cannot be eliminatively killed or merely opportunistically killed but only exploitatively killed (or gratuitously killed, unfortunately). Since Frowe mistakenly thinks that killing the knife-thrower in *Mob* is not exploitative, she does not even try to argue that the knife-thrower (and, by analogy, contributing civilians) might be liable to exploitative killing. It follows that Frowe's analysis of *Mob* does not support the liability of contributing civilians.

In my view, the knife-thrower might be liable to defensive killing even if he does not make Victim worse off (suppose the ringleader already has a knife) on the grounds that he jointly threatens Victim's rights together with the other mob members. Since contributing civilians do not jointly threaten anyone's rights together with their armed forces, my analysis of *Mob* does not support the liability of contributing civilians to exploitative killing. As we have seen, neither does Frowe's.

Conclusion

For almost two decades, the ethics of war has been dominated by two revisionist critiques: of the equality of combatants and of the equality of civilians. As we saw in Chapter 2, the first critique rests, in part, on a mistake. The law of war does not claim that combatants are permitted to fight for an unjust cause, only that states are prohibited from criminally prosecuting lawful combatants for acts that are not prohibited by the law of war. Just and unjust combatants are not morally equal. The mistake was thinking that the law of war claims otherwise.

As we have seen in this appendix, the second critique rests on a different kind of mistake. The law of war indeed prohibits the intentional killing of civilians not directly participating in hostilities. The mistake is thinking that the law of war is wrong to do so. Civilians are human beings with a basic right not to be killed or seriously harmed. They lose that right only by posing unjust threats directly, jointly with others, or indirectly through others they effectively control.

Moral philosophy can and should inform positive law. At the same time, positive law can serve as a repository and reminder of basic moral truths. Just war theory must not become a forum for devising ingenious arguments seeking to show that intentionally killing defenseless civilians, though always unlawful, is often morally permissible. Instead, the philosophical study of war should contribute to the interpretation, defense, and reform of the law of war, helping the law to achieve its constitutive aim of providing sound moral guidance to combatants and strong moral protection to civilians.

Bibliography

Aboodi, Ron, Adi Borer, and David Enoch, "Deontology, Individualism, and Uncertainty: A Reply to Jackson and Smith" (2008) 105 Journal of Philosophy 259.

Accordance with International Law of the Unilateral Declaration of Independence in Respect of Kosovo (Advisory Opinion) 2010 ICJ Rep 403.

African Commission on Human and Peoples' Rights, *General Comment No 3 on the African Charter on Human and Peoples' Rights: The Right to Life (Article 4)* (PULP 2015).

Akande, Dapo & Thomas Lieflander, "Clarifying Necessity, Imminence, and Proportionality in the Law of Self-Defense" (2013) 107 AJIL 563.

Allied Joint Publication AJP-5, Allied Joint Doctrine for Operational-Level Planning (2013).

Alston, Philip, Report of the Special Rapporteur on Extrajudicial, Summary or Arbitrary Executions, Study on Targeted Killings, Human Rights Council, UN Doc A/HRC/14124/Add.6 (May 28, 2010).

American Law Institute, Model Penal Code and Commentaries (1985) Associated Press, "Marine Accepts Plea Deal in Iraqi Civilian Deaths, Newsday," January 24, 2012, http://www.newsday.com/news/world/marine-accepts-plea-deal-in-iraqi-civillian-deaths-1.3474532.

Australian Defence Force, Australian Defence Doctrine Publication 06.4—Law of Armed Conflict (2006).

Barry, Christian & Gerhard Øverland, "The Implications of Failing to Assist" (2014) 40 Social Theory and Practice 570.

Baxter, Richard R, "So-Called 'Unprivileged Belligerency': Spies, Guerillas, and Saboteurs" (1951) 28 British Yearbook of International Law 323.

Bazargan, Saba, "Complicitous Liability in War" (2013) 165 Philosophical Studies 177

Bazargan, Saba, "Morally Heterogeneous Wars" (2013) 41 Philosophia 959.

Beit Sourik Village Council v Israel (Judgment) HCJ 2056/04, June 30, 2004.

Bergelson, Vera, "Rights, Wrongs, and Comparative Justifications" (2007) 28 Cardozo Law Review 2481.

Blum, Gabriella, "The Dispensable Lives of Soldiers" (2010) 2 Journal of Legal Analysis 69.

Bratman, Michael E, *Shared Agency: A Planning Theory of Acting Together* (OUP 2014)

British Ministry of Defence, JWP 0-01 British Defence Doctrine (1996).

Bureau of Investigative Journalism, "Covert Drone War," http://www.thebureauinvestigates.com/category/projects/drones/.

Cassese, Antonio, *International Criminal Law* (2nd edn OUP 2008).

Cassese, Antonio, "The Italian Court of Cassation Misapprehends the Notion of War Crimes" (2008) 6 J Int'l Crim Just 1077.

Chang, Ruth (ed), *Incommensurability, Incomparability, and Practical Reason* (Harvard UP 1997).

Clark, Roger S, "The Mental Element in International Criminal Law: The Rome Statute of the International Criminal Court and the Elements of Offences" (2002) 12 Crim L F 291.

Convention for the Protection of Human Rights and Fundamental Freedoms (opened for signature November 4, 1950, entered into force September 3, 1953) 213 UNTS 222.

Corn, Geoffrey S, Laurie R Blank, Chris Jenks, & Eric Talbot Jensen, "Belligerent Targeting and the Invalidity of a Least Harmful Means Rule" (2013) 89 International Law Studies 536.

Cryer, Robert, "Of Custom, Treaties, Scholars, and the Gavel: The Influence of the International Criminal Tribunals on the ICRC Customary Law Study" (2006) 11 J Conflict & Security L 239.

Dancy, Jonathan, *Ethics Without Principles* (OUP 2004).

Declaration Renouncing the Use, in Time of War, of Explosive Projectiles Under 400 Grammes Weight (St Petersburg Declaration) (entered into force December 11, 1868) 138 Consol TS 297, 18 Martens Nouveau Recueil (ser 1) 474.

Department of the Air Force, AFP 110-31, International Law—The Conduct of Armed Conflict and Air Operations (1976).

Dill, Janina *Legitimate Targets* (CUP 2015).

Dill, Janina & Henry Shue, "Limiting the Killing in War: Military Necessity and the St Petersburg Assumption" (2012) 26 Ethics & International Affairs 311.

Dinstein, Yoram, *War, Aggression and Self-Defence* (CUP 2005).

Dinstein, Yoram, *The Conduct of Hostilities under the Law of International Armed Conflict* (CUP 2010).

Dinstein, Yoram, "The Principle of Proportionality," in Kjetil Mujezinovic Larsen, Camilla Guldahl Cooper, & Gro Nystuen (eds) *Searching for a 'Principle of Humanity' in International Humanitarian Law* (CUP 2013) 72–85.

Dormann, Knut, *Elements of War Crimes under the Rome Statute of the International Criminal Court: Sources and Commentary* (CUP 2003).

Draper, Kai, *War and Individual Rights* (OUP 2015).

Dressler, Joshua, "Reforming Complicity Law: Trivial Assistance as a Lesser Offense?" (2008) 5 Ohio St J Crim L 427.

Duff, RA, "'I Might Be Guilty, But You Can't Try Me': Estoppel and Other Bars to Trial" (2003) 1 Ohio State Journal of Criminal Law 245.

Dunlap Jr, Charles J, "The DoD Law of War Manual and its Critics: Some Observations" (2106) 92 International Law Studies 85.

Fabre, Cécile, *Cosmopolitan War* (OUP 2012).

Fabre, Cécile & Seth Lazar (eds), *The Morality of Defensive War* (OUP 2014).

Feinberg, Joel, *The Moral Limits of the Criminal Law Vol 3: Harm to Self* (OUP 1989).

Ferzan, Kimberly Kessler, "Culpable Aggression: The Basis for Moral Liability to Defensive Killing" (2012) 9 Ohio State Journal of Criminal Law 669.

Fletcher, George P, & Jens David Ohlin, "Reclaiming Fundamental Principles of Criminal Law in the Darfur Case" (2005) 3 Journal of International Criminal Justice 539.

Fletcher, George P, & Jens David Ohlin, *Defending Humanity* (OUP 2008).

Frowe, Helen, *Defensive Killing* (OUP 2014).

Frowe, Helen, "Claims Rights, Duties and Lesser Evil Obligations" (2015) 89 Proceedings of the Aristotelian Society, Supplementary Volume, 267.

Gardner, John, *Law as a Leap of Faith* (OUP 2012).

Gebicke, Scott & Samuel Magid, "Lessons from around the World: Benchmarking Performance in Defense" (2010) 5 McKinsey on Government 1.

Geneva Convention (I) for the Amelioration of the Condition of the Wounded and Sick in Armed Forces in the Field (opened for signature August 12, 1949, entered into force October 21, 1950).

Geneva Convention (III) relative to the Treatment of Prisoners of War (opened for signature August 12, 1949, entered into force October 21, 1950).

Geneva Convention (IV) relative to the Protection of Civilian Persons in Time of War (opened for signature August 12, 1949, entered into force October 21, 1950).

Gilbert, Margaret, "Shared Intention and Personal Intention" (2009) 144 Philosophical Studies 167.

Goodman, Ryan, "The Power to Kill or Capture Enemy Combatants" (2013) 24 EJIL 819.

Hague Convention (II) with Respect to the Laws and Customs of War on Land (opened for signature July 29, 1899, entered into force September 4, 1900).

Hague Convention (IV) Respecting the Laws and Customs of War on Land (opened for signature October 18, 1907, entered into force January 26, 1910) 3 Martens Nouveau Recueil (ser 3) 461.

Hague Convention (IX) concerning Bombardment by Naval Forces in Time of War (opened for signature October 18, 1907, entered into force January 26, 1910).

Hanser, Matthew, "Killing, Letting Die, and Preventing People from Being Saved" (1999) 11 Utilitas 277.

Haque, Adil Ahmad, "Torture, Terror, and the Inversion of Moral Principle" (2007) 10 New Criminal Law Review 613 (2007).

Haque, Adil Ahmad, "Legitimacy as Strategy," in Paul H Robinson, Stephen Garvey, & Kimberly Ferzan (eds) *Criminal Law Conversations* (OUP 2009) 57.

Haque, Adil Ahmad, "Rights and Liabilities at War," in Paul H Robinson, Stephen Garvey, & Kimberly Ferzan (eds) *Criminal Law Conversations* (OUP 2009) 395.

Haque, Adil Ahmad, "Criminal Law and Morality at War," in RA Duff & Stuart Green (eds), *Philosophical Foundations of Criminal Law* (OUP 2011) 481.

Haque, Adil Ahmad, "International Crime: in Context and in Contrast," in RA Duff, Lindsay Farmer, SE Marshall, Massimo Renzo, & Victor Tadros (eds), *The Structures of Criminal Law* (OUP 2011) 106.

Haque, Adil Ahmad, "Protecting and Respecting Civilians: Correcting the Substantive and Structural Defects of the Rome Statute" (2011) 14 New Criminal Law Review 519.

Haque, Adil Ahmad, "Killing in the Fog of War" (2012) 86 Southern California Law Review 63.

Haque, Adil Ahmad, "Retributivism: The Right and the Good" (2013) 32 Law & Philosophy 59.

Haque, Adil Ahmad, "Law and Morality at War" (2014) 8 Criminal Law & Philosophy 79.

Haque, Adil Ahmad, "The US Model Penal Code's Significance for Complicity in the ICC Statute," December 13, 2014, http://jamesgstewart.com/the-u-s-model-penal-codes-significance-for-complicity-in-the-icc-statute-an-american-view/.

Haque, Adil Ahmad, "Human Shields," in Helen Frowe & Seth Lazar (eds), *The Oxford Handbook of the Ethics of War* (OUP 2015).

Haque, Adil Ahmad, "Off Target: Selection, Precaution, and Proportionality in the DoD Manual" (2016) 92 International Law Studies 31.

Haque, Adil Ahmad, "War Crimes and the Law of War", in Kevin Jon Heller, Frédéric Mégret, Sarah Nouwen, Jens Ohlin, & Darryl Robinson (eds), *The Oxford Handbook of International Criminal Law* (OUP, forthcoming 2017).

Henderson, Ian, *The Contemporary Law of Targeting: Military Objectives, Proportionality, and Precautions in Attack under Additional Protocol I* (Martinus Nijhoff 2009).

Hohfeld, Wesley, *Fundamental Legal Conceptions* (Yale University Press, 1919).

Hosein, Adam, "Are Justified Aggressors a Threat to the Rights Theory of Self-Defense?," in Helen Frowe & Gerald Lang (eds), *How We Fight: Ethics in War* (OUP 2014) 87–103.

Hurka, Thomas, "Proportionality in the Morality of War" (2005) 33 Philosophy & Public Affairs 34.

ibn Anas, Malik (ed), *Al-Muwatta* (circa 767 CE) (Diwan 4th edn 2015).

ICTY, Final Report to the Prosecutor by the Committee Established to Review the NATO Bombing Campaign Against the Federal Republic of Yugoslavia, June 8, 2000 (2000) 38 ILM 1257.

Instructions for the Government of Armies of the United States in the Field, General Order No 100 (April 24, 1863).

International Committee of the Red Cross, Commentary on the Additional Protocols of 8 June 1977 to the Geneva Conventions of August 12, 1949 (ICRC/ Martinus Nijhoff 1987).

International Committee of the Red Cross, *Customary International Humanitarian Law*, vol 1 (CUP 2009).

International Committee of the Red Cross, *Interpretive Guidance on the Notion of Direct Participation in Hostilities under International Humanitarian Law* (ICRC 2009).

International Covenant on Civil and Political Rights (ICCPR) (opened for signature December 19, 1966, entered into force March 23, 1976) 999 UNTS 171

International Criminal Court, Elements of Crimes (2011).

Israel Ministry of Foreign Affairs, *The 2014 Gaza Conflict: Factual and Legal Aspects* (2015).

Jackson, Frank, "Decision-Theoretic Consequentialism and the Nearest and Dearest Objection" (1991) 101 Ethics 467.

Jackson, Frank & Michael Smith, "Absolutist Moral Theories and Uncertainty" (2006) 103 Journal of Philosophy 267.

Jinks, Derek, "International Human Rights Law in Time of Armed Conflict," in Andrew Clapham et al, *Oxford Handbook of International Law in Armed Conflict* 656 (OUP 2014).

Jo, Hyeran & Beth A Simmons, "Can the International Criminal Court Deter Atrocity?" (unpublished ms).

Kamm, FM, *Intricate Ethics: Rights, Responsibility, and Permissible Harm* (OUP 2007)

Kasher, Asa & Amos Yadlin, "Military Ethics of Fighting Terror: An Israeli Perspective" (2005) 4 J Mil Ethics 3.

Kretzmer, David, "The Inherent Right to Self-Defence and Proportionality in *Jus Ad Bellum*" (2013) 24 EJIL 235.

Kirgis, Frederic L, "Custom on a Sliding Scale" (1987) 81 American Journal of International Law 146.

Kutz, Christopher, "Acting Together" (2000) 61 Philosophy and Phenomenological Research 1.

Lazar, Seth, "Responsibility, Risk, and Killing in Self-Defense" (2009) 119 Ethics 699.

Lazar, Seth, "The Morality and Law of War," in Andrei Marmor (ed), *Routledge Companion to Philosophy of Law* (Routledge 2012) 376.

Lazar, Seth, "Necessity in Self-Defense and War" (2012) 40 Philosophy & Public Affairs 3.

Lazar, Seth, "Associative Duties and the Ethics of Killing in War" (2013) 1 Journal of Practical Ethics 3.

Lazar, Seth, "On Human Shields" (August 5, 2014) Boston Review, http://www.bostonreview.net/world/seth-lazar-human-shields.

Lazar, Seth, "Risky Killing and the Ethics of War" (2015) 126 Ethics 91.

Lazar, Seth, "Authorization and the Morality of War" (2016) 94 Australasian Journal of Philosophy 211.

Lazar, Seth, *Sparing Civilians* (OUP 2016).

Lazar, Seth, "In Dubious Battle: Uncertainty and the Ethics of Killing" (unpublished ms).

Lee, Roy S (ed), *The International Criminal Court: Elements of Crimes and Rules of Procedure and Evidence* (Transnational 2001).

Lefkowitz, David, "Partiality and Weighing Harm to Non-Combatants" (2009) 6 Journal of Moral Philosophy 298.

Legality of the Threat or Use of Nuclear Weapons (Advisory Opinion) 1996 ICJ Rep 226.

Lieblich, Eliav, "Beyond Life and Limb: Exploring Incidental Mental Harm under International Humanitarian Law," in Derek Jinks, Jackson Nyamuya Maogoto, & Solon Solomon (eds), *Applying International Humanitarian Law in Judicial and Quasi-Judicial Bodies: International and Domestic Aspects* (TMC Asser 2014) 185.

Luban, David, "Military Necessity and the Cultures of Military Law" (2013) 26 Leiden Journal of International Law 315.

Luban, David, "Risk Taking and Force Protection," in Yitzhak Benbaji & Naomi Sussman (eds), *Reading Walzer* (Routledge 2014).

Luban, David, "Human Rights Thinking and the Laws of War," in Jens David Ohlin (ed), *Theoretical Boundaries of Human Rights and Armed Conflict* (OUP 2016) 45–77.

McMahan, Jeff, "Innocence, Self-Defense, and Killing in War" (1994) 2 Journal of Political Philosophy 193.

McMahan, Jeff, *The Ethics of Killing: Problems at the Margins of Life* (OUP 2002).

McMahan, Jeff, "The Ethics of Killing in War" (2004) 114 Ethics 693.

McMahan, Jeff, "The Basis of Moral Liability to Defensive Killing" (2005) Philosophical Issues 386.

McMahan, Jeff, "The Morality of War and the Laws of War," in David Rodin & Henry Shue (eds), *Just and Unjust Warriors* (OUP 2008) 19.

McMahan, Jeff, *Killing in War* (OUP 2009).

McMahan, Jeff, "The Just Distribution of Harm Between Combatants and Noncombatants" (2010) 38 Philosophy & Public Affairs 342.

McMahan, Jeff, "Who Is Morally Liable to be Killed in War" (2011) 71 Analysis 544.

McMahan, Jeff, "War Crimes and Wrongdoing in War," in RA Duff et al (eds), *The Constitution of Criminal Law* (OUP 2013) 151–84.

McMahan, Jeff, "Proportionate Defense" (2013–14) 23 Journal of Transnational Law and Policy 1.

McMahan, Jeff, "Proportionality and Necessity in Jus in Bello," in Helen Frowe & Seth Lazar (eds), *The Oxford Handbook of the Ethics of War* (OUP 2016).

McMahan, Jeff, "Liability, Proportionality, and the Number of Aggressors," in Saba Bazargan & Samuel Rickless (eds), *The Ethics of War* (OUP, forthcoming).

McNeal, Gregory S, "Are Targeted Killings Unlawful?: A Case Study in Empirical Claims Without Empirical Evidence," in Claire Finkelstein, Jens David Ohlin, & Andrew Altman (eds), *Targeted Killings: Law and Morality in an Asymmetrical World* (OUP 2012) 326.

McNeal, Gregory S, "Targeted Killing and Accountability" (2014) 102 Georgetown Law Journal 681.

Manacorda, Stefano & Chantal Meloni, "Indirect Perpetration versus Joint Criminal Enterprise" (2011) 9 Journal of International Criminal Justice 159.

Margalit, Avishai & Michael Walzer, "Israel: Civilians and Combatants," New York Review of Books, May 14, 2009.

May, Larry, *War Crimes and Just War* (CUP 2007).

Melzer, Nils, "Keeping the Balance Between Military Necessity and Humanity: A Response to Four Critiques of the ICRC's Interpretive Guidance on the Notion of Direct Participation in Hostilities" (2010) 42 New York University Journal of International Law & Politics 869.

Merriam, John J, "Affirmative Target Identification: Operationalizing the Principle of Distinction for US Warfighters" (2016) 56 Virginia Journal of International Law 83.

Merriam-Webster's Dictionary (2016).

Moreno-Ocampo, Luis, Chief Prosecutor, Memorandum to the International Criminal Court, February 9, 2006.

Muñoz-Rojas, Daniel & Jean-Jacques Frésard, "The Roots of Behaviour in War: Understanding and Preventing IHL Violations" (2004) 86 International Review of the Red Cross 189.

Nye, Howard, "Objective Double Effect and the Avoidance of Narcissism," in Mark Timmons (ed), *Oxford Studies in Normative Ethics*, vol 3 (OUP 2013) 280.

Office of the Prosecutor, Article 53(1) Report on the situation on Registered Vessels of Comoros, Greece and Cambodia, November 6, 2014.

Ohlin, Jens David, "Joint Intentions to Commit International Crimes" (2011) 11 Chicago Journal of International Law 693.

Ohlin, Jens David, "Targeting and the Concept of Intent" (2013) 35 Michigan Journal of International Law 79.

Oppenheim, Lassa, *International Law, Volume II: Disputes, War and Neutrality* (Hersch Lauterpacht ed, 7th edn 1952).

Osiel, Mark & Ziv Bohrer, "Proportionality in Military Force at War's Multiple Levels: Averting Civilian Casualties vs Safeguarding Soldiers" (2013) 46 Virginia Journal of International Law 747.

Oxford English Dictionary (2016).

Parfit, Derek, "Equality and Priority" (1997) 10 Ratio 202.

Parfit, Derek, *On What Matters*, vol 1 (OUP 2011).

Parks, W Hays, "Air War and the Law of War" (1990) 32 Air Force Law Review 1.

PBS, Quiz: The Tough Choices (February 19, 2008), http://www.pbs.org/wgbh/pages/frontline/haditha/etc/quiz.html.

PBS, Quiz Answers: The Tough Choices (February 19, 2008), http://www.pbs.org/wgbh/pages/frontline/haditha/etc/quiz.html.

Pictet, Jean, *Development and Principles of International Humanitarian Law* (Martinus Nijhoff 1985).

Porat, Iddo & Ziv Bohrer, "Preferring One's Own Civilians" (2015) 47 George Washington International Law Review 99.

Program on Humanitarian Policy and Conflict Research, Commentary on the HPCR Manual on International Law Applicable to Air and Missile Warfare (2010).

Prosecutor v Bemba, Decision on the Confirmation of Charges, ICC-01/05-01/08, Pre-Trial Chamber II, June 15, 2009.

Prosecutor v Blaškić (Judgment) IT-95-14-A, Appeals Chamber, 29 July 2004.

Prosecutor v Galić (Judgment) IT-98-29-T (December 5, 2003).

Prosecutor v Kupreškić (Judgment) IT-95-16-T (January 14, 2000).

Prosecutor v Lubanga, Decision on the Confirmation of Charges, 01/04-01/06, Pre-Trial Chamber, January 29, 2007.

Prosecutor v Perišić (Judgment) IT-04-81-T, Trial Chamber, September 6, 2011.

Prosecutor v Prlić (Judgment) IT-04-74, Trial Chamber, May 29, 2013.

Prosecutor v Rutaganda (Judgment) ICTR-96-3-T (December 6, 1999).

Prosecutor v Stakic (Judgment) IT-97-24-T, July 31, 2003.

Prosecutor v Strugar (Judgment) IT-01-42-A, Appeals Chamber, July 17, 2008.

Prosecutor v Tadić, Decision on the Defence Motion for Interlocutory Appeal on Jurisdiction, IT-94-1-AR72, Appeals Chamber, October 2, 1995.

Prosecutor v Taylor (Judgment) SCSL-01-01-A, Appeals Chamber, September 26, 2013.

Protocol Additional to the Geneva Conventions of 12 August 1949, and relating to the Protection of Victims of International Armed Conflicts (Protocol I) (adopted June 8, 1977, entered into force December 7, 1978) 1125 UNTS 3.

Protocol Additional to the Geneva Conventions of August 12, 1949, and relating to the Protection of Victims of Non-International Armed Conflicts (Protocol II) (adopted June 8, 1977, entered into force December 7, 1978) 1125 UNTS 609.

Public Committee Against Torture in Israel v Israel (Judgment) HCJ 769/02, December 11, 2005.

Quéguiner, Jean-François, "Precautions under the Law Governing the Conduct of Hostilities" (2006) 88 International Review of the Red Cross 804.

Quinn, Warren S, "Actions, Intentions, and Consequences: The Doctrine of Double Effect" (1989) 18 Philosophy & Public Affairs 334.

Quong, Jonathan, "Liability to Defensive Harm" (2012) 40 Philosophy & Public Affairs 46.

Raz, Joseph, *The Morality of Freedom* (OUP 1986).

Raz, Joseph, *Ethics in the Public Domain* (OUP 1994).

Raz, Joseph, *Practical Reason and Norms* (OUP 1999).

Raz, Joseph, *Between Authority and Interpretation* (OUP 2009).

Raz, Joseph, *From Normativity to Responsibility* (OUP 2011).

Regan, Donald H, "Authority and Value: Reflections on Raz's Morality of Freedom" (1989) 62 Southern California Law Review 1003.

Reichberg, Gregory M, "Just War and Regular War: Competing Paradigms," in David Rodin & Henry Shue (eds), *Just and Unjust Warriors: The Moral and Legal Status of Soldiers* (OUP 2008) 193.

Rickless, Samuel C, "The Moral Status of Enabling Harm" (2011) 92 Pacific Philosophical Quarterly 66.

Robinson, Paul H, "Criminal Law Defenses: A Systematic Analysis" (1982) 82 Columbia Law Review 199.

Rodin, David, "Morality and Law in War," in H Strachan & S Scheipers (eds), *The Changing Character of War* (OUP 2011) 446.

Rogers, APV, "Conduct of combat and risks run by the civilian population" (1982) Military Law & Law of War Review 310.

Rogers, APV, *Law on the Battlefield* (1996).

Rogers, APV, "Zero-Casualty Warfare" (2000) 82 International Review of the Red Cross 165.

Rome Statute of the International Criminal Court (opened for signature July 17, 1998, entered into force July 1, 2002) 2187 UNTS 90.

Ruys, Tom, *"Armed Attack" and Article 51 of the UN Charter* (CUP 2010).

Searle, John, "Collective Intentions and Actions," in P Cohen, J Morgan, & M Pollack (eds) *Intentions in Communication* (MIT 1990) 401–15.

Schmitt, Michael N, "The Principle of Discrimination in 21st Century Warfare" (1999) 2 Yale Human Rights and Development Law Journal 143.

Schmitt, Michael N, "Precision Attack and International Humanitarian Law" (2005) 87 International Review of the Red Cross 445.

Schmitt, Michael N, "Fault Lines in the Law of Attack," in Susan Breau & Agnieszka Jachec-Neale (eds), *Testing the Boundaries of International Humanitarian Law* (BIICL 2006) 277–307.

Schmitt, Michael N, "Human Shields in International Humanitarian Law" (2008) 38 Israel Yearbook on Human Rights 17.

Schmitt, Michael N, "The Interpretive Guidance on the Notion of Direct Participation in Hostilities: A Critical Analysis" (2010) 1 Harvard National Security Journal 5.

Schmitt, Michael N, "Military Necessity and Humanity in International Humanitarian Law: Preserving the Delicate Balance" (2010) 50 Virginia Journal of International Law 795.

Schmitt, Michael N, "Unmanned Combat Aircraft Systems and International Humanitarian Law: Simplifying the Oft Benighted Debate" (2012) 30 BU Int'l LJ 595.

Schmitt, Michael N, "Wound, Capture, or Kill: A Reply to Ryan Goodman's 'The Power to Kill or Capture Enemy Combatants'" (2013) 24 EJIL 860.

Schmitt, Michael N & John J Merriam, "The Tyranny of Context: Israeli Targeting Practices in Legal Perspective" (2015) 53 U Penn JIL 118.

Shue, Henry, "Proportionality in War," in Gordon Martel (ed), *The Encyclopedia of War* (Wiley 2012) 6.

Solf, Waldemar A, "The Status of Combatants in Non-International Armed Conflicts under Domestic Law and Transnational Practice" (1983) 33 American University Law Review 53.

Solis, Gary D, *The Law of Armed Conflict* (CUP 2010).

Spector, Horacio, "Decisional Nonconsequentialism and the Risk Sensitivity of Obligation" (2016) 32 Social Philosophy & Policy 91.

SS "Lotus" (France v Turkey) (Judgment) [1927] ICGJ 248.

Statute of the International Court of Justice (opened for signature 26 June, 1945, entered into force October 24, 1945) 33 UNTS 993.

Steinhoff, Uwe, "Jeff McMahan on the Moral Inequality of Combatants" (2008) 16 Journal of Political Philosophy 220.

Steinhoff, Uwe, "When May Soldiers Participate in War?" (2016) 8 International Theory 236.

Tadros, Victor, *The Ends of Harm* (OUP 2011).

Tadros, Victor, "Wrongful Intentions without Closeness" (2015) 43 Philosophy & Public Affairs 52.

Tadros, Victor, "Causal Contributions and Liability" (unpublished ms).

Tadros, Victor, "Duress and Duty" (unpublished ms).

Talmon, Stefan, "Determining Customary International Law: The ICJ's Methodology between Induction, Deduction and Assertion" (2015) 26 EJIL 417.

Tasioulas, John, "Custom, *Jus Cogens*, and Human Rights," in Curtis Bradley (ed), *Custom's Future: International Law in a Changing World* (CUP 2016) 95–116.

UK Ministry of Defense, *Law of Armed Conflict Manual* (OUP 2005).

United Nations Charter.

United States Manual for Courts-Martial (2012).

US Department of Defense, *The US Army and Marine Corps Counterinsurgency Field Manual* (US Army Field Manual No 3-24, 2006).

US Department of Defense, *Law of War Manual* (2015).

US Joint Chiefs of Staff, Joint Targeting (Joint Publication 3-60) (April 13, 2007).

US Joint Chiefs of Staff, Joint Targeting (Joint Publication 3-60) (January 13, 2013).

US Naval War College, Workbook on Joint Operations Planning Process, NWC 4111H, January 21, 2008.

US v Hamidullin, 114 F Supp 3d 365 (ED Va 2015).

US v List (American Military Tribunal, Nuremberg, 1948) 11 NMT 1230.

US v Von Weizsaecker et al (Ministries Case) (Nuremberg, 1949) 14 NMT 314.

Uzan, Elad, "Soldiers, Civilians, and in Bello Proportionality: A Proposed Revision" (2016) 99 The Monist 87.

Vattel, Emer de, *The Law of Nations* (1758) (Charles G Fenwick (tr), Carnegie 1916).

Vattel, Emer de, *The Law of Nations* (1758) (Thomas Nugent (tr), Liberty Fund 2008).

Vienna Convention on Consular Relations (opened for signature April 18, 1961, April 24, 1964) 500 UNTS 95.

Vienna Convention on the Law of Treaties (opened for signature May 23, 1969, entered into force January 27, 1980) 1155 UNTS 331.

von Hebel, Herman & Darryl Robinson, "Crimes within the Jurisdiction of the Court," in Roy S Lee (ed), *The International Criminal Court: The Making of the Rome Statute—Issues, Negotiations, Results* (Springer 1999) 104.

Waldron, Jeremy, *Torture, Terror, and Trade-offs* (OUP 2010).

Waldron, Jeremy, "Responses to Zedner, Haque and Mendus" (2014) 8 Criminal Law and Philosophy 137.

Walen, Alec, "Proof Beyond a Reasonable Doubt: A Balanced Retributive Account" (2015) 76 Louisiana Law Review 355.

Walzer, Michael, *Just and Unjust Wars* (2nd edn, Basic Books 1992).

Walzer, Michael, "Responsibility and Proportionality in State and Nonstate Wars" (2009) Parameters 40.

Walzer, Michael, "Can the Good Guys Win?" (2013) 24 European Journal of International Law 438.

Waxman, Matthew C, "Detention as Targeting: Standards of Certainty and Detention of Suspected Terrorists" (2008) 108 Columbia Law Review 1365.

Westlake, John, *International Law*, vol II (1907).

Wright, Jason D, "'Excessive' Ambiguity: Analysing and Refining the Proportionality Standard" (2012) 94 International Review of the Red Cross 819.

Zimmerman, Michael J, *Living with Uncertainty* (CUP 2009).

Zohar, Noam, "Risking and Protecting Lives: Soldiers and Opposing Civilians," in Helen Frowe & Gerald Lang (eds), *How We Fight: Ethics in War* (OUP 2014) 168.

Index